# Governance-First AI

## Board Authority. Architectural Precision. Governed AI at Enterprise Scale.

**Mohammad Maruf Hossain**
**Ahilan Ayyachamy Nadar Ponnusamy**

Apress®

***Governance-First AI: Board Authority. Architectural Precision. Governed AI at Enterprise Scale.***

Mohammad Maruf Hossain
Melbourne, VIC, Australia

Ahilan Ayyachamy Nadar Ponnusamy
Melbourne, VIC, Australia

ISBN-13 (pbk): 979-8-8688-3117-1
ISBN-13 (electronic): 979-8-8688-3118-8
https://doi.org/10.1007/979-8-8688-3118-8



Managing Director, Apress Media LLC: Welmoed Spahr
Acquisitions Editor: Abhideep Vijh
Editorial Assistant: Gryffin Winkler

Cover designed by eStudioCalamar

Distributed to the book trade worldwide by Springer Science+Business Media New York, 1 New York Plaza, New York, NY 10004. Phone 1-800-SPRINGER, fax (201) 348-4505, e-mail orders-ny@springer-sbm.com, or visit www.springeronline.com. Apress Media, LLC is a Delaware LLC and the sole member (owner) is Springer Science + Business Media Finance Inc (SSBM Finance Inc). SSBM Finance Inc is a **Delaware** corporation.

For information on translations, please e-mail booktranslations@springernature.com; for reprint, paperback, or audio rights, please e-mail bookpermissions@springernature.com.

Apress titles may be purchased in bulk for academic, corporate, or promotional use. eBook versions and licenses are also available for most titles. For more information, reference our Print and eBook Bulk Sales web page at http://www.apress.com/bulk-sales.

Any source code or other supplementary material referenced by the author in this book is available to readers on GitHub. For more detailed information, please visit https://www.apress.com/gp/services/source-code.

If disposing of this product, please recycle the paper

*To the true governors of our lives,*
*our wives,*

*Shamima and Kalpana.*

# Table of Contents

# About the Authors

**Dr Mohammad Maruf Hossain** named among the 2024 Global Top 100 Innovators in Data and Analytics, is Australia's leading Fractional Chief AI Officer (CAIO), providing strategic leadership in artificial intelligence to boards, consulting partnerships, and technology firms. He holds a PhD in Artificial Intelligence from the University of Melbourne, complemented by GAICD governance credentials.

Dr. Hossain's executive experience spans the enterprise and public sectors. As Chief AI Strategist at 42 Consulting.AI, he supports organizations worldwide in building sustainable AI capabilities. Previously, as Vice President of Data Science at ANZ Bank, he led large-scale AI adoption across banking operations. His earlier roles with Credit Clear, Telstra Global, IBM Global Business Services, Infosys Consulting, and the Australian Government involved establishing Data and AI Centers of Excellence and embedding responsible AI frameworks across regulated industries.

Author of several research papers, Dr. Hossain is recognized for aligning AI strategy with measurable organizational and governance outcomes.

**Ahilan Ayyachamy Nadar Ponnusamy** currently works as a specialist for Application Platform at Red Hat APAC. He enjoys working with customers on hybrid cloud architectures and cloud-native application development and delivery practices. He previously completed a Master of Computer Applications degree at Madurai Kamaraj University in India. His work history includes Philips CE in Eindhoven, the Netherlands; member of Customer-Centric Engineering and Support at BEA Technologies in India and the United States; pre-sales tech lead for the cloud platform team at Oracle USA; principal platform engineer at VMware; and global architect at Dell Technologies Singapore.

# About the Technical Reviewer

**Harsh Doshi** is a cybersecurity product leader working at the intersection of AI, data protection, and enterprise risk. Over the last 15 years, he has built security products used by some of the world's largest enterprises and has advised Fortune 500 CISOs on AI governance and security program design. He focuses on helping organizations adopt AI safely, balancing innovation with governance, compliance, and real-world security challenges.

# Acknowledgments

Every book has an origin, and this one began with a problem I could not put down: agentic AI (artificial intelligence) systems cannot reach production on enterprise architecture alone, because the governance they demand must be built into the solution architecture itself. That single realization became a book, and it became one because of the people who believed in it before the industry had the words for it.

My deepest gratitude belongs to Ahilan Ponnusamy, my co-author. When I first brought him the idea that governance belongs *inside* solution architecture rather than beside it, he did not need convincing—he saw it at once, and then he helped me build it. He designed the architecture diagrams that give this book its shape, and across 15 use cases (UCs) and 12 chapters, his judgment made every argument sharper than I could have made it alone. He did much of this work while unwell, yet you would never know it from the work itself; he kept showing up because the ideas still lit him up. This book carries his fingerprints on every page, and it simply would not exist without him.

I am deeply grateful to Sudhir Chaurasia, whose early confidence turned an idea into practice. His invitation to prepare solutions for a first set of use cases and his push to carry the thinking beyond banking into a broader industry landscape gave this work its first real proving ground and gave me the conviction to keep going.

And the questions at the heart of this book first came into focus during my years at ANZ, where the use cases that started it all were first imagined. For that beginning, I remain thankful.

# Introduction

Every enterprise leader has now heard the promise of generative AI (GenAI), and most have felt the disappointment that follows it. In 2025, MIT's NANDA initiative reported a finding that landed hard across boardrooms: of the corporate generative AI initiatives and pilots underway, 95% were failing to deliver any measurable financial return. Billions had been spent. Adoption was everywhere. Transformation was rare.

The usual explanations, whether model quality, talent, or regulation, do not survive contact with the evidence. The systems work. The demonstrations impress. And still, the initiatives stall on the way from pilot to production. This book is about why things are the way they are and what to do differently.

The argument at its center is simple to state and difficult to implement: **Governance cannot be a layer you add around an AI system. It has to be built into the solution architecture itself.** In most enterprises, governance lives in enterprise architecture, a separate plane of policies, reviews, and controls that sits beside the solution rather than inside it. For a generation of software, that separation was tolerable because a human always stood between the machine's recommendation and the action taken. If the recommendation was wrong, a person caught it. That safety net is precisely what agentic AI removes. When systems act on their own authority, at machine speed, governance that lives in a separate layer arrives too late to matter. It must be present at the moment of decision, or it is not present at all.

This realization did not arrive in the abstract. It came from practice. Leaving a major bank in late 2025, I carried with me a list of generative and agentic AI use cases I had wanted to build. They were approved and promising, but none of them reached production because the enterprise architecture around them could not support the governance an autonomous system would require. Working through the solution designs with my program director, Sudhir Chaurasia, we began preparing a first set of use cases and deliberately widened them beyond banking into a broader industry landscape. Somewhere in that drafting, the pattern became a thesis, and the thesis became a book.

I took the idea to Ahilan Ponnusamy, and he saw it at once. Over many conversations, we identified 15 use cases, each chosen to demonstrate a distinct component of a governance-first architecture, from foundational retrieval systems to fully autonomous, multi-domain agents. Those 15 became the spine of this book. Along the way, earning my company-director credential reshaped the thesis a second time: governance through architecture, yes, but governance ultimately answerable to the board. That is where the book's subtitle, *Board Authority*, comes from. *Architectural Precision*: authority for what an AI system may do originates with the board; precision is the discipline of building that authority into the architecture so it holds at runtime.

In the author's own enterprise deployments, foundational retrieval architectures of the kind described here have delivered efficiency gains in the range of 70–80 percentage points. The point is that gains like these are worthless to a regulated enterprise unless the system producing them can be governed, audited, and defended. This book is about earning the gains and keeping them.

What follows is organized in five parts.

**Part I, The Strategic Imperative**, makes the case for a governance-first posture. Chapter 1 establishes the book's constitutional foundation: three Governance Doctrines, the concept of delegated machine authority, and the engine that enforces board authority over what machines are permitted to do, set against the reality of Shadow AI filling the vacuum left by absent governance. Chapter 2 shows why the gap between consumer AI and enterprise AI is structural rather than technical and maps the 15 use cases onto the governance commitments an enterprise must actually keep.

**Part II, The Architectural Foundation**, builds the platform. Chapter 3 addresses risk classification and the choice between cloud and hybrid deployment. Chapter 4 details the security architecture that regulates AI demands: Zero Trust, document-level access control (DLAC) enforced at retrieval time, and immutable audit logging. Chapter 5 turns to LLMOps (Large Language Model Operations), the operational discipline that proves an AI system's outputs are not merely fast but correct, through Hybrid Search, re-ranking, and the Groundedness (Faithfulness) Score.

**Part III, Foundational Generative AI**, puts the foundation to work on retrieval systems. Chapter 6 presents the Efficiency Model, a retrieval-augmented assistant operating under mandatory human oversight. Chapter 7 escalates to the Compliance Model, engineered for regulated settings where a wrong answer carries legal weight. Chapter 8 addresses data integrity and optimization across a further set of use cases, in which each performance gain introduces a new governance risk to be managed.

**Part IV, The Frontier with Agentic and Autonomous AI**, crosses into systems that act. Chapter 9 marks the paradigm shift, introducing the constitutional machinery autonomy requires: the Machine Decision Authority Matrix (MDAM), the Autonomy Budget, and the Autonomy Levels that bound what an agent may do. Chapter 10 governs agents embedded in core business functions, in which non-human identity (NHI) becomes inseparable from what the agent is permitted to do. Chapter 11 reaches the highest-risk territory, multi-domain automation, where safety and accountability cannot be compromised at any point.

**Part V, Conclusion**, is a single chapter. Chapter 12 offers a roadmap to AI maturity, a four-stage model that maps all 15 use cases onto a governance continuum and lets an organization scale autonomy only as fast as its governance can demonstrably support.

This book is written for the people who must answer for AI in the enterprise: chief data, technology, information, and security officers; enterprise architects; and the risk and compliance leaders who sit beside them. It assumes you understand enterprise architecture and the fundamentals of generative AI. It does not assume that anyone has yet shown you how to make the two hold together. That is the work of the pages that follow.

# PART I

# The Strategic Imperative

# CHAPTER 1

# Building Future-Proof AI

A profound gap separates AI ambition from AI scale. Despite proven efficiency gains at the pilot level, the vast majority of organizations remain stuck, unable to translate localized success into enterprise-wide value. This scaling failure is, at its root, a failure of governance and architectural standardization, not of model capability.

Into this governance vacuum, the democratization of generative AI has introduced Shadow AI: unmanaged models and agents operating outside formal security, compliance, and authority controls. The financial, regulatory, and operational consequences of that sprawl constitute a direct and quantifiable burden on the enterprise: the Shadow Tax.

Beneath both failures lies a question most organizations have never formally answered: who holds decision authority in this organization, and how much of it has been delegated to machines? That question, not the choice of model or the size of the AI budget, is the constitutive governance question of the enterprise AI era. It is the founding question of the Enterprise Decision System (EDS) Governance Framework and its supreme constitutional instrument, the Governance Doctrine: the document that establishes the principles under which all machine decision authority must be delegated, bounded, and monitored.


M. M. Hossain and A. A. N. Ponnusamy, *Governance-First AI*,
https://doi.org/10.1007/979-8-8688-3118-8_1

The EDS Governance Framework is a governance architecture developed by the author and presented in this book; it is neither a standards body specification nor a separately published formal standard. It was designed to fill a gap that existing frameworks, NIST AI RMF (NIST AI 100-1, January 2023), ISO/IEC 42001:2023, and the EU AI Act (Regulation EU 2024/1689, entered into force August 1, 2024), do not address directly. Those frameworks ask whether the technology is safe and explainable. The EDS Governance Framework asks a prior and more fundamental question: *who holds decision authority in this organization*, and *how much of it has been delegated to machines*? Where existing frameworks govern the model, the EDS framework governs the authority that the model exercises. It is organized as a constitutional hierarchy: doctrines constrain principles, and principles constrain architecture, so that every technical decision in the enterprise is traceable back to a board-level governance commitment. This book is the operational implementation guide for that framework across the full spectrum of enterprise AI deployment.

Moving past the scaling bottleneck requires a governance-first approach: redefining AI not as a productivity tool but as a class of delegated decision authority, subject to the same board-level logic applied to senior executives. Operationalized through Platform Engineering, this approach channels AI demand into a secure, compliant architecture, making the governed path the path of least resistance.

This chapter establishes that scaling AI begins with a constitutional act, not a technical one. It proceeds in four movements: first, the reframe of AI from tool to delegated decision actor and the authority problem this creates; second, the three Governance Doctrines that form the constitutional foundation of the EDS framework; third, the governance case for why this approach is non-negotiable, including the post-pilot paradox, the failure of reactive governance, and the Shadow Tax; and fourth, the operationalization of constitutional mandates through North Star AI, Platform Engineering, and the Director's Mindset. By the end of this chapter, readers will understand why Certified Operational Velocity, the capacity to deploy AI at speed with board-level confidence, begins with governance, not engineering.

**How to Read This Chapter:**

**Governance Leaders and Board Members**: The constitutional framework and its business case are in the sections from "From Tool to Delegated Authority" through "Why Governance-First AI Is Non-negotiable."

**Architects and Practitioners**: The Platform Engineering operationalization begins at North Star AI.

**Key *Terms Used Early* and *Defined* in *Full Later*:**

- MANDATE (the framework)
- EDS (Enterprise Decision System)
- GMI (Governance Maturity Index; Chapter 4)
- MDAM (Machine Decision Authority Matrix; Chapter 9)
- ADAE (Autonomous Decision Authority Evaluation; Chapter 9)
- PDP/PEP (Policy Decision/Enforcement Point; Chapter 4)
- NHI (non-human identity; Chapter 10)
- DLAC (document-level access control; Chapter 4)
- ZTAI (Zero-Trust AI; Chapter 4)
- PaC (Policy-as-Code; Chapter 2)
- SRE (Safety Runtime Environment; Chapter 9)
- HITL (Human-in-the-Loop)/HOTL (Human-on-the-Loop)/HAL (Human-Above-the-Loop) (oversight models; Chapter 4)
- CAIO (Chief AI Officer)

## From Tool to Delegated Authority: The Constitutional Reframe

The conventional framing of AI in enterprise settings positions it as a tool, a productivity instrument wielded by human workers. This framing is no longer adequate. A modern autonomous AI agent does not assist a human to make a decision; it makes the decision itself, at speed, at scale, within whatever authority limits have been assigned to it. An autonomous pricing agent can reprice contracts across hundreds of thousands of customers. An autonomous collections agent can commit to arrangements on behalf of the organization. A multi-agent workflow can chain decisions together at machine speed across multiple business functions.

These systems exercise real decision authority on behalf of the organization: financial, operational, and customer-facing. The governance problem this creates is not a technology problem; it is an authority problem: the question of who holds that authority and whether the board has knowingly delegated it.

**THE CONSTITUTIONAL REFRAME: DECISION AUTHORITY AS GOVERNING LENS**

Boards govern organizations by controlling the delegation of decision authority. Human executives and machine systems are both decision actors operating under delegated authority. The board therefore governs the distribution of decision authority across the enterprise, not the underlying technology used by those actors.

This reframing delivers three governance advantages. First, it normalizes AI governance within existing board logic: boards already govern executives through delegation frameworks, authority limits, and accountability structures; autonomous AI agents are another class of decision actor, and the paradigm extends rather than rebuilds.

Second, it shifts the governance question to the correct level: not "Are our AI systems technically safe?" but "Who holds decision authority in this organization, and how much of it has been delegated to machines?"

Third, the Decision Authority Portfolio model is reusable beyond AI; it applies equally to algorithmic trading, robotic process automation, and autonomous supply chains. The board that governs AI through this lens is simultaneously prepared to govern the full spectrum of machine actors.

## MANDATE: Machine Authority Non-Delegable Autonomous Technology Enforcement

MANDATE, Machine Authority Non-Delegable Autonomous Technology Enforcement, is the constitutional governance product of the EDS framework, the board-level instrument through which machine decision authority is formally delegated, explicitly bounded, and continuously monitored. It is not a software product or a technical standard; it is the highest-order governance act the board undertakes regarding AI. No other EDS product—no policy, standard, operating manual, or assurance framework—can operate without the constitutional foundation MANDATE provides. Throughout this book, MANDATE is referred to by its acronym rather than its full name.

Three constitutional doctrines form the core of MANDATE. Each appears throughout this book as the governance lens applied to every blueprint, every architecture decision, and every Platform Engineering capability:

**DOCTRINE 1: DECISION AUTHORITY GOVERNANCE**

Autonomous systems are delegated decision actors operating within board-approved limits, governed through the same delegation logic applied to senior executives. The board's governance question is: *who holds decision authority in this organization*, and *how much has been delegated to machines*?

## DOCTRINE 2: GOVERNANCE-CONSTRAINED AUTONOMY

Organizations have repeatedly deployed autonomous systems faster than their governance capability could support. Doctrine 2 makes that gap constitutionally unacceptable. Autonomous decision authority may expand only where governance capability demonstrably supports that expansion. The Governance Maturity Index (GMI), the EDS framework's five-level certification scale that measures an organization's readiness to govern autonomous systems, is the binding constraint on autonomy scaling. No system may operate at an Autonomy Level exceeding the organization's certified GMI level. This constraint is constitutional and non-delegable.

## DOCTRINE 3: DELEGATED MACHINE AUTHORITY

Machine decision authority is governed using the same delegation logic applied to human executives. The board governs machine authority through three instruments: the Machine Decision Authority Matrix (MDAM), which defines the boundary between human and machine decision authority; the Autonomy Budget, the board-approved cap on aggregate delegated machine authority; and Governance Assurance and Monitoring, the four-layer assurance model that ensures machine decisions remain within board-approved limits at all times. Crucially, this authority is governed as a live condition, not a historical record. A decision that was admissible when authorized may become inadmissible as authority, conditions, exposure, or organizational context changes; the ability to explain how a decision once became valid does not answer whether it remains valid now. This principle of continuous admissibility is developed in full in the author's foundational treatment (Hossain, "Continuous Admissibility," 2026).

These three doctrines are the highest-order governance statements from which all other controls in this framework are derived. The six Governance Principles that operationalize these doctrines as architectural requirements are introduced and defined in Chapter 2: doctrines constrain principles, and principles constrain architecture. They are not redundant; they operate at different levels of authority and serve different audiences.

These three doctrines are the constitutional foundation to which this book returns in every chapter. Chapter 2 maps them to the regulatory compliance landscape. Chapters 4–8 apply the oversight models they mandate to specific use case blueprints. Chapters 9 and 10 operationalize the MDAM and Autonomy Budget for agentic and multi-agent systems (MASs); Chapter 11 establishes the certification and accountability standards that govern their highest-stakes deployments. Chapter 12 uses the complete EDS framework as a maturity assessment tool. The doctrine is the thread that runs through the entire book.

## The Governance Maturity Index

The Governance Maturity Index is the EDS framework's formal certification scale for measuring an organization's demonstrated readiness to govern autonomous AI systems. It is not a self-assessed maturity model or a benchmarking exercise. It is an externally verifiable certification standard, the board's constitutional instrument for answering the question below:

*Does this organization's governance infrastructure actually support the level of machine autonomy it is proposing to authorize?*

The GMI operates on five levels, as shown in Table 1-1. Each level defines the governance capability that must be demonstrably production-certified, not planned, not in progress, before the organization may deploy systems at the corresponding Autonomy Level. Advancement from one level to the next is a governance authorization decision, not a technical capability decision. The board may not approve GMI level advancement based on model performance, vendor assurances, or delivery schedules. The certification evidence must be produced, reviewed, and formally approved.

***Table 1-1.*** *The Governance Maturity Index—five certification levels, required governance controls, and autonomy deployment gates*

| GMI Level | Certification Name | Minimum Governance Controls Required | Autonomy Gate |
|---|---|---|---|
| 1 | Constitutional Foundations | Three Governance Doctrines formally adopted. Autonomy Register established. DLAC (document-level access control, defined in Chapter 4) enforced at the retrieval layer. Immutable audit logging deployed for all AI interactions. Personally Identifiable Information (PII) masking operational at ingestion. | Minimum gate before any production AI deployment, including simple RAG (Retrieval-Augmented Generation) assistants. No production deployment is authorized without GMI Level 1. |
| 2 | RAG Governance Certified | Zero-Trust RAG pipeline operational with DLAC, metadata lineage tagging, and WORM (Write-Once, Read-Many)-compliant immutable logging. Groundedness Score SLO (service-level objective) established and enforced as a production gate. HITL workflows operational, tested under load, and producing verifiable override rationales. MDAM entries approved for every deployed system. Autonomy Register current. | Minimum gate before any Autonomy Level 3 system enters production. |

(*continued*)

***Table 1-1.*** *(continued)*

| GMI Level | Certification Name | Minimum Governance Controls Required | Autonomy Gate |
|---|---|---|---|
| 3 | Agentic Governance Certified | Policy-as-Code (PaC) enforcement active across all agentic workflows. NHI (non-human identity—see below) Lifecycle Register complete for all deployed agents. Delegated Authorization Service operational. HOTL supervisors hold current certification for every Level 3 or above system. Decision Authority Scoring applied to every agent; MDAM entry approved per operational domain. | Minimum gate before any Autonomy Level 4 system enters production. |
| 4 | Safety-Critical Governance Certified | Ensemble reasoning certified for all regulated-domain decisions. ≥98% auditable rationale standard achieved and continuously monitored. Safety Runtime Environment enforcing span-of-control thresholds at infrastructure level. HAL supervisors hold Critical-tier endorsement for all Level 4–5 systems. Adversarial robustness testing active. KL/JS drift monitoring operational for all safety-critical models. | Minimum gate before any Autonomy Level 5 system enters production. |

*(continued)*

*Table 1-1.* (*continued*)

| GMI Level | Certification Name | Minimum Governance Controls Required | Autonomy Gate |
|---|---|---|---|
| 5 | Full Autonomy Governance Certified | Multi-agent orchestration governed end to end: Authority Matrix Rules Repository (the technical implementation of the Machine Decision Authority Matrix, defined fully in Chapter 9), NHI Lifecycle Register, GMI Gating Service, and Autonomy Budget Monitor all production-active and integrated. Continuous adversarial robustness testing in place. External assurance, independent third-party certification of governance controls, engaged and current. | Authorizes the full Autonomy Level 5 portfolio. The organization operates at the frontier of governed autonomy. |

The GMI is not assessed once and filed. It is a living certification maintained through continuous LLMOps monitoring, quarterly governance reviews, and formal recertification when operating conditions change, for example, when a new domain is added, an Autonomy Level is escalated, or a governance control degrades. Chapter 12 defines the full four-stage implementation roadmap for building and maintaining GMI certification, as well as the specific governance controls that must be production-certified at each stage.

## Authority versus Autonomy: The Five-Level Taxonomy

Autonomous decision-making exists on a five-level spectrum, as shown in Table 1-2. Each level places different demands on the governance architecture and requires a corresponding level of governance maturity before deployment can be authorized. The Autonomy Level taxonomy introduced here is the board's primary instrument for translating risk appetite into deployment constraints. It reappears in every blueprint chapter and is the central governance lens for Chapters 9–11.

***Table 1-2.*** *EDS Autonomy Level taxonomy*

| Autonomy Level | Classification | What the System Does | Oversight Model Required |
|---|---|---|---|
| Level 1 | Assistive AI | Recommends or drafts; human makes all final decisions. No autonomous execution. | Human-in-the-Loop (HITL): human approves each action. |
| Level 2 | Workflow Automation | Executes defined, rule-based tasks within narrow parameters. Human approves exceptions. | Human-in-the-Loop (HITL). |
| Level 3 | Supervised Autonomous Agents | Initiates and executes operational actions; human supervisor monitors in real time with active authority to intervene. | Human-on-the-Loop (HOTL): supervisor can intervene at any time. |

*(continued)*

*Table 1-2.* (*continued*)

| Autonomy Level | Classification | What the System Does | Oversight Model Required |
|---|---|---|---|
| Level 4 | Autonomous Execution Within Defined Limits | Executes complex, multi-step decisions within board-approved domain limits. Human reviews output batches. | Human-Above-the-Loop (HAL): periodic review before material commitment. |
| Level 5 | Multi-agent Orchestration | Autonomous AI systems coordinate with other AI systems to execute end-to-end workflows at machine speed. | HAL + external assurance; requires GMI Level 5 certification. |

One constitutional constraint governs the entire taxonomy: no autonomous system may operate at an Autonomy Level that exceeds the organization's currently certified GMI level. No business case, delivery timeline, or commercial pressure can override it.

Every blueprint in this book specifies an Autonomy Level and a required oversight model. These are not design preferences; they are constitutional requirements derived from Doctrine 2 and the MDAM. Each Autonomy Level additionally maps to a Delegation Tier that governs the intensity of oversight controls applied to a registered system. The Delegation Tier classification and its governance implications are formally introduced in Chapter 9.

# Why Governance-First AI Is Non-negotiable

Three structural failures make governance-first AI non-negotiable. The first is the post-pilot paradox: the persistent inability to translate localized AI success into enterprise-wide value. The second is Shadow AI:

the governance vacuum that fills that gap, exercising machine decision authority without board delegation, MDAM authorization, or Autonomy Budget allocation. The third is reactive governance: the assumption that policy documents and retrospective audits can control systems making decisions at machine speed. Each failure is examined in turn.

## Post-pilot Paradox

The inability to scale initial success is the key architectural failure obscuring the executive mandate for rapid AI deployment. While organizations report positive leading indicators, such as cost savings and revenue benefits at the individual use case level, this value frequently fails to translate into systemic organizational gains. Only 39% of companies report a measurable impact on Earnings Before Interest and Taxes (EBIT) at the enterprise level (McKinsey & Company, "The State of AI in 2025," 2025; this figure has remained constant across the 2023 and 2025 reports, underscoring the persistence of the governance scaling gap).

This disparity between localized success and enterprise-wide value realization suggests that the bottleneck is not technological novelty but rather a lack of structural operational maturity. The failure to scale is, fundamentally, a failure of governance and architectural standardization. Scaling AI requires embedding models and decision-making systems into critical, end-to-end business workflows. Without standardized infrastructure, clear policy enforcement, and reliable deployment practices, every pilot becomes a standalone island of technical debt and unmanaged risk.

Architectural standardization is the prerequisite for workflow transformation at enterprise scale. Where individual use cases generate isolated value without accumulating into top-line profitability, the constraint is governance and structural integrity, not model capability.

## Failure of Reactive Governance

The security perimeter has dissolved. Large language models (LLMs) and external AI services are accessible to every function in the organization without IT intermediation. Unlike legacy Shadow IT, which was confined to specific teams and tools, Shadow AI spans the full enterprise, from finance and legal to HR and operations, at a scale and speed that traditional reactive controls were never designed to handle.

This unmanaged sprawl leads to a critical erosion of the Decision Authority Portfolio, the aggregate set of machine decision authorities formally delegated by the board across the enterprise. Developers frequently integrate LLMs directly into applications without mandatory security reviews. Non-technical staff pastes proprietary information into public generative AI models. Each of these actions represents an unauthorized delegation of machine decision authority, a deployment that falls outside the MDAM, consumes no points from the Autonomy Budget, and generates no entries in the Autonomy Register, the EDS framework's live inventory of every AI system operating under formally delegated machine authority. From the perspective of the Governance Doctrine, this is not a compliance gap. It is a governance void.

Shadow systems are often a signal of genuine unmet need. Enforcement and suppression alone are counterproductive; they suppress the symptom while the cause persists. The strategic response is to channel that demand into secure, enterprise-grade architecture, making the governed path the faster path, not the bureaucratic one.

## The Unseen Crisis

The pace of Shadow AI proliferation is accelerated by organizational urgency, the fear of missing out (FOMO) on AI's competitive promise. This urgency compels developers and business units to bypass official channels, acquire licenses without governance review, and launch pilots without MDAM authorization. The result is not simply a compliance gap; it is a governance void in which machine decision authority is being exercised at scale with no board visibility.

## Defining the Shadow AI Threat Vector and the Impulse of FOMO

Shadow AI is any model or agent operating within the enterprise outside formal governance, security, and compliance controls. In the language of the Governance Doctrine, it is any autonomous system exercising decision authority without a corresponding MDAM entry, Autonomy Register record, or Autonomy Budget allocation. As no-code platforms and external AI vendors proliferate across decentralized teams, the governance gap compounds: policy enforcement becomes fragmented, and comprehensive model risk management becomes operationally impossible.

## Quantifying the Shadow Tax

The Shadow Tax is paid across three measurable domains: regulatory and confidentiality exposure, direct breach costs, and systemic operational fragility. Each is examined below.

### Regulatory and Confidentiality Exposure

The most immediate risk is the exposure of intellectual property (IP) and sensitive data. Employees routinely paste proprietary code, internal business documents, or customer personal data into third-party generative AI models. These actions constitute tangible breaches of confidentiality and IP and, under the Governance Doctrine, represent unauthorized extensions of machine decision authority into domains the board has never approved.

The regulatory implications are equally severe. Unapproved use of AI compromises compliance with major global mandates, including HIPAA, the Gramm–Leach–Bliley Act, and the General Data Protection Regulation (GDPR). The EU AI Act (Regulation EU 2024/1689), which is considered the world's first comprehensive regulatory framework for AI, introduces strict requirements for governance, transparency, and risk management, with prohibited practices applicable from February 2, 2025, and high-risk AI system obligations from August 2, 2026. Ignorance of unauthorized data transfer is not a defensible position when regulators investigate.

## Financial Toll

The financial consequence of Shadow AI control deficits has been measured. Organizations with high levels of unsanctioned AI systems incurred an average of $670,000 in additional breach costs compared with those with minimal Shadow AI exposure (IBM Security, "Cost of a Data Breach Report 2025," 2025). Breaches linked to Shadow AI environments also had longer detection and containment cycles and higher rates of customer PII compromise. Among organizations that experienced a Shadow AI–linked breach, 97% lacked proper AI access controls (IBM Security, 2025). Separately, 63% of surveyed organizations report having no formal AI governance policies (IBM Security, 2025).

## Systemic Operational Fragility

Beyond breach costs, decentralized Shadow AI deployments introduce systemic operational risk. Production AI requires deterministic latency, stable throughput, and guaranteed infrastructure. Ad hoc deployments cannot provide these prerequisites, introducing technical debt and scalability fragility that compound over time. When failures occur, and they do, there is no chain of accountability: no MDAM entry, no Autonomy Register record, no designated owner. The governance void becomes an operational void.

## Defining North Star AI

Moving from reactive governance to strategic scale requires a clear destination. North Star AI is that destination: a multi-horizon strategic vision for AI adoption anchored in the constitutional architecture of the EDS framework. It is not a technology vision; it is a governed deployment trajectory, bounded by Autonomy Levels, certified by the GMI, and authorized through the MDAM. Its three horizons map directly to the organization's governance maturity journey.

## Shifting AI from a Technical Problem to a Business Strategy

Governing AI at scale requires the board to own the question, not IT. Effective governance demands cross-functional leadership across security, legal, risk, and business operations, not because AI is complex, but because the authority it exercises touches every function in the organization.

Central to this shift is the establishment of clear strategic objectives. High-performing AI organizations understand that while efficiency is a primary goal (80% of organizations cite it; McKinsey & Company, "The State of AI in 2025," 2025), the true differentiator lies in setting complementary goals focused on growth and innovation, achieved by expanding governed autonomy rather than ungoverned sprawl.

## Aligning Policy Deployment

The pace of AI adoption makes slow, bureaucratic planning cycles obsolete. Alignment must be structured and executive-led: a long-term vision, mapped to corporate goals, and operationalized through ambitious three-year Objectives and Key Results (OKRs). The three-horizon model that follows provides the governance gateway for each planning phase.

## Defining the Time Horizons for AI Value

The North Star AI vision is operationalized across three strategic horizons, as shown in Table 1-3. Each horizon corresponds to a GMI certification level, the constitutional gateway that determines which Autonomy Levels the organization is authorized to deploy.

### Short-Term Success (0–12 Months)

The immediate imperative is AI Asset Visibility: establishing the Autonomy Register, scoring all known AI assets against the MDAM, and achieving initial coverage of the Decision Authority Portfolio. The primary deliverable is a comprehensive inventory of all AI systems operating within the enterprise: sanctioned, shadow, and embedded. Success metrics focus on eliminating quantifiable financial exposure to Shadow AI within the first year.

### Intermediate Success (1–3 Years)

With visibility established, the focus shifts to industrialization: achieving GMI Level 2–3 certification, enabling supervised autonomous agents under HOTL oversight, and automating compliance readiness against NIST AI RMF (NIST AI 100-1, January 2023), ISO/IEC 42001:2023, and the EU AI Act (Regulation EU 2024/1689; prohibited practices applicable from February 2, 2025; high-risk AI system obligations applicable from August 2, 2026). Success in this phase is measured by enterprise-level EBIT impact, not model count.

### Long-Term Success (3+ Years)

At full maturity, AI transitions from an optimization tool to a strategic differentiator. GMI Level 4–5 certification enables autonomous execution and multi-agent orchestration within board-approved authority limits.

Success is measured by competitive differentiation, governed revenue generation, and minimal material compliance failures under emerging global regulation.

***Table 1-3.*** *Strategic AI success horizons and metrics*

| Horizon | Strategic Focus Area | Key Governance Imperative | Measurement Examples (OKRs) |
|---|---|---|---|
| Short term (0–12 M) | Efficiency and stabilization | Autonomy Register established; MDAM coverage initiated; Shadow AI inventory completed | Reduce unsanctioned AI by X%; achieve 100% AI Asset Visibility; establish Autonomy Budget baseline. |
| Intermediate (1–3 Y) | Scale and workflow transformation | GMI Levels 2–3 certified; NIST AI RMF (NIST AI 100-1, January 2023) and ISO 42001 alignment; HOTL supervision program active | X% of EBIT influenced by governed AI; time-to-market for new models reduced by Z%; 50% of core workflows transformed. |
| Long term (3+ Y) | Growth and business reinvention | GMI Levels 4–5 achieved; MDAM covers all autonomous domains; proactive ethical and societal leadership | Launch N new growth markets driven by governed AI; achieve competitive advantage through trusted autonomy; zero material compliance failures. |

# Architectural Foundation

The strategy for North Star AI is operationalized not merely by creating models but by building the durable, compliant architecture that hosts them and enforces the constitutional constraints of the Governance Doctrine at the technical layer. This architectural mandate is realized through Platform Engineering: the discipline that builds the Internal Developer Platform (IDP) responsible for automatically enforcing governance policies. The Platform does not sit alongside governance; it is the technical enforcement mechanism through which the board's Autonomy Budget, MDAM domain restrictions, and GMI certification requirements are operationalized into every deployment pipeline.

## The Platform Is the Embodiment of Governance Policy

Scaling from individual pilots to enterprise-wide value requires moving beyond bespoke MLOps (Machine Learning Operations) pipelines to a standardized platform that automatically enforces governance policies across hundreds of models and multiple business units.

Platform Engineering is the critical discipline responsible for addressing this requirement. It focuses on building an IDP specifically engineered to accelerate software and AI delivery by empowering developers while embedding robust controls necessary for security, compliance, and operational stability. This approach ensures that governance requirements, such as data privacy, model risk management, bias mitigation, and authority limits, are not bolt-on checklists but inherent features of the production environment.

## Platform-as-a-Product Mindset

A cornerstone of Platform Engineering is adopting a product mindset, prioritizing the internal customer: data scientists, ML engineers, and development teams. If governance slows, burdens, or restricts the development process, developers will inevitably resort to unsanctioned Shadow AI tools to maintain velocity, generating unauthorized delegated machine authority that the board has never approved.

The strategic value of this approach lies in the Empowering Self-Service with Guardrails principle. The platform must reduce developers' cognitive load by automatically handling infrastructure provisioning, security checks, and policy adherence, which includes MDAM compliance verification and pre-scoring of authority exposure. This architectural approach shifts the compliance burden from individual developers to the platform itself, neutralizing the primary incentive to develop Shadow AI systems.

## Platform Principles Addressing Governance Deficits

To operationalize the AI vision, the architecture must actively address the inherent governance deficits. This is achieved by implementing the Platform-as-a-Product mindset, which prioritizes the developer experience, and delivering Empowering Self-Service with Guardrails. This principle is realized through two core components: the Model Service Catalog (a centralized, comprehensive inventory of all ML models and agents to combat fragmentation) and the Abstraction of Compliance, which converts complex governance requirements into simple, self-service APIs or Golden Paths.

## Model Service Catalog

To combat the fragmentation and lack of visibility inherent in Shadow AI, the platform must feature a centralized, high-UX Model Service Catalog. This catalog serves as the definitive internal marketplace and comprehensive inventory of all ML models operating across the enterprise. Under the EDS framework, it is the operational implementation of the Autonomy Register, the living source of truth for the Decision Authority Portfolio. Every entry maps to an MDAM domain, carries a decision authority score, and records the required oversight model.

## Abstraction of Compliance

The most powerful governance feature is the abstraction of complexity. By treating the platform as a product, sophisticated governance requirements, such as oversight model compliance, decision authority scoring, governance maturity gate clearance, and Human-on-the-Loop supervision provisioning, are converted into simple, easy-to-use, self-service APIs or pre-configured deployment templates, often referred to as Golden Paths. When the secure, compliant path is also the fastest and simplest path, the root cause of Shadow AI adoption is effectively mitigated.

# Balancing Velocity and Trust

To avoid over-restrictive policies and achieve the Certified Operational Velocity required for scaled AI, the Enterprise AI Platform cannot rely on a blanket-ban approach to governance. Instead, it must employ a nuanced taxonomy of controls that balances development speed with mandatory security and compliance. This is the Director's Mindset in practice: governance is not a brake on velocity but the certification mechanism that authorizes it.

The Governance Doctrine names this posture Guarded Innovation, the board's commitment to supporting autonomous AI where it demonstrably improves performance, while enforcing hard limits on uncontrolled autonomy, irreversible actions without circuit breakers, and unmonitored authority, as the constitutional foundation of Certified Operational Velocity. Guarded Innovation is not risk avoidance; it is risk-managed velocity. Chapter 12 establishes Guarded Innovation as the governing frame for all four AI maturity stages and defines its per-stage expression across the full deployment continuum.

## The Director's Mindset

The Governance Doctrine translates board-level accountability into five questions that must be answered before any autonomous system is deployed. These are not technical checkboxes; they are constitutional governance gates:

- Has the GMI been certified to the required level for this Autonomy Level?
- Is there a current MDAM entry authorizing this decision domain?
- Does the proposed decision authority score remain within the Autonomy Budget?
- Has the Chief AI Officer (CAIO) provided pre-release governance sign-off?
- Is the required oversight model (HITL, HOTL, or HAL) technically enforced, not merely policy-recommended?

If any answer is no, deployment does not proceed, regardless of business pressure or delivery timeline. This is what separates Certified Operational Velocity from ungoverned speed. The platform enforces these questions automatically through its four-tier control taxonomy.

## Taxonomy of Platform Controls

Effective governance within the Platform Engineering context requires a highly nuanced approach to controls. The EDS framework defines four named control types, each with a specific governance function:

- **Golden Paths:** Prescriptive, opinionated, end-to-end solution templates for everyday tasks. Golden Paths incorporate all necessary security, performance, MDAM compliance, and decision authority scoring by default, effectively steering developers toward the safest, most efficient workflow.
- **Guardrails:** Automated, preventative enforcement mechanisms designed to act as emergency stops. They monitor real-time activity and prevent actions that violate core policies, for example, enforcing the Autonomy Budget bands—holding deployments for Board Risk Committee review at 80% utilization, activating a moratorium at 90%, and treating any breach of the ceiling as a zero-tolerance event or missing a required GMI certification.
- **Safety Nets:** Resilience and recovery mechanisms to ensure operational stability. They include comprehensive monitoring, continuous tracking of system behavior against MDAM authority limits, and automated failure remediation features such as model rollbacks.

- **Manual Checkpoints:** Human oversight gates that enforce the oversight models (HITL, HOTL, HAL) mandated by the MDAM for each domain and Autonomy Level. They require explicit human intervention at critical lifecycle stages, particularly for systems at Level 3 and above.

# Operationalizing Compliance

Governance without automated enforcement is policy theater. The Enterprise AI Platform operationalizes constitutional mandates as executable architecture, serving as the Governance Engine that converts board-level commitments into automated controls and continuous visibility.

## Continuous Visibility and Risk Quantification

The platform must maintain continuous AI Asset Visibility, providing security and GRC leaders with real-time insight and control over all AI assets, including their authority scores, MDAM authorization status, and Autonomy Budget utilization. This living inventory enables executives to shift the discussion of AI risk from abstract policy debates to tangible material exposure and gives the board the evidence it needs to close the governance control loop.

## Automated Compliance Readiness

A key service component delivered by the platform is automated compliance readiness. This functionality automates the assessment of the organization's AI maturity against leading global standards, including the NIST AI RMF (NIST AI 100-1, January 2023), ISO/IEC 42001:2023, and mandatory elements of the EU AI Act (Regulation EU 2024/1689).

By continuously measuring compliance maturity, the platform enables teams to proactively identify performance gaps, moving the enterprise beyond costly, retrospective auditing toward demonstrable, proactive assurance. Table 1-4 demonstrates how different Platform Engineering Controls mitigates different Shadow AI risks, binds it to the constitutional layer and lists benefits this practice yields.

***Table 1-4.*** *Mitigating Shadow AI risks via Platform Engineering controls*

| Shadow AI Risk Area | Constitutional Gap (EDS Doctrine) | Platform Engineering Control | Benefit to Developer/User |
|---|---|---|---|
| Data exposure/ confidentiality | No MDAM data domain authorization; no Autonomy Register record | Golden Paths: pre-vetted data pipelines; Guardrails: automated PII and MDAM domain checks | Secure, compliant access to sensitive data without manual review delays (velocity) |
| Unauthorized machine decision authority (Shadow AI) | No decision authority scoring; no Autonomy Budget allocation; no governance maturity certification | AI Asset Visibility: mandatory Autonomy Register registration; automated compliance readiness (NIST AI RMF—NIST AI 100-1, January 2023; ISO/IEC 42001:2023, EU AI Act—Regulation EU 2024/1689) | Clear inventory, guaranteed compliance status, faster governance approval (trust) |

(*continued*)

***Table 1-4.*** *(continued)*

| Shadow AI Risk Area | Constitutional Gap (EDS Doctrine) | Platform Engineering Control | Benefit to Developer/User |
|---|---|---|---|
| Operational fragility/bias | No Safety Runtime Environment; no kill-switch architecture; no oversight model enforcement | Safety Nets: continuous monitoring and drift detection; Manual Checkpoints: mandatory HOTL/HAL supervision gates at Level 3+ | High reliability metrics and enforced trustworthiness in production (stability) |
| Scaling and cost overruns | No Autonomy Budget tracking; no deployment moratorium trigger; no authority ceiling enforcement | Golden Paths: standardized infrastructure provisioning with authority exposure pre-scoring; Guardrails: mandatory Board Risk Committee review at 80% utilization (Amber); automatic deployment moratorium at 90% (Red); breach of the ceiling (100%) is a zero-tolerance event | Predictable, cost-efficient infrastructure setup; eliminates ad hoc sprawl (efficiency) |

## The Constitutional Architecture: Operationalizing MANDATE

The Shadow AI crisis is not a technology problem; it is an authority vacuum. MANDATE is the EDS framework's constitutional instrument for closing that vacuum. It is not a software product or a technical standard; it is the board-level instrument through which the organization establishes that machine decision authority is formally delegated, explicitly bounded, and continuously monitored. To realize its full power, that authority must be anchored in a technical enforcement architecture that translates board-level policy into automated, real-time controls, making the governed path the only path. The Constitutional Engine is that architecture: the operational expression of the Governance Doctrine in code, configuration, and infrastructure. Executive leadership must authorize its construction as the direct technical counterpart to the constitutional act of adopting the MANDATE. This is not a standard technology stack; it is a governance-native architectural layer designed to ensure that no machine decision ever occurs outside of a board-delegated authority. This architecture evolves to include a mix of autonomous machine decisions and verification workflows as AI adoption matures and organizational confidence in these systems increases. Building these layers to be configuration-driven ensures that the system evolves through simple policy adjustments rather than requiring the recoding or reconstruction of modules from scratch.

## The Architecture Disruption: From Blueprints to Velocity

To understand why the Constitutional Engine is necessary, we must first look at how enterprise systems were traditionally constructed. For decades, software engineering was a discipline of rigid blueprints. Organizations spent months on requirement gathering and architectural design before a single line of code was written. This was a deterministic world where logic was hard-coded or statically configured via rule engines, paths were predictable, and calculation results were always certain. Architecture was the anchor that ensured safety, security, and compliance.

The arrival of generative AI and agentic AI has fundamentally disrupted this orderly progression. The probabilistic nature of large language models has introduced a development style that feels like agile on steroids, where deployment speed often outpaces the maturity of the underlying control framework. Projects can move from pilot to production at breakneck speed, often fueled by the democratization of tools that let business units bypass central IT guardrails. While this velocity is a competitive advantage, it often discards the structural discipline required for enterprise safety and creates fertile ground for the Shadow Tax discussed earlier. The Constitutional Engine is the architectural response to this shift. It is designed to bring the traditional rigors of blueprinting to the modern speed of AI, ensuring that innovation does not outpace institutional control.

## The Authority Gap: Why Policy Is Not Enough

In traditional enterprise settings, automated and system-driven governance often lags because it occurs through retrospective audits or manual checklists. In the age of delegated machine authority, where decisions happen at machine speed, lagging governance is effectively no governance at all. This creates the Authority Gap, which is the distance between the board's risk appetite and the autonomous agent's actual execution.

To close this gap, the architecture must move from detective controls to preventative interdiction. This is achieved through the Constitutional Engine, an integrated architecture spanning four layers: the governance strategy and doctrine layer, the business actor layer, the application component layer, and the physical and data layer. Figure 1-1 presents the complete Architectural Building Block (ABB) Catalog, mapping each layer from board-level constitutional doctrine through to the runtime data infrastructure that enforces it. At the execution layer of this architecture, four specific components serve as the runtime enforcement controls, the instruments that act at the moment of decision, within the authority boundaries pre-authorized by GMI certification. Figure 1-2 identifies these runtime components as the primary instruments for enforcing authority.

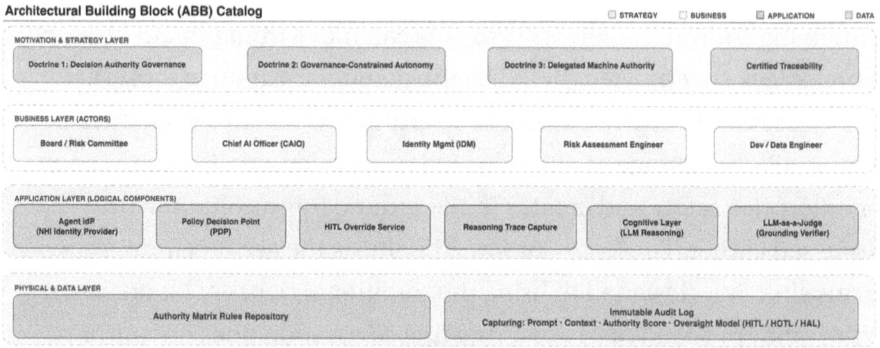


***Figure 1-1.*** *The EDS Architectural Building Block (ABB) Catalog—four-layer constitutional architecture spanning the motivation and strategy layer, the business layer, the application layer, and the physical and data layer*

# Non-human Identity and Access Governance

A fundamental requirement for any Constitutional Engine is establishing a rigorous identity framework for machine actors. In a governed enterprise, an autonomous agent cannot exist as an anonymous script or a generic service account. Every agent must be assigned a unique and verifiable NHI within the corporate identity management (IM) system.

This identity is the foundation of the entire authority chain. Just as a senior executive is granted specific financial sign-off limits based on their role, an AI agent is granted decision authority based on its verified identity or none at all, which will be the case in most early-stage adoptions.

Any attempt to deploy a model or agent that bypasses these enterprise access control rules must be treated as an extreme risk and addressed as an immediate threat to the organization's constitutional integrity. By anchoring agent identities in the existing IM infrastructure, the board ensures that machine actors in the enterprise are subject to the same lifecycle management and security reviews as human employees. The system must support immediate identity revocation to act as a technical kill switch for any agent exhibiting unauthorized or emergent behavior. This identity discipline is not merely a security control; it is the human dimension of the Director's Mindset applied to machine actors: every NHI in the enterprise must be as accountable as the executive who authorized its deployment.

## The Authority Loop: Policy Decision Point and the HITL Override Service

At the heart of the Constitutional Engine lies the PDP, the component that intercepts every proposed agent action before execution and evaluates it against the authority policy. Every time an AI agent proposes a significant action, such as repricing a contract or approving a credit line, the PDP intercepts the proposal before it is executed. To perform this assessment, the PDP must query a deterministic source of truth: the Authority Matrix Rules Repository.

The Authority Matrix Rules Repository is the technical implementation of the Machine Decision Authority Matrix (the Authority Matrix), the board instrument that defines the boundaries of machine decision authority across all operational domains. Throughout this book, "**the Authority Matrix**" refers to the board-level governance policy. The Authority Matrix Rules Repository is its digital manifestation: a hardened configuration store that translates high-level policy into specific, machine-readable rules that the PDP can evaluate at runtime. This separation is critical because it enables the board to adjust risk appetite and authority limits through simple configuration updates to the repository rather than requiring recoding of the model integration layer.

The PDP queries this repository to answer a single, critical question: does this agent hold the delegated authority for this decision domain, as defined in the Authority Matrix Rules Repository?

If the action is indexed and within the pre-approved authority score, the PDP permits the transaction and records it in the Immutable Audit Log. However, if the decision is unindexed, meaning the AI has encountered a novel scenario for which the board has not yet delegated authority, the system does not simply fail or proceed blindly. It triggers the HITL Override Service.

The HITL Override Service is the technical embodiment of Doctrine 2 (Governance-Constrained Autonomy). It ensures that machine autonomy never outpaces the organization's ability to govern it. When the PDP flags a high-risk or unindexed decision, the HITL Override Service dynamically routes the request based on the risk score:

- **Low-Risk Anomalies:** These are logged and routed for notification and review under the applicable oversight model, rather than triggering a real-time halt.
- **High-Risk Anomalies:** These trigger a mandatory halt and route the decision to a certified Human-on-the-Loop (HOTL) supervisor for immediate, real-time intervention.
- **Autonomy Budget Breaches:** If a proposed action would breach the Autonomy Budget ceiling, it is blocked absent prior Board Risk Committee approval; the system alerts the CAIO, and expanding the ceiling itself requires a formal Full Board resolution.

The routing above is a simplified preview. In every case, the proposed action is held—paused, queued, or awaiting confirmation—before execution; what differs is the oversight response, which is governed by the deployment's oversight model (HITL, HOTL, or HAL). Chapter 4 defines these execution behaviors precisely.

This mechanism ensures that the Director's Mindset, which is the ability to ask who holds this authority, is technically enforced. It prevents the Shadow AI tax by making the unauthorized path technically impossible. Figure 1-2 illustrates the runtime enforcement layer of the Constitutional Engine, showing how the board's three doctrines flow through the Policy Decision Point and HITL Override Service to the business actors responsible for oversight, with alert routing differentiated by risk level to the risk assessment engineer, HOTL supervisor, and CAIO.

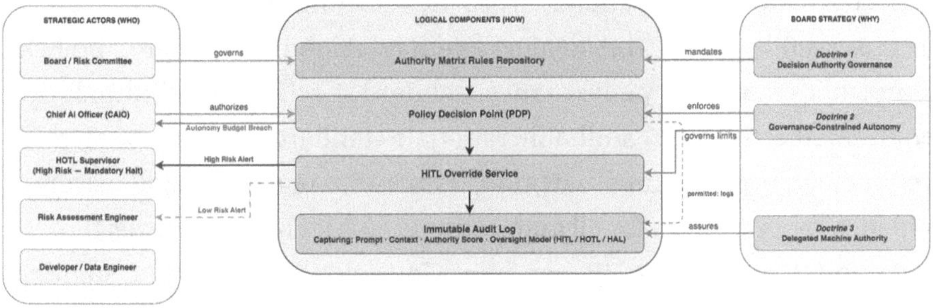


***Figure 1-2.*** *The runtime enforcement layer of the Constitutional Engine—showing the flow from the three Governance Doctrines (right) through the Authority Matrix Rules Repository, Policy Decision Point, HITL Override Service, and Immutable Audit Log (center) to the business actors (left): Board Risk Committee governing the repository, Chief AI Officer receiving Autonomy Budget breach alerts, HOTL supervisor receiving high-risk alerts, and risk assessment engineer receiving low-risk alerts. These four runtime components enforce the authority boundaries that GMI certification has pre-authorized; they do not determine those boundaries—they enforce them.*

## End-to-End Traceability and Reasoning Observability

Traditional systems are built to log results, but they are rarely designed to explain their own logic. In a deterministic world, the code is the explanation. However, in the world of generative AI, the path to a decision is often as important as the decision itself. This necessitates a new approach to observability that captures and analyzes machine reasoning.

Every execution of an agent must be assigned a unique Execution ID, the session/task identifier that threads every log entry for a single workflow into a reconstructible, ordered audit trail. This ID is passed end to end through every service and component involved in the transaction, serving as the correlation thread that binds the original query to the internal reasoning steps and finally to the resulting action captured in the observability layer. The Logging and Explainability Standard, the EDS framework's mandatory governance standard specifying minimum logging requirements, the ≥98% auditable rationale standard, decision audit trail architecture, override capability obligations, and regulatory defensibility evidence requirements for all autonomous AI systems, formalizes the Execution ID as one of its 18 mandatory log fields. The complete Standard, including its full 18-field log schema, is formally established in Chapter 11. Critically, the architecture must now capture the model's intermediate reasoning steps. This is a significant shift for many enterprises because deterministic systems do not reason and therefore do not produce reasoning logs. The Constitutional Engine treats reasoning as a primary data source for governance. The Reasoning Trace Capture infrastructure does not merely record correct answers. It monitors the model's logical path to ensure it remains within ethical and operational boundaries. Any reasoning trace that exhibits deceptive or manipulative logic must automatically trigger an alert and an enterprise review. This review process allows the organization to develop mitigation plans before an erratic thought process leads to a catastrophic operational failure.

## The Immutable Audit Log: The System of Record for AI

The final component of the architecture in the scope of this chapter is the Immutable Audit Log, the system of record for every machine decision. In a regulated environment, trust is not an emotion but a verifiable trail. Unlike standard application logs, the Immutable Audit Log captures a comprehensive governance trace, including intent, context, the authority score, and the full reasoning trace, all correlated via the Execution ID. It also records the applicable oversight model—Human-in-the-Loop (HITL), Human-on-the-Loop (HOTL), or Human-Above-the-Loop (HAL)—and the specific version of that model used.

By establishing the Immutable Audit Log as the system of record, the organization achieves Certified Operational Velocity. Auditors no longer need to investigate how the model works; they need only review the Log to confirm that every decision remained within the board's constitutional limits, as defined in the Authority Matrix.

## Summary

This chapter established the constitutional foundation of the EDS framework, the governing law that every subsequent architectural decision in this book must satisfy. The key takeaways are as follows:

- **Governance precedes architecture.** The Constitutional Engine is not a layer added to the AI system; it is the condition under which the AI system may operate. The Authority Matrix, the Policy Decision Point, the HITL Override Service, and the Immutable Audit Log are not optional enhancements; they are the minimum infrastructure required before any autonomous action is authorized.

- **The GMI certification system translates the board's risk appetite into deployment permissions.** The five GMI levels, from Constitutional Foundations to Full Autonomy, define which Autonomy Levels a system may operate at, which oversight model applies, and what circuit-break controls must be technically enforced. A system that has not been certified cannot be deployed at scale; certification is the governance gate, not the compliance report.
- **Human primacy is a constitutional principle, not a quality guideline.** The HITL gate is not triggered because the system performed poorly. It is triggered because the board has determined that certain categories of decisions require human accountability regardless of machine confidence. That determination is encoded in the Authority Matrix and enforced by the separation between the Policy Decision Point (PDP)—the analytical engine that evaluates every candidate output against the board-approved rules and returns a deterministic Allow or Deny verdict—and the Policy Enforcement Point (PEP), the physical gatekeeper and sole component authorized to act on that verdict, releasing the response on Allow or blocking it on Deny. (The PDP and PEP are defined in full in Chapter 4.)
- **The Execution ID is the thread that makes governance auditable.** Every autonomous action—retrieval, generation, gating decision, HITL invocation—is tagged with a single session identifier that threads the complete audit trail into a coherent, ordered record. Without it, governance is policy; with it, governance is evidence.

- **The oversight model is the first architectural constraint, not the last.** Before latency, cost, or capability is considered, the deployment team must determine which oversight model, HITL, HOTL, or HAL, applies to this use case at this Criticality Tier. That determination constrains every subsequent architectural choice in the stack.

The next chapter begins not with architecture but with a diagnosis of why the newly established constitutional framework is necessary in the first place and what the enterprise must clear away before any of it can be built.

**Before You Continue:** The tables below map every governance instrument introduced across this book—what it governs, where it is formally defined, and where it first appears in a blueprint. Return to it whenever a new term requires anchoring.

# EDS Governance Framework: Reference Card

This card is a navigational reference for the full book. Each instrument is formally defined in the chapter listed; return to this page whenever a new term requires anchoring.

| **CONSTITUTIONAL LAYER *Board-Level Authority*** | | | |
|---|---|---|---|
| **Instrument** | **What It Governs** | **Defined In** | **First Applied** |
| **MANDATE** | Supreme constitutional act: formally delegates, bounds, and monitors all machine decision authority. No EDS instrument operates without it. | Chapter 1 | Chapter 1—three doctrines |
| **Three Governance Doctrines** | Decision Authority Governance · Governance-Constrained Autonomy · Delegated Machine Authority. Constitutional constraints that no business case may override. | Chapter 1 | Every chapter |
| **Governance Maturity Index (GMI)** | Five-level certification scale. No system may operate at an Autonomy Level exceeding the org's certified GMI level. Certification evidence must be formally approved. | Chapter 1 | Chapter 1 Table 1-1; Chapter 12 roadmap |
| **Autonomy Level taxonomy** | Five levels (1 Assistive ➤ 5 Multi-agent). Determines the required oversight model and governance controls for every deployment. GMI level is the hard ceiling. | Chapter 1 | Every blueprint chapter |

(*continued*)

| **CONSTITUTIONAL LAYER *Board-Level Authority*** | | | |
|---|---|---|---|
| **Instrument** | **What It Governs** | **Defined In** | **First Applied** |
| **Guarded Innovation** | Board risk posture: autonomous AI supported where it improves performance; zero tolerance for uncontrolled autonomy or irreversible actions without circuit breaks. | Chapter 1 | Chapter 3; Chapter 12 |
| **Autonomy Register** | Live inventory of every AI system operating under formally delegated machine authority. No production deployment without a registered entry. | Chapter 1 | Chapter 2—Governance Principles |
| **North Star AI** | Three-horizon strategic vision bounded by Autonomy Levels, certified by GMI, and authorized through MDAM. Operationalizes constitutional framework into a governed deployment trajectory. | Chapter 1 | Chapter 1; Chapter 12 roadmap |

| **OVERSIGHT and ACCOUNTABILITY** ***Human Control Instruments*** | | | |
|---|---|---|---|
| **Instrument** | **What It Governs** | **Defined In** | **First Applied** |
| **Human-in-the-Loop (HITL)** | Levels 1–2. Human approves every individual action before execution. Hard stop enforced at orchestrator—cannot be bypassed by the system's own logic. | Chapter 1 | Chapter 4—oversight decision matrix |
| **Human-on-the-Loop (HOTL)** | Level 3. Certified supervisor monitors in real time with active authority to intervene, adjust, or halt. System executes autonomously between interventions. | Chapter 1 | Chapter 4—oversight decision matrix |
| **Human-Above-the-Loop (HAL)** | Levels 4–5. Supervisor reviews output batches and approves before any material commitment is executed. | Chapter 1 | Chapter 4—oversight decision matrix |
| **AI System Criticality Classification** | Four tiers: Critical, High, Moderate, Low. Assigned before any architecture decision. Determines the minimum oversight model and audit obligations. | Chapter 3 | Chapter 4—decision matrix Table 4-1 |
| **HOTL Certification Framework** | Five-component program certifying supervisors can genuinely challenge autonomous decisions. Tests automation bias resistance. Valid 12 months. Lapse = system suspension. | Chapter 11 | Chapter 11—UC11–15 blueprints |

(*continued*)

| **OVERSIGHT and ACCOUNTABILITY** ***Human Control Instruments*** | | | |
|---|---|---|---|
| **Instrument** | **What It Governs** | **Defined In** | **First Applied** |
| **Span-of-control thresholds** | Max decisions/hour a single HOTL supervisor may oversee: Critical ≤50 · High ≤100 · Moderate ≤200 · Low ≤500. Exceeding = governance breach. SRE shifts to HITL at threshold. | Chapter 11 | Chapter 11—Table 11-1 |

| **AUTHORITY QUANTIFICATION** ***Agentic AI Instruments*** | | | |
|---|---|---|---|
| **Instrument** | **What It Governs** | **Defined In** | **First Applied** |
| **ADAE—Autonomous Decision Authority Evaluation** | Four-dimensional scoring: Financial Authority 40% · Customer Reach 30% · Operational Reach 20% · Decision Velocity 10%. Produces composite score determining Autonomy Level and Delegation Tier. | Chapter 9 | Chapter 9—UC6 worked example |
| **Delegation Tier** | Three governance bands derived from ADAE score: Supervised (Levels 1–2) · Monitored (Level 3) · Delegated (Levels 4–5). Governs intensity of oversight controls. | Chapter 9 | Chapter 9—Table 9-1 |
| **Machine Decision Authority Matrix (MDAM)** | Board instrument authorizing which operational domains agents may act in, at what maximum magnitude, under which oversight model. No agent may act in an unauthorized domain. | Chapter 9 | Chapter 9; applied Chapters 10 and 11 |

(*continued*)

| **AUTHORITY QUANTIFICATION *Agentic AI Instruments*** | | | |
|---|---|---|---|
| **Instrument** | **What It Governs** | **Defined In** | **First Applied** |
| **Autonomy Budget** | Board-approved aggregate ceiling on total delegated machine authority (illustrative only—set per board resolution; see Chapter 9). Prevents invisible concentration of authority. Utilization is tracked against the ceiling: at 80% (Amber), no further deployment proceeds until the Board Risk Committee approves a management plan; at 90% (Red), an automatic deployment moratorium applies; reaching 100% is a zero-tolerance breach. The ceiling itself may be changed only by Full Board resolution. | Chapter 9 | Chapter 9; Chapter 12 portfolio tracker |
| **Maximum action magnitude (MAM)** | Per-system single-transaction ceiling on authority exercised without human confirmation. Set at infrastructure level within the board-authorized MDAM domain limit. | Chapter 9 | Chapter 11—mandatory log field |

| **SECURITY and ACCESS ARCHITECTURE** ***Identity and Enforcement*** | | | |
|---|---|---|---|
| **Instrument** | **What It Governs** | **Defined In** | **First Applied** |
| **Document-level access control (DLAC)/Security Trimming** | Least privilege enforced at retrieval: access filters applied per query, per user, per chunk. Resolves the Isolation Paradox without fragmenting the knowledge corpus. | Chapter 4 | Chapter 4; every RAG blueprint |
| **Zero-Trust AI (ZTAI)** | Extends Zero Trust to non-human identities: every agent action verified, least-privileged, and logged regardless of network origin. | Chapter 4 | Chapter 9—agentic deployments |
| **NHI Lifecycle Governance (JML Framework)** | Governs provisioning, modification, and deprovisioning of non-human identity credentials for all agentic systems. Orphan NHI = zero-tolerance breach. Mirrors system lifecycle. | Chapter 10 | Chapter 10—all five UC blueprints |
| **Policy-as-Code (PaC)/Governance-as-a-Service (GaaS)** | Real-time enforcement of governance rules at execution. Policy Conflict Resolution Engine applies strict priority: Safety > Regulatory > Security > Efficiency. | Chapter 9 | Chapter 9; Chapter 10 |

*(continued)*

| **SECURITY and ACCESS ARCHITECTURE** ***Identity and Enforcement*** | | | |
|---|---|---|---|
| **Instrument** | **What It Governs** | **Defined In** | **First Applied** |
| **Delegated Authorization Service** | Enforces Permission Mirroring: agent's permissible actions technically constrained to systems and operations in the board-authorized authority scope. | Chapter 9 | Chapter 9; Chapter 10 |

| **QUALITY, ASSURANCE & LOGGING** ***Accuracy and Audit Standards*** | | | |
|---|---|---|---|
| **Instrument** | **What It Governs** | **Defined In** | **First Applied** |
| **Deterministic Shell** | Five-component control sequence transforming a probabilistic LLM into a governed asset: PDP → PEP → Groundedness Check → HITL Gate → Immutable Audit Log. | Chapter 2 | Chapter 2; every blueprint |
| **Groundedness (Faithfulness) Score** | 0–1 metric: how faithfully the LLM's answer is supported by retrieved sources. 1.0 = fully entailed. Measures citation fidelity to retrieved sources, not independent factual correctness. Legal proxy for factual authority. Enforced at Citation Threshold by PDP/PEP chain. | Chapter 5 | Chapter 5; every RAG blueprint |

(*continued*)

| **QUALITY, ASSURANCE & LOGGING** ***Accuracy and Audit Standards*** | | | |
|---|---|---|---|
| **Instrument** | **What It Governs** | **Defined In** | **First Applied** |
| **LLMOps/Accuracy Engine** | Continuous governance assurance: Dual-stage retrieval · Groundedness monitoring · Drift detection · CRAG feedback loop. Detects Threshold Drift, Supervisor Drift, and Prompt Drift before they become governance failures. | Chapter 5 | Chapter 5; Chapter 6 onward |
| **Corrective RAG (CRAG)** | Closed feedback loop: HITL overrides become active index-optimization signals, continuously improving retrieval quality in production. | Chapter 5 | Chapter 6—UC1 enhancement |
| **Logging and Explainability Standard/≥98% auditable rationale standard** | ≥98% of regulated-domain decisions must generate a complete auditable rationale before execution (write-before-execute). Below 98% in any quarter = Board Risk Committee escalation. Seven-year minimum retention. | Chapter 11 | Chapter 11—UC11–15 blueprints |
| **Immutable Audit Log** | Tamper-proof record of every agent decision, HITL event, override rationale, and NHI action. Captures the complete accountability chain—not merely model output. | Chapter 4 | Chapter 4; every blueprint |

*(continued)*

| **QUALITY, ASSURANCE & LOGGING** ***Accuracy and Audit Standards*** | | | |
|---|---|---|---|
| **Instrument** | **What It Governs** | **Defined In** | **First Applied** |
| **Safety Runtime Environment (SRE)** | Always-on infrastructure enforcing span-of-control thresholds, triggering automatic HITL mode shifts at threshold, and enforcing fail-closed when logging infrastructure is unavailable. | Chapter 11 | Chapter 11—UC11–15 |

| **MATURITY and DEPLOYMENT FRAMEWORKS** ***Sequencing and Scaling*** | | | |
|---|---|---|---|
| **Instrument** | **What It Governs** | **Defined In** | **First Applied** |
| **EDS blueprint template** | Unified five-section structure for all 15 use cases: Business Problem · Governance Instrument · Technical Architecture · Governance Delta · Board Outcome. Governance stated before architecture in every instance. | Chapter 6 | Chapters 6–12 |
| **AI risk taxonomy (eight categories)** | Decision Velocity · Cascade Failure · Governance Drift · Model Behavior · Prompt Drift · Accountability Diffusion · Concentration · Regulatory Explainability. Governs workload classification before any deployment model is selected. | Chapter 3 | Chapter 3; Chapter 12 Table 12-1 |

*(continued)*

| MATURITY and DEPLOYMENT FRAMEWORKS *Sequencing and Scaling* | | | |
|---|---|---|---|
| **Instrument** | **What It Governs** | **Defined In** | **First Applied** |
| **Safety Constraint Engineering (SCE)** | Stage 4 instrument: pre-verified safety specifications enforced by a Runtime Monitor before every agent action. Non-negotiable safety rules always override conflicting objectives and policy logic. | Chapter 12 | Chapter 12—Stage 4 systems |
| **Orchestration-based Saga Pattern** | Distributed transaction management for agentic workflows: predefined compensating transactions for each forward action; idempotent commands preventing unintended retry side effects. | Chapter 9 | Chapter 10; Chapter 11—UC11–15 |

# References


Hossain, M Maruf. 2026. Continuous Admissibility: A Temporal Governance Framework for Delegated Machine Authority in Regulated Enterprises. Preprint. Zenodo. `https://doi.org/10.5281/zenodo.20580716`.

IBM Security. 2025. Cost of a Data Breach Report 2025. Armonk, NY: IBM Corporation. `https://www.ibm.com/reports/data-breach`.

McKinsey & Company. 2025. The State of AI in 2025: Agents, Innovation, and Transformation. New York: McKinsey & Company. `https://www.mckinsey.com/capabilities/quantumblack/our-insights/the-state-of-ai`.

CHAPTER 2

# From Chatbot Hype to Enterprise Reality

Chapter 1 established the three Governance Doctrines, the concept of delegated machine authority, and the Constitutional Engine that enforces the board's risk appetite at the infrastructure layer. This chapter begins not with architecture but with diagnosis: the structural reasons why the constitutional framework is necessary in the first place and what the enterprise must construct before any AI system can be trusted with consequential decisions. Every organization experimenting with generative AI is, in some form, running the same pilot. A capable model is connected to an internal knowledge base or a business workflow, the initial results impress, and the business case is made. Then the attempt to scale begins and fails. Not because the model was wrong, but because the model was never the constraint. The constraint was the governance architecture that no one had built around it.

The gap is structural, not technical. Consumer AI tools are designed for a world in which the cost of a wrong answer is inconvenience. Enterprise AI operates in a world where a wrong answer can be a regulatory breach, a financial liability, a safety failure, or an unauthorized commitment made on behalf of the organization by a system that was never formally authorized to make such a commitment. Closing that gap requires moving from a model selection problem to a governance architecture problem,


M. M. Hossain and A. A. N. Ponnusamy, *Governance-First AI*,
https://doi.org/10.1007/979-8-8688-3118-8_2

from asking "Which LLM should we use?" to asking "What control layer must surround it before we are permitted to deploy it?" The answer to the second question is the subject of this book.

Chapter 1 established the constitutional governance framework: the three doctrines and the concept of delegated machine authority. This chapter operationalizes that framework in light of the realities of enterprise deployment, beginning by introducing and defining the six Governance Principles that translate those doctrines into architectural requirements. It does so through the lens of 15 high-value use cases spanning the full spectrum of AI complexity, from simple RAG-based knowledge retrieval to fully autonomous, mission-critical agentic systems, and demonstrates that each one is governed not by the intelligence of the underlying model but by the robustness of the deterministic control layer surrounding it.

This chapter is organized into five movements. First, it diagnoses the structural reasons why AI fails to scale: the illusion of autonomy, the inherent non-determinism of LLMs, the trust deficit they create, and the attack surface that autonomous action introduces. Second, it establishes the governance-first mandate and translates the six Governance Principles defined in this chapter into specific architectural requirements. Third, it maps the 15 use cases across four strategic value pillars, showing how governance complexity scales with business value and risk. Fourth, it previews the four non-negotiable architectural controls—Zero-Trust access enforcement, immutable audit logging, the Deterministic Shell, and the Policy Enforcement Engine—which form the common foundation every use case inherits. Fifth, it introduces the Deterministic Shell in detail: the five-component control sequence that transforms a probabilistic LLM core into a governed, certifiable enterprise asset. Each use case chapter from Chapter 6 onward follows a unified five-section blueprint structure—Business Problem, Governance Instrument, Technical Architecture, Enhancement, and Board Outcome—with governance established before architecture in every instance.

**Governance Leaders**: The six Governance Principles and the four strategic value pillars are your primary sections.

**Architects and Practitioners**: The Deterministic Shell and its five components are the technical entry point.

## The Central Thesis of This Book

The central thesis of this book, that governance is the strategic accelerator, is built on an architectural analysis of 15 high-value generative AI use cases. These use cases span the full spectrum of enterprise AI complexity, from foundational RAG to the highest-risk, autonomous, agentic systems in areas such as predictive maintenance (PdM) and financial fraud monitoring.

Each use case is governed by a specific Autonomy Level (1–5) and a corresponding oversight model—Human-in-the-Loop (HITL), Human-on-the-Loop (HOTL), or Human-Above-the-Loop (HAL)—derived from the constitutional Governance Principles introduced in Chapter 1. These are not design preferences; they are mandatory governance requirements that the surrounding architecture must technically enforce.

Before diving into the governance mandates these demands necessitate, Table 2-1 provides a quick reference to the use case (UC) identifiers that will be referenced throughout the remainder of the book.

***Table 2-1.*** *15 Enterprise AI use cases used in this book*

| Use Case | Title | Primary Objective |
|---|---|---|
| **UC1** | AI-powered frontline knowledge assistant | Improve staff efficiency and reduce query resolution time. |
| **UC2** | Enterprise knowledge and regulatory compliance platform | Maximizing operational velocity and achieving certifiable regulatory assurance. |
| **UC3** | Intelligent document quality and consistency uplift | Enhance data integrity by reducing documentation errors and eliminating conflicting information. |
| **UC4** | Domain-specific AI stylist and language adapter | Ensure AI outputs are technically precise and adhere to the firm's proprietary language, brand, or executive voice. |
| **UC5** | Predictive customer insight and proactive service support | Enhance customer experience and proactive engagement with real-time, predictive recommendations. |
| **UC6** | Autonomous IT service resolution agent | Automate the end-to-end resolution of high-volume, repetitive IT support and back-office issues. |
| **UC7** | End-to-end insurance claims agent | Automate the entire claims processing workflow from intake to payment/denial, enhancing speed and accuracy. |
| **UC8** | Autopilot market intelligence system | Deliver real-time, synthesized market intelligence reports and strategic recommendations autonomously. |
| **UC9** | Financial risk and fraud monitoring agent | Proactively detect and mitigate high-impact financial risk events, fraud, and anomalies in real time. |

(*continued*)

*Table 2-1.* (*continued*)

| Use Case | Title | Primary Objective |
|---|---|---|
| **UC10** | Hotel dynamic pricing and booking agent | Offer a fully autonomous, conversational booking experience while dynamically optimizing room rates. |
| **UC11** | Restaurant waitlist and preference agent | Autonomously manage waitlists, optimize table turnover, and capture detailed customer preferences. |
| **UC12** | Event ticket and seat upgrade agent | Autonomously handle complex ticket exchanges, secure seat upgrades, and manage event logistics inquiries. |
| **UC13** | Aircraft predictive maintenance | Enhance aircraft reliability and safety by scheduling preventive maintenance at the optimal point in a component's Remaining Useful Life (RUL). |
| **UC14** | Predictive maintenance for defense equipment | Enhance operational readiness, safety, and longevity of defense assets through AI-driven preventive maintenance. |
| **UC15** | Predictive maintenance for manufacturing equipment | Improve production uptime and reduce equipment failure through AI-enabled preventive maintenance. |

## Illusion of Autonomy

The public consciousness, shaped by the pervasive accessibility of consumer-grade generative tools, operates under the illusion of autonomy: the idea that successful enterprise AI deployment is a simple matter of selecting a powerful LLM and connecting it to a corporate data source. Users experience immediate, often dazzling, conversational prowess, leading to the dangerous executive expectation that complex business processes, from underwriting a loan to approving a critical repair, can be solved with this simple, plug-and-play approach.

This illusion, however, collapses the moment a proof of concept (PoC) touches sensitive, regulated, or high-stakes data. The structural and cultural gap separating consumer hype from enterprise reality is defined by a profound shift in stakes:

- In the consumer world, an ungrounded AI response (a hallucination) is a novelty, a technical oddity, or a minor inconvenience.
- In the enterprise world, a single ungrounded hallucination can result in a catastrophic audit failure, a major data leakage event, or a liability that cannot be insured against.

This book's fundamental analysis demonstrates that the successful integration of LLMs is not defined by the model's inherent intelligence, which is fast becoming a commodity, but by the robust, auditable governance architecture that surrounds it. The true challenge is not teaching the AI to talk, but building a system that, under regulatory scrutiny, can demonstrate why it spoke, what data it used, and who was authorized to retrieve that information. Only through this governance-first lens can the enterprise move past pilot purgatory and achieve sustained, compliant value.

## Unfulfilled Promise of Simple Generative AI

The initial enthusiasm for generative AI focused almost entirely on its conversational and content generation capabilities. However, enterprise deployment demands systems capable of executing complex, goal-oriented, multi-step workflows. In this domain, general LLMs routinely fall short of operational standards, resulting in stalled pilot projects and a widening gap between capability and reliable production use.

Research indicates a significant baseline performance gap: the best language models can complete only approximately 30% of the agentic workplace tasks they are tested on in the TheAgentCompany benchmark, meaning they fail roughly 70% of the time in scenarios requiring complex planning, tool use, and data synthesis (Xu et al., "TheAgentCompany," arXiv:2412.14161v3, 2025). This inherent unreliability in executing multi-step enterprise workflows fundamentally counters the consumer-facing hype surrounding autonomous capabilities. This high failure rate necessitates treating orchestration and governance not as optional add-ons but as foundational prerequisites for achieving enterprise scalability and reliability. A surrounding deterministic architecture must correct the inherent probabilistic nature of the base LLM to ensure production viability.

The unreliability is often exacerbated by integration complexity. Enterprise tasks require LLMs to interact with internal APIs, legacy systems, and proprietary databases, for example, updating an asset record, calculating costs, or retrieving prices from internal documents. The critical failure point often lies in the technical integration gap: the probabilistic LLM struggles to reliably map its creative, natural-language reasoning onto the rigid input requirements of existing enterprise APIs. To address this challenge and ensure reliable autonomous execution, the architecture mandates an intermediary layer: the Tool Schema Definition and Translation Layer (defined fully in Chapter 9), which standardizes API access for agents. This mechanism ensures that tool definitions adhere to robust standards, maximizing the accuracy of autonomous execution and securing documented efficiency gains.

## Core Distinction: Perception, Reasoning, and Action

The enterprise market is rapidly moving beyond simple, read-only RAG assistants to powerful, read/write agentic AI systems capable of autonomous action. This transition from consultation (answering questions) to transaction (executing business processes) fundamentally escalates the risk profile, demanding a corresponding increase in governance maturity.

AI agents are defined by their ability to perceive their environment, process information, reason about goals, and take autonomous actions to complete a specific task without constant human intervention. This shift from generating simple text to executing critical, multi-step transactions means the risk profile instantly moves from factual inaccuracy (hallucination) to catastrophic financial, compliance, and safety breaches (i.e., unauthorized action). While the value derived from agentic AI is massive, this operational value is only safely accessible if the system can manage the inherent risks associated with autonomy. This requires explicit architectural controls, such as Agent Scope Enforcement (Sandboxing), and mandatory oversight enforcement tied directly to the Autonomy Level classification.

Despite the compelling promises of this emerging technology, executive hesitation remains high. Current data shows that while 23% of organizations have launched AI agent pilots and a further 61% are still exploring, only 2% have deployed AI agents at full scale, and trust in fully autonomous agents has dropped from 43% to 27% in a single year (Capgemini Research Institute, "Rise of Agentic AI: How Trust Is the Key to Human-AI Collaboration," 2025). This significant lag between technological capability and enterprise adoption is directly attributed to pervasive concerns over unchecked autonomy, governance maturity, and the complexity of managing agent sprawl. This evidence reinforces the central thesis: the technological capability to deploy autonomous systems has been demonstrated, but the governance architecture necessary to scale and maintain these systems safely remains the primary bottleneck.

## Enterprise Trust Deficit

The security and reliability concerns inherent in LLMs have become the primary inhibitor to enterprise-wide scaling, creating a critical trust deficit that must be addressed through architectural mandates rather than reactive patching:

- **Systemic Fear of Hallucination**: The potential for LLM hallucination, the generation of factually incorrect or fabricated information, such as citing nonexistent policies or fake legal cases, is a major source of executive and user concern. This fear is widespread; only 19% of IT application leaders surveyed expressed high or complete trust in their vendor's abilities to protect against AI hallucinations (Gartner, "Gartner Survey Finds Just 15% of IT Application Leaders Are Considering, Piloting, or Deploying Fully Autonomous AI Agents," press release, September 30, 2025). This persistent fear demands architectural mitigation. The system must implement mandatory GRC controls, such as grounding verification, which generates a Support Score, the raw numerical output from which the Groundedness (Faithfulness) Score (a 0–1 measure of how faithfully the LLM's answer is supported by retrieved source documents; formally defined in Chapter 5) is derived, to factually verify the LLM's claims against retrieved sources before the output is delivered to the user.

- **Prompt Injection As the New Attack Vector**: The capability for autonomous action dramatically increases the system's vulnerability to manipulation. A large majority of IT application leaders (74%) believe AI agents represent a new attack vector for their organizations (Gartner, "Gartner Survey Finds Just 15% of IT Application Leaders ...," 2025). This vector is dominated by prompt injection, which is ranked number one on the Open Web Application Security Project (OWASP) Top 10 for LLM Applications (OWASP Foundation, LLM01: 2025). Prompt injection attacks exploit the LLM's fundamental design by manipulating inputs to cause the model to abandon its original, benign instructions. This can enable the agent to exfiltrate private information, generate restricted content, or execute unauthorized code. The risk is further compounded in multi-agent systems by indirect prompt injection, in which malicious instructions can be embedded in a single compromised resource, causing the payload to propagate across collaborating agents.

- **Security Governance Disparity**: While leadership aligns on the strategic risks of autonomy, practitioners (engineers) often prioritize tactical implementation issues. Security practitioners tend to prioritize security and data governance controls more than executives do. This difference in perception underscores the urgent need for a unified strategy: the tactical mandates of security teams, such as Personally Identifiable Information (PII) or Protected Health Information (PHI) leakage prevention via retrieval-time access enforcement (Security Trimming) and foundational data classification checks during ingestion, must be elevated to strategic investment priorities by executive leadership. This alignment ensures that necessary controls are implemented from the architecture's inception, rather than applied as costly, reactive patches.

## Governance-First Mandate

The strategic analysis of enterprise risk and the inherent unreliability of general-purpose LLMs in multi-step workflows lead to one inescapable conclusion: governance is the strategic accelerator, not an afterthought. This conclusion is not merely a best practice; it is the operational expression of the constitutional Governance Principles established in Chapter 1. The EDS framework's Principle 5, Governance Primacy Over Delivery, introduced later in this chapter, applies directly here: no delivery timeline, commercial pressure, or cost considerations override the requirement to establish governance controls before a system goes to production.

The governance-first mandate demands a paradigm shift in how AI budgets are allocated and projects are sequenced. It rejects the piecemeal, use-case-by-use-case development model. This path inevitably leads to crippling repetition as every team must rebuild the same security, auditing, and grounding controls, resulting in fragmented compliance and unsustainable operating costs.

This mandate directs the organization to prioritize developing a non-negotiable, common architectural foundation (the subject of Part II) before any high-value use case is allowed to proceed to production. This foundation is not merely a set of guardrails; it is the System of Record for AI Compliance, providing a centralized, comprehensive synthesis of mandatory controls:

- **ZTAI**: Enforcing the least-privilege principle across every data retrieval
- **Immutable Audit Logging**: Creating a tamper-proof record of every agent decision and transaction for full regulatory traceability
- **Groundedness Verification**: Ensuring factual integrity across all LLM outputs

By establishing this robust, certifiable layer on day one, the enterprise moves from managing risk reactively to proactively engineering trust. This is the only path to achieving Certified Operational Velocity, the ability to deploy high-value, high-risk generative AI systems (such as the autonomous agents in UC6–15) at speed, with the assurance that the underlying architecture inherently manages compliance and security.

## The Six Governance Principles in Practice

The six principles in this chapter are the operational layer beneath the three constitutional doctrines established in Chapter 1. The doctrines express the board's governing commitments: that machine authority must be quantified, that autonomy must be constrained by governance, and that human accountability must be preserved. The principles translate those commitments into specific architectural requirements that system designers, engineers, and governance teams must implement. Where a principle and a doctrine appear to share a name or concept, Governed

Autonomy (Principle 1) reflecting Governance-Constrained Autonomy (Doctrine 2) or Quantified Delegation appearing in both frameworks, this is intentional: the principle is the implementation specification for the doctrine's constitutional commitment, not a duplicate of it.

The EDS framework's Agentic AI Governance Policy, the organization's binding operational policy for autonomous system deployment, owned by the CAIO and authorized by the board, translates the constitutional Governance Doctrine from Chapter 1 into six binding organizational principles. These principles are not aspirational guidelines; they are mandatory constraints that the enterprise architecture must technically enforce. Each one directly shapes the architectural decisions made throughout this book. A note on usage: Throughout this book, "mandatory" applied to architectural controls and governance requirements refers to requirements of the EDS framework unless a specific statute or regulation is cited. EDS framework requirements derive their authority from the board's adoption of the Governance Doctrine, not from external law, though many align with or exceed applicable regulatory obligations.

### PRINCIPLE 1: GOVERNED AUTONOMY

*The organization does not deploy unconstrained agentic AI. Every agentic system operates within a defined autonomy boundary that has been explicitly approved before deployment. Autonomy is a governance decision, not a technical default.*

**Implication for Architecture**: No agentic AI system may be deployed into production without an Autonomy Level classification, a registered entry in the Autonomy Register (the EDS framework's live inventory of all authorized AI deployments, introduced in Chapter 1), and formal approval from the CAIO.

## PRINCIPLE 2: QUANTIFIED DELEGATION

*Machine decision authority is a form of institutional authority. The organization quantifies the total decision authority delegated to agentic AI systems using a structured scoring methodology and manages that aggregate against a board-approved budget ceiling.*

**Implication for Architecture**: Every deployment must be scored for its delegated decision authority before go-live. The Platform Engineering layer must track aggregate authority utilization across the entire AI estate and block deployments that would breach the board-approved ceiling.

## PRINCIPLE 3: HUMAN PRIMACY

*Human authority over agentic AI systems is non-negotiable and non-delegable. Every agentic system at Autonomy Level 3 or above must have a certified Human-on-the-Loop supervisor with active authority to intervene, adjust, or halt the system. No commercial, operational, or efficiency consideration overrides the obligation to maintain human primacy.*

**Implication for Architecture**: The oversight model (i.e., HITL, HOTL, or HAL) specified for each use case in this book is a constitutional requirement, not a design option. The architecture must technically enforce it.

## PRINCIPLE 4: MANDATORY HALT CAPABILITY

*Every agentic AI system in production must have a kill-switch capability that allows an authorized operator to halt, suspend, or roll back the system immediately and unconditionally. The kill switch must operate independently of the system's own decision logic.*

**Implication for Architecture**: Kill-switch design is a non-negotiable component of every agentic blueprint in Parts III and IV. A system without a functioning kill switch is not approved for production deployment.

## PRINCIPLE 5: GOVERNANCE PRIMACY OVER DELIVERY

*Governance controls are not subject to override by delivery timelines, commercial pressures, or cost considerations. Where a technology delivery schedule or business objective conflicts with a governance requirement, the governance requirement prevails.*

**Implication for Architecture**: The common architectural foundation in Part II must be fully certified before any high-value use case proceeds to production. No project sponsor may instruct the governance function to bypass or defer a mandatory control to meet a deployment deadline.

## PRINCIPLE 6: ACCOUNTABILITY FOLLOWS AUTHORITY

*The organization is accountable for the decisions and actions of agentic AI systems operating on its behalf, regardless of whether those systems were built internally or procured from vendors. Accountability cannot be contracted away.*

**Implication for Architecture**: Vendor-supplied agentic systems are subject to the same governance requirements as internally built systems. Procurement contracts for agentic AI must include mandatory governance terms covering telemetry access, circuit-break capability, incident notification, and audit rights.

## Governance As the Accelerator, Not the Brake

Effective risk management is the mechanism that unlocks scale and speed, fundamentally transforming GRC from a bureaucratic burden into a competitive advantage:

- **Governance As the Unlock for Scale**: Governance is the foundational enabler of modernization and AI adoption, fueling innovation by building trust and aligning strategy with business value for scalable transformation. Firms leading the charge in generative AI deployments strongly emphasize that strict governance is not a brake; it is the accelerator. This confidence, built on making data and AI decisions fit for purpose, is what drives the achievement of strategic objectives. The resulting strategic impact is profound: with governance in place, organizations gain the confidence to use modern architecture and advanced analytics effectively, delivering insights that are both action-ready and trusted.
- **Shift to Proactive Assurance**: AI-driven GRC represents a profound shift from a reactive, manual compliance model to a proactive assurance strategy. AI can automate and continuously test controls across systems, detecting failures or exceptions in near real time. This continuous monitoring reduces reliance on periodic, lagging assessments and enables organizations to proactively address compliance gaps before they escalate into breaches. This includes essential capabilities such as regulatory change management, in which Natural Language Processing (NLP) can scan and analyze thousands of regulatory

documents and legal updates daily, immediately aligning existing internal controls with new rules and frameworks.

- **Data Governance As the Foundational Enabler**: Robust governance is critical to protecting the organization's master data, the single, authoritative dataset for core business entities such as customers and patients. Research consistently shows that poor data foundations actively undermine AI progress. The architectural mandate for Data Lineage Tagging during the ingestion phase is a direct technical mechanism to enforce this foundational data quality and records retention requirement across all enterprise use cases.

## LLM Failure Is a Governance Failure

Public and internal LLM failures are not inherent, unavoidable defects in the underlying large language model technology; they are symptomatic of missing or insufficient architectural governance controls needed to manage probabilistic output in a deterministic enterprise context:

- **Failure to Enforce Policy**: An LLM failure, such as providing factually incorrect or inconsistent advice, occurs when the overall system fails to enforce external, auditable constraints. The fault lies in the lack of governance controls, for example, failing to check the Groundedness (Faithfulness) Score against a predefined threshold or to trigger a HITL review for low-confidence answers. The LLM may hallucinate, but the system failed to prevent the hallucination from reaching the user or executing an action on its basis.

- **Non-repudiable Audit Requirement**: For regulated domains, reproducibility and traceability are both a regulatory obligation and an EDS framework requirement, enabling auditors to verify decision paths. The system design must therefore center on creating an immutable record of all transactions and reasoning steps. This necessity is enforced by the immutable audit logging service, which often requires WORM storage to prevent post-incident tampering. Logs must capture comprehensive forensic data, including the complete RAG chain and security metadata tags, for every user request.

## Certified Operational Velocity As the Strategic Metric

The ultimate strategic payoff of a governance-first approach is the operational velocity it unlocks. By guaranteeing trust and auditability through robust architectural controls, the enterprise gains the confidence necessary to move complex, high-impact AI solutions from pilot to scaled production:

- **Defining Certified Operational Velocity**: This concept represents the highest state of AI maturity, the synchronous achievement of dramatic operational efficiency (speed/velocity) and the complete mitigation of systemic regulatory exposure (certified assurance). The objective shifts from generating a merely fast answer to generating a contextualized, compliant, and source-cited response. This transforms the LLM output into an auditable artifact by requiring direct source citations, establishing a foundation for certifiable regulatory assurance.

- **Quantifying the GRC ROI**: Governance is the multiplier that accelerates the quantifiable business case. Automated and embedded governance reduces triage effort, for example, by cutting the time spent detecting and remediating data handling errors—thereby reclaiming engineering hours that can be reinvested into innovation. This efficiency gain directly supports core business objectives, including a predicted 70–80% productivity uplift for frontline staff (UC1). This efficiency, however, is conditional: staff will realize this uplift only if they trust the system's accuracy and compliance, a trust engineered by the underlying governance framework.

## Non-determinism and the Necessity of Hybrid Architecture

The fundamental constraint that drives the governance-first mandate stems from the LLM's core nature: non-determinism. An LLM is a probabilistic engine; it does not operate on traditional enterprise logic (IF/THEN), but instead chooses the next word based on statistical likelihood. This means the same critical query, run twice, can yield two different, often contradictory, responses.

While this inherent flexibility fuels creativity in consumer tools, it introduces intolerable operational and regulatory risks for enterprises. For any use case related to finance (UC9), compliance (UC2), or safety (UC13), system outcomes must be deterministic, repeatable, and auditable—every time. This failure rate renders a pure LLM core entirely unsuitable for anything beyond simple, low-risk content generation.

The Hybrid AI Architecture is the only viable solution for enterprise generative AI. This architecture dictates a strict separation of concerns:

1. **Probabilistic Core**: The LLM is used exclusively for its non-deterministic strengths: synthesizing large volumes of data, processing natural-language queries, and generating creative drafts.

2. **Deterministic Shell**: The probabilistic core is tightly bound by engineered components that enforce logic, safety, and control. This shell includes the RAG pipeline for grounding, the agentic orchestrator for step-by-step logic, and GRC layers, such as mandatory audit logging and Security Trimming.

Only by successfully marrying the LLM's flexible intelligence with a rigid, auditable, and deterministic control layer can the enterprise achieve the safety, reliability, and certified performance required to unlock the high-value, autonomous use cases that drive true organizational value.

## Probabilistic Challenge

The core issue of LLM output variability undermines auditability and debugging, leading to irreproducible results even when identical prompts are used, an unacceptable outcome in regulated environments:

- **The Inconsistency Problem**: Deterministic systems, such as rule-based fraud filters, guarantee consistent, repeatable, and explainable results. In contrast, non-deterministic LLMs embrace adaptability and learning by injecting randomness or relying on learned parameters, leading to shifts in phrasing, tone, or even facts across identical runs, even when using greedy sampling (i.e., temperature set to 0). This unpredictability fundamentally conflicts with the enterprise's need for perfect repeatability and traceability.

- **Batch Invariance Failure**: The randomness is not often attributed to the combination of floating-point non-associativity and concurrent execution on GPUs. That explanation identifies a real mechanism of numerical deviation but is incomplete: as recent work demonstrates, the deeper source is that many GPU inference kernels are not batch-invariant—their output for a given request varies with the overall batch size, which itself fluctuates with server load (He and Thinking Machines Lab, 2025). The numerical result for an individual user request varies subtly with the unpredictable batch size in which it is processed, a factor entirely outside the user's control. Since the server's load is constantly changing, the batch size is unpredictable for the user, resulting in a final output that appears non-deterministic.
- **Regulatory Violation**: When an LLM decision lacks deterministic reproducibility, auditors cannot verify that the decision is traceable and repeatable. This creates a high-stakes compliance gap in regulated domains, which the EU AI Act (Regulation EU 2024/1689) explicitly emphasizes.

## Architectural Response

The fundamental conflict between the need for creative, flexible solutions (probabilistic LLM) and the requirement for auditable, consistent results (deterministic GRC) is optimally resolved through the Hybrid AI Architecture:

- **Hybrid Architecture Design Principle**: Hybrid AI combines predictable, rule-based, and auditable logic with non-deterministic methods that handle novelty and adapt to complex situations. This separation of concerns is the mandated design choice for systems with mixed requirements, such as those balancing high novelty (e.g., generative AI) with high regulatory requirements (e.g., compliance and auditability).
- **Separation of Concerns and the Role of the Orchestrator**: In the hybrid model, the two paradigms are assigned distinct, isolated responsibilities, with the orchestrator managing their interactions:
    1. The LLM's role is restricted to reasoning, generating text, and proposing action plans (probabilistic, creative).
    2. The role of deterministic systems is to validate, enforce policy, execute transactions, and securely log the decision (i.e., in a deterministic, auditable manner).

For example, in UC9, Financial Risk Monitoring, advanced models such as Graph Neural Networks (GNNs) may produce a probabilistic risk score. Still, the Policy Enforcement Engine, a deterministic system, dictates whether the subsequent action (e.g., freezing funds) is legal, compliant, and within the agent's delegated scope of authority.

## Unprecedented Attack Surface

The read/write capabilities of agentic AI introduce systemic security and compliance risks, demanding new Zero-Trust concepts for AI assets and a dedicated governance layer to manage the complexity of autonomous action:

- **ZTAI**: The proliferation of non-human AI identities, which can rapidly outnumber human users in enterprise environments, requires a security framework based on Zero-Trust principles, treating the LLM-integrated application and the agent itself as dynamic, untrusted entities. The architecture must mandate ZTAI, which requires assigning the agent a strong, verifiable identity (e.g., a PKI Certificate) via an AI Agent Identity Provider (IdP) to enable non-repudiable authentication. Crucially, this framework must include the capability for a rapid kill switch and instant revocation of agent credentials to neutralize compromised or rogue agent instances.

- **Controlling Execution and Tool Use**: The agent's ability to call external APIs must be rigorously controlled by the orchestrator, which serves as the central point of control and a potential source of compliance failures. This is enforced through a dual layer of control:

    1. Agent Scope Enforcement (Sandboxing) strictly limits the agent's functional capabilities, including financial transaction limits or resource consumption caps, to prevent emergent or runaway behavior.

    2. Delegated Authorization Service intercepts agent action plans to ensure the proposed action complies not only with the agent's technical service account but also with the authenticated human agent's specific RBAC (Role-Based Access Control) permissions before execution.

- **Governing Agent Logic**: Uncontrolled agent sprawl and emergent behavior must be managed through codified rules. This requires a robust Governance-as-a-Service (GaaS) framework. The GaaS includes a rule engine that functions as a PDP to dynamically validate the legality and compliance of every planned agent action against the current policy set. Real-time policy enforcement is essential to maintaining control over autonomous systems.

## Mapping Risk to Reward Across 15 Use Cases

To effectively manage investment, the enterprise must map the risk profile of a generative AI application directly against its potential return on investment (ROI). This strategic analysis, driven by the demands of the 15 use cases, reveals a clear four-pillar progression from low-risk, internal efficiency gains to high-risk, autonomous revenue drivers.

The 15 use cases serve as the organizational blueprint, grouped not just by business function, but by the escalating complexity of the required governance architecture. By using the 15 use cases as a framework for this risk-to-reward mapping, the organization is forced to recognize that the most lucrative applications (Pillars 3 and 4) are wholly inaccessible until the common architectural foundation (Part II) is in place to manage the complexity and risk they introduce.

## Pillar 1: Operational Efficiency and Productivity Uplift

These foundational use cases, also known as the RAG-Based Efficiency Model, focus on enabling internal staff and achieving efficiency gains through rapid, fact-based knowledge retrieval. The primary governance focus is on access control and quality assurance, which are necessary to build staff trust and drive adoption.

## Strategic Objective and Value

The primary goal is to drastically improve staff efficiency by eliminating the time sink of manual search and addressing information fragmentation. This objective translates directly into a quantifiable benefit: an expected 70–80% productivity uplift for frontline staff by reducing search and analysis time, consistent with the productivity potential McKinsey identifies for generative AI in knowledge work (McKinsey & Company 2023). Furthermore, UC3, Intelligent Document Quality, promises a 60–70% reduction in manual data validation and entry effort by leveraging AI for semantic consistency checks.

## Governance Delta

The Governance Delta defines the incremental architectural controls this pillar requires beyond the common foundation established in Part II. To support efficiency, the architecture must ensure security and quality. The focus is on Security Trimming (or DLAC), which is mandatory for enforcing least-privilege access at the data retrieval layer. Continuous LLM Operations (LLMOps) is the discipline for managing the LLM lifecycle, performance, and governance in production; it is required to maintain the ultra-low-latency target (typically 10–15 seconds) and manage costs, preventing staff from reverting to manual searches due to slow response times.

## Example Use Case Integration

- **Use Case 1—Frontline Knowledge Assistant**: This use case establishes the baseline RAG deployment, mandating core features such as Hybrid Search and the Corrective RAG (CRAG) via a HITL (a feedback mechanism that initiates additional retrieval cycles when grounding quality falls below the Citation Threshold; defined in full in Chapter 5). This continuous feedback loop transforms human expertise into a continuous, data-driven tool for refining the underlying retrieval architecture and index, ensuring the system remains relevant as enterprise knowledge evolves.

- **Use Case 4—Domain-Specific AI Stylist**: This use case achieves efficiency by automating brand consistency and language adaptation using Parameter-Efficient Fine-Tuning (PEFT) or Low-Rank Adaptation (LoRA). The governance challenge lies in securing this multi-tenant architecture, which requires a stringent User Access Management (UAM) framework to map users to authorized security domains. This is necessary to enforce multi-tenant isolation and prevent unauthorized stylistic or proprietary leakage between isolated business units. The access control and quality assurance disciplines established in Pillar 1 are prerequisites for the higher-stakes deployment model that follows: without proven retrieval fidelity and security governance, the regulated compliance use cases in Pillar 2 cannot be safely authorized.

## Pillar 2: Regulatory Assurance and Compliance Shield

These use cases, also known as the High-Stakes Compliance Model, operate in regulated domains (e.g., finance, legal, compliance) and mandate enhanced RAG architectures and explicit governance mechanisms to achieve auditable, legally defensible outcomes.

## Strategic Objective and Value

The goal is to maximize operational velocity while simultaneously achieving certifiable regulatory assurance. The system acts as a preventative compliance control by minimizing the human error driven by systemic information friction. This commitment mitigates the risk of severe regulatory fines and costly litigation and delivers quantifiable value by achieving potential productivity gains of up to four hours per week for legal and compliance professionals, equivalent to adding an additional colleague for every ten team members (Thomson Reuters, "Future of Professionals Report 2024," 2024).

## Governance Delta

Compliance rigor requires non-negotiable architectural mandates: WORM storage for source data, AES-256 encryption, and an immutable audit logging service to guarantee post-incident integrity. The orchestrator is elevated to a regulatory gatekeeper that uses the calculated Faithfulness (Groundedness) Score as a risk-gating mechanism, explicitly programmed to refuse generation or trigger a HITL review for low-confidence claims.

## Example Use Case Integration

- **Use Case 2—Compliance Intelligence Platform**: This platform requires advanced retrieval techniques, such as Hierarchical RAG and custom parsing, to preserve the stringent logical structure of complex legal and policy documents, thereby mitigating the compliance risk posed by fragmented context. It also enforces Data Residency Zoning at the ingestion layer to ensure compliance with regulations such as the GDPR.

- **Use Case 3—Intelligent Document Quality**: This scenario focuses on semantic consistency and requires RBAC to strictly enforce Separation of Duties (SoD). For instance, the person who writes a document cannot be the final approver of its quality review, thereby mitigating operational risk. The system also uses a sophisticated Contradiction Taxonomy (e.g., Temporal, Numerical, Authority, Policy Reversal) to classify and route semantic conflicts efficiently, thereby enhancing audit efficiency and the compliance posture. The immutable logging, WORM storage, and HITL governance mandated by Pillar 2 form the accountability infrastructure that Pillar 3's agentic, transactional use cases depend on, where a compliance failure is not a log entry but a financial liability.

## Pillar 3: Revenue Generation and Optimization

These use cases, also known as the Agentic Monetization Model, transition to the transactional domain, leveraging agent autonomy, planning, and tool execution to optimize financial outcomes and capture ancillary revenue. This introduces the complexity of managing distributed financial transactions and of adhering to regulatory standards such as the Payment Card Industry Data Security Standard (PCI DSS).

### Strategic Objective and Value

The goal is to autonomously optimize pricing, yield, and ancillary sales based on real-time market factors and personalized customer profiles. The expected quantified value includes a potential increase in Average Daily Rate (ADR) of 3–5% and a focus on maximizing the core metric, Revenue Yield per Interaction (RYI).

## Governance Delta

Managing high-impact agent actions requires dedicated security protocols. The architecture mandates Secure Payment Offload and Tokenization via a dedicated gateway to achieve PCI DSS compliance by strictly isolating the LLM-driven Cognitive Layer from raw cardholder data (CHD). This is necessary because if the LLM were to capture sensitive financial data, the entire system would fall under strict PCI scope. Furthermore, the system requires a formal Ethical Pricing Framework with continuous bias audits to ensure that profit maximization does not lead to discriminatory or trust-eroding outcomes.

## Example Use Case Integration

- **Use Case 10—Hotel Dynamic Pricing Agent**: Requires a sophisticated Memory Subsystem (integrating Episodic and User-Specific Memory) to provide the granular context necessary for personalized negotiation and loyalty-based pricing. The architectural resilience mandates an explicit Agent Failover Strategy that automatically reverts to human-assisted channels or established fixed pricing when the LLM agent or critical external systems fail, ensuring business continuity.
- **Use Case 12—Event Ticket Agent**: This use case requires the Orchestration-based Saga Pattern (defined fully in Chapter 9; the mandated approach for distributed transaction integrity in agentic deployments) to manage the complex, distributed seat-upgrade transaction (Inventory ➤ Pricing ➤ Payment ➤ Ticketing) across disparate microservices. For resilience and auditability, all steps in the Saga must be defined as idempotent commands to prevent

unintended side effects (such as double-charging a customer) during mandatory retry attempts following transient failures. Pillar 3 proves that agentic AI can generate direct revenue, but only within tightly bounded authority limits. Pillar 4 extends the same architecture into environments where the consequence of a governance failure is not a financial loss but a safety incident.

## Pillar 4: Safety, Resilience, and Mission Criticality

These use cases, also known as the Autonomous High-Risk Model, involve autonomous actions that directly impact physical safety, operational readiness, or mission-critical infrastructure and therefore mandate the most stringent governance, Machine Learning Operations (MLOps), and XAI controls.

### Strategic Objective and Value

The goal is to proactively prevent catastrophic failures, reduce unplanned downtime, and ensure equipment is available and mission-capable in extreme and unpredictable conditions. The quantifiable value is substantial, including reductions in unplanned downtime of up to 25% and maintenance cost savings of 10–25% across industry implementations (Deloitte, Industry 4.0 research, 2023). This directly translates into enhanced mission readiness by reducing unscheduled downtime for UC14.

## Governance Delta

The operation of mission-critical agents mandates the highest level of security and control. This requires ZTAI for agent identity and a high-risk GRC framework aligned with external regulatory bodies, such as the Federal Aviation Administration (FAA), the European Union Aviation Safety Agency (EASA), and the EU AI Act (Regulation EU 2024/1689; high-risk AI system obligations applicable from August 2, 2026, for Annex III systems; embedded product systems from August 2, 2027). For decision integrity, the system mandates ensemble reasoning (requiring consensus among multiple specialized agents, such as a Diagnostic Agent validated by a Digital Twin Agent) and Reasoning Trace Capture (logging the LLM's ReAct (Reasoning and Action) logic) to provide full auditability and XAI evidence.

## Example Use Case Integration

- **Use Case 13—Aircraft Predictive Maintenance**: This solution requires a Hybrid AI Architecture that separates responsibilities: deep learning for RUL prognostics (prediction), GenAI/RAG for diagnostics (explanation/procedure), and a multi-agent system (MAS) for scheduling (execution). Governance mandates MLOps monitoring of statistical divergence metrics, such as the Kullback–Leibler (KL) or Jensen–Shannon (JS) divergence, to detect data drift and ensure the model remains accurate in a safety-critical context. A mandatory HITL sign-off is required for any unscheduled aircraft grounding.

- **Use Case 14—Defense Equipment Predictive Maintenance**: This use case demands maximum resilience through a structured Edge–Fog–Cloud architecture optimized for disconnected, intermittent, and low-bandwidth (DIL/DOL) environments. The MAS includes specialized agents, such as the Safety Risk Agent (SRA), which issues mandatory halt flags, and the Audit and Compliance Agent (ACA), which enforces real-time governance by generating an Immutable Audit Log that aligns with regulatory and ethical mandates before any action is executed.

The synthesis of the 15 use cases demonstrates that enterprise value is achieved across four distinct pillars, each requiring a specific and escalating set of governance mandates. Table 2-2 listed some examples and potential benefits of different enterprise AI use cases and linked them to four value pillars.

***Table 2-2.*** *The four pillars of strategic enterprise AI value*

| Value Pillar | Strategic Objective (the "Why") | Example of Quantifiable Benefit | Example Use Case |
|---|---|---|---|
| Operational efficiency | Eliminate information fragmentation and manual search time. | 70–80% productivity uplift; up to 70% reduction in manual triage effort. | AI-powered frontline knowledge assistant (UC1) |
| Regulatory assurance | Achieve certifiable legal defensibility and risk mitigation. | Certifiable assurance; measurable reduction in regulatory fines. | Enterprise knowledge and regulatory compliance intelligence (EKRCI) platform (UC2) |
| Revenue generation | Autonomously optimize pricing, yield, and ancillary sales. | 3–5% increase in Average Daily Rate (ADR); maximize Revenue Yield per Interaction (RYI). | Hotel dynamic pricing and booking agent (UC10) |
| Safety and resilience | Proactively prevent catastrophic failures and maintain mission readiness. | Reductions in unplanned downtime up to 25%; maintenance cost savings 10–25%; enhanced mission readiness. | Aircraft predictive maintenance (UC13) |

# Previews of the Architectural Non-negotiables

The strategic mapping of risk to reward across the 15 use cases immediately forces a confrontation with the non-optional architectural components. These elements, detailed in the following chapters (Part II), constitute the non-negotiable floor, the Minimum Viable Governance (MVG) layer, that must be fully certified before any high-value AI system can enter production.

This chapter introduces these core requirements not as abstract concepts, but as mandatory solutions to specific, high-stakes risks identified in the use cases:

- **ZTAI via Retrieval-Time Access Enforcement**: This is the most critical mandate for RAG-based systems (UC1–5). Because a user query often traverses multiple security boundaries to retrieve source documents, the system cannot rely on simple application-level security. The mechanism enforces DLAC by using security metadata (e.g., clearance level, department) to security-trim retrieved documents before the LLM ever sees them. This prevents the primary risk of PII leakage or unauthorized access, guaranteeing the principle of least privilege within the AI workflow.
- **Immutable Audit Logging (GRC Layer)**: For high-risk, transactional systems (UC2, UC7, and UC9), every single decision must be traceable. This component mandates a tamper-proof, time-sequenced ledger that records the original query, the source documents retrieved, the agent's intermediate steps, and the final LLM output. This creates a non-repudiable transaction

record essential for meeting regulatory audits and legal compliance requirements, ensuring the system can always explain why a decision was made.

- **Deterministic Hybrid Engine**: To overcome the LLM's inherent non-determinism and multi-step failure rate, the architecture must strictly separate roles. The AI's creative core is tightly bound by a Deterministic Shell built from traditional code and structured data. This shell includes
    - **Grounding Verification**: Factual checks that tie the LLM's answer back to the source text and generate a Support Score to mitigate hallucination
    - **Policy-as-Code (PaC) Guardrails**: Explicit rules that prevent the LLM from taking unauthorized actions during agentic workflows

These previews establish the book's core thesis: the path to enterprise AI value is not about choosing the right model; it is about flawlessly architecting the surrounding governance layer to control the model's behavior and risk profile. These foundational components form the structure that Part II will detail, ultimately enabling the safe deployment of the most lucrative use cases in Parts III and IV.

## Security and Trust

Security must be implemented at the data retrieval layer to rigorously enforce the principle of least privilege, a non-negotiable requirement for compliance and mitigating data leakage:

- **Retrieval-Time Access Enforcement (Security Trimming or DLAC)**: This mechanism is mandatory for all RAG use cases, ensuring that users receive only authorized documents, even when the LLM can find semantically related but unauthorized information. The process is enforced by embedding required permissions as metadata tags during ingestion. At runtime, the Retrieval Engine uses the user's Identity and Access Management (IAM) identity to execute the semantic search constrained by this security filter, ensuring that only authorized chunks are retrieved for prompt augmentation. This meticulously enforces the principle of least privilege, thereby mitigating the Isolation Paradox: the tension between indexing the full corpus for RAG performance and restricting per-user access for compliance and preventing PII leakage.

- **The ZTAI Mandate for Non-human Identities**: As autonomous agents become pervasive, they must be treated as untrusted, privileged entities by default. ZTAI requires strong identity validation and continuous authentication controls for these non-human identities. Agents must be assigned a verifiable identity, typically via an AI Agent Identity Provider (e.g., a PKI Certificate), for non-repudiable authentication. This also requires implementing a rapid, centralized kill switch to revoke access rights for any compromised or rogue agent.

## Accountability and Auditability

Audit readiness demands a complete, immutable record of all data transformations and LLM decisions to enable forensic reconstruction and justify outcomes to regulators. This capability moves logging beyond debugging to legal defensibility:

- **Immutable Audit Logging**: The solution must record a complete, timestamped transaction trace for every interaction using WORM storage to prevent post-incident modification and guarantee integrity. This comprehensive audit trail is essential for forensic reconstruction and auditability.
- **Data Lineage Tagging** :To ensure compliance with records retention policies and data privacy regulations (e.g., the right to be forgotten), the ingestion process must enforce strict data provenance requirements. The Pre-processing Engine must act as a Data Lineage Tagger, appending compliance and lineage metadata (such as retention classification and original system ID) to every single data chunk. This architecture enables the immediate identification and deletion of all corresponding vectors when a source document is removed or updated, ensuring the RAG index remains compliant with data lifecycle mandates.
- **Mandatory Reasoning Trace Capture**: For complex agentic decisions, logging only the final action is insufficient for accountability. The logs must capture the LLM's intermediate decision points, the ReAct loop logic (i.e., Thought, Action, Observation) and the exact RAG context used. Capturing this step-by-step reasoning is mandatory to establish accountability, allowing compliance officers to fully reconstruct how a complex decision was reached and thereby fulfilling the XAI and contestability requirements.

## Operational Integrity

LLMOps, the practice of managing the lifecycle, performance, and stability of LLM applications, is shifting from a performance tool to a critical component of Continuous Regulatory Control. It ensures the system maintains quality and consistency despite the inherent risks of adaptive AI and evolving data:

- **Sustaining Factual Accuracy (Groundedness)**: The paramount technical metric for LLM trust is faithfulness (groundedness), which assesses the percentage of claims directly supported by the retrieved, authorized context. A high Faithfulness Score directly equates to lower hallucination rates and greater user trust. This is quantified using the Groundedness Score, derived from the raw Support Score returned by the Grounding Verifier. Continuous monitoring of this metric is necessary to ensure that technical quality reinforces the business objective of process efficiency and prevents staff from reverting to manual verification.
- **Corrective RAG (HITL) Feedback Loop**: A HITL workflow is mandatory for continuous quality improvement and safety-critical checks. When HITL feedback identifies a failure, such as a user tagging a response as incorrect, this signals a problem with the retrieval or chunking strategy. This information triggers a Corrective RAG (CRAG) feedback loop to refine the ingestion pipeline (e.g., updating the index or refining the chunking strategy), ensuring that human expertise continuously drives the refinement of the underlying retrieval architecture.

- **Continuous Drift Monitoring**: LLM applications are highly susceptible to silent performance degradation caused by model drift over time. The LLMOps framework must integrate a Model Drift Monitoring Service to continuously track semantic quality and consistency. This involves running synthetic, "*golden*" test queries at regular intervals and comparing the resulting Faithfulness and Answer Relevance scores against historical baselines. For safety-critical systems (UC13), this monitoring involves statistical divergence metrics, such as KL/JS divergence, applied to input features to trigger automated retraining when operational profiles shift, thereby maintaining regulatory compliance.

## Autonomy Control

For agentic use cases, control mechanisms must be implemented to prevent emergent, unplanned behavior and enforce policy mandates in real time, leveraging the orchestrator as the enforcer:

- **Orchestrator As Policy Gatekeeper**: The LLM orchestrator serves as a risk-gating mechanism, enforcing mandatory guardrails against malicious prompt injection, PII leakage, and toxic language. This is essential for enterprise security, and the monitoring of these guardrails must be continuous to adapt to evolving attack vectors.

- **Policy Enforcement Engine (PaC)**: The most critical control for autonomous action is the dedicated external Policy Enforcement Engine (PaC) within the GaaS framework. This serves as a final, deterministic gateway that validates the agent's proposed action plan against high-level legal and business rules before the action is executed. This mechanism ensures that autonomy does not circumvent policy mandates.
- **Agent Scope Enforcement and XAI**: To control the risk of autonomous action, Agent Scope Enforcement (Sandboxing) strictly limits the agent's functional capabilities (e.g., financial limits or access to tools) within defined boundaries. This must be complemented by mandatory XAI microservices that generate clear, human-readable decision rationales (e.g., using SHAP) for all high-risk decisions. This ensures that the human agent can confidently explain the model's logic to a customer or regulator, fulfilling the mandate for transparency.

Table 2-3 summarizes the governance-first mandate of non-negotiable architectural controls.

***Table 2-3.** The governance-first mandate of non-negotiable architectural controls*

| Governance Requirement | Function/Problem Solved | Preview of Architectural Mechanism | Primary Risk Mitigated |
|---|---|---|---|
| Security/access control | Enforcing the principle of least privilege for knowledge retrieval | Retrieval-time access enforcement (Security Trimming or DLAC) | Unauthorized data leakage/Isolation Paradox |
| Accountability/ auditability | Guaranteeing non-repudiable proof of decision-making rationale | Immutable audit logging and Data Lineage Tagging | Compliance failure/right to be forgotten/data tampering |
| Quality/trust | Sustaining factual accuracy and minimizing fabrication | Faithfulness (Groundedness) Score, Hybrid Search, or re-ranker | Hallucination risk |
| Autonomy control | Preventing emergent behavior from exceeding authorized scope | Policy Enforcement Engine (PaC) and Agent Scope Enforcement (Sandboxing) | Unchecked agent autonomy or prompt injection |

# Building the Confidence to Scale

The enterprise imperative is to move from cautious, siloed experimentation to strategic, enterprise-wide scaling. The synthesis of the 15 detailed use cases conclusively shows that AI success is not a function of model quality alone, but rather a direct function of architectural discipline and governance maturity. Governance is the foundational enabler of modernization, allowing innovation to scale further and earn the trust of all stakeholders, from the frontline staff to external regulators.

The analysis of the four strategic value pillars demonstrates the direct link between governance investment and high-value returns. By investing in robust governance controls, specifically DLAC, immutable audit logging, and continuous LLMOps, organizations gain the confidence to pursue high-value, high-risk use cases (Pillars 3 and 4) that directly drive revenue and resilience (e.g., measurable reductions in unplanned downtime and maintenance costs in predictive maintenance: UC13–UC15; Deloitte, 2023). The non-deterministic nature of LLMs ensures that hybrid systems, balancing the probabilistic LLM cores with deterministic GRC controls, are the only viable architecture for long-term enterprise adoption.

## Architecture for Enterprise Reality: The Deterministic Shell

The Deterministic Shell is the technical architecture that enforces the board's constitutional commitment to governed autonomy in the production environment. Its five components, the Evaluation Baseline Service, Security Trimming, the LLM Council, the LLM-As-a-Judge, and Streaming Anomaly Detection, operate in sequence to ensure that no probabilistic output reaches a user or triggers an action without passing through a deterministic control gate.

## The Logic of the Deterministic Shell

The Deterministic Shell is a logical layer of traditional software and fixed business rules that tightly bounds the probabilistic core of the artificial intelligence. It ensures that every request and every response is filtered through a series of deterministic gates. These gates are not optional recommendations but are technical mandates that the architecture enforces before any information is exchanged with the user or any transaction is executed.

The Deterministic Shell serves as the technical infrastructure that enables the organization to achieve a specific GMI, the EDS framework's five-level certification scale. For example, an organization cannot achieve GMI Level 2 certification without a production-ready Deterministic Shell that enforces real-time grounding and Security Trimming. GMI Level 2 corresponds to the operationalized maturity stage established in Chapter 12, where the Zero-Trust RAG pipeline, Groundedness SLO, and immutable audit logging are fully operational. By inserting this shell between the user and the Cognitive Layer, the enterprise transforms the model from a black box into a governed component of the wider system. The shell provides the necessary structure to meet the four strategic pillars of value: operational efficiency, regulatory assurance, revenue generation, and mission criticality. All architectural blueprints within this section use a structured enterprise architecture notation to ensure a unified visual language across the strategic and application layers.

## Beyond the Chatbot Hype: Why the Direct Link Fails

The consumer experience of AI creates a deceptive mental model: a user asks a question, and the model produces an answer. Connecting an enterprise knowledge base to a large language model with this same "direct link" architecture is the most common and most costly mistake in enterprise AI deployment. When a user query traverses the entire corporate knowledge base without access controls, the LLM synthesizes whatever it retrieves, including documents the user has no right to see, outdated policies that have been superseded, and information from domains entirely unrelated to the user's role. The probabilistic nature of the model means no two queries produce identical results, making reproducibility and auditability structurally impossible. The result is not a chatbot with occasional inaccuracies; it is a system that is ungovernable by design. The Deterministic Shell exists precisely to close this gap: to insert the deterministic control gates that the direct link omits.

The Deterministic Shell is not a single component but a sequence of control gates, and the sequence is the governance. Figure 2-1 shows how a user request must pass through pre-deployment certification and Zero-Trust access control before reaching the Cognitive Layer and how every output from that layer is then subjected to grounding verification and anomaly detection before it can be released to the user or trigger an action.

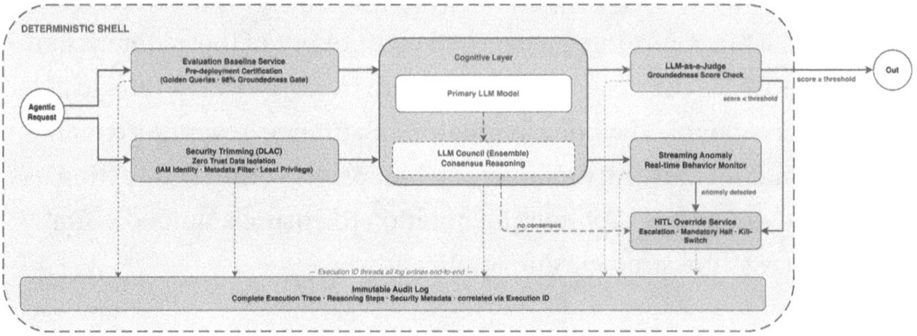


***Figure 2-1.*** *The Deterministic Shell—five sequential control gates that every request and response must traverse: the Evaluation Baseline Service (pre-deployment certification), Security Trimming (Zero-Trust access enforcement at retrieval), the LLM Council (ensemble reasoning in the Cognitive Layer), LLM-As-a-Judge (post-generation grounding verification), and Streaming Anomaly Detection (real-time drift and manipulation monitoring). No output reaches the user without passing all five gates*

## Pre-deployment Governance: The Evaluation Baseline Service

Architecture for trust begins long before a model or an agent reaches production. It is critical to recognize that models are just a small part of the overall system. Traditionally, models were selected based on their general performance on public benchmarks. For a governed enterprise, general performance is irrelevant. What matters is the performance of the entire system on specific organizational domains.

The Evaluation Baseline Service is a mandatory application component that functions as the certification registry for all models and agents. Before a system is permitted to enter the Cognitive Layer, it must be scored against a set of golden queries. These queries are high-quality and human-verified examples of the specific tasks the model will perform in production.

The service provides a configuration-driven environment in which the risk assessment engineer can define minimum performance thresholds for both groundedness and safety. If a model falls below a 98% Groundedness Score during this pre-flight certification, it is automatically blocked from deployment. This pre-deployment groundedness threshold is distinct from the 98% auditable rationale standard introduced in Chapter 1 (and detailed in Chapter 11), which governs the proportion of live decisions that must generate a complete rationale log. The two share a numeric value but measure different things: answer groundedness at certification versus log completeness in production. This ensures that only models with proven reliability are integrated into the enterprise ecosystem, effectively mitigating the risk of hallucinations before they can impact the business. The Evaluation Baseline Service is the pre-deployment gate component; Chapter 5 develops the full LLMOps framework within which it operates, extending this pre-deployment certification into continuous production assurance through the Gate Trigger Rate, Threshold Drift, and Groundedness SLO metrics (all defined in Chapter 5).

## Zero-Trust Data Access: Security Trimming and DLAC

One of the most significant risks in enterprise AI is the unauthorized exposure of sensitive information. While Retrieval-Augmented Generation is the gateway to using proprietary data, it requires a control layer to remain safe. The Deterministic Shell provides that layer by enforcing the principle of least privilege at the moment of data retrieval. This mechanism, Security Trimming, or DLAC, ensures that the Retrieval Engine surfaces only information that the requesting identity is authorized to see.

This process maximizes the utility of enterprise data by unlocking the value of proprietary documents without risking a security breach. Every data chunk in the enterprise repository is tagged with security metadata that aligns with the organization's existing identity management rules. This metadata filtering occurs before the large language model ever sees the data, thereby enforcing Zero Trust at the data layer and ensuring the Cognitive Layer is never exposed to unauthorized information. The full technical implementation of Security Trimming, including metadata tagging at ingestion and constrained search at runtime, is established in Chapter 4. What matters here is the architectural principle: security is enforced at the chunk level, at the moment of retrieval, not at the application boundary.

## The Cognitive Layer: LLM Council and Consensus Logic

For high-stakes decisions, relying on a single large language model is a point of failure. The EDS architecture positions the LLM as the Cognitive Layer, with the probabilistic reasoning component governed by the Deterministic Shell. This is consistent with the *"Deterministic Shell"* framing established earlier in this chapter and carried through Chapters 9–11, where the same separation is described as the Cognitive Layer bounded by the Deterministic Core. For high-stakes decisions, the Cognitive Layer can include a mix of a primary model and an Ensemble Reasoning service, known as the LLM Council (introduced here; Chapter 5 references the LLM Council in the context of retrieval-quality optimization and model selection).

To maintain strict accountability, every action performed by the LLM Council is explicitly tracked and correlated via the Execution ID (the session/task identifier that threads all log entries for a single workflow into a complete audit trail, as formalized in the Logging and Explainability Standard established in full in Chapter 11). This ensures that the consensus reached by the ensemble is non-negotiable and traceable back to the original user intent.

The LLM Council models can be assigned dynamic roles. For instance, one model might focus on security for one execution and then be dynamically reassigned to a compliance verification task for the next. Alternatively, the architecture can apply an Ensemble Reasoning approach, requiring all models to perform the same task and selecting the most common outcome as the final decision by consensus. This is the same consensus mechanism developed in depth in Chapter 9's "Safety-Critical Governance" section. If the Council cannot reach consensus or if a dissenting reasoning trace is detected, the system triggers the HITL Override Service, routing the decision to a certified HOTL supervisor. This ensures that the most sensitive machine actions are backed by a collective intelligence far more robust than any individual model.

## Post-execution Validation: LLM-As-a-Judge and Anomaly Detection

The final layer of the Deterministic Shell consists of post-execution validation services that monitor the Cognitive Layer's output in real time. Even with pre-deployment certification and secure data access, the core's probabilistic nature means an erratic response is always possible.

The LLM-As-a-Judge component acts as a real-time validator. It performs a specific groundedness check by comparing the model's response against the retrieved source documents. It calculates a Groundedness (Faithfulness) Score for the output, derived from the Support Score that quantifies how much of the answer is based on verified, retrieved facts rather than model fabrication. If the Groundedness Score falls below the board-approved threshold, the response is discarded or escalated to the HITL Override Service for human review. Chapter 4 establishes the Groundedness Score as the mandatory governance gate SLO, and Chapter 5 develops the full LLMOps quality framework within which it operates.

Simultaneously, the Streaming Anomaly Detection service monitors the system for volatility and drift. This component looks for spikes in decision velocity or unusual patterns in the Execution ID correlation thread. If the system detects that an agent is making a series of increasingly risky decisions or if the reasoning trace shows signs of manipulation, the component triggers the HITL Override Service, the automated circuit breaker that immediately halts agent execution and routes the decision for human review. Chapter 5's LLMOps quality framework formalizes the specific metrics (Threshold Drift, Supervisor Availability Drift, Prompt Drift) that this monitoring layer evaluates. This real-time monitoring ensures that the enterprise maintains continuous control over its autonomous assets and can intervene before a technical drift becomes a material liability.

# Summary

This chapter established the Deterministic Shell as the enforcement layer of the constitutional framework, the control architecture that operates at the moment of inference to ensure that every output the system produces is governed, auditable, and contestable. The key takeaways are as follows:

- **The Deterministic Shell converts constitutional policy into technical reality**. The Authority Matrix Rules Repository defines what is permitted. The PDP evaluates every candidate's output against those rules. The PEP acts on that evaluation. The HITL Override Service routes low-confidence or policy-violating outputs to human review. The Immutable Audit Log records the complete chain. None of these components is optional; removing any one of them breaks the governance chain on which the others depend.
- **Hybrid Search and the re-ranking stack are governance controls, not retrieval optimizations**. The specific retrieval mechanisms that deliver this (hybrid lexical and vector search, rank fusion, and Cross-Encoder Re-ranking) are defined and applied in Chapter 5. The governance point here is that an answer can only be as grounded as its retrieved context; retrieval quality is therefore a prerequisite for compliance, not a mere performance optimization.

- **Zero Trust is the access model for the retrieval layer**. Security Trimming enforces document-level access control at the moment of retrieval, not at the application layer, where it can be bypassed, but at the infrastructure layer, where it cannot. Every retrieval call is an authentication event. Every chunk that reaches the prompt generator has been verified against the user's current permissions.
- **The LLM Council and LLM-As-a-Judge create a verification loop inside the Cognitive Layer**. A single model cannot adjudicate its own output. The multi-model council architecture separates generation from evaluation, ensuring that the Groundedness Score the PDP acts on is produced by a different model than the one that generated the candidate answer. That separation is what makes the Groundedness Score meaningful as a governance signal.
- **Streaming Anomaly Detection is the real-time circuit breaker**. It operates during token generation, not after. If the output stream begins to deviate—semantic drift, policy violation, or anomalous pattern—the Streaming Anomaly Detection service halts generation before a non-compliant response is fully formed. This is the difference between governance as a post hoc check and governance as an active control.

The next chapter takes a step back before moving forward: before specifying any security control or access architecture, it asks where the AI physically runs and establishes why that question has a governance answer, not just a technical one.

# References

Capgemini Research Institute. 2025. Rise of Agentic AI: How Trust Is the Key to Human-AI Collaboration. Paris: Capgemini Research Institute. https://www.capgemini.com/insights/research-library/ai-agents/.

Deloitte. 2023. Industry 4.0: Using Predictive Technologies for Asset Mainte nance. New York: Deloitte Insights. https://www2.deloitte.com/us/en/insights/industry/manufacturing-industrial-products/industry-4-0/using-predictive-technologies-for-asset-maintenance.html.

Gartner. 2025. Gartner Survey Finds Just 15% of IT Application Leaders Are Considering, Piloting, or Deploying Fully Autonomous AI Agents. Press release, September 30. https://www.gartner.com/en/newsroom/press-releases/2025-09-30-gartner-survey-finds-just-15-percent-of-it-application-leaders-are-considering-piloting-or-deploying-fully-autonomous-ai-agents.

He, Horace, and Thinking Machines Lab. 2025. Defeating Nondeterminism in LLM Inference. Thinking Machines Lab: Connectionism, September. https://thinkingmachines.ai/blog/defeating-nondeterminism-in-llm-inference/.

OWASP Foundation. 2025. OWASP Top 10 for Large Language Model Applications: LLM01:2025 Prompt Injection. OWASP Foundation. https://genai.owasp.org/llmrisk/llm01-prompt-injection/.

Thomson Reuters. 2024. *Future of Professionals Report 2024.* Toronto: Thomson Reuters Institute. https://www.thomsonreuters.com/en/c/future-of-professionals.html.

McKinsey & Company. 2023. The Economic Potential of Generative AI: The Next Productivity Frontier. McKinsey & Company, June. https://www.mckinsey.com/capabilities/mckinsey-digital/our-insights/the-economic-potential-of-generative-ai-the-next-productivity-frontier.

Xu, Frank F., Yufan Song, Boxuan Li, Yuxuan Tang, Kritanjali Jain, Mengxue Bao, Zora Z. Wang, Xuhui Zhou, Zhitong Guo, Murong Cao, Mingyang Yang, Hao Yang Lu, Amaad Martin, Zhe Su, Leander Maben, Raj Mehta, Wayne Chi, Lawrence Jang, Yiqing Xie, Shuyan Zhou, and Graham Neubig. 2025. TheAgentCompany: Benchmarking LLM Agents on Consequential Real World Tasks. arXiv:2412.14161v3. `https://arxiv.org/abs/2412.14161`.

# PART II

# The Architectural Foundation

# CHAPTER 3

# Architecting for Governance and Scale

Chapter 1 established what the organization is constitutionally committed to governing. Chapter 2 mapped those governance commitments across 15 use cases and established the Deterministic Shell that enforces them at the point of inference. This chapter addresses the question that precedes both: where does the AI actually run, and what does that choice mean for governance, cost, and control? The answer is rarely straightforward. For regulated enterprises, the deployment model is not a technical preference; it is the physical expression of the governance framework, and the wrong choice makes the right governance impossible.

The foundational constraint is risk. Before any deployment architecture is selected, the organization must classify its AI workloads using a structured risk taxonomy. This taxonomy determines which deployment options are even permissible, which oversight models are required, and which circuit-break controls must be embedded at the infrastructure layer rather than the application layer. The eight risk categories introduced in this chapter are not a compliance checklist; they are the governing constraints from which every deployment decision in this book flows.


M. M. Hossain and A. A. N. Ponnusamy, *Governance-First AI*,
https://doi.org/10.1007/979-8-8688-3118-8_3

The second constraint is economics. AI cost structures bear little resemblance to traditional IT spend. Token billing, embedding calls, retrieval queries, orchestration steps, and agent actions each generate distinct cost signals that are fragmented across teams, environments, and vendors. Traditional FinOps frameworks were not designed for this. The financial governance model must be rebuilt from first principles, with cost controls embedded directly in the MLOps pipeline rather than applied retrospectively through finance reporting.

This chapter is organized into five movements. First, it establishes the AI risk taxonomy and Criticality Classification framework that governs all deployment decisions. Second, it explains the governance accountability model and the role of MLOps as a compliance enforcement mechanism. Third, it analyzes the strategic choice between cloud-only and hybrid architectures, considering data sovereignty, TCO, latency, and vendor concentration risk. Fourth, it addresses the core technology stack decision as a governance choice rather than a developer preference. Fifth, it introduces the Agent Hub, the operational execution environment that ties the deployment model to the constitutional governance framework established in the preceding chapters.

**Governance Leaders**: The AI risk taxonomy, Criticality Classification, and the strategic deployment model decision are your primary sections.

**Architects and Practitioners**: The technology stack decision, Agent Hub architecture, and FinOps governance model begin at Beyond Compute.

# AI Risk Taxonomy: Classifying Deployment Risk Before Architecture

Risk classification precedes architecture. The taxonomy below governs which deployment options are permissible, which oversight models are mandatory, and which circuit-break controls must be embedded at the infrastructure layer.

## The Eight AI-Specific Risk Categories

The following risk taxonomy formally classifies the AI-specific risks inherent in any deployment of an autonomous decision system. These categories fall within the enterprise's existing operational, financial, and compliance risk classes; they are not separately governed. Understanding which risk categories apply to a given workload is a prerequisite for selecting the deployment model.

**DECISION VELOCITY RISK**

*Autonomous systems execute decisions faster than governance oversight can detect or interrupt, creating irreversible outcomes before controls can respond.*

**Architectural Implication:** Real-time agentic workloads require on-premises or edge deployment with circuit-break thresholds and HOTL supervision embedded at the infrastructure layer.

**CASCADE FAILURE RISK**

*A failure in one autonomous agent propagates across dependent or orchestrated agents, amplifying operational impact beyond the scope of a single system.*

**Architectural Implication:** Multi-agent deployments require isolated execution environments and kill-switch architecture that operates independently of the system's own decision logic. Hybrid deployments must enforce failure domain isolation across on-premises and cloud boundaries.

## GOVERNANCE DRIFT RISK

*Governance controls become progressively misaligned with deployed Autonomy Levels over time, particularly where capability or usage expands without a corresponding governance maturity advancement.*

**Architectural Implication:** The MLOps pipeline must enforce continuous governance maturity certification gates. Autonomy-Level changes require reclassification of the workload's deployment requirements, not just redeployment.

## MODEL BEHAVIOR RISK

*An AI model produces materially different outputs following a version update, fine-tuning event, or input distributional shift, without the change being detected through governance controls.*

**Architectural Implication:** Model drift monitoring and QA regression pass rates are mandatory infrastructure components, not optional LLMOps enhancements. Deployment models must support immutable model versioning and rollback at the infrastructure layer.

## PROMPT DRIFT RISK

*Iterative prompt changes, each individually classified as standard changes, cumulatively expand the system's effective decision authority, behavioral boundaries, or oversight bypass conditions beyond the approved authority scope, without triggering a material change classification.*

**Architectural Implication:** The control is prompt version control coupled with an approved Prompt Authority Scope Statement (PASS) for each production prompt: a record of the decision domains, action types, and authority limits the prompt is permitted to operate within. The MLOps pipeline must version every prompt change, log its version identifier and scope-statement reference on each decision and reconcile the cumulative effect of those changes against the prompt's approved scope at each quarterly review, flagging any system whose accumulated changes have pushed its effective authority beyond the domain authorized for it in the Machine Decision Authority Matrix (MDAM). This differs from Model Behavior Risk monitoring, which tracks output drift from model or version changes rather than cumulative authority creep from prompt edits, so the two require separate controls. (the Prompt Authority Scope Statement is defined in Chapter 11; the Machine Decision Authority Matrix is defined in Chapter 9).

## ACCOUNTABILITY DIFFUSION RISK

*Responsibility for an AI-driven decision cannot be clearly attributed to an accountable human actor, creating audit gaps and potential regulatory exposure.*

**Architectural Implication:** Every autonomous decision must be traceable to a named human accountable executive via the oversight model (HITL, HOTL, or HAL) specified for that workload. Immutable audit logging must capture this accountability chain, not merely the model output.

## CONCENTRATION RISK

*Excessive dependency on a single AI model provider, infrastructure vendor, or agent platform, analogous to third-party concentration risk in prudential operational risk management.*

**Architectural Implication:** No single provider should represent more than 40% of the organization's aggregate Autonomous Decision Authority Evaluation score (the framework's measure of delegated machine authority, defined in Chapter 9). This 40% ceiling is an established EDS framework threshold, set as a deliberately conservative concentration limit; hybrid and multi-cloud architectures are therefore not merely cost optimization tools but concentration risk mitigation strategies.

## REGULATORY EXPLAINABILITY RISK

*Autonomous decision-making in regulated domains (credit, pricing, collections, reporting) fails to meet explainability, fairness, or audit trail obligations under applicable law.*

**Architectural Implication:** The Deterministic Shell of the Hybrid AI Architecture must generate an auditable rationale for at least 98% of decisions in regulated domains; this is the minimum compliance threshold under the EDS Logging and Explainability Standard (the framework's mandatory governance standard governing minimum logging requirements, the ≥98% auditable rationale standard, audit trail architecture, override capability obligations, and regulatory defensibility evidence requirements; formally established in Chapter 11), not a quality target. Falling below 98% in any quarter is a Board Risk Committee escalation event requiring a management action plan within ten business days of quarter-end.

## AI System Criticality Classification

Before any workload is deployed, it must be assigned a Criticality Tier based on the potential impact if the system fails or acts incorrectly, not its technical complexity or degree of autonomy. The EDS framework's AI System Criticality Classification is a mandatory four-tier governance instrument that translates this impact assessment into specific deployment constraints. This classification determines the minimum oversight model and governs the minimum governance requirements at each Autonomy Level. Table 3-1 links the AI system criticality classification with minimum oversight requirements.

***Table 3-1.** AI System Criticality Classification and minimum oversight requirements*

| Criticality Tier | Definition | Example Use Cases | Minimum Oversight (Level 3+) |
|---|---|---|---|
| Critical | Failure would cause material financial loss, regulatory breach, or significant customer harm. | Credit approval, fraud response, regulatory reporting | HOTL with Board Risk Committee notification; quarterly audit; CRO sign-off |
| High | Failure would cause significant operational disruption or reputational harm. | Customer communications, pricing adjustments, claims processing | HOTL required; CRO sign-off; semi-annual audit |
| Moderate | Failure would cause contained operational impact recoverable within normal business processes. | Internal analytics, workflow routing, scheduling optimization | HOTL required; CRO review |
| Low | Failure would cause minor, easily reversible operational inconvenience. | Internal document processing, data formatting, administrative automation | Human-Above-the-Loop (HAL); Chief AI Officer approval |

Criticality Tier is the first filter in deployment design. A Critical-tier system at Autonomy Level 3 or above cannot run cloud-only unless that environment can technically enforce HOTL supervision and circuit-break controls at the infrastructure layer. Where it cannot, the deployment model is mandated, not chosen.

## Architectural Accountability

MLOps is the enforcement mechanism for governance, not an efficiency framework. When implemented correctly, the MLOps pipeline is the persistent, auditable record that continuously demonstrates responsible AI usage and mitigates legal liability. For regulated enterprises, this is not optional: the pipeline must serve as the system of record for every model in production.

Operationalizing governance through MLOps requires four embedded steps: classify the use case and assign a Criticality Tier; assign ownership and formalize data handling policies for PII, sector regulations, and regional mandates; embed those policies in the MLOps platform; and establish continuous monitoring to maintain the compliance posture throughout the model's production lifetime.

More complex deployment models, hybrid or multi-cloud, increase the architectural burden and must be justified by specific non-cost requirements, such as data residency, low-latency performance, or concentration risk mitigation. Complexity for its own sake is a governance liability.

## Strategic Deployment Models

The analysis that follows is directed at two audiences simultaneously: governance leaders who will authorize the deployment model and architects who will implement it. The filters are governance constraints first; technical and economic preferences follow. The deployment decision is not abstract. The question is not "Cloud or hybrid?"; it is which architecture can actually satisfy the governance constraints that apply to this workload. Data sovereignty rules out cloud-only for many regulated datasets. Latency rules out cloud-only for real-time agentic systems. Concentration risk rules out cloud-only for organizations approaching the 40% single-provider limit. What remains after those filters is the required architecture, not a preferred one.

## Data Sovereignty and Residency

Legal geography constrains infrastructure placement. Where GDPR, national privacy law, or sector-specific regulation requires personal data to remain within a defined boundary, that boundary determines the deployment model. A cloud zone guarantee is not a substitute for on-premises control; regulators assess where data physically resides, not where the vendor contractually promises to store it.

For multinational enterprises, the patchwork of jurisdictional requirements across the EU, Japan, Australia, Brazil, and others creates a compliance surface that a cloud-only model struggles to satisfy consistently. The practical implication is that many regulated enterprises find that data residency requirements have already determined their deployment architecture before any technical analysis begins.

## Hybrid Architecture As a Governance Enforcer

Raw data stays local. Sensitive data, such as customer records, transaction history, and clinical data, remains behind the on-premises perimeter and is never directly exposed to cloud infrastructure. This is not a preference; it is the boundary established by residency law.

Derived data can move, but only after passing through the data-gating control. This mandatory pre-processing step applies anonymization, tokenization, or aggregation before any data crosses the perimeter. Anonymization removes direct identifiers so that the output cannot be traced to an individual. Tokenization replaces sensitive values with opaque references that retain relational structure without exposing the underlying data. Once processed through these controls, the derived output is no longer subject to the same residency restrictions as the raw source, making cloud-burst training and inference permissible. This is the architectural step that makes hybrid deployment operationally viable rather than theoretically appealing.

Federated learning handles the cases where even derived data cannot leave its origin, a common situation in multi-institution healthcare and cross-bank fraud detection. Rather than centralizing any data, federated learning trains a shared model across distributed nodes, with only gradient updates (not raw data or processed outputs) transmitted between participants. While this significantly reduces data exposure compared with centralized training, gradient updates may still be vulnerable to gradient inversion attacks under adversarial conditions, in which an adversary reconstructs private training data from the shared gradients; additional privacy-preserving techniques, such as differential privacy, may be required in highly sensitive contexts. The result is a collaboratively trained model that no single institution's data has ever produced in raw form.

Table 3-2 summarizes the governance trade-offs between the two core deployment models, mapped against the risk taxonomy categories that each architecture must address.

***Table 3-2.*** *Comparative analysis of AI deployment models*

| Dimension | Cloud-Only Model | Hybrid/On-Premises Model | Governance Impact/ Risk Category |
|---|---|---|---|
| Primary TCO profile | High variable OpEx; explosive volatility due to fragmented costs (tokens, embeddings) | High fixed CapEx; predictable OpEx, 30–50% savings if utilization > 65% | Embedded FinOps controls required at source. Mitigates Decision Velocity Risk |
| Data residency | High compliance risk; depends on regional zone guarantees | Low risk; sensitive data secured within organizational perimeter | Enforces GDPR and data sovereignty compliance. Mitigates Regulatory Explainability Risk |
| Scalability | Instantaneous, automatic elasticity for variable peak workloads | Slower scaling; baseline capacity optimized, burst capacity reserved for the cloud | Policy enforcement required for SKU and scale management. Mitigates Concentration Risk |
| Latency/ workload | Potential network latency; best for latency-tolerant batch inference | Low latency required for real-time/ agentic autonomous decision-making | Enables real-time mission-critical operations. Mitigates Decision Velocity Risk |
| Vendor risk | High risk of vendor lock-in via proprietary AI services and cloud APIs | Reduced lock-in; portability easier using open standards (Kubernetes) | Reduces dependency via open standards and multi-cloud distribution. Mitigates Concentration Risk |

Table 3-2 reinforces one conclusion: there is no universally superior deployment model. Cloud-only is operationally simpler and elastically scalable, but fails the residency test for regulated data and the latency test for real-time agentic workloads. A hybrid satisfies both at the cost of architectural complexity. For most regulated enterprises, the hybrid model is not a choice but a constraint imposed by the intersection of residency law, latency requirements, and concentration risk limits.

## Financial Dimensions

AI cost structures do not resemble traditional IT economics. The core tension is between stable, high-CapEx on-premises infrastructure and variable, consumption-based cloud OpEx, but the AI-specific wrinkle is that cloud costs fragment across token billing, embedding calls, retrieval queries, orchestration steps, and agent actions, each tied to an engineering decision rather than an infrastructure configuration. This fragmentation makes traditional cost forecasting unreliable and embeds the financial governance problem directly into the decision about the deployment architecture.

## TCO Comparison

Cloud costs are elastic but carry a significant premium at scale: at high sustained utilization, cloud-based AI infrastructure can cost substantially more than equivalent on-premises hardware. That premium is justified when demand is volatile; organizations with inference demands that fluctuate significantly can avoid provisioning and paying for on-premises capacity sized to peak load. On-premises becomes the superior choice when demand is stable and predictable: above a high, sustained utilization threshold, the economics favor owned infrastructure, because the fixed CapEx commitment is recovered and amortized, whereas below it, the variable, pay-as-you-go cloud model wins. For real-time agentic systems at the Critical tier, this financial analysis is secondary: the requirement for local compute is driven by governance, not economics; the oversight controls cannot be technically enforced elsewhere.

## Operational Overhead and AI FinOps

Traditional FinOps was designed for compute and storage. In AI systems, spend appears in prompts, retrieval queries, orchestration steps, and agent actions, each tied to an engineering decision rather than an infrastructure configuration. Practitioner experience consistently shows that a single prompt change can multiply token consumption by an order of magnitude or more overnight. Static budgets and periodic reporting cannot govern this.

## Context Tax and the Mandate for Context Hygiene

The Context Tax is the cost and performance penalty incurred from processing irrelevant data within the model's reasoning window. It is distinct from the Information Tax, the productivity cost to human workers of information fragmentation and manual search time, the hours spent navigating disconnected knowledge systems rather than creating value, which Chapter 6 quantifies as the primary inefficiency the RAG architecture addresses. For cloud-hosted LLMs, the Context Tax is a direct billing problem: irrelevant tokens are charged at the same rate as useful ones. For self-hosted models, the tax is paid differently through increased GPU resource consumption, higher inference latency, and reduced output quality, but the penalty is equivalent. Including a 500-word irrelevant policy document in every retrieval response is not a minor inefficiency; it is a financial drain in the cloud model and a performance drain in the self-hosted model, and in both cases it can increase hallucination risk by diluting the relevant context the model has to reason over. The architectural response is context hygiene: programmatic filtering that ensures only the highest-density, most relevant information reaches the Cognitive Layer. An architecture that ignores context hygiene is authorizing waste at the infrastructure layer, regardless of where the model runs.

Managing the Context Tax is one reason the hybrid model is financially superior at scale. Fixed on-premises GPUs process high-volume baseline workloads at a predictable cost, while the cloud handles elastic demand. Three operational controls govern this spend: chargeback assigns spend to the consuming business unit in real time; visibility gives engineers granular cost data at the point of the engineering decision, where it can still be changed; and engineer-facing cost gates enforce policy-based spending limits before agent actions execute, preventing runaway consumption from recursive loops or token spikes.

# Architectural and Operational Trade-Offs

The deployment model also shapes the operational parameters of a system once it is in production. Three axes determine the right placement: latency tolerance (which drives where the workload runs), infrastructure complexity (which determines how the hybrid environment is managed), and vendor dependency (which is a concentration risk regardless of latency profile). Each is examined below.

## Latency, Scalability, and Specialized Hardware

Latency requirements are the primary technical factor determining where an AI workload must reside. The strategic distinction is made between batch and real-time inference:

- **Batch Inference**: This method is optimal for high throughput and computational efficiency when immediate responses are not required. It operates asynchronously, processing large datasets on a schedule, and tolerates delays of minutes or hours. Batch workloads are ideal for placement on public cloud infrastructure, leveraging its scalability and cost-effectiveness for offline processing.

- **Real-Time (Online) Inference and Agentic AI**: Real-time processing is essential for continuous data streams where immediate insights and dynamic decision-making are crucial. Agentic AI handles complex, multi-step decision workflows autonomously. To operate smoothly and without latency issues, these agents require substantial, low-latency computing power. Network latency inherent to public cloud environments can degrade the performance of mission-critical agents, often necessitating on-premises deployments using local high-performance resources, such as NVIDIA AI GPUs, for real-time processing. Critically, this is also where Decision Velocity Risk is highest; the system is executing consequential decisions at machine speed, and the deployment architecture must embed circuit-breaker and oversight controls at the infrastructure layer, not the application layer.

Standardized, cloud-native technologies, such as Kubernetes and serverless compute, manage distributed hybrid resources consistently. For architects specifying workload placement, latency-sensitive, high-stakes workloads require local or edge compute, with circuit-break and oversight controls embedded at the infrastructure layer, not the application layer.

## Vendor Lock-In and Multi-cloud Complexity

Vendor lock-in is a governance problem before it is a sourcing problem. When a single vendor controls a significant portion of the organization's autonomous decision-making infrastructure, two dependencies arise: operational and oversight. The second is more dangerous: if the organization's right to halt an autonomous system depends on contractual terms with the vendor, the kill-switch mandate from Chapter 1 is no longer technically enforceable; it is contingent on the contract. The EDS framework's 40% concentration limit exists precisely to prevent this.

The mitigation is open standards and multi-cloud distribution. Containerization, microservices architecture, and interoperable APIs reduce both operational and oversight dependencies by enabling the organization to enforce governance controls independently of any single vendor.

The operational cost of increased complexity is managed through centralized governance platforms that enforce consistent IAM, cost tagging, and resource location policies across all environments.

# Core Technology Decision

The technology stack decision is a governance decision about production suitability, not a developer preference about tooling. The governance-relevant question is not which language has the best AI libraries, but which ecosystem provides the stability, auditability, and lifecycle maturity required to govern autonomous systems in production. Model Behavior Risk and Cascade Failure Risk are harder to contain in rapidly evolving ecosystems; Accountability Diffusion Risk is more effectively mitigated in environments with mature, auditable lifecycle tooling. Two ecosystems serve distinct roles in this framework. Table 3-3 links these risk categories or operational overheads with technology stacks.

# Ecosystem, Talent, and Velocity

Python is the velocity layer. Its ecosystem, including NumPy, Pandas, TensorFlow, LangChain, and LlamaIndex, provides the fastest path from model research to a working prototype, with the widest talent pool for AI engineering. It is the right choice for rapid experimentation, model development, RAG-heavy applications, and R&D workloads where iteration speed is the primary constraint.

Java and the JVM are the reliability layer. The ecosystem is smaller and slower to adopt new AI frameworks, but offers the stability, security maturity, and enterprise integration depth that high-stakes production systems require. For Critical-tier and High-tier autonomous systems at Autonomy Level 3 or above, where a framework-breaking change is a governance event rather than a maintenance task, the JVM provides a cleaner production baseline.

***Table 3-3.*** *Technology stack evaluation for enterprise AI*

| **Dimension** | **Python (Standard AI Stack)** | **Java/.NET (Enterprise Stack)** | **Operational Overhead/Risk Category** |
| --- | --- | --- | --- |
| Ecosystem and talent | Superior ecosystem and dominant AI/ML tooling adoption. Python's advantage for AI deployments lies in its unmatched AI/ML ecosystem and framework depth, not in raw developer count (see note). | Deep enterprise engineering talent pool. Java's advantage lies in production stability and enterprise integration maturity, not in AI/ML tooling breadth (see note). | Lower immediate overhead for feature development; higher long-term overhead for security and dependency management |
| Production stability | Rapidly evolving frameworks (e.g., LangChain and LangGraph reached their first stable 1.0 releases only in October 2025; LangChain 2025a, 2025b). | High stability, robustness, and maturity; preferred for continuous, large-scale integration. | Elevated Model Behavior Risk and Governance Drift Risk from frequent framework updates. Mitigated by strict MLOps governance policies |

*(continued)*

***Table 3-3.*** *(continued)*

| Dimension | Python (Standard AI Stack) | Java/.NET (Enterprise Stack) | Operational Overhead/Risk Category |
|---|---|---|---|
| Enterprise integration | Often requires complex API bridging to core, legacy enterprise systems. | Seamless integration with existing core business platforms (finance, healthcare). | Reduced integration complexity and reduced bridging cost. Lower Accountability Diffusion Risk due to cleaner audit trails |
| Security foundation | Higher vulnerability surface due to package ecosystem (injections, malicious packages). | Stronger inherent security features and mature libraries; robust access control mechanisms. | Higher diligence required in MLOps pipeline hardening, version locking, and CVE analysis. Directly mitigates Cascade Failure Risk from supply-chain attacks |

# Governance Implications of Stack Choice

The governance implications of the Python ecosystem are elevated Model Behavior Risk and Governance Drift Risk: rapid framework evolution means that a version update can alter system behavior without a corresponding governance review. The JVM trades velocity for stability, the right trade for Critical-tier autonomous systems at Autonomy Level 3 or above, where a framework-breaking change is a governance event, not a maintenance task.

---

**Note** SlashData's Developer Nation Survey (29th wave, 2025) reports that Python and Java each have approximately 23 million active developers globally, so raw developer population does not distinguish between them. The decision rests on ecosystem fit: Python leads in AI/ML tooling and framework depth, while Java leads in production stability and enterprise integration maturity.

---

## Governance, Security, and Operational Overhead

The stack choice determines the governance overhead of dependency management, observability, and auditability. In many regulated enterprises, these concerns outweigh the raw compute economics of the deployment decision.

### Lifecycle Governance Controls

Governance must be embedded in the software lifecycle, not bolted on at the end. Four lifecycle controls matter: dependency management (version-locked, CVE-monitored, with isolated environments per project), observability (every prompt, output, and execution metric logged to the central governance platform), secure release discipline (no model reaches production without passing the MLOps certification gates established in the Criticality Tier classification), and HITL logging (every human intervention recorded with full context, not just the outcome). In the Python ecosystem, Poetry provides the isolated virtual environment management that makes the first control enforceable, and LangSmith provides the observability layer that makes the second control visible; both are operational prerequisites for a compliant Python MLOps stack.

# Actionable Recommendation

The optimal technology strategy is one of stratification:

- **Velocity Layer (Python)**: Use Python for rapid experimentation, model development, R&D, and RAG-heavy applications, thanks to its high velocity and extensive ecosystem. This layer must be constrained by strict MLOps governance policies and robust dependency management to mitigate Model Behavior Risk and Governance Drift Risk.
- **Reliability Layer (Java/.NET)**: Transition mission-critical, high-traffic production models, especially autonomous agentic AI orchestration hubs, to the Java or .NET environment. This layer leverages the stability, superior enterprise integration, and inherent security maturity of the JVM to ensure maximum production uptime, auditability, and compliance with the oversight model requirements for Critical-tier and High-tier workloads.

Table 3-4 presents a final decision matrix that aligns core business drivers with the optimal deployment architecture and technology stack under a governance-first mandate, with the risk taxonomy category most directly implicated by each governance driver.

***Table 3-4.** Strategic decision matrix for drivers of deployment architecture by governance*

| Primary Governance Driver | Low Volatility/ Batch Workloads | High Volatility/ Real-Time Agentic Workloads | Recommended Technology Stack |
|---|---|---|---|
| Cost optimization (TCO focus) | Hybrid (on-premises base load; cloud for off-peak bursts to utilize cost efficiency) | Hybrid/cloud-only (pay-as-you-go elasticity for unpredictable inference spikes) | Python (for rapid prototyping and RAG-heavy workflows) |
| Strict data sovereignty [mitigates: Regulatory Explainability Risk] | On-premises/ private cloud (raw training data contained locally) | Hybrid (local inference; utilize federated learning techniques for training) | Java/.NET (for integrating with existing robust enterprise identity and security controls) |
| High performance/ low latency [mitigates: Decision Velocity Risk] | On-premises (local GPU/TPU access) | On-premises/hybrid edge (AI agent deployed near the execution layer with embedded circuit-break controls) | Java/.NET (for speed, low GC latency, and stability; mandatory for Critical-tier Autonomy Level 3+ systems) |
| Operational simplicity/ speed [monitors: Governance Drift Risk] | Cloud-only (managed MLOps services, immediate deployment) | Cloud-only (focus on unified API gateways for deployment via managed agent-serving platforms such as LangSmith Deployment, formerly LangGraph Platform) | Python (faster prototyping, wider immediate toolkit access; requires compensating governance controls) |

## The Operational Architecture: Hybrid Deployment and the Agent Hub

The Agent Hub is the operational execution environment where governance meets infrastructure. It hosts the Deterministic Shell and serves as the gateway between business applications and hybrid infrastructure. Four control functions make the governance framework viable at enterprise scale.

## The Platform Decision: Convergence versus Divergence

Every enterprise implementing this book's governance framework must make a foundational platform decision: whether to extend its existing enterprise application infrastructure to support AI (the Convergence Model) or to maintain a dedicated, parallel AI platform alongside its existing systems (the Divergence Model). This is not a technology preference; it is a governance complexity decision that directly affects the cost and coherence of the controls described throughout this book.

The Convergence Platform approach builds upon the existing Enterprise Application Platform, which currently serves cloud-native workloads. By extending the existing container-based infrastructure to include artificial intelligence capabilities, the organization inherits years of security, identity, and compliance foundations. In this model, the AI is treated as another service within the established Enterprise Application Platform ecosystem. The advantage of convergence is a unified governance pane and a single set of operational tools that the IT team already understands. The Convergence Platform is the technical vehicle for the hybrid deployment strategy recommended in this chapter. Critically, it inherits a single governance pane—one identity framework, one compliance control set, and one audit trail—which significantly reduces the operational overhead of implementing the Authority Matrix, NHI Lifecycle Governance (the EDS-mandated process for provisioning, monitoring, and revoking non-human agent identities throughout their operational lifetime), and Immutable Audit Log requirements described in later chapters.

The Divergence Platform approach involves leveraging an established, specialized cloud AI platform from a major provider such as Amazon Web Services, Google Cloud, or Microsoft Azure. This is a Divergence Model because it requires the enterprise to maintain two distinct platforms: one for traditional cloud-native applications and another specifically for artificial intelligence. While this approach allows for faster access to the latest model innovations and proprietary provider features, it introduces significant fragmentation. The organization must now manage dual security stacks, dual identity frameworks, and two different sets of compliance controls. For regulated enterprises implementing this book's governance framework, the fragmentation cost of divergence is material: dual NHI registries, dual Policy Decision Points, and dual audit trails that must be reconciled for board reporting. Unless a compelling model capability gap justifies the overhead, convergence is the governance-efficient default.

This book's governance architecture is deployment model–agnostic: the Constitutional Engine, Deterministic Shell, and Agent Hub described in Chapters 1–3 can be implemented under either model. The Convergence Model reduces governance complexity; the Divergence Model may be justified when access to the frontier model is a strategic necessity. The choice should be driven by tolerance for governance overhead, not by technology preference alone.

## Operationalizing the Agent Hub

The four components operate as follows:

- **The FinOps Interceptor**: The FinOps Interceptor monitors token consumption and dollar spend for every agentic request in real time. It enforces policy-based cost gates, blocking actions that would breach a business unit's budget, and prevents the runaway model scenario in which a recursive agent loop exhausts the monthly budget within hours.
- **Hybrid Sync Layer**: The Hybrid Sync Layer keeps the Authority Matrix Rules Repository and the Immutable Audit Log synchronized across on-premises and cloud nodes. This allows the Cognitive Layer to run in the cloud while governance controls remain behind the corporate firewall.
- **Agent Proxy and Gateway**: The Agent Proxy and Gateway provide a standardized interface for all agents. It enforces the Tool Schema Definition layer, ensuring probabilistic models interact with deterministic legacy systems through verified protocols, and injects the Execution ID (the unique session identifier that threads all downstream transaction log entries into a single, ordered audit trail) into every downstream transaction, threading all activity into a single auditable chain.
- **HITL Override Service and Resilience**: The HITL Override Service operates as both an automated circuit breaker (triggered by Streaming Anomaly Detection) and an operator-initiated kill switch. When an agent is flagged as erratic, it is decoupled from the production environment before the failure can propagate.

The Agent Hub's governance value is not in any single component but in how the four components operate as a unified control layer. The FinOps Interceptor prevents runaway cost before an action executes; the Hybrid Sync Layer keeps the Authority Matrix and Immutable Audit Log consistent across deployment boundaries; the Agent Proxy enforces the Tool Schema and injects the Execution ID that threads every transaction into a single auditable chain; and the HITL Override Service provides the circuit-break and kill-switch capability that Chapter 1 mandates for any system operating at Autonomy Level 3 or above. Figure 3-1 shows how these four components connect and why removing any one of them breaks the governance chain on which the others depend.

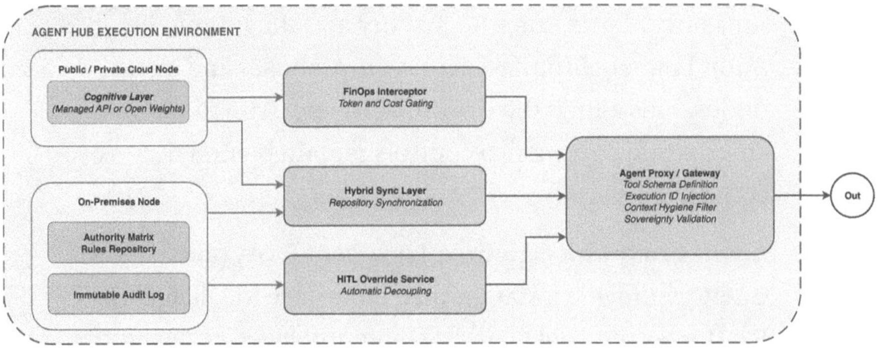


***Figure 3-1.*** *The Agent Hub as a unified governance control layer—showing the interaction between the FinOps Interceptor (cost gating and runaway prevention), the Hybrid Sync Layer (Authority Matrix and Audit Log synchronization across on-premises and cloud boundaries), the Agent Proxy and Gateway (Tool Schema enforcement and Execution ID injection for end-to-end traceability), and the HITL Override Service (automated circuit break and operator kill switch). The four components operate in concert: a cost breach detected by the FinOps Interceptor triggers the HITL Override Service; a sync failure in the Hybrid Sync Layer halts the Agent Proxy until consistency is restored. Governance is enforced at the infrastructure layer, not the application layer*

# AI Sovereignty: An Emerging Governance Dimension

AI Sovereignty is the governance question that data residency does not answer. An enterprise can satisfy every data residency requirement while remaining entirely dependent on a foreign model provider for the reasoning capability that acts on that data. Sovereignty requires the organization to control three things: the model weights (self-hosted or contractually guaranteed), the inference location (which jurisdiction processes the reasoning), and the data masking boundary (what governed data the model is ever permitted to see). It must also assess a fourth dimension, geopolitical dynamics: the risk that supply-chain disruption or regulatory change in a foreign jurisdiction could suddenly disable a critical reasoning capability. The first three are levers the organization holds; the fourth is an exposure it must monitor. An enterprise that cannot control where its intelligence runs cannot fully govern how it is used. Table 3-5 lists different AI sovereignty dimensions.

***Table 3-5.*** *AI Sovereignty dimension*

| Dimension | Description |
|---|---|
| **Model weight control** | The ability to host and control the model parameters within a private environment rather than relying on a provider's black-box API. |
| **Inference location** | Geopolitical considerations regarding where the actual computation occurs and which jurisdictions have legal access to the reasoning process. |
| **Geopolitical dynamics** | The risk of supply-chain disruptions or regulatory changes in foreign jurisdictions that could suddenly disable critical enterprise intelligence. |
| **Data masking** | Critical governed data is protected from unapproved AI exposure outside the safe boundaries defined by the governance rules. |

Sovereignty decisions should be made at deployment time, not discovered at crisis time when a provider changes its terms, faces regulatory intervention, or experiences a service disruption.

# Summary

This chapter established that deployment architecture is a governance decision, not a technology preference. Every architectural choice, cloud-only versus hybrid, on-premises versus edge, Python versus Java, carries a distinct risk profile that must be assessed against the AI risk taxonomy before provisioning infrastructure. For most regulated enterprises, the hybrid deployment model is not optional: it is the only architecture capable of simultaneously satisfying data residency obligations, latency requirements for real-time agentic systems, and concentration risk limits. The key takeaways are as follows:

- **Risk classification precedes architecture**. The eight AI-specific risk categories—Decision Velocity, Cascade Failure, Governance Drift, Model Behavior, Prompt Drift, Accountability Diffusion, Concentration, and Regulatory Explainability—are the governing constraints that determine which deployment models are permissible, which oversight models are mandatory, and which circuit-break controls must be embedded at the infrastructure layer. Every deployment decision in this book is filtered through this taxonomy.

- **Criticality Tier is the first deployment filter**. Before TCO or latency is considered, the workload's Criticality Tier determines whether a given deployment model is even permissible. Critical-tier systems at Autonomy Level 3 or above cannot run cloud-only unless the cloud environment can technically enforce HOTL supervision and circuit-break controls at the infrastructure layer. Where it cannot, the deployment model is mandated rather than chosen.

- **The hybrid model is the governance enforcer.** Hybrid architecture is not a compromise between cloud convenience and on-premises control. It is the architecture that enforces compliance boundaries, keeps sensitive data behind the organizational perimeter, embeds oversight controls near the execution layer, and reduces concentration risk by distributing decision authority across environments. Its operational complexity is the price of satisfying governance requirements that simpler architectures cannot meet.

- **AI economics requires embedded financial governance.** Token billing, embedding calls, retrieval queries, orchestration steps, and agent actions each generate separate cost signals. Traditional FinOps frameworks were not designed for this fragmentation. Cost controls must be embedded directly in the MLOps pipeline through chargeback, engineer-facing visibility, and policy-based cost gates. The Context Tax, the cost and performance penalty of processing irrelevant data in the reasoning window, must be addressed through architectural context hygiene, not post hoc budget adjustments.

- **The Agent Hub completes the operational triad.** The Constitutional Engine provides the governance law. The Deterministic Shell provides the inference control layer. The Agent Hub provides the operational execution environment that ties to both the physical infrastructure and the agent. Its four components—the FinOps Interceptor, Hybrid Sync Layer, Agent Proxy and Gateway, and HITL Override Service—enforce governance mandates at the infrastructure layer, not just at the application layer.

The next chapter opens with a question that must be settled before any security component is specified: which human oversight commitment applies to this system, and what does that determination require of everything built around it?

# References

LangChain. 2025a. LangChain 1.0 Now Generally Available. Changelog, October 22. `https://changelog.langchain.com/announcements/langchain-1-0-now-generally-available`.

LangChain. 2025b. LangGraph 1.0 Is Now Generally Available. Changelog, October 22. `https://changelog.langchain.com/announcements/langgraph-1-0-is-now-generally-available`.

SlashData. 2025. Developer Nation Survey, 29th Wave. London: SlashData. `https://www.developernation.net/developer-reports/dn29/`.

CHAPTER 4

# Governing Access and Lineage

The deployment of generative AI in regulated and risk-averse enterprises has exposed a governance gap that traditional security architecture was never designed to close. Enterprise knowledge bases contain data that is simultaneously valuable for AI-driven productivity and subject to strict access, residency, and retention obligations. The moment an LLM is connected to that knowledge base, even via a well-intentioned RAG pipeline, the organization has created a new attack surface, a new data lineage problem, and a new accountability obligation. The question is not whether the AI system is capable. The question is whether the governance architecture surrounding it is adequate to ensure that its decisions are auditable, its access controls are enforceable, and its human oversight obligations are technically binding rather than merely declared.

The answer demands moving beyond the traditional network perimeter model. In a Zero-Trust architecture (ZTA), no entity, human or machine, is trusted by default, regardless of where it sits in the network. Every request is verified, every action is least-privileged, and every decision is logged. For RAG systems operating in regulated environments, this is not a design aspiration; it is a compliance mandate. The shift to cloud-native infrastructure has eliminated the perimeter as a meaningful control boundary. What replaces it is a governance control plane that operates at the transaction level: verifying identity before retrieval,


M. M. Hossain and A. A. N. Ponnusamy, *Governance-First AI*,
https://doi.org/10.1007/979-8-8688-3118-8_4

enforcing access policy at the chunk level, and recording every decision in a tamper-evident ledger that can withstand a regulatory audit or a legal challenge.

This chapter establishes the control plane. It defines the universal Zero-Trust security and governance architecture that underpins every use case blueprint in Parts III and IV of this book. Every component described here, from the oversight model decision matrix and the orchestrator as a singular PEP to Security Trimming, Data Lineage Tagging, and Reasoning Trace Capture, is a non-negotiable architectural requirement, not a recommended practice. Architects building on the use case blueprints in later chapters must implement these controls as preconditions, not as optimizations.

The chapter is organized around a critical Governance Principle: the human oversight model, whether HITL, HOTL, or HAL, is not a policy annotation appended after engineering is complete. It is the first architectural constraint. It determines how the LLM orchestrator must be configured, what the Audit Log must capture, and what supervisor interface the system must expose. Before any component is specified, that determination must be made from the EDS oversight model decision matrix introduced in this chapter. The remainder of the chapter then defines the four technical planes—the Identity Plane, the Control Plane, the Data and Lineage Plane, and the Accountability Plane—that together enforce whatever oversight commitment has been made.

**Governance Leaders**: The oversight model decision matrix and the four technical planes at a conceptual level are your primary entry points.

**Architects and Practitioners**: Every section from "Oversight Models As Architectural Requirements" onward is your working specification.

# Oversight Models As Architectural Requirements

The three oversight models derive from the constitutional governance framework established in Chapter 1 and are each mandated by the intersection of the deployment's Autonomy Level and Criticality Tier (Chapter 3). They are not interchangeable.

## Defining the Three Oversight Models

Each oversight model places a different technical demand on the governance control plane:

**AUTONOMY LEVELS 1–2: HUMAN-IN-THE-LOOP (HITL)**

*A human must approve each individual action before the system may execute it. The LLM orchestrator must be configured to pause execution at every decision point, present its reasoning to a human reviewer, and proceed only upon explicit approval. No action proceeds without a positive human confirmation signal.*

**Architectural Requirement:** The orchestrator must implement a synchronous approval gate, a hard stop that cannot be bypassed by the system's own logic. For RAG systems, this means the orchestrator holds the augmented prompt and proposed response pending human sign-off before generation or output delivery. This is the minimum standard for Critical-tier systems at any Autonomy Level.

## AUTONOMY LEVEL 3: HUMAN-ON-THE-LOOP (HOTL)

*A certified human supervisor monitors autonomous system outputs in real or near real time and retains active, unimpeded authority to intervene, adjust, or halt the system. The system executes autonomously, but the supervisor has a live override capability at all times.*

**Architectural Requirement:** The orchestrator must expose a real-time intervention interface accessible to the certified supervisor. The Audit Log must record every instance where the supervisor could have intervened but did not, creating a positive attestation trail. The kill-switch capability required by Principle 4 (Mandatory Halt Capability) of the governance framework must be accessible to the supervisor at all times during system operation.

## AUTONOMY LEVELS 4–5: HUMAN-ABOVE-THE-LOOP (HAL)

*A human supervisor periodically reviews agent output batches and approves before any material commitment is executed. The system operates with high autonomy between review cycles but cannot execute material commitments without batch approval.*

**Architectural Requirement:** The orchestrator must classify outputs as material or non-material according to the Machine Decision Authority Matrix entry for the deployment domain. Non-material outputs are streamed to users directly. Material outputs are queued for batch approval before execution. The boundary between material and non-material must be defined in the Autonomy Register entry for the system, not inferred at runtime by the model.

## EDS Oversight Model Decision Matrix

Table 4-1 maps each of the 15 use cases in this book to its required oversight model, Autonomy Level, and Criticality Tier. This mapping governs the orchestrator configuration, the audit logging standard, and the Human-on-the-Loop supervision requirements for each deployment. Architects must consult this matrix before specifying any component of the governance control plane.

***Table 4-1.*** *Oversight model requirements for all 15 use cases*

| Use Case | Autonomy Level | Criticality Tier | Required Oversight Model | Key Architectural Enforcement |
|---|---|---|---|---|
| UC1—Frontline knowledge assistant | Level 2 | Moderate | HITL (approval gate for low-confidence answers) | Orchestrator enforces HITL review when Groundedness Score falls below threshold. No ungrounded answer delivered without human sign-off. |
| UC2—Regulatory compliance platform | Level 2 | Critical | HITL (mandatory for all regulatory-domain outputs) | Orchestrator blocks generation and mandates HITL review for any response in a regulated legal or compliance domain. CRO approval required per Chapter 3 criticality matrix. |

(*continued*)

***Table 4-1.*** *(continued)*

| Use Case | Autonomy Level | Criticality Tier | Required Oversight Model | Key Architectural Enforcement |
|---|---|---|---|---|
| UC3—Document quality uplift | Level 2 | Moderate | HITL (Separation of Duties enforcement) | Author and approver must be different identities. Orchestrator enforces Separation of Duties via RBAC metadata check before releasing quality review output. |
| UC4—AI stylist and language adapter | Level 2 | Low | HITL (human approves stylistic outputs before release) | Each stylistic output is presented for human approval before release. No brand or voice commitment is published without explicit sign-off. |
| UC5—Predictive customer insight | Level 2 | High | HITL (human approves recommendations before they are acted upon) | Each customer-facing recommendation is presented for human approval before it is acted upon. |
| UC6—IT service resolution agent | Level 3 | High | HOTL (supervisor monitors automated resolutions) | Supervisor monitors resolution actions in real time. Kill switch accessible at all times. Escalation to HITL for any resolution above defined cost threshold. |

*(continued)*

***Table 4-1.*** *(continued)*

| Use Case | Autonomy Level | Criticality Tier | Required Oversight Model | Key Architectural Enforcement |
|---|---|---|---|---|
| UC7—Insurance claims agent | Level 3 | Critical | HOTL + HITL circuit break for payment decisions | All payment or denial decisions above threshold trigger mandatory HITL gate. Supervisor monitors all other actions in real time. Board Risk Committee notification required per Critical-tier mandate. |
| UC8—Market intelligence system | Level 3 | High | HOTL (supervisor monitors report generation) | Supervisor reviews autonomous report generation in real time. Material strategic recommendations queued for HAL batch review before distribution. |
| UC9—Financial risk and fraud agent | Level 3 | Critical | HOTL + HITL for irrceversible financial actions | Any action that freezes funds, flags a customer, or triggers a regulatory report requires HITL approval. All other monitoring actions are HOTL-supervised. |

*(continued)*

*Table 4-1.* (*continued*)

| Use Case | Autonomy Level | Criticality Tier | Required Oversight Model | Key Architectural Enforcement |
|---|---|---|---|---|
| UC10—Hotel dynamic pricing agent | Level 3 | High | HOTL (supervisor monitors pricing decisions) | Pricing commitments above ADR threshold queued for HAL batch review. All other booking actions are HOTL-supervised. |
| UC11—Restaurant waitlist agent | Level 3 | Moderate | HOTL (supervisor monitors guest interactions) | Supervisor monitors all guest-facing actions. No operational commitment (table assignment, hold cancellation) executed without HOTL coverage. |
| UC12—Event ticket and seat upgrade agent | Level 3 | High | HOTL + HITL for payment execution | Payment execution step of Saga Pattern requires HITL gate. All other steps are HOTL-supervised with idempotent retry logging. |

(*continued*)

*Table 4-1.* (*continued*)

| Use Case | Autonomy Level | Criticality Tier | Required Oversight Model | Key Architectural Enforcement |
|---|---|---|---|---|
| UC13—Aircraft predictive maintenance | Level 4 | Critical | HAL + mandatory HITL for grounding decisions | HAL batch review for all maintenance scheduling. Any unscheduled grounding recommendation mandates HITL sign-off before execution. Continuous monitoring required. As a Critical-tier system, it requires Board Risk Committee notification, quarterly audit, and CRO sign-off; Board Risk Committee approval is additionally required where its maximum action magnitude (MAM) limit exceeds the defined threshold. |

(*continued*)

***Table 4-1.*** *(continued)*

| Use Case | Autonomy Level | Criticality Tier | Required Oversight Model | Key Architectural Enforcement |
|---|---|---|---|---|
| UC14—Defense equipment maintenance | Level 4 | Critical | HAL + HITL for safety-critical halt flags | Safety Risk Agent halt flags require HITL confirmation before operational impact. All other scheduling is HAL batch-reviewed. External assurance required. |
| UC15—Manufacturing equipment maintenance | Level 4 | High | HAL (batch approval for maintenance scheduling) | Maintenance scheduling queued for HAL batch review. Unplanned shutdown recommendations require HITL gate to prevent operational disruption. |

Figure 4-1 illustrates how the oversight model determines when each supervision mode is activated and how authority shifts between HITL, HOTL, and HAL across the five Autonomy Levels.

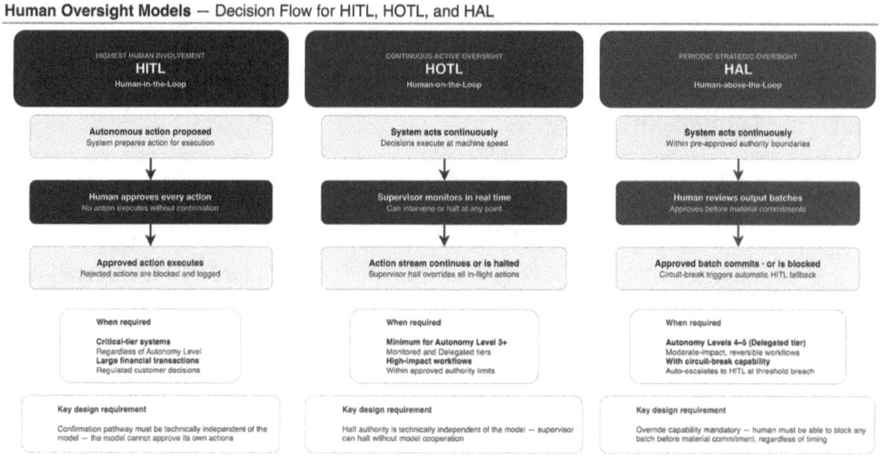


***Figure 4-1.*** *Human oversight models—decision flow for HITL, HOTL, and HAL: when each model activates, what the supervisor's authority is, and how the oversight mode shifts between them across the five Autonomy Levels*

This matrix is the governing reference for every blueprint in Parts III and IV. The Autonomy Level and oversight model specified here are constitutional requirements derived from the Governance-Constrained Autonomy principle established in Chapter 1. Architects may not select a lower-oversight model for convenience, cost, or velocity. Where a deployment's real-world risk profile would justify a higher level of oversight than the matrix specifies, that higher standard applies.

# Zero-Trust Access Matrix for RAG

Applying Zero-Trust tenets requires mapping specific security controls to the core RAG components. This matrix confirms that every stage of the RAG pipeline must function as a continuous enforcement mechanism, moving the system beyond a simple application and into the realm of mission-critical, governed infrastructure. Table 4-2 lists different Zero-Trust tenets and advice on how they should be enforced.

***Table 4-2.*** *Zero-Trust access matrix for RAG*

| Zero-Trust Tenet | RAG System Component | Technical Enforcement Mechanism |
|---|---|---|
| Verify explicitly | LLM orchestrator or PEP | IAM verification of user identity before context augmentation. For HOTL/HAL deployments, supervisor identity is also verified and logged at each oversight checkpoint. |
| Use least privilege | Retrieval Engine or vector DB | Retrieval-time access enforcement or Security Trimming. Constrained to the human operator's current RBAC permissions in HITL/HOTL deployments. |
| Assume breach | Audit logging or guardrails | Immutable log capture; output sanitization and classification. For HOTL/HAL deployments, logs must also record supervisor intervention events and non-intervention attestations. |

# Architecting the Governance Control Plane

The governance control plane is organized around four technical planes: the Identity Plane, the Control Plane, the Data and Lineage Plane, and the Accountability Plane. Before specifying any of these components, the architect must confront the foundational design tension that motivates the entire architecture: the Isolation Paradox.

## Isolation Paradox

The architectural design of an enterprise knowledge base presents a fundamental tension known as the Isolation Paradox. Optimal RAG performance requires indexing the entire corporate knowledge corpus together to maximize semantic search value. By combining all documents, the RAG system can find semantically related information across vast stores that might otherwise be missed. However, being overly permissive with access can lead to compliance nightmares, particularly for regulated data (e.g., HIPAA, SOX, GDPR).

DLAC is the mandated mechanism to resolve this paradox. By enforcing the Zero-Trust principle of least privilege, the system allows the corpus to be indexed holistically for maximum efficiency while ensuring that access filters are applied at retrieval. This means that the RAG pipeline ensures least privilege is maintained not just per user, but granularly, per query, based on the user's current identity and role. This architectural requirement is non-negotiable for operating RAG in a secure enterprise environment.

The LLM orchestrator must be designated as the mandatory PEP: the singular gateway through which every governance check is enforced and which no request or response can bypass. This designation is non-negotiable because the orchestrator directly bridges external user queries with sensitive corporate data. It is important to note that the orchestrator serves a dual role in this architecture: it functions simultaneously as the PEP (enforcing policy verdicts) and as the cognitive coordinator (assembling context, sequencing tool calls, and managing the reasoning flow). These two responsibilities are logically distinct even when implemented within the same component; the PEP function must never be bypassed by the orchestrator's own reasoning logic.

Figure 4-2 illustrates the four-plane control architecture across which the orchestrator operates as PEP: the Identity Plane (ZTAI and NHI registration), the Control Plane (PDP verdict and PEP enforcement), the Data and Lineage Plane (DLAC, Security Trimming, and ingestion governance), and the Accountability Plane (Immutable Audit Log, Reasoning Trace Capture, and Data Provenance Log). The orchestrator's configuration for each deployment, synchronous approval gates for HITL, real-time intervention interfaces for HOTL, or material/non-material batch queuing for HAL, must be locked at deployment time and governed as a material change rather than an operational preference.

## Defining the Single Gateway for Control

The orchestrator functions as a risk-gating mechanism: for high-stakes enterprise use cases, compliance is non-negotiable and takes precedence over efficiency.

Its core responsibilities in the inference phase are centered on control and verification:

1. It receives the filtered, DLAC-approved context and performs the necessary context assembly or augmentation to formulate the detailed prompt for the LLM.
2. It must integrate the grounding verification service to explicitly check the generated answer candidate against the retrieved facts (cited chunks).
3. It manages the Citation Threshold, the minimum acceptable Groundedness Score for an answer to be released to the user. When the score falls below the mandatory threshold, it executes the oversight model-appropriate safety action: for HITL deployments, it pauses and requests human approval; for HOTL deployments, it alerts the live supervisor and awaits override or confirmation; for HAL deployments, it queues the output as a material item for batch review.

The architecture must recognize that the orchestrator's operational failure modes are not merely technical bugs but represent audit failures. If the orchestrator fails to check permissions, enforce a grounding threshold, or invoke the correct oversight model gate, it has violated a compliance mandate. This inherent risk necessitates the immutable, specific logging of the orchestrator's decision rationales, not just the outcome, to ensure complete, auditable proof of its governance function.

## Centralized Policy Decision Flow

The orchestrator is the runtime enforcer of compliance policies. It enforces the Groundedness policy using the Groundedness Score. If this score falls below a predefined threshold, signifying insufficient or questionable context, the orchestrator must be programmed to execute a predefined safety action: either refuse generation, trigger a Corrective RAG (CRAG) loop to seek better context, or escalate to the oversight model's review gate. The specific action taken, and the identity of the human who reviewed and approved or rejected it, must be captured in the Audit Log as a non-repudiable governance record. It is important to note that the Groundedness Score addresses a specific hallucination failure mode: confabulation, in which the model generates claims unsupported by the retrieved context. A second and distinct failure mode, faithful hallucination, where the model accurately reproduces an error or contradiction present in the source documents themselves, is not detectable by the Groundedness Score alone. Faithful hallucination requires source integrity controls operating upstream of retrieval, specifically the Contradiction Detection Module (CD-Module) described in Chapter 8. Architecturally, these are complementary controls: the Groundedness Score governs output fidelity relative to the retrieved context; source integrity controls govern the trustworthiness of the context itself.

For autonomous agentic systems, the orchestrator's role as PEP extends to Policy Conflict Resolution: dynamically validating every planned action against multiple, potentially conflicting Governance-as-a-Service (GaaS) rules before execution. The governance framework must operate under a defined and non-negotiable priority hierarchy. Consider the example: A financial fraud agent (UC9) identifies a suspicious transaction at 2:14 AM. Its efficiency policy mandates the immediate freezing of accounts to minimize exposure to fraud. Its human oversight policy requires HITL approval (a P1 mandate) before any irreversible customer action. These two rules conflict directly. The PEP must resolve this before any action is taken.

The resolution follows a strict priority order. Safety and HITL mandates (P1) are never overridden; they block all conflicting rules regardless of business justification. Regulatory compliance rules (P2) override security and efficiency rules, but a CRO-approved exception can be granted on record. Data security rules, including DLAC and ZTAI enforcement (P3), override efficiency rules; any override requires a Chief Information Security Officer (CISO) escalation event in the Audit Log. Operational efficiency rules (P4) are the lowest priority and are applied only after P1–P3 are satisfied. In the fraud agent example, the HITL mandate (P1) wins unconditionally. The account freeze is queued as a material action pending HITL approval, not executed autonomously. The efficiency policy is overridden, and the conflict resolution outcome is recorded as a non-repudiable governance event in the Immutable Audit Log.

## Mandatory Guardrails

The orchestrator integrates a dedicated Guardrail Service that enforces proactive security against malicious input and sensitive output leakage.

During the pre-processing phase (Input Guardrail), this service inspects the incoming user query to actively scan for and block malicious encodings or prompt injection attempts.

During the post-processing phase (Output Guardrail), the orchestrator performs a final compliance review of the LLM's final output before releasing it to the user. This review includes confirming the successful insertion of mandatory citations and verifying adherence to high-level content policies. Most critically, the Guardrail Service must actively scan for and block PII leakage in the generated answer. Any detected guardrail violation must be logged as a critical compliance event in the Immutable Audit Log, thereby providing auditable proof of the execution of ethical and safety features. For HITL and HOTL deployments, guardrail violation events must also be surfaced to the human reviewer in real time; they are not silent background controls. Table 4-3 illustrates how LLM orchestrator can be used as the PEP.

***Table 4-3.*** *LLM orchestrator as the Policy Enforcement Point*

| Policy Control Enforced | Mechanism | Failure Action (Risk Gating) |
|---|---|---|
| Access filtering (DLAC) | Verifies user identity against retrieved chunk metadata (i.e., Security Trimming) | Blocks unauthorized retrieval; logs compliance failure. For HOTL deployments, alerts supervisor immediately |
| Grounding/ trust | Enforces minimum Groundedness Score threshold | Triggers oversight model gate: HITL approval pause, HOTL supervisor alert, or HAL material queue. Logs threshold breach and resolution |
| Security guardrails | Scans inputs (prompt injection) and outputs (PII leakage) | Blocks prompt/redacts output; logs violation as critical event. Surfaces to human reviewer in real time for HITL/ HOTL deployments |

# Governing Access

Security Trimming (retrieval-time access enforcement) is the runtime enforcement of DLAC: the corpus is indexed holistically for maximum semantic breadth, but every query is constrained to the requesting identity's verified ACL (Access Control List) scope at the chunk level. This resolves the Isolation Paradox without sacrificing retrieval quality. The implementation operates across two phases.

## Metadata Integration and Constrained Search

The process of Security Trimming is meticulously enforced in two distinct phases of the RAG pipeline:

- **Step 1—Metadata Integration (Ingestion)**: During ingestion, the Pre-processing Engine must perform dual duties: pulling content and simultaneously extracting or mapping existing source metadata. Critical security attributes, such as security group IDs, organizational roles, or Access Control Lists (ACLs), are extracted or mapped from the source system (e.g., SharePoint permissions) and attached as metadata to each text chunk. This meticulous, granular tagging creates the essential secure access points needed for runtime enforcement.

  A key technical constraint for enterprise architects involves the underlying vector database implementation. Vector fields themselves are typically not filterable in Approximate Nearest Neighbor (ANN) search algorithms used by vector databases. This means that security policies cannot be embedded solely within the semantic vector itself. Instead, filtering must be applied to separate, filterable non-vector fields in the same index, such as string or numeric fields. This technical reality fundamentally requires that security permissions be stored as explicit metadata tags alongside the vector chunk.

- **Step 2—Access Filtering and Constrained Search (Runtime)**: At runtime, the user's identity is verified via enterprise Identity and Access Management (IAM) systems (e.g., Single Sign-On). The Retrieval Engine uses this verified identity to generate a dynamic filter query against the security metadata field in the vector index. The vector database then executes the semantic search constrained by this filter. This ensures that the search only retrieves authorized chunks for prompt augmentation, rigorously enforcing the principle of least privilege.

This meticulous enforcement, while non-negotiable for compliance, introduces complexity and a marginal cost to query performance, a necessary performance tax paid for operating a compliant Zero-Trust system in a regulated environment.

Table 4-4 demonstrates how governance control can be placed in RAG and other agentic layers.

***Table 4-4.*** *Governance control placement—RAG and agentic layers*

| Control | Layer | Purpose | Failure Mode |
|---|---|---|---|
| **Identity verification (ZTAI)** | Identity (IAM/NHI Register) | Authenticates every human and NHI before any request is processed | Unregistered NHI operates in production (Shadow AI). |
| **PDP policy evaluation** | Control Plane (Authority Matrix) | Returns deterministic Allow/Deny verdict before every action | PDP bypassed: action executes without policy check. |
| **PEP enforcement (LLM orchestrator)** | Control Plane (orchestrator) | Intercepts every request, enforces verdict, and invokes HITL/HOTL/HAL gate, guardrails, and delegated auth | Audit failure: orchestrator skips a governance check (permission, grounding, or oversight gate). |

(*continued*)

*Table 4-4.* (*continued*)

| Control | Layer | Purpose | Failure Mode |
|---|---|---|---|
| **Security Trimming (DLAC)** | Data Plane (Retrieval Engine/vector DB) | Filters retrieved chunks to the requesting identity's authorized ACL scope at query time | Unauthorized chunk surfaces in LLM context window (Isolation Paradox breach). |
| **Data Lineage Tagging** | Lineage Plane (ingestion pipeline) | Appends provenance, security, and retention metadata to every chunk at ingestion | Chunk is untagged: right to erasure and source attribution cannot be enforced. |
| **Immutable Audit Log** | Accountability Plane (Audit Service) | Records complete RAG chain, oversight model events, and guardrail violations in tamper-evident storage | Incomplete log: audit trail non-compliant; oversight model events missing. |
| **Reasoning Trace Capture** | Accountability Plane (Agentic Audit) | Captures every Think–Act–Observe step for full decision reconstruction and contestability | Only final output logged: reasoning failure versus policy violation cannot be distinguished. |
| **Delegated Authorization Service** | Control Plane (proxy layer) | Intercepts agent API calls and checks proposed action against the human operator's RBAC scope | Excess Agency: agent executes a privileged action the human principal cannot authorize. |

## Data Residency Zoning and Geo-fencing

The DLAC principle is extended to address global data sovereignty and residency mandates. For organizations operating across multiple regulatory jurisdictions, unauthorized cross-border data transfers pose a severe risk.

The ingestion layer must enforce Data Residency Zoning by applying metadata tags that explicitly mandate the physical storage location (e.g., region, country) for each document and its corresponding vector chunks.

At runtime, the Retrieval Engine uses the user's inferred location or the organization's compliance policy as an additional filter query against the Data Residency Zone metadata. This mechanism ensures that semantic search is geographically confined, preventing the LLM from accessing or synthesizing data that must remain within designated geographic boundaries (e.g., EU data stays in the EU), providing a critical layer of jurisdictional compliance.

# Governing Data Lineage

The ingestion pipeline is the primary governance control point: every indexed chunk must be fully traceable, tamper-evident, and erasable on demand to satisfy records retention and right-to-erasure mandates.

## Mandate for Non-repudiable Data Lineage Tagging

The indexing process must enforce strict data provenance requirements to support records retention compliance and privacy rights such as right to erasure, through both physical and logical safeguards.

Architecturally, all source data must be stored in WORM formats to prevent tampering or modification after ingestion. Furthermore, comprehensive protection, including mandatory AES-256 encryption for data at rest, must be implemented to secure enterprise and regulatory data.

The Pre-processing Engine acts as a crucial initial security gateway for data ingress. It must perform a data classification check against enterprise policy to prevent highly sensitive, unapproved data (e.g., certain PII or confidential client data) from ever being indexed and embedded. This classification check is a mandatory preventive security control, complemented by poisoning mitigation through rigorous source verification to detect document anomalies and resist malicious data injection attempts. These ingestion-layer controls are the architectural defense against faithful hallucination: the failure mode in which the model accurately reproduces an error or contradiction already present in the source. Where the Groundedness Score governs fidelity to the retrieved context, source integrity controls govern the trustworthiness of the context itself, a distinction developed in full in the "Centralized Policy Decision Flow" section above.

## Pre-processing Engine As the Data Lineage Tagger

The Pre-processing Engine must function as the Data Lineage Tagger, appending compliance and lineage metadata to every text chunk before it is embedded.

This lineage tag is stored alongside the vector in the vector database and recorded in a dedicated Data Provenance Log. Table 4-5 lists different metadata fields and justifies why they should be logged.

A direct operational benefit: The lineage tag enables immediate identification and deletion of all corresponding vectors when a source document is removed, enforcing right-to-erasure compliance.

***Table 4-5.*** *Data Lineage Tagging—mandatory metadata fields for provenance*

| Metadata Field | Purpose/Justification |
|---|---|
| Ingestion timestamp | Non-repudiable audit trails and data freshness validation |
| Original system ID | Tracing content back to source system (e.g., SharePoint site ID) |
| Retention classification | Compliance with data disposal and retention policies (right to erasure) |
| Security attributes (ACLs) | Required permissions (e.g., security group ID, org role) for DLAC/Security Trimming |
| Data classification | Preventing highly sensitive data (PII/PHI) indexing (critical preventive control) |

## Continuous Index Fidelity

The operational reliability of any RAG system is directly dependent on the freshness of its source data; stale facts will inevitably undermine user trust. Therefore, the ingestion pipeline must run asynchronously to avoid affecting real-time user experience.

This asynchronous process requires establishing automated, incremental update processes. This is managed through two primary methods: deploying real-time listeners for highly critical, volatile data (e.g., immediate policy changes) or utilizing periodic batch processing for less frequently updated documentation.

Since updating vector indexes, especially if the underlying embedding model changes, can be computationally costly, the architecture must strictly prioritize dynamic, incremental index updates for modified or new documents. This approach maintains continuous index fidelity while managing the computational cost of index maintenance.

## Agent Governance

The ZTAI mandate extends identity verification beyond human users to every NHI. In a HOTL deployment, the human supervisor must be able to verify in real time which agent identity is executing which action; an agent without a registered identity is, by definition, unsupervisable.

## Securing Autonomous Agents

The ZTAI mandate requires treating the LLM-integrated application and the agent itself as dynamic, untrusted entities, a constant application of the "Never trust, always verify" principle.

To achieve this, agents must be assigned durable, verifiable digital identities, often backed by PKI Certificates, to enforce non-repudiable authentication for all communications and actions. This ensures that every action taken by the agent can be definitively attributed to a specific digital principal.

The centralized identity management system must support immediate PKI Certificate revocation, an instant kill switch that neutralizes a compromised agent before systemic damage occurs. This is the technical implementation of Principle 4 (Mandatory Halt Capability) established in Chapter 2.

## Delegated Authorization Service

Excess Agency arises when an agent's service account privileges exceed those of the human it acts on behalf of. An AI assisting a customer service representative must not approve a financial transaction that the representative is not authorized to approve.

To mitigate this, the architecture mandates the use of a Delegated Authorization Service. This service acts as a proxy layer, intercepting the LLM's planned external API call and performing a dynamic check against the authenticated human agent's RBAC permissions. Only if the proposed action is within the human agent's defined scope is the API call allowed to proceed. This enforces least privilege for every autonomous action. As a policy enforcement function, the Delegated Authorization Service operates within the Control Plane, acting as a specialized enforcement point alongside the orchestrator's PEP role. In HITL deployments, the check precedes the human review gate. In HOTL deployments, the result surfaces to the supervisor's intervention interface in real time.

## Enforcing Accountability

Accountability is enforced through a centralized, tamper-proof logging architecture purpose-built for forensic analysis and litigation readiness. The standard varies by oversight model: A HITL deployment must log the identity of the approving human, the content they reviewed, and their explicit approval or rejection. A HOTL deployment must log every supervisor intervention event and every non-intervention as a positive attestation that the supervisor was present and aware. A HAL deployment must log the batch review decision and the reviewer's identity for every material commitment. Without these model-specific log fields, the audit trail is incomplete and non-compliant.

## Logging the Complete RAG Chain

Logs must capture the forensic data required to reconstruct every decision, enabling failure attribution to specific pipeline stages (retrieval failure versus generation failure).

A critical component of this logging is providing proof of compliance for all internal security and ethical controls. The logs must include the guardrail violation trace, detailing whether a prompt injection was detected and blocked or if PII was redacted from the output. This record provides auditable proof that the system's security and ethical guardrails are being enforced.

***Table 4-6.** Mandatory fields for immutable audit logging and forensic traceability*

| Log Field | Justification |
|---|---|
| System identifier | The unique identifier of the RAG deployment as registered in the Autonomy Register. Correlates every log entry to the system's governance record, oversight model, and accountable executive. |
| Execution ID (session identifier) | Unique identifier for the task or session. Threads every log entry for a single RAG workflow into a complete, ordered audit trail. Mandatory for forensic reconstruction and oversight model compliance verification. |
| Timestamp | Millisecond-precision timestamp generated by the logging infrastructure at the moment of decision. Establishes temporal integrity and is the primary evidence of contemporaneous log generation required for regulatory defensibility. |
| Autonomy Level | The Autonomy Level (1–5) under which the decision was made, as registered in the Autonomy Register. A mismatch between the logged level and the registered level is a governance anomaly requiring immediate escalation. |
| User query and applied ACLs | The original user query and the Access Control List permissions applied at retrieval time. Provides accountability for what was requested and verifies that Security Trimming enforced least privilege correctly. Essential for investigating prompt injection attempts. |
| Augmented prompt and retrieved context | The exact prompt supplied to the LLM including all retrieved chunks, with document and chunk IDs recorded. Enables full reconstruction of the decision context and links output to source lineage. Required for Faithfulness failure investigation and right-to-erasure enforcement. |

*(continued)*

*Table 4-6.* (*continued*)

| Log Field | Justification |
|---|---|
| Groundedness Score | The Groundedness (Faithfulness) Score for the output, quantifying how much of the answer is supported by retrieved source documents. Records the threshold applied and whether the score triggered the oversight model gate. The primary technical proxy for legal defensibility of the response. |
| Model and prompt version identifiers | The specific model version and prompt version active at inference time. Enables forensic investigation to reproduce the decision context and detect whether a model or prompt change caused a behavioral deviation. Mitigates Model Behavior Risk and Prompt Drift Risk. |
| Decision output | The answer or recommendation produced by the RAG system, including any citations or source references provided to the user. The record against which Groundedness Score is evaluated and against which a HITL reviewer makes their approval decision. |
| Guardrail violation trace | Record of any guardrail events during the request: prompt injection attempts detected and blocked at input; PII leakage detected and redacted at output. Provides auditable proof of compliance with security and ethical controls. Surfaced to the human reviewer in real time for HITL and HOTL deployments. |
| Oversight model event record | For HITL: the approver's identity, content reviewed, approval or rejection decision, and timestamp. For HOTL: every supervisor intervention and every non-intervention (as a positive attestation that the supervisor was present and monitoring). For HAL: the batch review decision, reviewer identity, and timestamp for every material commitment. Without these model-specific fields, the audit trail is non-compliant. |

**Note** Table 4-6 presents fields 1–11 of the mandatory log schema—the RAG-context subset. The complete 18-field schema adds seven agentic and safety-critical fields (fields 12–18): tool calls, decision output, action taken, MAM authority check, SRE evaluation result, anomaly flags, and override record. All 18 fields are defined in the EDS Logging and Explainability Standard, set out in full in Appendix A, and established in Chapter 11.

## Auditing Autonomous Systems

The shift to autonomous systems requires a new logging standard known as Reasoning Trace Capture. For complex decision-making processes, logging only the final action or the augmented prompt is insufficient.

Since an LLM agent reaches its conclusions via multi-step reasoning chains (often following the ReAct paradigm of Think-Act-Observe), the Audit Log must capture these intermediate decision points. This includes the LLM's internal monologue (thought), the tool used (action), and the response received (observation) at each step.

Capturing the ReAct trace ensures that the AI's complex decision logic can be reconstructed in its entirety. This capability guarantees that autonomous decisions are fully auditable and, critically, contestable by a human reviewer or regulator. This elevated standard of forensic data is mandatory for fulfilling the accountability layer required for all agentic systems. For HOTL deployments, the reasoning trace must be surfaced to the supervisor in a human-readable form, not stored only in machine logs, to enable meaningful real-time oversight, not nominal supervision.

# Component Specifications and Implementation Standards

Three implementation standards govern the Zero-Trust RAG pipeline beyond the security mandate: continuous index fidelity, context-preserving pre-processing, and full-stack observability for non-deterministic component management.

## Advanced Pre-processing

Generic, fixed-size text splitting strategies are insufficient for complex enterprise documents, such as procedural manuals or contracts. These documents require preserving the logical relationship between text elements to ensure that the retrieved content is meaningful to the LLM.

The foundational requirement is implementing Document-Based Chunking. This specialized method parses documents based on their intrinsic structure (e.g., splitting by Markdown headings, HTML tags, or PDF sections). This approach is mandatory because it maintains the logical unit of content, ensuring that a retrieved chunk retains sufficient surrounding context to be comprehensible and usable as a precise, verifiable citation.

## Non-deterministic Component Management

Generative AI systems are inherently non-deterministic, meaning the same input may yield different outputs, complicating debugging and trust. To manage this, full-stack observability via an LLMOps (Large Language Model Operations; the discipline for managing LLM lifecycle, performance, and governance in production) framework is mandatory. This framework must capture the complete execution trace for every user request, enabling rapid root-cause analysis (RCA) across all pipeline stages, from retrieval and re-ranking to final generation. Specifically, the tracing must identify which components contribute most to latency (e.g., slow vector retrieval versus LLM generation time) to enable continuous optimization and maintenance of performance targets.

## The Governance Architecture: Securing Access and Lineage

This section synthesizes the governance control plane components across the four planes introduced in Figure 4-2, which illustrates the Identity Plane, the Control Plane, the Data and Lineage Plane, and the Accountability Plane, and shows how each sub-section maps to one plane; together they form the non-repudiable chain through which every machine action is authorized, every data access is filtered, and every decision is recorded.

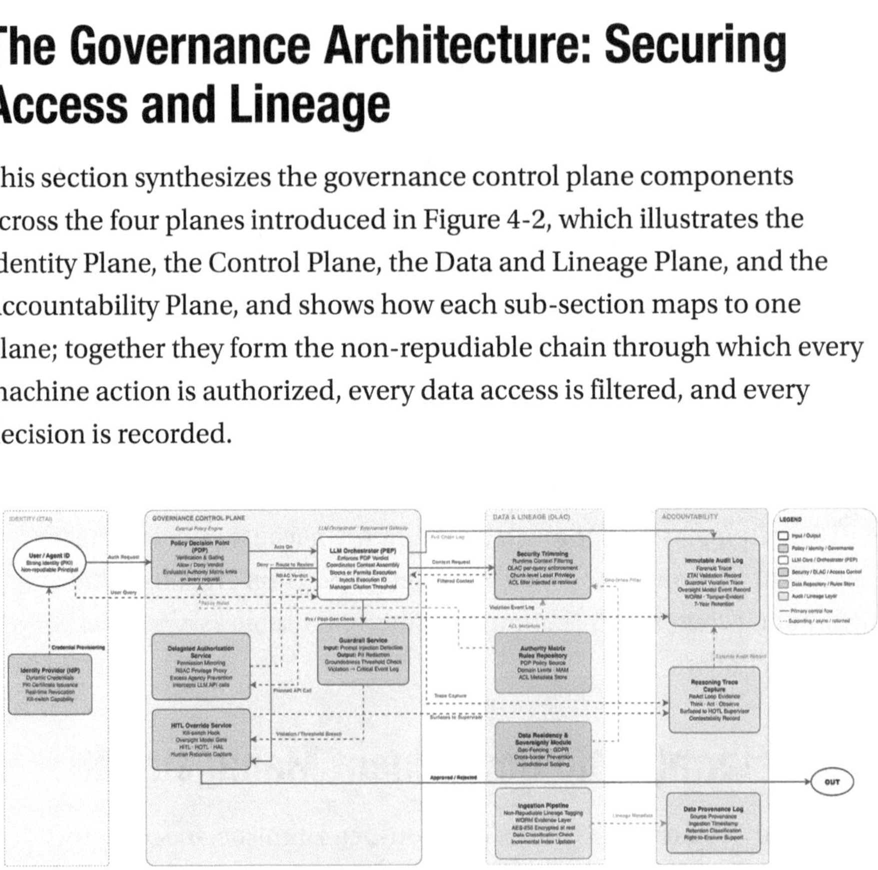


***Figure 4-2.*** *The Zero-Trust RAG governance architecture—end-to-end control flow across the Identity (ZTAI), Control Plane (PDP and PEP), Data and Lineage (DLAC), and Accountability layers, illustrating how verified identities, policy enforcement, Security Trimming, and immutable audit logging combine to form a non-repudiable governance chain*

In a governed enterprise, ZTAI begins before an agent's first action: every non-human identity must be registered in the NHI Lifecycle Register and associated with its authorized decision authority scope before it may operate in production. An NHI without a register entry is, by definition, a Shadow AI risk. Three of the board's six mandatory internal audit domains (Autonomy Register Completeness, NHI Lifecycle Governance, and Shadow AI Detection) treat its discovery as an immediate escalation event. The six domains in full are those three, plus Oversight Failure, Circuit-Break Reliability, and Regulatory Compliance of Automated Decisions. Once registered, agents are assigned unique digital identities backed by PKI Certificates, and the central identity system must support instant certificate revocation as the technical kill switch that neutralizes a compromised or rogue agent before it can cause systemic damage.

## PEP and the HITL Override Service

The LLM orchestrator operates within this architecture as the PEP, the physical gateway that enforces the PDP's decisions. While the PDP is the external policy engine (established in Chapter 1 as the Authority Matrix Rules Repository query layer) that returns a deterministic Allow/Deny verdict, the PEP is the orchestrator itself: the component that intercepts every request; enforces the PDP's verdict; coordinates the interaction between the user query, the security filters, and the generation process; and ultimately blocks or permits execution.

One of the most critical functions of the PEP is the invocation of the HITL Override Service, the technical manifestation of human primacy. When the system encounters a high-risk scenario or the Groundedness Score falls below the board-approved threshold, the PDP returns a Deny decision, and the PEP acts on it by pausing execution and routing the decision to the HITL Override Service for human review.

The Immutable Audit Log is the system of record for all machine decisions, capturing the complete RAG execution chain in tamper-evident storage as specified in Table 4-6. For agentic systems, this standard is extended by Reasoning Trace Capture.

## The Role of Reasoning Trace Capture

For complex agentic systems, the organization must also implement Reasoning Trace Capture. Because an agent reaches a conclusion through multiple steps of internal monologue and tool use, logging the final act is insufficient for a regulatory audit. Reasoning Trace Capture records every intermediate step of the reasoning process, often following the Think–Act–Observe loop.

This level of forensic detail allows auditors to reconstruct not just what the system decided, but why it decided it. If an agent proposes a pricing adjustment that appears irregular, the Reasoning Trace Capture provides the evidence needed to determine if the logic followed the approved doctrines or if the model experienced a reasoning failure. This capability is essential to meeting the requirements of explainability and contestability in regulated industries.

# Summary

This chapter established the mandatory security architecture that every EDS deployment must technically enforce, the controls that operate below the application layer and make governance claims verifiable rather than aspirational. The key takeaways are as follows:

- **The oversight model is the first architectural constraint, not a compliance afterthought**. Every security control in this chapter—DLAC, Data Lineage Tagging, and immutable audit logging—exists to make the oversight model enforceable in production. A HITL gate that cannot be proven to have fired is not a governance control; it is a policy statement. The security architecture converts policy statements into forensic evidence.

- **Document-level access control is enforced at retrieval, not at presentation.** DLAC operates before the retrieved context reaches the prompt generator. A user cannot receive a document they are not authorized to see, not because the application layer filters it, but because the retrieval layer never surfaces it. This is the distinction between access control as a boundary and access control as a guarantee.
- **Data Lineage Tagging creates the provenance chain that the board requires.** Every chunk that enters the vector index is tagged with its source document, version, access classification, and ingestion timestamp. When a response is generated, the lineage tags travel with the retrieved context through the PDP evaluation and into the Immutable Audit Log. The board can verify not only what the system said, but which version of which document authorized it to say it.
- **The Immutable Audit Log is the system of record for every autonomous action.** The 11 RAG-context log fields defined in Table 4-6—system identifier, Execution ID, timestamp, Autonomy Level, user query and applied ACLs, augmented prompt and retrieved context, Groundedness Score, model and prompt version identifiers, decision output, guardrail violation trace, and oversight model event record—constitute

the minimum forensic dataset required to reconstruct any RAG decision for litigation or regulatory examination. The complete 18-field mandatory log schema, which extends these fields with agentic and safety-critical additions, is defined in the EDS Logging and Explainability Standard and fully established in Chapter 11. The log is append-only; post-incident modification is architecturally impossible.

- **The Policy Conflict Resolution hierarchy prevents governance from becoming ambiguous under pressure**. When multiple policies apply to a single transaction, privacy versus disclosure, residency versus availability, regulatory versus operational, the P1–P4 priority hierarchy determines which policy governs. The orchestrator does not negotiate between conflicting policies at runtime; it applies the hierarchy. This is what makes governance deterministic rather than probabilistic.

The next chapter addresses how the accuracy and reliability of the Cognitive Layer are continuously validated in production, the LLMOps controls that ensure the system remains trustworthy over time, not just at deployment.

# CHAPTER 5

# Operationalizing Quality and Accuracy with LLMOps

Chapter 4 established who can access what and proved that every decision was made. This chapter addresses a harder problem: proving that those decisions were *correct* and that they remain correct over time. A governance architecture that enforces access control and logs every action is necessary but not sufficient. An LLM system can be fully compliant with every access policy and still hallucinate, producing confident, well-formatted, auditably logged falsehoods that no guardrail has been configured to catch. The discipline that closes this gap is Large Language Model Operations (LLMOps).

LLMOps is the operational counterpart to the governance architecture established in Chapter 4. Where Chapter 4 defines the control plane, the policies, enforcement points, and audit trail, LLMOps defines the assurance plane: the continuous monitoring, evaluation, and self-correction mechanisms that determine whether the control plane is actually doing its job in production. A HITL threshold set at deployment may be miscalibrated six weeks later because the underlying embedding model has drifted. A HOTL supervisor may be nominally present but effectively absent due to automation bias. A prompt that was within its


M. M. Hossain and A. A. N. Ponnusamy, *Governance-First AI*,
https://doi.org/10.1007/979-8-8688-3118-8_5

approved scope of authority at go-live may have accumulated incremental changes, expanding its effective decision-making authority beyond what the oversight model permits. None of these failures is visible in the access logs. They require a different kind of monitoring entirely, one that treats quality metrics as governance signals, not just operational Key Performance Indicators (KPIs).

This chapter establishes the mandatory technical framework for that assurance function. It defines LLMOps not as a performance-engineering discipline bolted onto a deployed system, but as a continuous governance mechanism that is architecturally inseparable from the oversight model commitments made in Chapter 4. The chapter covers three non-negotiable technical pillars in sequence. First, retrieval integrity: the dual-stage retrieval pipeline, Hybrid Search followed by Cross-Encoder Re-ranking, that ensures the LLM operates on the highest-density, most authoritative context the knowledge base can provide. Second, factual authority: the Groundedness (Faithfulness) Score, the 0–1 metric that quantifies how much of an LLM's answer is directly supported by retrieved source documents, where 1.0 indicates every claim is fully entailed by the retrieved context, as the legal proxy for factual grounding, enforced at the Citation Threshold by the PDP/PEP governance chain. Third, continuous assurance: the full-stack observability, drift detection, and closed CRAG feedback loop that together ensure the system's quality, and therefore its governance compliance, is maintained not just at go-live but throughout the system's operational lifetime.

The chapter also introduces a fourth obligation that connects directly to Chapter 4's oversight model matrix: Oversight Model Continuity. The three risk types—Threshold Drift, Supervisor Availability Drift, and Prompt Drift Expanding Decision Authority—represent the specific ways in which a governance-compliant deployment can silently become non-compliant after go-live. LLMOps is the mechanism that detects and remediates each of them before they become governance failures, audit findings, or regulatory events.

**Governance Leaders:** The "Oversight Model Continuity" section and its three risk types are your primary concern—these are the conditions under which a governance-compliant deployment silently becomes non-compliant.

**Architects and Practitioners:** The three technical pillars (dual-stage retrieval, Groundedness Score, continuous assurance) are the full specification.

# Mandate for Trust

The deployment of generative AI has shifted the conversation from technological capability to the far more critical issues of enterprise adoption and compliance. For any regulated or risk-averse organization, the core strength of this material lies in its focus on governance, risk, and auditability, the non-negotiable requirements that dictate whether AI value can be realized.

True enterprise value remains inaccessible if an AI system cannot demonstrate consistent factual accuracy, traceability, and verifiable compliance. The objective is not merely to deploy AI, but to achieve Certified Operational Velocity, the capacity to move fast only because trust and auditability are natively embedded into the foundational architecture. This section establishes the mandatory technical framework, LLMOps, required to convert the probabilistic nature of generative models into predictable, auditable enterprise assets, beginning with the unique operational challenges they present.

## Extending MLOps for Generative Non-determinism

The core technical challenge driving the need for LLMOps is the inherent non-determinism of generative models. Unlike traditional machine learning models, LLMs can yield inconsistent or contradictory outputs from the same input across successive runs. This probabilistic behavior introduces significant operational volatility that must be managed to maintain continuous quality and reproducibility, establishing the implementation as a persistent governance challenge. LLMOps provides the systematic, structured approach required to operate amid non-determinism, primarily through rigorous, iterative testing, automated evaluation against synthetic benchmarks, and streamlined deployment strategies that prioritize resource allocation and latency optimization.

Furthermore, the unique requirements of generative AI place high demands on the underlying infrastructure. LLMOps must handle the massive computational complexity and associated high costs, specifically by managing the allocation of specialized resources such as Graphics Processing Units (GPUs) and Tensor Processing Units (TPUs) and by continuously tracking variable token-based billing. The practical constraint is infrastructure cost: LLMOps must manage GPU and TPU allocation, track variable token-based billing, and enforce latency SLOs simultaneously. These operational pressures make structured lifecycle management not a choice but an architectural requirement.

## Quality As a Regulatory Control

In enterprise contexts, particularly those involving regulatory compliance platforms (UC2) or autonomous decision systems (UC7), AI failure is not merely an operational error; it is fundamentally a failure of governance.

Metrics are therefore elevated to the status of technical controls, providing the verifiable, auditable evidence that the system adheres to mandated service-level objectives (SLOs) and regulatory requirements.

The foundation of enterprise adoption is trust. If operational staff do not trust the AI's accuracy due to concerns about hallucination or inconsistent quality, they will inevitably revert to manual processes, immediately defeating the core efficiency objectives. For mission-critical deployments, compliance LLMOps must prioritize factual accuracy and grounding above all other objectives. Key metrics, such as the Groundedness Score, are classified as mandatory compliance SLOs that directly correlate low hallucination rates with legal defensibility and certifiable assurance.

The LLM orchestrator acts as the central control plane and governance gateway, enforcing policies and utilizing these quality metrics in real time to govern the generative output. For instance, a low Groundedness Score triggers the appropriate oversight model gate. For Autonomy Level 1–2 deployments, this means mandatory HITL review; for Autonomy Level 3 systems, a live HOTL supervisor alert; for Autonomy Levels 4–5, the output is classified and queued for batch review by the designated oversight authority.

# LLMOps Framework for Enterprise Resilience

The integrated set of LLMOps controls defined in this chapter is referred to throughout as the Accuracy Engine: the governance-native framework that converts probabilistic model outputs into auditable enterprise assets. The four components operate in sequence: dual-stage retrieval surfaces high-density context; the Groundedness Score enforces factual authority at inference time; continuous monitoring detects silent degradation before it becomes a governance failure; and the CRAG feedback loop drives self-correction at the index level.

A resilient LLMOps framework is essential for providing the architectural infrastructure necessary to support continuous operation, financial oversight, and ongoing quality maintenance across the entire application stack. The framework must ensure system resilience, which starts with the non-negotiable requirements of traceability and reproducibility.

Traceability and reproducibility require versioning and logging across three distinct asset classes:

**Governance Assets**: The oversight model configuration, Citation Thresholds, and prompt authority scope must be versioned so that any change can be audited against the Machine Decision Authority Matrix entry for the deployment.

**Technical Assets**: LLM versions, embedding models, chunking strategy, and retrieval configuration must be tracked so that any output can be reproduced for forensic analysis.

**Evidence Artifacts**: Immutable Audit Log entries, HITL override rationales, and drift reports must be retained as the evidentiary record that the system operated within its approved governance parameters at the time of every decision.

The technical controls required to sustain quality in a generative AI system are consolidated into three non-negotiable architectural pillars that operationalize trust: optimizing the retrieval pipeline for context quality, rigorously quantifying and enforcing factual grounding, and implementing continuous Operational Monitoring and Drift Control.

## Oversight Model Continuity: Sustaining Governance Through Operations

The oversight model assigned to a deployment in Chapter 4, HITL, HOTL, or HAL, is not a static configuration set once at go-live. It is a live governance commitment that depends on the system continuing to operate within the parameters that justified the original assignment of the oversight model. LLMOps is the operational mechanism that ensures this commitment is honored continuously, not just at the point of deployment.

Three operational dynamics can silently erode oversight model compliance after deployment, and each requires a specific LLMOps control to detect and remediate it:

### OVERSIGHT MODEL RISK 1: THRESHOLD DRIFT

***Failure Mode**: The Groundedness Score that governs HITL escalation may degrade due to embedding drift, model updates, or index staleness. The system appears to escalate correctly, but the threshold is no longer measuring what it was calibrated to measure; the governance gate is compromised without any visible alert.*

**LLMOps Control:** Monitor the Groundedness Score continuously against golden-query baselines. Any sustained divergence triggers a mandatory governance review and threshold recalibration, logged as a governance event and reviewed by the deployment's oversight authority.

### OVERSIGHT MODEL RISK 2: SUPERVISOR AVAILABILITY DRIFT (HOTL/HAL)

***Failure Mode:** A supervisor is nominally on duty but rubber-stamping outputs without genuine engagement. Silent degradation of supervisor engagement quality, through rubber-stamping, automation bias, or skill atrophy, renders the oversight model non-compliant even if the system logs show the supervisor as "on duty."*

**LLMOps Control:** Track supervisor intervention patterns in the Audit Log. An anomalously low intervention rate on a HOTL deployment, particularly alongside a declining Groundedness Score, is a governance escalation signal, not a technical one.

Consider a recalibration example. A regulatory compliance assistant (UC2) is deployed at Autonomy Level 3 with a HOTL supervisor reviewing all outputs with a Groundedness Score below 0.78 (illustrative). Because UC2 operates in a regulated domain, its threshold is set above the 0.65–0.75 band acceptable for non-critical HOTL outputs, consistent with the regulated-domain floor of 0.75 or above established earlier in this chapter. At the six-week review, the LLMOps dashboard shows the Gate Trigger Rate has dropped from a baseline of 18% to 4%, and the supervisor has not intervened on any routed item in 11 days. This is the anomaly: over the same period, the Groundedness Score baseline has declined from 0.83 to 0.76. A falling score distribution should have pushed more outputs below the fixed 0.78 threshold and driven the trigger rate up, not down. A trigger rate that declines as groundedness declines signals that the gate is no longer functioning as intended, while the supervisor's unbroken non-intervention indicates that the human check has degraded into rubber-stamping.

This pattern indicates threshold miscalibration compounded by automation bias. The correct recalibration sequence is as follows:

1. Immediately escalate to the governance authority; the oversight model is effectively non-functional.

2. Temporarily raise the Citation Threshold to 0.82 (illustrative), so that the now-lower-scoring outputs are once again routed for review and the escalation rate is restored to baseline while the root cause is investigated.

3. Run a mandatory supervisor competency review and re-brief the supervisor on intervention obligations.

4. Initiate an index staleness check for the document domains with the lowest Groundedness Scores.

5. Log the full recalibration sequence as a governance event with the oversight authority's sign-off before restoring normal operations.

The recalibration is complete only when the Gate Trigger Rate returns to within 5% of the original baseline for two consecutive weeks.

*Threshold values in this example are illustrative; organizations should calibrate against their own deployment baseline and domain risk profile, subject to the minimum floors established earlier in this chapter.*

**OVERSIGHT MODEL RISK 3: PROMPT DRIFT EXPANDING DECISION AUTHORITY**

***Failure Mode***: *Individually minor prompt changes can cumulatively expand the system's effective decision authority beyond the Autonomy Level that justified the original oversight model assignment, until it operates at a higher effective Autonomy Level than its oversight model permits. A system originally classified as Autonomy Level 2 (HITL required) may, through accumulated prompt modifications, be operating at an effective Autonomy Level 3 capability without the corresponding HOTL supervision.*

**LLMOps Control:** Track cumulative prompt changes in the Audit Log against the approved authority scope. At each quarterly review, compare the current prompt configuration against the original Machine Decision Authority Matrix entry and flag any scope expansion for formal reclassification.

Taken together, these three risks establish the operational scope of LLMOps. The framework is not merely a performance monitoring tool; it is a continuous governance assurance mechanism. The quality metrics described in the remainder of this chapter are not just operational KPIs; they form the evidence base for determining whether the oversight model commitment made in Chapter 4 is being honored in production.

## Optimizing Retrieval Quality and Context

The performance of any RAG system is bounded by the quality and density of the context it retrieves. Without architectural intervention, naive retrieval yields fragmented or overly broad contexts that force the LLM to generalize and fabricate; the architecture must enforce retrieval integrity as a primary technical control.

## Failure of Naïve Vector Search

While vector search provides the crucial capacity for semantic relevance, that is, finding content based on conceptual meaning, relying on pure, single-stage vector search is often insufficient. It introduces critical failure modes in complex enterprise data environments.

A common failure mode is low recall, as semantic search struggles to reliably capture exact identifiers. Enterprise queries frequently combine conceptual questions (e.g., "What is the policy on leave?") with precise, unique tokens, such as policy numbers, form identifiers, or specific procedure codes (e.g., "Form 42B-1"). Pure semantic search, which relies on embedding similarity, often misses exact keyword matches, resulting in incomplete or non-compliant responses.

Conversely, single-stage retrieval often suffers from low precision, resulting in contextual noise. The retrieval may return conceptually related but irrelevant documents or large, undifferentiated chunks, diluting the LLM's context window. This increases the cognitive burden on the language model, making it more susceptible to fabrication and undermining the objective of providing high-density, actionable information. The architectural solution must resolve this fundamental RAG trade-off by achieving both high recall (i.e., broad coverage) and high precision (i.e., high-quality context).

# Mandating Dual-Stage Retrieval

To strategically resolve the retrieval trade-off, enterprise systems must mandate a dual-stage retrieval paradigm: a fast, high-recall stage for broad coverage, followed by a computationally intensive, high-precision stage for specialized filtering.

## Hybrid Search and Reciprocal Rank Fusion

The first stage is architected to maximize the pool of candidate documents and prevent critical token-specific information from being overlooked. The system must implement Hybrid Search as a foundational component, combining vector-based semantic search with traditional sparse keyword search methods, such as BM25. This approach is mandatory because it ensures the system captures both the conceptual relevance of the query (via vectors) and the token-specific, critical identifiers (via keywords), thereby maintaining high accuracy and preventing significant compliance constraints from being missed.

The strategic integration of both search methods requires an intelligent fusion algorithm. Reciprocal Rank Fusion (RRF) is the standard mechanism for intelligently merging the rankings from semantic and keyword searches. RRF calculates a combined score by summing the inverse rankings across lists, giving higher weight to documents that appear consistently high in both the keyword and vector rankings. This process provides a unified, highly reliable result set, crucial for queries involving complex enterprise terminology and specific document IDs.

## Cross-Encoder Re-rankers

The second stage of retrieval focuses solely on maximizing precision, selecting the smallest set of candidate documents with the most significant informational value before they reach the LLM.

A dedicated re-ranker model is applied to the top K retrieved documents (e.g., the top 5–10 candidates) provided by the Hybrid Search. This process evaluates the contextual fit of these documents relative to the user query and prioritizes only the most relevant passages. Re-rankers are typically structured as cross-encoders that process the query and document together as a single concatenated input. This architecture enables self-attention mechanisms to model the deep, nuanced interactions between query and document words, yielding a direct, highly accurate relevance score.

This precision-focused step is essential for optimizing the use of the LLM's limited context window. By supplying only the highest-quality source material, the re-ranker directly enhances grounding quality and significantly reduces the risk of factual hallucination. For specialized applications, such as the enterprise knowledge and regulatory compliance platform (UC2), fine-tuned re-rankers can prioritize regulatory documents over general market analysis, making them indispensable for meeting specialized audit requirements.

You may leverage the same model used for the LLM-As-a-Judge evaluation use case, or one of the models used in the LLM Council ensemble (the multi-model ensemble introduced in Chapter 2), for this task, based on model capability and deployment context.

As agentic AI gains prominence, RAG architecture might be replaced with agentic standards such as agent skills and tools, but the overall governance architecture discussed in this section remains the same.

## Context Density and Latency Mitigation

While the pursuit of maximum factual accuracy through robust context retrieval is crucial, it introduces a critical architectural tension: maximizing context density often conflicts with meeting mandated low-latency SLOs, such as the 10–15-second resolution target in mission-critical RAG systems.

Techniques required for compliance, such as Hierarchical RAG and Document-Based Chunking, are necessary to preserve complex document structure and contextual fidelity. Document-Based Chunking is a general requirement for complex enterprise documents established in Chapter 4, not a UC2-specific control; UC2 (regulatory compliance) is simply a use case where its importance is most pronounced, given the legal consequences of fragmenting a clause or procedure across chunk boundaries. Still, they result in a significant increase in the final token payload sent to the LLM. This heavier context payload directly increases the computational time required for LLM generation. To prevent this from degrading the user experience, the architecture requires countermeasures.

The design must incorporate advanced latency mitigation controls, such as sophisticated caching and GPU-accelerated retrieval pipelines. However, the most strategic control lies in the precision layer: the Cross-Encoder Re-ranker. By ensuring that only the absolute minimum set of the most relevant, highest-density chunks is passed to the generation model, the re-ranker acts as an efficient compression filter, minimizing the final prompt token count while maximizing informational value, thereby protecting the stringent latency targets.

## Quantifying and Enforcing Factual Trust

Factual trust is the cornerstone of any enterprise generative AI application. Yet the fundamental challenge lies in systematically measuring, enforcing, and proving that an LLM's output is not a confident fabrication or hallucination but rather a statement grounded in authorized, proprietary knowledge. This metric is non-negotiable for any enterprise AI application, especially those impacting financial, legal, or safety outcomes (UC2, UC7, UC13).

The non-deterministic nature of the LLM necessitates the adoption of a technical proxy: a quantifiable metric that can withstand internal auditing and regulatory scrutiny. This shifts the focus from judging the model's fluency to verifying its claims against a verified knowledge base. The most rigorous measure of this integrity is the Groundedness (Faithfulness) Score, which must be engineered into the core application loop as a mandatory technical control. Consequently, the second non-negotiable architectural pillar of LLMOps is the implementation of a robust, real-time factual grounding and enforcement service.

## Groundedness Score

The cornerstone of factual trust and reliability in generative systems is the Faithfulness metric, also known as the Groundedness Score.

**Definition and Measurement:** Faithfulness is the paramount technical metric, assessing the percentage of claims in the generated answer that are directly supported by the retrieved, authorized context. The score is calculated by comparing the answer candidate against the provided facts (cited chunks) and typically ranges from 0.0 to 1.0. Higher scores indicate that the output is more grounded and less prone to hallucination, with 1.0 representing the best possible score, where the facts wholly entail every claim.

**Compliance and Operational Impact:** A high Groundedness (Faithfulness) Score directly correlates with lower hallucination rates and greater user trust. Continuous monitoring of this metric is necessary to maintain the technical quality that reinforces process efficiency, preventing staff from reverting to manual verification due to distrust. Furthermore, in regulated domains, the Groundedness Score is considered the technical proxy for legal defensibility. If an audit or legal review questions an AI-generated claim, the score provides auditable evidence that the claim was factually supported by a source document authorized at the time of retrieval. Critically, a sustained decline in this score is also an oversight model compliance signal: if the score falls below the threshold that triggers HITL review more than a configurable percentage of the time, this indicates a system in need of governance remediation, not merely technical optimization.

## Citation Threshold and Refusal Policy

**Grounding Verification Service:** The LLM orchestrator must integrate a dedicated grounding verification service (or API) that explicitly checks the answer against the retrieved facts (cited chunks) and provides a Support Score, the raw numerical output from which the Groundedness Score is derived. This service is designed for speed, ensuring it can be called during each inference without significant slowdown.

**Citation Threshold and Active Gatekeeping:** The system must enforce a non-negotiable Citation Threshold. This threshold dictates the minimum acceptable Groundedness Score for an answer to be released to the user. If the generated answer's Support Score falls below this critical threshold, the orchestrator acts as a risk-gating mechanism. It must be programmed to execute one of several compliance actions determined by the deployment's assigned oversight model:

1. **Refuse Generation:** When the Groundedness Score indicates no usable supporting context (a score at or near zero), the system refuses to generate a substantive answer, instead routing it for review and returning an explicit inability-to-answer response. This is the most severe of the compliance actions and is the mandated floor for all deployments: a

claim with no grounding is never released and is never substituted with a hedged or partial answer. It is distinct from the sub-threshold-but-nonzero case below, where the score is low enough to fail the Citation Threshold but high enough that human review (rather than outright refusal) is the appropriate response.

2. **Trigger the Oversight Model Gate:** For HITL deployments, the transaction is flagged for immediate human approval before any output is delivered. For HOTL deployments, the live supervisor is alerted, and the output is held pending either intervention or explicit attestation of non-intervention. For HAL deployments, the output is classified as a material item and queued for batch review.

3. **CRAG Loop:** The orchestrator initiates a request for additional context to enable more reliable generation and then re-evaluates before invoking the oversight model gate.

This refusal policy and the mandatory Source Citation (i.e., providing a direct link to the original document) are the primary architectural controls that establish end-to-end accountability and build user confidence.

Figure 5-1 illustrates the complete LLMOps accuracy architecture. A verified user query enters the dual-stage Retrieval Engine, where Hybrid Search and Cross-Encoder Re-ranking surface the highest-density context from the knowledge index under DLAC filters; the Grounding Verifier then scores factual faithfulness and passes the Groundedness Score to the Policy Decision Point, which either permits generation through the Cognitive Layer or triggers one of three enforcement actions: refusal,

CRAG-driven retrieval retry with index refinement, or HITL escalation. In parallel, LLM-As-a-Judge, the Adversarial Testing Module, and the Drift Monitor continuously stress-test and recalibrate the system, the Drift Monitor feeding retraining signals back to the ingestion pipeline and threshold recalibration signals to the PDP, while every override decision is captured in the Reasoning Trace Capture as a contestability record.

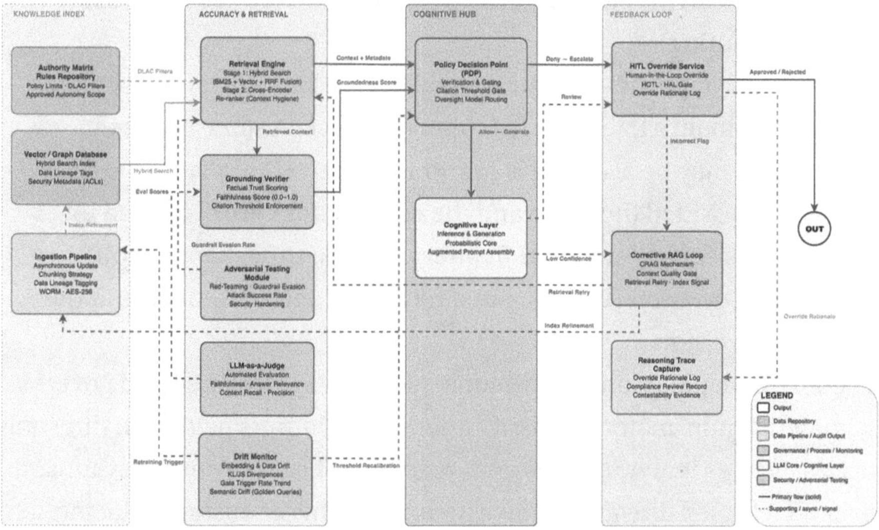


***Figure 5-1.*** *The LLMOps accuracy architecture—from dual-stage retrieval and factual grounding through PDP-governed oversight routing, continuous drift and adversarial monitoring, and the closed corrective feedback loop to the knowledge index*

## Defining Citation Thresholds in Practice

Setting a defensible Citation Threshold requires balancing legal risk against operational availability. The threshold is not a universal constant; it must be calibrated for each deployment based on the Autonomy Level, the Criticality Tier, and the domain's risk profile. The following guidance applies across deployment types.

For HITL deployments (Autonomy Levels 1–2), the Citation Threshold should be set conservatively, typically at 0.75 or above for regulated domains such as legal, financial, or clinical use cases. Any answer scoring below this threshold must be withheld from the user and routed to the HITL queue. The system must not present a partial or hedged answer as a substitute; the routing is mandatory, and the queue entry must include the retrieved context, the candidate answer, and the Groundedness Score at the time of routing.

For HOTL deployments (Autonomy Level 3), the threshold should reflect the domain's tolerance for supervised risk. A score between 0.65 and 0.75 may be acceptable for non-critical outputs surfaced to a supervisor, provided the score and the cited chunks are displayed to the supervisor in the intervention interface. The supervisor's explicit attestation of non-intervention must be logged against the score at the time of the decision.

For HAL deployments (Autonomy Levels 4–5), the threshold governs the material/non-material classification gate. Outputs below the threshold are classified as material items and queued for batch review; they must never be released directly to downstream systems or customer-facing channels. The threshold floor for any HAL deployment in a regulated domain should not be set below 0.70 without a documented risk acceptance signed by the Chief Risk Officer.

These figures represent the minimum permissible floors for each deployment type; individual deployments should establish a board-approved SLO above the floor, as illustrated by the 95% threshold in UC1's Board Outcome.

The low-confidence refusal policy must specify three things unambiguously: the score range that triggers each action (refuse, CRAG retry, or HITL/HOTL/HAL gate); the maximum number of CRAG retry cycles permitted before the transaction is escalated to human review regardless of score; and the audit log entry format that records the threshold, the score, the action taken, and the oversight model event. These three specifications are the minimum for a Citation Threshold policy to be considered audit-ready.

## Continuous Factual Validation Using LLM-As-a-Judge

LLM-As-a-Judge evaluation scales quality assessment beyond manual review by running programmatically within the production pipeline. The minimum viable evaluation layer covers both generation and retrieval:

1. **Generation Assessment:** This verifies how the LLM uses the provided context:
   - **Groundedness (Faithfulness):** Assesses the ratio of claims supported by the retrieved context
   - **Answer Relevance:** Confirms that the final response directly and informatively addresses the user's original query intent
2. **Retrieval Assessment:** This ensures the pipeline successfully found the correct information:
   - **Context Recall:** Measures how completely the retrieved context covers all the information required for the ideal answer. Low recall poses a significant risk because it forces the LLM to respond with incomplete data, potentially leading to non-compliant procedural advice.
   - **Context Relevance:** Assesses precision, the concentration of useful information within the retrieved chunks, aiming to minimize irrelevant noise.

For high-stakes decisions, the system must employ Compliance-Specific Benchmarks, that is, specialized evaluation frameworks (e.g., LegalBench-RAG; Pipitone and Houir Alami, 2024) that rigorously test Question-Answering tasks in which miscitation or hallucination can have severe compliance repercussions. This systematic measurement ensures adherence to mandated SLOs. Table 5-1 sets out the LLMOps quality metrics that operationalize these controls as a service-level and KPI matrix, pairing each metric with its measurement focus and its compliance or trust impact for technical validation.

***Table 5-1.*** *LLMOps quality metrics (SLO/KPI matrix) for technical validation*

| KPI Category | Metric Name | Formula/Measurement Focus | Compliance/Trust Impact |
|---|---|---|---|
| Factual accuracy (SLO) | Groundedness (Faithfulness Score) | Ratio of claims directly supported by retrieved, authorized context (range: 0.0–1.0). Sustained decline triggers oversight model re-evaluation. | Paramount metric; directly mitigates hallucination risk; ensures legal defensibility. Governs HITL/HOTL/HAL escalation threshold calibration. |
| Retrieval quality | Context recall | Measures completeness: how much of the required information for the ideal answer was retrieved. | Mitigates risk of incomplete procedural advice (e.g., missing policy steps). |
| Retrieval quality | Context relevance | Assesses precision: concentration of useful information within retrieved chunks. | Maximizes informational density for the LLM; reduces noise. |

(*continued*)

***Table 5-1.*** *(continued)*

| KPI Category | Metric Name | Formula/Measurement Focus | Compliance/Trust Impact |
|---|---|---|---|
| User value | Answer relevance | Confirms that the final response directly addresses the user's intent. | Ensures output is actionable and valuable; high score reinforces productivity uplift. |
| Security (SLO) | DLAC Filter Efficacy Rate | Measures successful filtering of unauthorized documents at the retrieval layer. | Non-negotiable security boundary integrity (e.g., for document-level access control). |
| Oversight model compliance | Gate Trigger Rate vs. baseline | Frequency with which the Groundedness (Faithfulness) Score triggers the oversight model gate, tracked against deployment baseline. | Sustained increase above baseline indicates system degradation that may be eroding oversight model compliance. Triggers governance review. |

Taken collectively, these metrics prove two things: that the system is finding the right information (context recall and context relevance) and that it is using that information correctly (Groundedness Score and answer relevance). The Gate Trigger Rate is the bridge between the two; a sustained increase signals that the retrieval or grounding layer is degrading in a way that is beginning to erode oversight model compliance, not just quality.

## Continuous Quality Assurance

Operational quality hinges on robust LLMOps practices to proactively manage costs and performance, maintain model integrity and guardrails, and defend against drift and adversarial attacks. This effort fulfills LLMOps' continuous assurance mandate, which is essential to preserving enterprise readiness.

In any complex, distributed, and non-deterministic system, such as an enterprise RAG pipeline, failures are inevitable, making root-cause analysis impossible without comprehensive operational monitoring. Continuous quality assurance mandates four requirements—full-stack observability, operational and financial monitoring, proactive drift detection, and guardrail security hardening—each targeting a distinct failure mode across the request lifecycle. This ensures the system is not only accurate but also stable, performant, and cost-efficient. Crucially, this capability moves the system beyond simply checking the final answer to proactively detecting degradation in the underlying components (i.e., the retriever, embedding model, and knowledge base) before a user reports a failure. The overriding goal is to maintain a state of perpetually high operational health, dramatically minimizing Mean Time to Resolution (MTTR) for critical issues.

## Full-Stack Observability

The first requirement is comprehensive tracing. LLM systems are distributed and non-deterministic, making traditional monitoring insufficient for root-cause analysis and forensic reconstruction.

**End-to-End Traceability:** Logging must capture the complete execution trace for every user request, spanning the frontend, the orchestrator, the RAG layer, vector search, and the final LLM API calls. This diagnostic tracing is indispensable for reliably identifying bottlenecks or failure points, for example, determining whether a slow vector retrieval, a generation error, or an external tool timeout in an agentic system is causing a performance issue.

**Forensic Context Logging (Auditability):** For robust auditability and litigation readiness, logs must explicitly capture all forensic data required to reconstruct the decision-making process. This includes recording the original user query, the exact final augmented prompt supplied to the LLM, and, critically, the complete set of retrieved documents or chunks, including their security metadata tags. The most critical layer for advanced observability is the orchestration layer, which tracks prompt–response pairs, retries, and tool execution timing. Logging the complete RAG chain and the final confidence score provides the necessary data to attribute failures to specific pipeline stages (e.g., context recall failure versus groundedness failure). As established in Chapter 4, logs must also capture the oversight model event record: the identity of the human reviewer, the content reviewed, and the approval, rejection, or non-intervention attestation with timestamp, for all HITL, HOTL, and HAL deployments.

## Operational and Financial Monitoring

The second requirement extends observability to cost. This discipline, FinOps for generative AI, focuses on meeting SLOs while managing the variable economics of token-based billing.

**Performance and Latency SLOs:** Continuous monitoring of end-to-end request duration (typically tracked via P95 Latency) is essential to verify that strict resolution targets are consistently met (e.g., a 10–15-second target). Detailed analysis of traces must pinpoint which components contribute most to latency, enabling proactive optimization.

**Cost Analytics and Token Tracking:** Tracking token consumption per query is mandatory for accurate cost prediction and management, helping prevent unexpected charges due to the variable pricing of LLM interactions. FinOps principles require integrating cost observability into MLOps pipelines, tagging resources by project, and setting budget thresholds up front. The LLMOps framework must facilitate A/B testing of different models or configurations to compare their performance against associated token costs, ensuring deployment decisions maximize sustainable ROI.

# Proactive Drift Detection for Model Integrity

The third requirement moves from reactive monitoring to proactive detection. LLM applications are highly susceptible to silent degradation caused by model drift, a decline in performance that may not surface as user complaints until governance thresholds have already been breached. Drift detection is also the primary mechanism for detecting Oversight Model Risk 1 (Threshold Drift) and Oversight Model Risk 3 (Prompt Drift Expanding Decision Authority).

## Monitoring Embedding Consistency and Statistical Divergence

Drift detection must systematically monitor deviations in both the input data (data drift) and the model's behavior (semantic drift).

**Data Drift (Input Consistency):** This involves tracking the statistical properties of the incoming production data (e.g., term frequency, entity distribution) and comparing them against the training baseline. Metrics such as the Kullback-Leibler (KL) or Jensen-Shannon (JS) divergence quantify the information loss, triggering alerts when the divergence in key input features exceeds a predefined threshold.

**Embedding Drift (Silent Semantic Degradation):** A critical form of drift is the degradation of the embedding model. The Model Drift Monitoring Service must continuously track the similarity distribution of new vectors relative to the established index baseline to detect whether the embedding model has functionally changed or whether the input data distribution has shifted in a way that compromises vector space integrity.

**Semantic Drift (Output Consistency):** This tracks model behavior by running synthetic, golden test queries (i.e., queries with known ground truth) at regular intervals. The resulting Groundedness (Faithfulness) and answer relevance scores are compared against historical baselines, often utilizing an LLM-As-a-Judge.

### Automated Retraining Triggers

If the calculated drift score, derived from statistical or semantic divergence, exceeds a predefined threshold, the system must automatically trigger alerts for the Model Risk Officer (MRO), the EDS-designated governance role responsible for continuous evaluation of model integrity, bias, and drift across all production AI deployments. Systematic failures or persistent drift that cannot be remediated operationally is escalated by the MRO to the Model Governance Board (MGB), the cross-functional governance body that reviews portfolio-level model performance, approves material changes to oversight model configurations, and reports to the Board Risk Committee. For persistent drift, the integrated MLOps pipeline must trigger an automated retraining loop that fetches the latest feedback data, updates model parameters, and restores predictive power. Where drift is associated with a change in the Groundedness (Faithfulness) Score baseline, the oversight model Citation Threshold must be re-evaluated concurrently with the retraining cycle.

## Guardrail Efficacy and Security Hardening

The fourth requirement is active security hardening. Guardrails are mandatory at the orchestrator level, but their efficacy must be continuously verified rather than assumed.

**Continuous Guardrail Monitoring:** This includes tracking and logging attempts to inject malicious prompts, detecting PII leakage in inputs and outputs, and detecting toxic language. Analyzing the effectiveness of these detection mechanisms allows for dynamic adjustment of guardrail configurations.

**Adversarial Testing (Red-Teaming):** The LLMOps framework must integrate an Adversarial Testing Module to support periodic Red-Teaming activities. The system must continuously track the Guardrail Evasion Rate and Attack Success Rate. These metrics formally validate the AI system's continuous security performance, moving beyond passive logging to proactive security hardening. Table 5-2 extends this from point-in-time validation to continuous operation, mapping the operational monitoring dimensions that keep an LLMOps deployment within its governance envelope once it is live.

***Table 5-2.*** *LLMOps operational monitoring dimensions*

| Dimension | Key Metric | Measurement Focus/ Technology | Risk Mitigation Focus |
|---|---|---|---|
| Performance | P95 End-to-End Latency | End-to-end request duration via distributed tracing | SLO compliance and user abandonment |
| Financial control | Token Cost per Query | Input/output token consumption via FinOps tagging | Budget compliance and ROI |
| Model integrity | Data drift/KL divergence | Statistical shift in input distribution versus baseline (KL/JS divergence) | Model decay and Citation Threshold re-evaluation trigger |
| RAG system health | Embedding consistency | Similarity distribution of new vectors versus index baseline | Silent semantic degradation; Oversight Model Risk 1 indicator |
| Security | Guardrail Evasion Rate | Frequency of successful prompt injection or PII leakage attempts | Data breach risk and attack surface hardening |
| Oversight compliance | Gate Trigger Rate trend | Trend in oversight gate invocations versus deployment baseline | Risk 1 and 3 indicator; governance review trigger |

## Closed Feedback Loop

The most significant technical capability of a robust LLMOps architecture is its ability to learn from failure and drive perpetual self-improvement through a closed feedback loop. This mechanism transforms every operational failure, whether a hallucination or an irrelevant answer, from a system flaw into a data point for refinement. This feedback cycle is the engine of continuous integrity, ensuring that the system's knowledge base and retrieval strategy remain perpetually aligned with ground truth. The loop is anchored by two distinct mechanisms: HITL, the governance signal layer responsible for safety and compliance review, and CRAG, the technical remediation layer responsible for index correction and retrieval quality improvement. These are complementary but separate: HITL identifies that something is wrong; CRAG fixes the underlying data condition that caused it.

## Human-in-the-Loop (HITL) Architecture

The HITL architecture functions as the final ethical and compliance safety layer, ensuring human experts review and validate outputs before high-risk actions are executed. In the context of LLMOps, HITL serves a dual function: it is both a real-time governance gate (as established in Chapters 1, 2, and 4) and a continuous improvement signal. Every HITL intervention generates structured feedback that must be fed back into the system's quality metrics and, where appropriate, into the calibration of its oversight model.

**Mandatory Intervention Triggers:** Human intervention is automatically triggered when the LLM's Groundedness Score falls below the Citation Threshold or when the user explicitly flags an answer as incorrect, misleading, or unclear. For accountability, the HITL workflow must require the human reviewer to log an explicit rationale for any override or veto, creating a clear, auditable record for post-incident analysis and compliance review. The accumulation of HITL override rationales is also a governance signal: a pattern of overrides in a specific decision domain indicates that the system's authority scope in that domain may need to be reviewed.

## Corrective RAG and Data-Driven Index Optimization

The key function of the feedback loop is to move beyond simple post hoc error correction and establish a mechanism for continuous refinement of the knowledge base, thereby addressing the root causes of retrieval failures.

**Failure Attribution:** When a user flags a response as incorrect, the system must assess the failure point. If the LLM was faithful to the retrieved context but the answer was still wrong, the fundamental failure lies in the retrieval quality or the chunking strategy (i.e., index quality).

**CRAG Mechanism:** The technical solution for this is the CRAG feedback loop. CRAG introduces a quality gate by critically evaluating the relevance and quality of the retrieved context before the generation phase. If the initial retrieval fails to meet a relevance threshold, CRAG initiates corrective steps or, most importantly, signals a deep failure in the index itself.

**Data-Driven Index Optimization:** The HITL feedback is captured as a signal of index quality. When human reviewers provide structured feedback, it directly informs remediation actions in the asynchronous ingestion pipeline (e.g., refining the Document-Based Chunking strategy or initiating an urgent check for data staleness). This process continuously refines the index, ensuring that human expertise fuels the continuous refinement of the underlying data infrastructure.

## Remediation by Failure Type

The CRAG loop's value lies in precision: it attributes each failure to a specific root cause and applies targeted remediation rather than a generic retraining cycle. The system must distinguish between four failure types and respond to each differently.

Retrieval failure occurs when the model is faithful to the retrieved context, but that context is incomplete or incorrect. The correct answer exists in the knowledge base but was not surfaced. **Remediation:** Trigger an urgent staleness check on the relevant document domain, review the chunking strategy for that source type, and re-index with finer chunk granularity or adjusted overlap parameters. The failure must be logged as an index quality event, not a model quality event.

Generation failure occurs when the retrieved context was complete and correct, but the model produced an unfaithful answer, a genuine hallucination against its own context. **Remediation:** Flag the prompt template used for that query type for mandatory review, increase the Citation Threshold for the affected query category by 0.05, and log the event as a model calibration signal for the next scheduled fine-tuning cycle.

Coverage failure occurs when the knowledge base lacks the information needed to answer the query. The model correctly refused or produced a low-confidence answer, but the root cause is a gap in the index. **Remediation:** Route the query to the content governance team as an urgent ingestion request, tag the document domain as "coverage-incomplete" in the index metadata, and ensure the system refuses similar queries until coverage is confirmed.

Threshold miscalibration occurs when the HITL gate is triggering at an anomalously high or low rate relative to the deployment baseline. If the Gate Trigger Rate has risen more than 15% above the baseline without a corresponding change in query volume or domain, the Citation Threshold itself may be too sensitive. If it has fallen more than 15% below baseline, the threshold may be too permissive. Either condition triggers a mandatory threshold recalibration event, which must be treated as a governance event rather than an operational tuning exercise and approved by the deployment's oversight authority.

# Summary

This chapter established the LLMOps framework as the continuous assurance plane, the operational layer that ensures the AI system remains accurate, trustworthy, and governable in production, not just at the moment of deployment. The key takeaways are as follows:

- **Deployment is not the end of governance; it is the beginning of the hardest part.** A model that passes pre-deployment evaluation can still drift, degrade, or fail silently in production. The LLMOps framework exists to detect that degradation before it becomes a compliance failure, through continuous evaluation, drift monitoring, and structured feedback loops that keep the knowledge base current and the oversight model calibrated.
- **The Groundedness Score is the primary governance signal, not a quality metric.** A Groundedness Score below the Citation Threshold is not a performance indicator requiring investigation; it is a constitutional trigger requiring a HITL invocation. The distinction matters: treating it as a quality metric invites discretion; treating it as a governance signal requires action. The threshold is board-approved and cannot be waived at the application layer.

- **Citation Thresholds must be calibrated to the deployment context, not set once at go-live.** A threshold appropriate for an internal knowledge assistant is not appropriate for a regulated-domain compliance system. The chapter establishes Citation Threshold calibration guidance organized by oversight model: HITL deployments (Autonomy Levels 1–2), HOTL deployments (Autonomy Level 3), and HAL deployments (Autonomy Levels 4–5), each with distinct minimum Groundedness Score floors, with regulated domains requiring the most conservative settings. Threshold recalibration is a board-level governance event, not an engineering decision.
- **The CRAG feedback loop converts human review into architectural improvement.** When a HITL reviewer rejects or overrides a response, that decision is not merely a quality correction; it is a structured signal that the retrieval pipeline, the chunking strategy, or the knowledge index has a systematic flaw. The CRAG protocol attributes the failure to the correct pipeline layer and initiates targeted remediation, ensuring that the knowledge base improves continuously rather than degrading silently.
- **The Model Risk Officer is the human accountable for what the model does in production.** The MRO is not a technical role; it is a governance role. Responsibility for monitoring drift, approving threshold recalibrations, authorizing version updates, and escalating systematic failures to the Model Governance Board rests with a named individual rather than the engineering team. This assignment of personal accountability is

what makes AI governance meaningful rather than organizational. The MGB receives MRO escalations, reviews portfolio-level model performance, approves material changes to oversight model configurations, and provides the Board Risk Committee with evidence that the production AI estate operates within approved governance parameters. While the MRO is accountable for the integrity of individual models, the MGB is accountable for the integrity of the entire governed AI portfolio.

The next chapter applies this complete governance stack: constitutional framework, Deterministic Shell, deployment model, security architecture, and LLMOps assurance plane to the first high-impact production use case: the AI-powered frontline knowledge assistant.

## Reference

Pipitone, Nicholas, and Ghita Houir Alami. 2024. LegalBench-RAG: A Benchmark for Retrieval-Augmented Generation in the Legal Domain. arXiv:2408.10343. `https://arxiv.org/abs/2408.10343`.

# PART III

# Foundational Generative AI

# CHAPTER 6

# The Efficiency Model

In regulated enterprises, information fragmentation is not a technology problem; it is a governance problem. The information exists; the architecture to surface it reliably and accurately, with a verifiable audit trail, does not. This chapter introduces the Efficiency Model, the first of the EDS framework's five enterprise deployment models, through the lens of Use Case 1: the AI-powered frontline knowledge assistant. Its central claim is that, in the author's deployment experience, a 70–80% productivity uplift for frontline staff is achievable, but only when speed is built on embedded trust rather than by bypassing governance controls.

The chapter's governance instrument is straightforward: UC1 operates at Autonomy Level 2 under a mandatory Human-in-the-Loop oversight model. Every response below the Citation Threshold must be reviewed by a named human reviewer before delivery. This is not a quality recommendation; it is a constitutional requirement enforced at the orchestrator level. The efficiency gain is realized precisely because the HITL gate removes the need for ad hoc manual verification by frontline staff, replacing unstructured human judgment with a structured, auditable governance event.

Parts I and II established the constitutional framework, the Deterministic Shell, the deployment model, the security architecture, and the LLMOps accuracy layer. This chapter applies all five to the first high-impact production use case: the AI-powered frontline knowledge assistant.


M. M. Hossain and A. A. N. Ponnusamy, *Governance-First AI*,
https://doi.org/10.1007/979-8-8688-3118-8_6

Every architectural control described here—Hybrid Search, grounding verification, the PDP/PEP handshake, and the CRAG feedback loop—is the operational expression of Governance Principles already established.

The chapter follows the EDS unified blueprint structure in five sections: the Business Problem that defines the productivity cost of information fragmentation; the Governance Instrument that establishes the constitutional constraint; the Technical Architecture that implements the dual-pipeline solution; the Governance Delta that defines the grounding, HITL, and LLMOps controls specific to this use case; and the Board Outcome that closes the governance loop with measurable, auditable evidence of ROI. The following sections ground this blueprint in the operational reality that necessitates the governance architecture.

**Governance Leaders:** The Governance Instrument and Board Outcome sections define the constitutional commitment and its measurable evidence.

**Architects and Practitioners:** The Technical Architecture and Governance Delta sections contain the full implementation specification.

# Operational Cost of Fragmented Knowledge

Frontline staff in regulated enterprises spend the majority of their working hours not serving customers but searching for information. A contact center representative must navigate internal wikis, SharePoint repositories, archived contract databases, Customer Relationship Management (CRM) systems, and static policy manuals; each query requires a separate manual search across disconnected systems. This is not an edge case; it is the default operating condition for frontline knowledge work in regulated sectors.

The economic cost is quantifiable. Poor data quality and the time knowledge workers spend searching for information rather than creating value impose high, well-documented costs on organizations. In a contact center of 1,000 agents, time lost to inefficient information retrieval is capital consumed at full-employment cost, with zero customer value delivered.

The RAG solution is justified purely by its capacity to reverse this time sink. Information fragmentation causes excessive search time; excessive search time causes delayed service and low productivity; automated, governed retrieval eliminates the search step. That causal chain is the ROI anchor for this architecture.

## Quantifiable Efficiency via RAG

The solution is a RAG-powered knowledge assistant that serves as a unified conversational layer across the organization's full content library, including SharePoint, Confluence, internal databases, and proprietary policy repositories, replacing manual, multi-system searches with a single natural-language query.

The practical outcome of this deployment is a radical simplification of the agent's task. Instead of initiating multiple manual searches across various sources, the frontline agent asks the AI assistant a natural-language question, such as "How much notice is required for a large withdrawal from a retirement fund?" The RAG system instantly scans the relevant policies and procedures across all integrated platforms, synthesizing a single, definitive answer. The core capability is the rapid delivery of contextualized, compliant, and source-cited responses, typically within a 10–15-second target window. This commitment to ultra-low latency is the architectural foundation of the entire Efficiency Model.

External evidence supports the efficiency target:

- McKinsey estimates that applying generative AI to customer care functions can increase productivity by 30–45% of current function costs (McKinsey & Company, The Economic Potential of Generative AI, June 2023).
- Beyond this consulting estimate, vendor implementations of Retrieval-Augmented Generation report substantial reductions in resolution and retrieval time, though such figures are vendor-reported and not independently verified.

## Defining Certified Operational Velocity

Certified Operational Velocity is the chapter's governing concept: speed is only possible because trust is embedded, not assumed. If the system's output is untrustworthy, hallucinated, or based on outdated sources, frontline staff will add a manual verification step, negating the 10–15-second speed advantage entirely. The HITL gate is not an obstacle to velocity; it is the certification mechanism that makes velocity trustworthy. A system that bypasses HITL under time pressure ceases to be an Efficiency Model and becomes a source of Shadow AI risk.

The architecture also delivers secondary strategic benefits:

- The system ensures consistent, accurate, and source-cited responses across all branches and service channels, thereby improving customer satisfaction and credibility.
- It measurably reduces the Time-to-Competency (TTC) required for new hires. The assistant serves as an accelerator for talent development, helping

new employees reach target productivity faster by providing them with grounded, on-demand access to institutional knowledge that would otherwise take months to absorb.

- It accelerates time-to-value across the customer lifecycle, from onboarding through support and upsell.

## Blueprint: UC1—AI-Powered Frontline Knowledge Assistant

The following blueprint applies the unified five-section structure. Governance requirements are stated before architecture; every deployment closes with a board-level outcome that the CFO and COO can attest to. All deployments in this chapter operate within the board's Guarded Innovation risk posture; autonomous capability is enabled when it demonstrably improves performance and constrained by governance controls that ensure every action remains visible, accountable, and reversible.

## 1. The Business Problem

Frontline staff in regulated enterprises, contact center representatives, bank tellers, and legal support staff spend the majority of their time resolving queries manually, searching across fragmented knowledge systems. The resulting delays, inconsistent response quality, and diminished staff productivity are directly attributable to informational fragmentation. The quantifiable cost provides the ROI anchor: in the author's deployment experience, a 70–80% productivity uplift is achievable by automating the single highest-friction function in the workflow.

# 2. The Governance Instrument

| GOVERNANCE STACK: UC1—AI-Powered Frontline Knowledge Assistant | |
|---|---|
| **Instrument** | **Active Setting for This Deployment** |
| **Autonomy Level** | Level 2 (Workflow Automation). |
| **Criticality Tier** | Moderate. |
| **Oversight model** | Human-in-the-Loop (HITL)—human must approve every response below the Citation Threshold before delivery; hard stop enforced at orchestrator level. |
| **Delegation Note** | No autonomous action authority; system generates and presents; human approves. |
| **Groundedness threshold** | Groundedness (Faithfulness) Score threshold: ≥0.75 for regulated domains; responses below threshold held at HITL gate pending named reviewer approval. |
| **DLAC enforcement** | Security Trimming enforced at retrieval layer per user identity and role; no cross-boundary chunk delivery. |
| **Logging standard** | Immutable Audit Log capturing full RAG chain including HITL event records with named reviewer identity. |
| **Governing Principles** | Human Primacy (Principle 3) · Governance Primacy Over Delivery (Principle 5). |
| **Latency versus governance** | 10–15-second target does not override HITL; system waits for approval regardless of time pressure. |

# 3. The Technical Architecture

Dual-pipeline architecture (asynchronous ingestion + inference pipeline) with Hybrid Search (vector + BM25), Reciprocal Rank Fusion (RRF), Cross-Encoder Re-ranker, grounding verification service, and mandatory

Source Citation. The pipeline is separated because embedding generation is computationally intensive and cannot share a latency budget with real-time query resolution. DLAC/Security Trimming is enforced at the retrieval layer. Immutable audit logging captures the complete RAG chain, including HITL event records. Full details in the "Architectural Delta" section below.

## 4. The Enhancement

Parameter-Efficient Fine-Tuning (PEFT)/Low-Rank Adaptation (LoRA) for domain-specific language adaptation (covered in Chapter 8). For this use case, the primary enhancement is the Corrective RAG (CRAG) feedback loop, which transforms HITL overrides from passive corrections into active index optimization signals, thereby continuously improving retrieval quality in production.

## 5. The Board Outcome

The board attests that the system delivers a sustained 70–80% reduction in query cycle time while maintaining a Groundedness Score above the board-approved service-level objective of 0.95. All low-confidence responses are systematically intercepted at the HITL gate prior to delivery, ensuring that output quality and risk controls operate within defined tolerance levels. This 0.95 service-level objective and the 0.75 floor established in Chapter 5 for HITL regulated-domain deployments are the same metric, the Groundedness Score, measured on the same 0-to-1 scale; the board has set this deployment's operational target (0.95) above the Chapter 5 minimum (0.75), which is the compliance floor, not the performance target.

Audit and risk reporting should confirm that governance controls are functioning as designed: no confidential documents are retrieved outside authorized access boundaries (DLAC enforcement), all responses below the Citation Threshold are reviewed and approved by a named human reviewer (HITL event records), and the system consistently operates within its designated Autonomy Level 2 classification, with no unauthorized autonomous actions observed.

Exception rates, HITL interventions, and access control violations are continuously monitored and escalated according to board-defined thresholds. Based on this evidence, the board confirms that the deployment is delivering its expected return on investment, the oversight model is being enforced in practice, and the system remains within the organization's approved risk appetite.

## Governance Delta

Sustained efficiency gains are entirely contingent upon frontline staff trusting the AI's output. Therefore, the governance framework focuses on three pillars: technical verification (i.e., grounding), continuous learning (i.e., feedback loops), and operational stability (i.e., LLMOps). These pillars are designed to convert the LLM's probabilistic nature into a reliable, auditable enterprise asset, reinforcing the Certified aspect of the operational velocity mandate.

The Governance Delta for this use case is defined by the HITL oversight model requirement. Every governance control in this section exists to either enforce the HITL gate correctly or to maintain the conditions under which the HITL gate remains meaningful.

## Grounding Verification

Trust is the foundation of user adoption. If staff do not trust the AI's accuracy, they will revert to manual searching, thereby immediately defeating the efficiency objective. The Support Score and mandatory Source Citation are, therefore, the core technical controls that enable efficiency in this model.

- **Grounding Verification Mechanism:** To ensure the LLM's generation is verifiable, the orchestrator integrates a grounding verification service. This service explicitly checks the generated answer candidate against the retrieved facts (cited chunks).
- **Support Score:** A value between 0 and 1 returned by the Grounding Verifier, quantifying how faithfully the answer is locked to the retrieved context, as established in Chapter 5.
- **Citation Threshold:** The minimum acceptable Groundedness Score for answer release, as defined in Chapter 5. This is the technical trigger for the HITL gate.
- **Mandatory Source Citation:** The LLM is strictly prompted to lock its answers to the retrieved sources, providing a direct citation that allows the user to reference the specific source document (e.g., "Section 4.2 of Policy X"). This provides clear audit trails and builds user confidence. In the HITL workflow, the citation also enables the human reviewer to directly verify the grounding claim.

## The Anatomy of a Trustworthy Citation

In the Efficiency Model, a citation is not merely a link to a document; it is the governance control that makes grounding verifiable by a human reviewer. It is a technical control that enables accountability. For a citation to be valid within this architecture, it must meet three specific criteria.

First, it must be granular. The citation must point to the specific chunk or section of the document that supported the claim, not just the document as a whole. Second, it must be point-in-time accurate. The system must use the lineage tags from the Immutable Audit Log to prove exactly which version of the policy was active when the answer was generated. Third, it must be verifiable. The HITL Override Service provides an interface in which a human can view the source and the machine's claim side by side to attest to their alignment.

## Continuous Improvement Loop

A continuous feedback loop using the HITL architecture is implemented not only to correct immediate outputs but also to optimize data-driven indexes. This approach transforms human feedback from a passive review into an active learning and architectural maintenance process.

- **HITL Triggers:** Human intervention is automatically triggered when the LLM's Groundedness Score falls below the Citation Threshold or when the user explicitly flags an answer as incorrect, misleading, or unclear. The HITL event: The reviewer's identity, the content reviewed, and the rationale for approval or rejection are logged as a mandatory audit record as described under the field oversight model event record in Table 4-6.
- **CRAG Protocol:** Structured feedback is captured as a signal of index quality failure, not merely as a model correction. Before any remediation is taken, the system performs failure attribution using the four-category taxonomy established in Chapter 5: a retrieval failure, where the correct information exists but was not surfaced (remediation: refine chunking or metadata strategy, logged as an index quality event); a generation failure, where the retrieved context was correct but the model produced an unfaithful answer (remediation:

flag the prompt template, raise the Citation Threshold for the affected query category, and log a model calibration signal; if the failure pattern is systemic, the MGB may authorize a fine-tuning cycle or version rollback); a coverage failure, where the information is absent from the index entirely (remediation: initiate an urgent ingestion request and mark the domain as coverage-incomplete); and threshold miscalibration, where the HITL gate is triggering at an anomalously high or low rate relative to baseline (remediation: a governance-approved recalibration event). This attribution step ensures each correction is applied to the right pipeline layer.

- **Model Governance Board (MGB):** The EDS framework's designated oversight body for model risk, ethical compliance, and version governance (introduced in Chapter 5). It approves model version changes, reviews HITL override patterns at each governance cycle, and issues threshold recalibration instructions when drift is detected.

## Lifecycle Governance

The long-term viability of the efficiency gains depends on the health of the oversight model, not just the system's health. A technically performant deployment that has experienced Threshold Drift is no longer delivering Certified Operational Velocity; it is delivering ungoverned speed. The LLMOps framework is the monitoring layer that detects differences and provides the board with evidence that governance controls are functioning as designed, not merely that the system is running.

- **LLMOps Framework:** Provides end-to-end tracing, cost monitoring (tracking token consumption), and guardrail monitoring to maintain system performance, reliability, and security compliance. Beyond these baseline controls, it monitors two categories of governance indicators. Leading indicators like the Gate Trigger Rate trend and the Groundedness Score trajectory signal governance risk before it becomes a compliance failure. Lagging indicators such as error rate, HITL intervention frequency, and index rebuild cost confirm the impact of drift once it has occurred. The Gate Trigger Rate is the primary leading indicator: a sustained increase signals Threshold Drift; a near-zero rate may indicate automation bias or threshold miscalibration.
- **Model Drift Monitoring:** Tracks the semantic consistency of the embedding model and LLM over time. Early detection allows the Model Risk Officer (the EDS-designated governance role established in Chapter 5) to initiate targeted remediation, fine-tuning, or adjustments to retrieval parameters before a major model update forces a full index rebuild. An index rebuild is computationally expensive and temporarily degrades retrieval quality, making early drift detection a cost control and a governance control simultaneously. The specific risk being managed is Semantic Drift: the degradation of the embedding model's semantic consistency, which causes retrieval quality to decline silently without triggering obvious errors. Left undetected, Semantic Drift eventually

forces a complete index rebuild, which is expensive and operationally disruptive and temporarily degrades retrieval quality for every user. Early detection protects the enterprise's capital investment in the knowledge index.

- **Adversarial Testing (Red-Teaming):** Periodic Adversarial Testing (Red-Teaming) is mandatory to proactively harden security guardrails and test the system's resilience against new attack vectors. This moves security management from reactive detection to proactive hardening.

## Operationalization and ROI Quantification

The measurement framework connects technical quality to business return. The architecture must support continuous KPI measurement to prove the business case to the board, not just at go-live but on an ongoing basis, because the board's attestation in the Board Outcome section is a standing commitment, not a one-time sign-off. Cost avoidance from reduced manual effort is the primary financial mechanism: for a contact center of 1,000 agents, a 20% reduction in handle time translates into millions of dollars in annual FTE savings, and new-hire productivity is accelerated through assistants that compound returns by compressing time-to-value across the workforce. Both benefits must translate into FTE cost savings and onboarding cost reductions to satisfy the board's formal ROI standard.

## Governing Trust

These metrics ensure technical quality and directly reinforce the efficiency objective:

- **Groundedness (Faithfulness):** This is the paramount technical metric, assessing the percentage of claims in the generated answer that are directly supported by the retrieved context. Constant monitoring is necessary to ensure that technical quality reinforces efficiency and prevents staff from reverting to manual verification.
- **Context Recall:** Measures how completely the retrieved context covers the information required for the ideal answer.
- **Answer Relevance:** Confirms that the final response directly addresses the intent of the user's original query, ensuring the output is actionable and valuable.
- **Retrieval Quality:** Metrics such as precision, recall, F1 Score, and Normalized Discounted Cumulative Gain (NDCG) evaluate how accurately the system retrieves and presents relevant, correct, and context-aware information from internal sources.
- **Gate Trigger Rate:** Tracks the frequency with which the Groundedness Score falls below the Citation Threshold, triggering the HITL gate. The baseline rate established at deployment serves as the governance reference: a sustained increase signals Threshold Drift; a near-zero rate may indicate automation bias or an improperly calibrated threshold. Both are compliance concerns under the oversight model requiring governance review.

## Measuring Productivity and Competency

Establishing baseline metrics (manual search cycle time, error rates) before deployment is essential to demonstrate quantitative improvements.

- **Cycle Time Reduction (CTR):** This measures the total time a frontline employee requires to resolve a query, from the initial request to the final documented answer. For example, in a contact center, CTR maps to Average Handle Time (AHT). CTR is more precise for the AI assistant because it isolates search and analysis time, specifically the AI's core efficiency function. The baseline-versus-assisted comparison is the primary proof point for efficiency gains.
- **Time-to-Competency (TTC) Reduction:** This metric measures the time required for new hires to achieve target productivity levels with the assistance of the RAG system, compared with the traditional manual training curriculum. This capability reduces onboarding cost and accelerates time-to-productivity, supporting the business case.
- **Accuracy and Throughput:** Tracking the frequency of errors, rework, or compliance violations attributable to incorrect or inconsistent information (i.e., Error Rate Reduction) is critical. Error reduction must be explicitly valued as a financial benefit in the ROI calculation, as consistent, accurate responses across channels minimize high-impact, low-frequency events such as litigation risk and external regulatory fines.

## Justifying the Investment

Financial return is primarily measured by cost avoidance resulting from reduced manual effort. The hours saved through faster resolution (e.g., CTR) and reduced training time (e.g., TTC reduction) must be rigorously translated into FTE cost savings.

The KPIs in Table 6-1 provide the board with two accountability lenses simultaneously: business value metrics (cycle time, competency) demonstrate the efficiency case, while governance health metrics (Gate Trigger Rate, drift score) demonstrate that the controls are functioning and the oversight model has not eroded. The formal ROI calculation is

*ROI = (Financial Benefits - System Operational Costs) / System Operational Costs*

System operational costs must encompass token usage tracking, infrastructure hosting for the LLM and vector database, and the continuous management overhead associated with the LLMOps framework.

***Table 6-1.*** *Key Performance Indicators (KPIs) for Efficiency Model ROI quantification*

| KPI Category | Metric Name | Measurement Focus/ Compliance Standard | Efficiency Model Target |
|---|---|---|---|
| Efficiency and speed | Average query cycle time (CTR)/ AHT | Time from query submission to final response (manual baseline versus AI-assisted). | 70–80% reduction. |
| Quality and trust | Groundedness (Faithfulness) Score | Ratio of claims supported by retrieved context (0–1). Governs HITL Citation Threshold calibration. | >0.95 (SLO). |

(*continued*)

*Table 6-1.* (*continued*)

| KPI Category | Metric Name | Measurement Focus/ Compliance Standard | Efficiency Model Target |
|---|---|---|---|
| Oversight compliance | Gate Trigger Rate versus baseline | Frequency of HITL gate invocations versus deployment baseline. Sustained change triggers governance review. | Stable within ±10% of baseline; any sustained divergence triggers MGB review. |
| Staff development | Time-to-Competency (TTC) reduction | Average time (days/weeks) for new employees to achieve target productivity levels. | Measurable reduction (target set per deployment). |
| Operational health | Model drift score | Tracks semantic consistency of Embedding Model/LLM output over time. | Automated alert trigger if threshold exceeded. |
| Accuracy | Task execution accuracy/error rate | Frequency of errors/ compliance violations attributable to inconsistent information. | Measurable reduction. |

# Phased Deployment Strategy

The deployment must follow a structured, three-phased approach to manage risk and validate the expected ROI against established manual performance baselines. This disciplined methodology ensures that technical functionality is verified against real-world metrics and that critical security and governance controls are fully integrated before enterprise-wide scaling. The entire strategy is designed to rigorously prove the quantitative improvements required to justify the substantial investment.

## Phase 1: Establishing Baseline Through PoC

Technical validation and baseline measurement. The ROI calculation depends entirely on the accuracy of these baselines.

- **Objective:** Technically validate the core RAG pipeline and establish measurable manual performance baselines.
- **Scope:** Index a single, non-sensitive, well-defined knowledge domain (e.g., a specific set of IT Helpdesk FAQs).
- **Key Activities:** Configure Data Connectors, implement basic chunking, and deploy an LLMOps framework with end-to-end tracing. The most crucial activity is to measure and document the current manual average query cycle time (CTR) and error rate for the chosen domain. Establish the Gate Trigger Rate baseline at zero (pre-AI) for comparison after deployment.

## Phase 2: Pilot, Security Hardening, and HITL Integration

Security hardening and HITL integration in a restricted pilot environment.

- **Objective:** Introduce core enterprise requirements, specifically security (least-privilege access) and advanced quality control, to a restricted pilot group (e.g., 50 trained frontline staff).
- **Key Activities:**
    - **Security Implementation:** Implement retrieval-time access enforcement (Security Trimming) by enforcing access filters during retrieval.

- **Quality Enhancement:** Deploy Document-Based Chunking techniques and integrate the hybrid retrieval and re-ranker mechanism to optimize context quality.
- **Governance and Feedback Loop:** Establish the mandatory citation process and the HITL workflow, triggered by low confidence or user flags. Configure the Audit Log to capture oversight model event records for every HITL invocation. All decision audit logs and HITL override records are subject to a minimum seven-year retention obligation under the EDS Logging and Explainability Standard (formally established in Chapter 11), or for as long as applicable law requires, whichever is longer; where data protection obligations such as erasure rights apply, retention is reconciled with those requirements rather than overriding them. Train HITL reviewers on their governance obligations. They are not performing an optional quality review; they are executing a constitutional requirement.

## Phase 3: Scaling, Validation, and ROI Formalization

Full operational scaling and formal ROI validation.

- **Objective:** Full operational scaling across the organization and formal quantification of the business value and ROI.

- **Key Activities:**
    - Roll out the assistant to all target staff and complete integration/indexing of all remaining enterprise knowledge sources.
    - Formal ROI quantification is achieved by comparing post-implementation KPIs (e.g., CTR, TTC, Groundedness Score, Gate Trigger Rate) against Phase 1 baselines to validate the targeted productivity uplift.
    - This phase also involves leveraging continuous LLMOps monitoring and HITL data to refine indexing and retrieval strategies and presenting the Gate Trigger Rate trend to the Model Governance Board as evidence of sustained compliance with the oversight model. The MGB reviews the accumulated failure attribution data from the CRAG loop and determines whether the Citation Threshold remains calibrated or requires formal recalibration before the next governance cycle.

# Architectural Delta

The Efficiency Model is built on the dual-pipeline architecture: a strict separation between asynchronous data preparation (the ingestion phase) and real-time query handling (the inference phase). It builds upon the foundational security and logging components, DLAC and immutable audit logging, established in Chapters 4 and 5. The Architectural Delta describes what is unique to this use case, not what is universal. This separation is not a performance optimization; it is lineage control. Every chunk is tagged with security and provenance metadata before any user ever queries it, so the audit trail is built into the data at source. Speed in the inference phase is trustworthy precisely because integrity was enforced at ingestion. The Information Tax, the productivity cost of human search time lost to informational fragmentation, is the precise inefficiency this architecture addresses. This is distinct from the Context Tax introduced in Chapter 3, which quantifies the compute and token cost penalty of poorly structured AI context. Both taxes erode enterprise value; the dual-pipeline architecture addresses the human productivity dimension of that cost.

As agentic AI matures, the execution method may shift from traditional RAG to agent skills and tools. The governance architecture remains unchanged: the rules of authority and the gates of oversight are independent of whether the model retrieves a document or calls an automated tool.

## Dual-Pipeline Model for Continuous Index Fidelity

The enterprise-grade RAG solution utilizes a dual-pipeline architecture to maintain performance and scalability. This design rigorously separates the offline data preparation and indexing stage (i.e., ingestion phase) from the real-time query handling stage (i.e., inference phase). This segregation is critical because it allows computationally intensive tasks, such as embedding generation, to run asynchronously without impacting the end user latency during query resolution.

### Asynchronous Ingestion Phase

This phase is responsible for preparing the proprietary enterprise knowledge and laying the foundation for the semantic search capability.

- **Data Sourcing:** Structured and unstructured data are pulled from enterprise data sources (e.g., SharePoint, Confluence, policy databases) via robust Data Connectors.
- **Indexing and Storage:** Processed chunks are transformed into high-dimensional numerical vectors by the Embedding Model and stored, along with associated metadata, in the vector database, creating the indexed, semantically aware knowledge repository.
- **Data Freshness Protocol:** The reliability of RAG is entirely contingent on the freshness of its source data. The architecture must strictly prioritize dynamic, incremental index updates for newly added or modified documents to maintain continuous index fidelity. This is achieved by establishing automated, incremental update processes, such as real-time listeners for highly critical, volatile data (e.g., immediate policy changes) and periodic batch processing for less frequently updated documentation.

## Intelligent Content Structuring

The quality of the final response is inextricably linked to the integrity and structure of the underlying index.

- **Document-Based Chunking:** For complex enterprise content like procedural manuals and contracts, generic, fixed-size text splitting is inadequate. The architecture mandates Document-Based Chunking, which parses documents based on their intrinsic structure (e.g., splitting by Markdown headings, HTML tags, or PDF sections). This maintains the logical unit of content, ensuring that a retrieved chunk is fully comprehensible and usable as a precise citation. Chunking is a governance decision: each chunk must be granular enough to serve as an accurate, verifiable citation. In a HITL deployment, the human reviewer must be able to verify the claim against a coherent, self-contained unit of policy or procedure without ambiguity.

- **Metadata Enrichment:** Before the embedding process, critical security and contextual attributes must be appended to every single text chunk. This enrichment creates the granular, secure access points necessary for the Downstream Access Control (i.e., DLAC) mechanism, which is enforced during retrieval.

## Inference Pipeline

The inference phase must operate with high recall and precision to meet the demanding 10–15-second resolution target. The strategy involves resolving the inherent tension between the need for both concept and token accuracy.

- **Hybrid Search Strategy:** Frontline queries often combine specific token identifiers (e.g., form names, policy codes) with broader conceptual requests. Pure semantic search may miss exact matches, while pure keyword search fails to capture conceptual relevance.
    - The system must implement Hybrid Search, combining vector-based semantic search with traditional sparse keyword search (e.g., BM25).

    - Results from both techniques are merged using Reciprocal Rank Fusion (RRF), producing a single ranked set of top K documents that satisfies both token and conceptual relevance within the latency target.

- **Re-ranking for Context Optimization:** The initial retrieval phase, though fast, can still contain noise. A slower, more precise, dedicated re-ranker model is applied to the top K retrieved documents.

    - This model evaluates the contextual fitness of these documents relative to the user query and prioritizes only the most relevant passages at the very top.

    - This step optimizes the LLM's context window for informational density, directly improving grounding quality and reducing hallucination risk. The re-ranker is the culmination of the retrieval stack: retrieval quality flows directly into grounding quality, and grounding quality determines whether the HITL gate is invoked.

## Policy Enforcement: The Handshake Between PDP and PEP

The EDS framework enforces a strict functional separation between two components: the PDP, which evaluates every proposed action against the board-approved governance rules and returns a deterministic verdict, and the PEP, which receives that verdict and is the sole component authorized to act on it. This separation ensures that governance logic remains independent of execution machinery; the PDP can be updated to change risk tolerance without modifying application code, and the PEP cannot release a response without a PDP verdict.

## PDP As the Analytical Engine

The PDP is the analytical engine within the governance layer. It resides conceptually within the Authority Matrix Rules Repository environment. When a generated response is produced, the Grounding Verifier calculates a Support Score. The PDP evaluates this score and other request attributes against the board-approved rules. It returns a deterministic "Allow" or "Deny" verdict.

The PDP never acts directly on the data stream; instead, it provides the intelligence needed for a decision. This allows the organization to change its risk tolerance or Citation Thresholds in a single central location without modifying the underlying application code or re-registering the models.

## PEP As the Physical Gatekeeper

The Policy Enforcement Point is the physical gatekeeper, typically implemented as the AI gateway or orchestrator. The PEP receives the verdict from the PDP and is the only component authorized to release information to the user.

If the verdict is Allow, the PEP releases the source-cited response. If the verdict is Deny, the PEP physically blocks the delivery and triggers the HITL Override Service. The PEP is also responsible for injecting the unique Execution ID (the session/task identifier that threads all log entries for a single workflow into a complete, ordered audit trail) into the transaction and ensuring every step, including the PDP verdict, is recorded in the Immutable Audit Log. This separation ensures a clear division of duties that satisfies even the most rigorous regulatory audits.

Figure 6-1 illustrates the complete governance architecture of the frontline assistant. A verified user query enters the Retrieval Engine, which surfaces context from the vector database under Authority Matrix rules; the probabilistic core generates a candidate answer; the Grounding Verifier scores it and passes the Support Score to the PDP, which returns a deterministic Allow or Deny verdict to the orchestrator (PEP), releasing the response on Allow or triggering the HITL Override Service on Deny. Low-confidence outputs route to the corrective feedback loop, sending an Index Remediation Signal back to the vector database; the LLMOps Monitor continuously tracks drift and Gate Trigger Rate, feeding threshold review signals to the PDP and escalating to the Model Governance Board, which closes the oversight loop with threshold recalibration back to the Authority Matrix.

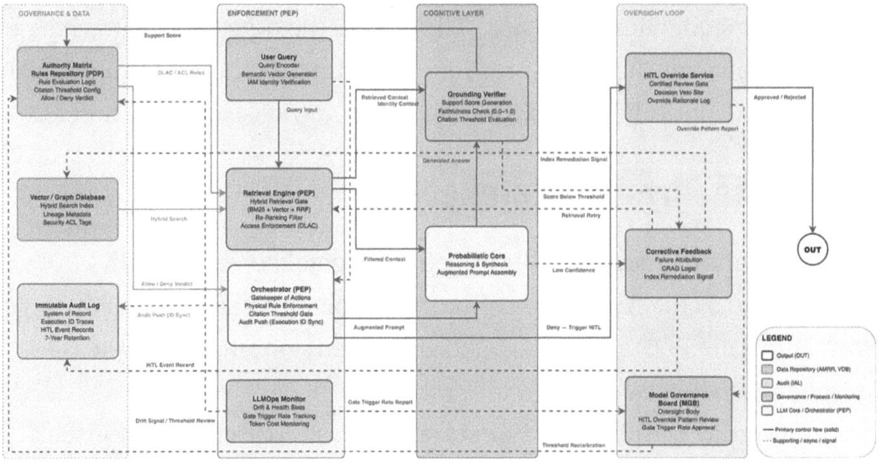


***Figure 6-1.*** *End-to-end governance architecture of the AI-powered frontline knowledge assistant—from identity-verified query ingestion and hybrid retrieval through PDP-governed enforcement, HITL oversight, and the closed corrective feedback loop to the knowledge index and Model Governance Board*

# Summary

This chapter established that the 70–80% productivity uplift the Efficiency Model targets is structurally dependent on the governance architecture surrounding the model, rather than incidental to it. Every technical control exists to enforce a single principle: speed is only trustworthy when trust is embedded in the infrastructure layer, not assumed at the application layer. The key takeaways are as follows:

- **Governance is the precondition for efficiency, not the constraint on it.** The HITL gate is not a bottleneck; it is the mechanism that makes the efficiency claim defensible. A system that bypasses HITL under time pressure ceases to deliver Certified Operational Velocity and instead generates Shadow AI risk. The productivity uplift is achievable only when frontline staff trusts the output enough to act on it without independent verification.
- **The dual-pipeline architecture is a lineage control, not a performance optimization.** Tagging every chunk at ingestion means the audit trail is built into the data before any query is processed; the Groundedness Score the PDP evaluates is only meaningful because the retrieval pool was governed at source.
- **The PDP/PEP separation is the architectural expression of board-level accountability.** The Policy Decision Point evaluates; the Policy Enforcement Point acts. This separation ensures that governance logic—risk tolerance, Citation Thresholds, and HITL gate conditions—can be updated in one central location without modifying application code. It also ensures that no response reaches a user without a formal, auditable governance verdict.

- **CRAG transforms human feedback into architectural improvement.** It attributes each failure to the correct pipeline layer, retrieval, coverage, or reasoning, and applies targeted remediation rather than a generic model retrain.
- **The Efficiency Model establishes the measurement vocabulary**, including Cycle Time Reduction, Groundedness Score, Gate Trigger Rate, Time-to-Competency, and model drift score, that the board will apply as the evidence standard to every subsequent blueprint in this book.

The next chapter applies this foundation to the Regulatory Shield model, where Hierarchical RAG and strict access controls enable certifiable regulatory compliance in high-stakes, audit-intensive domains.

# Reference

McKinsey & Company. 2023. The Economic Potential of Generative AI: The Next Productivity Frontier. McKinsey & Company, June. https://www.mckinsey.com/capabilities/mckinsey-digital/our-insights/the-economic-potential-of-generative-ai-the-next-productivity-frontier.

# CHAPTER 7

# The Compliance Model

Chapter 6 established the Efficiency Model: a RAG architecture that delivers a 70–80% productivity uplift for frontline staff by replacing manual search with governed, auditable retrieval. This chapter escalates that architecture into the Compliance Model, the EDS framework's reference deployment for regulated-domain knowledge retrieval, instantiated as UC2: the enterprise knowledge and regulatory compliance intelligence (EKRCI) platform. The escalation is not technical but constitutional: where UC1 triggers Human-in-the-Loop review when confidence falls below a threshold, UC2 mandates HITL for every regulated-domain output regardless of confidence. A high-confidence wrong answer in a regulated domain carries the same legal consequences as a low-confidence one.

The business case for this escalation is straightforward. Compliance officers and frontline staff in regulated enterprises spend significant time manually searching fragmented policy and legal repositories. Under time pressure, staff may inadvertently rely on outdated knowledge, exposing the organization to regulatory fines and litigation. The EKRCI platform resolves this by transforming knowledge retrieval from a manual, error-prone process into a governed, auditable, and legally defensible one, achieving operational efficiency and regulatory assurance simultaneously rather than trading one against the other.


M. M. Hossain and A. A. N. Ponnusamy, *Governance-First AI*,
https://doi.org/10.1007/979-8-8688-3118-8_7

The Compliance Model introduces six architectural controls that have no equivalent in the Efficiency Model: Hierarchical RAG with custom parsing (structural fidelity for legal documents), WORM storage with AES-256 encryption (data non-repudiation), Geographic Metadata Tagging with Retrieval-Time Residency Filter (jurisdictional sovereignty), External Regulatory Feed Service (continuous knowledge currency), ACL Delta Sync Index (real-time privilege integrity), and a Multidimensional Confidence Score that aggregates retrieval relevance, grounding faithfulness, and DLAC enforcement confidence. Each control addresses a compliance risk that the Efficiency Model was not designed to manage.

The chapter follows the unified EDS blueprint structure. It begins with the governance instrument establishing UC2's constitutional constraints, then details the Governance Delta and Architectural Delta that distinguish the Compliance Model from its predecessor, and then covers the MLOps framework for continuous compliance, the threat and ethics model, and the three-phase deployment strategy. The summary closes with the Board Outcome: verifiable evidence that the system is functioning as a Regulatory Shield, actively preventing regulatory exposure rather than logging compliance failures after the fact.

**Governance Leaders:** The Governance Instrument, Board Outcome, and the distinction from UC1 are your primary sections.

**Architects and Practitioners:** The Governance Delta, the Architectural Delta, and the MLOps compliance framework are your working specification.

# Blueprint: UC2—Enterprise Knowledge and Regulatory Compliance Intelligence Platform

The following blueprint applies the unified five-section template to UC2. This use case is a direct governance escalation of UC1: the same foundational RAG architecture is retained, but every governance parameter is elevated to reflect the Critical Criticality Tier and the mandatory HITL requirement for all regulated-domain outputs.

## 1. The Business Problem

In regulated domains, the cost of human error is not operational inconvenience but regulatory breach. Compliance officers and frontline staff searching fragmented policy repositories under time pressure may rely on outdated knowledge, producing advice that is factually wrong and legally indefensible. The objective is certifiable regulatory assurance: every output must be traceable to a specific, current, verified policy version, and every output must pass human review before delivery.

## 2. The Governance Instrument

**GOVERNANCE STACK: UC2—Enterprise Knowledge and Regulatory Compliance Platform**

| Instrument | Active Setting for This Deployment |
|---|---|
| **Autonomy Level** | Level 2 (Workflow Automation). |
| **Criticality Tier** | Critical. |
| **Oversight model** | HITL—mandatory for ALL regulated-domain outputs regardless of confidence score; not triggered only by low-confidence responses as in UC1. |

*(continued)*

**GOVERNANCE STACK: UC2—Enterprise Knowledge and Regulatory Compliance Platform**

| Instrument | Active Setting for This Deployment |
|---|---|
| **Delegation Note** | No autonomous action authority; every regulated-domain output requires named human reviewer approval before delivery. |
| **Groundedness threshold** | Multidimensional Confidence Score (aggregates retrieval relevance, grounding faithfulness, DLAC enforcement confidence); any output in a regulated domain requires HITL regardless of score. |
| **DLAC enforcement** | Geographic Metadata Tagging with Retrieval-Time Residency Filter; ACL Delta Sync Index for real-time privilege integrity; WORM storage with AES-256 encryption. |
| **Logging standard** | Immutable Audit Log with complete HITL event record per output; Policy Versioning with Delta Indexing for temporal traceability to the policy version active at time of query. |
| **Governance escalation from UC1** | UC1 triggers HITL below Citation Threshold only; UC2 mandates HITL for every regulated-domain output—Critical Criticality Tier requires this universal gate. |
| **Constitutional constraints** | Governance Primacy Over Delivery (Principle 5) · Accountability Follows Authority (Principle 6). |
| **Board attestation requirement** | CRO approval required per Critical-tier mandate; quarterly audit; Board Risk Committee notification for any SLO breach. |

## 3. The Technical Architecture

Hierarchical RAG with custom parsing (preserves logical structure of legal documents), WORM storage with AES-256 encryption (data non-repudiation), Geographic Metadata Tagging with Retrieval-Time Residency Filter (data sovereignty), External Regulatory Feed Service (continuous knowledge currency), ACL Delta Sync Index (real-time privilege integrity), Multidimensional Confidence Score (aggregates retrieval relevance, grounding faithfulness, and DLAC enforcement confidence), mandatory HITL gate for all regulated-domain outputs, immutable audit logging capturing the complete oversight model event record. Full details in the "Architectural Delta" and "Governance Delta" sections below.

## 4. The Enhancement

**Compliance-Specific Benchmarks (e.g., LegalBench-RAG; Pipitone and Houir Alami,** 2024**)**: For continuous quality validation of regulatory reasoning tasks, where miscitation carries severe legal consequences

**Automated Regulatory Reporting**: Regulator-specific evidence bundles generated from the Immutable Audit Log

**Policy Versioning with Delta Indexing**: Every document versioned to enable explicit traceability to the policy version active at the time of any given query, a paramount requirement for regulatory audits

## 5. The Board Outcome

The board attests that the system delivers a sustained 70–80% reduction in query cycle time for compliance operations while operating within board-approved regulatory risk and data governance thresholds. All regulated-domain outputs are subject to mandatory Human-in-the-Loop (HITL) review prior to delivery, with each decision recorded as a verifiable HITL event linked to a named reviewer.

Audit and compliance reporting should confirm that no unauthorized cross-jurisdictional data transfers have occurred and that DLAC and data residency controls consistently enforce access and location policies. Every output is fully traceable to the specific policy version in force at the time of the query, ensuring temporal accuracy and legal defensibility. The Immutable Audit Log provides a complete forensic chain of evidence suitable for regulatory examination.

The board receives ongoing reporting on Critical Compliance SLOs, including the Groundedness (Faithfulness) Score and DLAC Filter Efficacy Rate, with any deviations or exceptions escalated in accordance with defined governance thresholds. Based on this evidence, the board confirms that the system is functioning as a Regulatory Shield, enabling operational efficiency while maintaining full compliance, integrity, and adherence to the organization's risk appetite.

## Governance Delta

The orchestrator component is elevated well beyond a simple workflow coordinator; it functions as a sophisticated risk-gating mechanism where efficiency concerns are strictly secondary to mandatory compliance requirements. The orchestrator is the critical single point of control and a potential source of compliance failure. Its core responsibility is to enforce the DLAC mandate and the mandatory guardrails, ensuring that no unauthorized or low-confidence responses reach the end user.

The fundamental difference from UC1 is this: In UC1, the HITL gate is triggered by a below-threshold Support Score. In UC2, the HITL gate is triggered by any regulated-domain output, regardless of confidence score. A high-confidence wrong answer in a regulated domain is no less dangerous than a low-confidence one. The HITL requirement at this Criticality Tier is categorical, not conditional.

## PEP: Security Trimming and DLAC Enforcement

The system enforces access control at the retrieval layer, a process known as Security Trimming or DLAC. The orchestrator's role is to execute this DLAC as a pre-generation filtering mandate. This involves first verifying the user's authorization against the ACLs associated with the retrieved documents.

This process ensures that only authorized chunks, the documents that pass the strict permission check, proceed to the prompt generator, rigorously upholding the principle of risk containment. This architectural choice elevates the Retrieval Engine's primary function: it must move from merely finding relevant data to finding authorized, relevant data. This meticulous enforcement of the principle of least privilege, while potentially introducing marginal complexity and latency, is a non-negotiable requirement for compliance in regulated environments. Technical enforcement relies on Attribute-Based Access Control (ABAC) or RBAC to enforce real-time access controls based on granular user and context attributes. In cross-jurisdictional deployments, the DLAC enforcement must also apply the Retrieval-Time Residency Filter, ensuring that a user in one jurisdiction does not receive policy documents from another.

## Mandatory Guardrails

The LLM orchestrator must implement mandatory security guardrails at the software level to actively monitor and filter both the input query and the generated output, serving as a crucial defensive layer. This dual-sided filtering is essential to prevent unauthorized actions and the circumvention of ethical boundaries by detecting malicious inputs, such as prompt injection, and by actively scanning the output for sensitive data leakage, such as PII leakage. These guardrails are mandatory for systems in regulated environments, providing the final software-level defense against both intentional attacks and accidental data breaches. Additionally, as a final safety measure, the orchestrator conducts a final compliance review and response sandboxing of the LLM's output to confirm mandatory direct source citations and verify adherence to predefined content policies before releasing the response to the user.

## Proactive Input and Output Filtering

The orchestrator integrates a dedicated Guardrail Service designed for continuous inspection. On the input side, this service must actively detect and block malicious inputs designed to manipulate the LLM, including prompt injection and jailbreaking attempts. This is essential to prevent unauthorized actions or the circumvention of ethical boundaries.

On the output side, the service must actively scan for and block sensitive data leakage. This includes detecting PII leakage in the generated answer, toxic or biased language, and inadvertent disclosure of proprietary or commercially sensitive information. The system can be configured to detect standard PII formats or customized sensitive information using organization-specific regular expressions.

## Final Compliance Review and Response Sandboxing

As a final safety measure, the orchestrator conducts a final compliance review of the LLM's output before releasing it to the user. This review confirms the successful insertion of mandatory direct source citations and verifies that the response adheres to predefined content policies. This step functions as a final, proactive guardrail against the inadvertent disclosure of confidential enterprise data that might have been retrieved.

## Faithfulness Enforcement and Risk-Gating Mechanisms

To ensure certifiable assurance, the system must enforce the Faithfulness and Groundedness policy. The Groundedness Score is a critical technical metric that quantifies the degree to which the retrieved documents directly support the LLM's answers. For this Critical-tier compliance system, this metric is expanded into a Multidimensional Confidence Score. This score provides a comprehensive, quantifiable risk assessment for the transaction, acting as the operational lever that balances mandatory compliance rigor with the overall efficiency objective. If the score falls below a predefined threshold, the orchestrator must take immediate risk-gating action.

## Multidimensional Confidence Score

For this Critical-tier compliance system, the standard Groundedness Score is expanded into a Multidimensional Confidence Score. This score aggregates several critical sub-scores reflecting confidence in (1) retrieval relevance, (2) grounding faithfulness, and (3) the successful enforcement of DLAC. This multifaceted score provides a comprehensive, quantifiable risk assessment for the transaction.

The multidimensional score serves a dual governance function in UC2: it is both a quality gate (does this answer meet the Faithfulness SLO?) and a compliance confirmation (did the DLAC enforcement succeed?). A high score on grounding faithfulness, combined with a low score on DLAC enforcement confidence, is still a compliance failure and must be routed to HITL regardless of the grounding result.

## Mandatory Risk-Gating Action

The confidence score acts as the operational lever that balances mandatory compliance rigor with the efficiency objective. If the generated answer's multidimensional Support Score falls below a predefined acceptable threshold, signifying insufficient context or questionable veracity, the orchestrator is mandated to take immediate action.

The available risk-gating actions include programming the orchestrator to refuse generation, triggering a Corrective RAG (CRAG) loop to seek better context, or flagging the transaction for immediate HITL review. In UC2, every regulated-domain output is additionally subject to the mandatory HITL gate regardless of the confidence score; the score determines whether additional remediation steps are required before the HITL reviewer sees the output. The crucial point is that the orchestrator's failure modes are treated as audit failures. This necessitates specific, immutable logging of the rationales for access control and risk-gating decisions, providing clear accountability and forensic evidence for every refusal and every HITL invocation.

## Policy Enforcement: The Categorical Escalation

The EDS framework maintains the strict functional separation between evaluation and enforcement, but for the Compliance Model, the logic is escalated to manage the Critical Criticality Tier.

### PDP As the Categorical Logic

In the Efficiency Model, the PDP returned an Allow verdict based on a conditional Groundedness Score. In the Compliance Model, the PDP logic becomes categorical. For any query tagged as being in a regulated domain, the PDP returns a Deny for direct release, regardless of the confidence score. This ensures that human primacy is not conditional on machine confidence but is a mandatory requirement for any legal or compliance statement.

## PEP As the Hardened Gate

The PEP physically executes this escalation. It receives the categorical Deny from the PDP and physically routes the transaction to the HITL Override Service. The PEP ensures that the output remains in a secure state until a certified officer provides sign-off. It is also responsible for injecting the unique Execution ID (the session/task identifier that threads all log entries for a single workflow into a complete, ordered audit trail) and for recording the complete transaction, including the PDP verdict and the human sign-off, in the Immutable Audit Log.

Figure 7-1 illustrates the complete compliance architecture of the EKRCI platform: the Retrieval Engine retrieves authorized chunks from the Hierarchical DB under Authority Matrix rules before the orchestrator (PEP) applies categorical gating, routing every regulated-domain output via Mandatory HITL Route to the certified reviewer for sign-off, while the probabilistic core's generated answer is scored by the Grounding Verifier and the multidimensional score feeds the Authority Matrix (PDP) for categorical evaluation; the Guardrail Service performs dual-sided inspection with Failure Trace Logs to the Immutable Audit Log and Category 2 HITL triggers on violation; the Compliance Monitor tracks Critical Compliance SLOs, feeding drift/SLO signals to the Authority Matrix and Gate Invocation Rate reports to the Model Governance Board, which closes the oversight loop with Policy/Threshold Updates back to the Authority Matrix; and the External Regulatory Feed Service continuously synchronizes both the Authority Matrix and the Hierarchical DB to maintain regulatory currency.

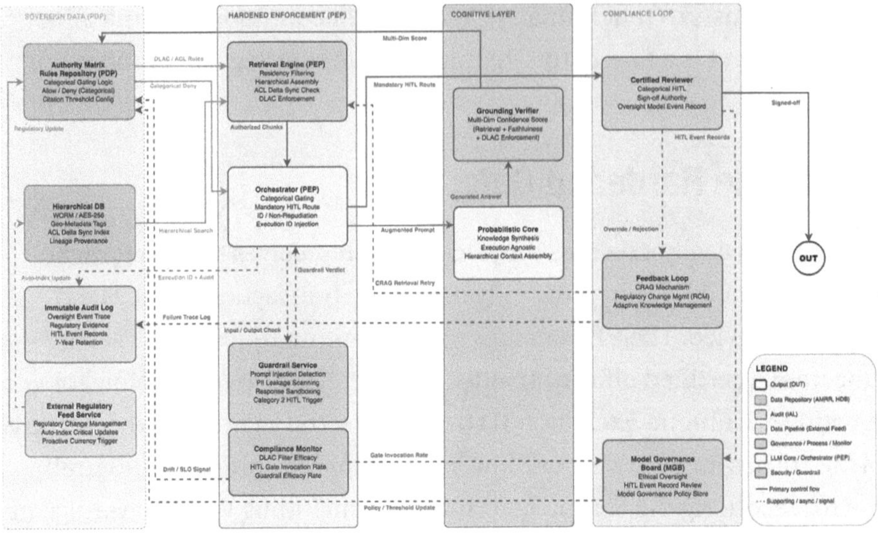


***Figure 7-1.*** *The EKRCI platform compliance architecture—hardened enforcement flow across sovereign data, hardened enforcement (PEP), Cognitive Layer, and compliance loop, with categorical HITL gating, mandatory guardrails, continuous compliance monitoring, and closed regulatory feedback to the Authority Matrix and Hierarchical DB*

# Architectural Delta

The mandate for certifiable regulatory assurance requires significant architectural specialization beyond the standard RAG pipeline, with a focus on contextual fidelity, data residency, source integrity, and continuous knowledge management. This specialization is crucial because the inherent risks in regulated environments demand explicit, non-negotiable controls to guarantee the system's output is legally defensible and fully auditable. These specialized techniques elevate the EKRCI platform from a basic search tool to a Critical-tier compliance engine.

## Contextual Fidelity

Traditional RAG implementations often fail when processing complex, structured legal and procedural documents. The simple, fixed-size text splitting used in standard methods risks context fragmentation, in which text chunks lose their logical relationship to parent articles or governing definitions, leading to inconsistent and potentially non-compliant interpretation by the LLM.

To overcome this, the architecture mandates two specialization techniques:

- **Custom Parsing and Structured Enrichment:** Implement custom parsing strategies to handle complex documentation. These strategies often leverage vision models to intelligently identify and extract various semantic objects, including text blocks, tables, and nested enumerated lists. These components, which may be multimodal, must then be translated into a consistent, structured output format to ensure the LLM receives rich, organized context.

  This is essential because legal and financial compliance data frequently resides in tables or visual layouts. Ignoring the visual layout during chunking severely impairs RAG fidelity and creates a compliance vulnerability. Custom parsing solves this by ensuring that all critical structural components are extracted, normalized, and made available for semantic search, preventing the downstream model from missing vital context embedded outside pure running text.

- **Hierarchical RAG for Logical Structure Preservation:** The system must deploy Hierarchical RAG, an advanced strategy engineered to preserve the stringent, hierarchical structure of legal and policy documents. This involves explicitly linking a specific clause or sub-section to its governing parent article or top-level policy definition.

  This preservation of structure mitigates the direct compliance risk posed by scope fragmentation. If an LLM is inadvertently provided only a sub-clause without its governing top-level article, the system risks misinterpreting the rule's scope—for instance, incorrectly applying a policy intended only for the Asia Pacific (APAC) region globally. Hierarchical RAG provides the comprehensive logical framework needed for accurate legal or procedural interpretation, ensuring that the compliance advice generated is robustly scoped and well-defined. The comprehensive chunking strategy forms a primary control point for auditability and risk mitigation. This is also the critical enabler of the HITL reviewer's ability to verify a citation: the reviewer must be able to trace any claim to its parent article, not merely to an isolated sub-clause.

## Data Residency Zoning

Global compliance requires strict adherence to data sovereignty laws in each jurisdiction, such as the GDPR. The architecture explicitly separates data handling according to these jurisdictional requirements, ensuring that all PII and regulatory compliance data remain within their designated geographical boundaries (e.g., EU data stays within the EU). This separation is both a regulatory obligation under applicable data sovereignty law and an EDS framework requirement, ensuring the legal defensibility of the system's operations across multiple jurisdictions.

This is technically implemented through Geographic Metadata Tagging at the ingestion layer. Metadata tags are applied to each document and its corresponding vector chunks, explicitly mandating the physical storage location (region, country). This tagging, performed during the offline ingestion phase, directly enables a Retrieval-Time Residency Filter during inference, ensuring a verifiable log that proves adherence to data sovereignty rules.

## Third-Party Risk Management for External LLMs

Organizations in regulated sectors are fully responsible for the compliance of all their downstream sub-processors, including cloud providers and external LLM vendors. Uncontrolled data leakage via unmonitored prompts to external LLMs creates severe legal liability.

A mandatory due diligence process and formal vendor risk assessment must be established for all external LLM APIs. This involves rigorously auditing the LLM provider's policies to ensure that customer data and prompts are not used for model training or retained beyond the necessary transaction time and to align with stringent data residency and privacy laws. Furthermore, the architecture must mandate and document a contingency plan (failover strategy) to switch between LLM providers or internal models in the event of a service outage or a critical security/compliance failure by the primary vendor.

## Data Integrity

To ensure data non-repudiation and the legal defensibility of the knowledge base, source data must be secured in a Write-Once, Read-Many (WORM) format. WORM storage prevents tampering or modification of source documents post-ingestion, ensuring the integrity of historical policy evidence and guarding against claims of retrospective alteration.

Mandatory data confidentiality controls complement this integrity. Comprehensive protection must be implemented using AES-256 or an equivalent standard for data-at-rest encryption, along with mandatory encryption in transit as data moves across internal services.

## Poisoning Mitigation

The ingestion process is susceptible to subtle yet catastrophic attacks. Malicious actors could insert invisible character sequences designed to subtly influence the LLM's final output, leading to compliance failures or dangerous decision-making. To mitigate this, poisoning mitigation is mandatory, requiring explicit data validation protocols and rigorous source verification during ingestion to detect document anomalies. This acts as a critical preventive security control against data corruption in a highly sensitive system.

## Continuous Knowledge Management

Regulations and policies are dynamic. The platform must continuously ensure its internal knowledge base remains synchronized with external law to prevent decisions based on stale facts. This requires integrating the ingestion pipeline with an External Regulatory Feed Service. This service, often sourced from commercial compliance intelligence providers, proactively flags and automatically indexes critical, high-impact external regulatory changes (e.g., a new GDPR ruling) as soon as they are released. This mechanism drastically reduces the time a compliance team spends assessing applicability and identifying obligations.

## ACL Delta Sync Index

The integrity of the DLAC mechanism relies entirely on the freshness of the Access Control List (ACL) metadata. The ingestion pipeline must maintain a real-time or near-real-time Delta Sync Index to update ACL metadata whenever user permissions or document sensitivities change within the central IAM system. This continuous synchronization ensures that newly revoked access permissions are immediately reflected in the vector index metadata, preventing privilege drift, the condition in which a user's effective access expands beyond their currently approved scope, and subsequent DLAC failures. A stale ACL is not merely a technical issue; in a Critical-tier deployment with mandatory HITL, a DLAC failure is an audit failure that must be logged as a critical compliance event regardless of whether the HITL reviewer catches the error. Table 7-1 sets out the architectural delta required to specialize the platform for regulatory context.

*Table 7-1. Architectural Delta of specialization for regulatory context*

| Foundational Requirement | UC2 Specialization (Architectural Delta) | Compliance Benefit |
|---|---|---|
| Data chunking | Hierarchical RAG and custom parsing | Preserves logical structure, mitigating fragmentation risk in legal/policy interpretation. Enables HITL reviewers to verify citations against parent articles |
| Data storage | WORM storage/ AES-256 encryption | Guarantees data non-repudiation, ensuring source integrity and confidentiality |
| RAG source management | External Regulatory Feed Service | Ensures index freshness against dynamic legal changes (regulatory change management) |
| Data filtering | Data Residency Zoning (metadata tagging) | Enforces jurisdictional compliance for regulated data. Prevents cross-border data transfer violations |

# MLOps for Continuous Compliance

Sustaining a Regulatory Shield requires a comprehensive MLOps framework that ensures auditability and continuous adaptation to evolving knowledge and regulations. This framework encompasses three critical areas: auditability and immutable traceability, which guarantee every transaction is legally defensible; adaptive knowledge management, which uses human feedback to refine the underlying data infrastructure; and benchmarking LLM quality, which enforces specific Critical Compliance Service-Level Objectives (SLOs) to mitigate AI risk.

## Auditability and Immutable Traceability

Formal LLMOps practices are mandatory for managing the lifecycle, performance, stability, and ethical compliance of this Critical-tier RAG system. The foundation of this practice is the immutable audit logging service, which must rigorously record the full transaction trace for compliance reporting, ensuring integrity and legal defensibility. This critical section details two mandates: the non-negotiable requirements of the immutable audit logging service itself and the necessity of Automated Regulatory Reporting derived from these timestamped logs.

### Immutable Audit Logging Service

The immutable audit logging service is mandatory enterprise infrastructure. It must rigorously record the full transaction trace for compliance reporting using immutable, timestamped storage (e.g., append-only logs) to prevent post-incident modification and guarantee integrity. This log serves as the foundation for transparency and interpretability by tracking data provenance.

The logs must explicitly capture the forensic data necessary to reconstruct the decision-making process for auditability and litigation readiness. This forensic data includes the user ID and the specific ACLs applied, the complete retrieved context (listing the document IDs and chunk IDs used), the exact augmented prompt supplied to the LLM, the final confidence score, and a mandatory record of all active guardrail checks—the guardrail violation trace. For UC2, every log entry for a regulated-domain output must also include the oversight model event record: the HITL reviewer's identity, the content reviewed, the reviewer's approval or rejection decision, and the rationale. This record is not optional; it is the primary evidence of compliance with the Human Primacy Governance Principle.

Logging the complete RAG chain provides the necessary evidence to attribute failures to specific pipeline stages (e.g., context recall failure versus faithfulness failure). This ensures that every piece of advice given can be traced back to an authorized policy version, serving as a powerful litigation defense tool. The system must also support Automated Regulatory Reporting, producing regulator-specific reports and redacted evidence bundles from these audit logs. All decision audit logs, HITL override records, and oversight model event records generated by this system are subject to a minimum seven-year retention obligation under the EDS Logging and Explainability Standard (formally established in Chapter 11) or longer as required by applicable regulatory law.

## Adaptive Knowledge Management

Adaptive knowledge management is the EDS framework's continuous learning mechanism: it treats HITL feedback, system exceptions, and retrieval failures as structured data signals for knowledge index refinement rather than as isolated incidents. The system captures the full failure trace and feeds it back into an automated workflow, treating each failure as an indicator of a flaw in the underlying vector index or ingestion pipeline.

### CRAG Feedback Loop

The HITL architecture serves as the final ethical and compliance guardrail and as a continuous feedback mechanism. When human users provide structured feedback (e.g., flagging an answer as incorrect), this signal is captured as an indicator of potential index failure (e.g., poor retrieval or stale data).

If retrieval fails, the system must trigger a CRAG feedback loop to log the query and the failure trace. This workflow informs remediation actions in the ingestion pipeline, such as refining the chunking strategy for that document type or initiating an urgent check for data staleness. This mechanism ensures that human expertise directly fuels the continuous refinement of the underlying data infrastructure, perpetually enhancing the index and retrieval mechanisms. In UC2, the pattern of HITL reviewer rejections and override rationales is also fed into the adaptive knowledge management system: a pattern of rejections within a specific policy domain signals a systematic failure in retrieval quality in that domain, not merely individual errors.

## Robust Policy Versioning and ACL Synchronization

Continuous regulatory compliance requires robust control over knowledge assets. The system mandates version control across the entire knowledge base (data, code, and models) to ensure reproducibility. By leveraging technologies that support Delta Indexing, a necessity for handling rapid changes without costly full-index rebuilds, the system ensures that every document is versioned. This provides explicit traceability to the specific policy or regulation version that was active at the time of the user's query, a paramount requirement for external regulatory audits. The integrity of the DLAC is maintained through the ACL Delta Sync Index, which updates access permissions in real time.

The Immutable Audit Log captures the complete RAG chain, including the human reviewer's identity and their specific approval rationale. The system leverages this log to produce automated regulatory evidence bundles. This capability allows the organization to respond to audits in minutes rather than weeks, proving that every machine action remained within the board-approved risk appetite.

# Benchmarking LLM Quality for Risk Mitigation

Compliance LLMOps must prioritize factual accuracy and grounding above all else. This is enforced through continuous, rigorous evaluation using LLM-As-a-Judge methods directly in the production pipeline, which serves as a Continuous Regulatory Control system.

The architecture mandates specific Critical Compliance SLOs to mitigate inherent AI risks:

1. **Groundedness (Faithfulness):** This is the paramount technical metric. It assesses the percentage of claims in the generated answer that are directly supported by the retrieved, authorized context. Continuous monitoring of a high Groundedness Score is required, as it directly correlates with lower hallucination rates and is a critical control against compliance-related hallucinations.

2. **DLAC Filter Efficacy Rate:** A mandatory security KPI that measures the successful filtering of unauthorized documents at the retrieval stage, ensuring the integrity of the security boundary. In UC2, a DLAC failure on a cross-jurisdictional query is a reportable compliance event regardless of whether the HITL reviewer caught and rejected the response.

3. **Guardrail Efficacy Rate:** This SLO measures the percentage of successful detections and blocks against known prompt injection and PII leakage attempts, formally validating the continuous performance of the AI safety features.

4. **Contextual Recall:** This metric ensures that the retrieved context contains all necessary information to synthesize a complete, fully compliant output. Low recall poses a significant risk because it forces the LLM to provide legal or procedural advice based on incomplete data, potentially resulting in insufficient or incorrect advice.

5. **HITL Gate Invocation Rate:** The frequency with which the mandatory HITL gate is invoked, tracked against the total volume of regulated-domain outputs. In UC2, this should approach 100% for regulated-domain outputs. A rate significantly below 100% indicates a system misconfiguration: outputs are bypassing the mandatory gate, a zero-tolerance governance breach.

Table 7-2 defines the critical compliance SLOs and their performance metrics.

***Table 7-2.*** *Performance metrics (Critical Compliance SLOs)*

| KPI Category | Metric Name | Measurement Focus/ Compliance Standard | Target Business Impact |
|---|---|---|---|
| Risk and quality (SLO) | Faithfulness (Groundedness Score) | Ratio of claims supported by retrieved, authorized context. | Lower hallucination rates; ensures legal defensibility. |
| Risk and quality (SLO) | DLAC Filter Efficacy Rate | Measures successful filtering of unauthorized documents. Cross-jurisdictional failures are reportable events. | Non-negotiable security integrity. |
| Ethical/ security (SLO) | Guardrail Efficacy Rate | Percentage of successful block/redaction of PII leakage/prompt injection. | Prevents data breach; mitigates attack surface. |
| Oversight compliance (SLO) | HITL Gate Invocation Rate | Frequency of HITL gate invocation versus total regulated-domain outputs. Should approach 100%. | Confirms Human Primacy principle is being enforced. Rate < 100% is a zero-tolerance governance breach. |

# Threat Modeling, Ethical Safety, and AI Risk Assessment

The deployment of a compliance-focused generative AI system requires moving beyond reactive security fixes to proactive, continuous risk mitigation. This mandate is enforced through a structured process that identifies, quantifies, and treats AI-specific risks. This crucial section outlines three mandates: continuous threat modeling to adapt to adversarial inputs, the deployment of an ethical safety policy to prevent misuse, and the establishment of risk quantification and treatment to measure and mitigate the system's residual risk profile.

## Continuous Adversarial Testing and Risk Assessment

A formal, continuous threat modeling process must be integrated to proactively identify and mitigate emerging AI-specific and regulatory risks. This requires continuous Adversarial Testing (e.g., Red-Teaming) to assess the resilience of the orchestrator's guardrails and the LLM's resistance to hallucination and data leakage. This testing moves beyond passive monitoring to proactively hardening the system against new attack vectors.

Furthermore, to manage the introduction of new risks, a formal, periodic AI Compliance Impact Assessment (similar to a Data Protection Impact Assessment) must be conducted to evaluate the ethical, legal, and operational risks introduced by new model versions or system updates before production deployment.

## MGB and Ethical Oversight

The system must operate under a formal mandate of the MGB, the EDS framework's designated oversight body for model risk, ethical compliance, and version governance, introduced in Chapter 5. This board is responsible for defining and enforcing the EDS Model Governance Policy Store, a governed configuration repository, owned by the MGB, that defines the approved list of LLMs, their permitted configuration parameters, and ethical use constraints.

A designated Model Risk Officer (the EDS-designated governance role introduced in Chapter 5) is responsible for continuous risk evaluation, focusing specifically on

- **Bias and Fairness:** Assessing and mitigating potential systemic biases introduced by the LLM or embedding model that could lead to unfair or inconsistent responses across different user groups.
- **Version Drift Control:** Approving and managing the transition between different model versions, ensuring that backward-compatibility testing and quality baselines are met before deployment. A model version update in UC2 requires a formal AI Compliance Impact Assessment before deployment.
- **Mandatory Documentation:** Comprehensive documentation (e.g., Model Cards) must be maintained for all production-deployed LLMs and re-ranker models, detailing their training data, known limitations, and performance against fairness and bias metrics.

## Mandatory High-Risk HITL Review

The HITL architecture serves as the final ethical and compliance guardrail. In UC2, the mandatory HITL scope extends beyond the standard low-confidence trigger. These are independent triggers for mandatory HITL, not an exhaustive classification of outputs: an output may satisfy one or both, and because UC2 is scoped as a regulated-domain compliance platform, effectively every output falls under Category 1. There is no residual baseline path in UC2 that escapes mandatory HITL; the conditional, confidence-based trigger of UC1 does not apply here. Two categories of mandatory HITL invocation apply:

**Category 1—All Regulated-Domain Outputs:** Every output in a regulated legal or compliance domain is subject to mandatory HITL review, regardless of the confidence score. This is the UC2 escalation from UC1 and reflects the Critical Criticality Tier.

**Category 2—Guardrail Violation Triggers:** Any response flagged by the Guardrail Service (e.g., potential PII leakage or a close-call prompt injection attempt) must automatically trigger a mandatory HITL review before the response is finalized or logged. This ensures a human security expert validates the outcome of the compliance control and provides an added layer of safety in the event of an attempted breach.

Both categories must be logged as oversight model event records. The distinction between Category 1 and Category 2 invocations must be captured in the log; a Category 2 invocation is a security event requiring separate tracking and escalation, not merely a quality review. Table 7-3 maps the orchestrator's risk-gating mechanisms and their controls.

*Table 7-3. Orchestrator risk-gating mechanisms*

| Gatekeeper Function | Control Mechanism | Compliance SLO | Risk Mitigated |
|---|---|---|---|
| Access enforcement | Document-level access control (DLAC) + Retrieval-Time Residency Filter | DLAC Filter Efficacy Rate | Unauthorized data exposure/cross-jurisdictional privilege escalation |
| Output quality control | Multidimensional Confidence Score (faithfulness + DLAC + retrieval) | Groundedness Score/Refuse Generation Threshold | Compliance-related hallucination and legal misstatement risk |
| Input/output safety | Guardrail Service (PII leakage/prompt injection) | Guardrail Efficacy Rate | Malicious attack and sensitive data leakage |
| Third-party control | Vendor Due Diligence and Audit | Data Usage/Privacy Audit Score | Supply-chain risk and data retention violation |

# Phased Deployment Strategy

Successful adoption and the realization of the projected productivity uplift depend on a carefully managed, incremental deployment that builds staff trust and minimizes organizational risk. This approach ensures that the system's core promise, the simultaneous delivery of efficiency and compliance, is validated empirically before a full rollout. The strategy is structured around three key phases: Building the Minimum Viable Compliance (MVC) Core to establish foundational governance; Pilot Deployment and Validation to empirically demonstrate efficiency and compliance SLOs; and Full-Scale Expansion, which integrates the system across the enterprise.

## Phase 1: Building the Minimum Viable Compliance Core

The initial focus is on technical validation and establishing measurable baselines against manual processes.

- **Key Security Activities:** Finalize the foundation for physical and logical security. This includes establishing the WORM format for source data and implementing Geographic Metadata Tagging to comply with data residency requirements.
- **Key GRC Activity:** Conduct initial LLM and Third-Party Risk Assessment to vet the external LLM provider's security and data usage policies, ensuring the vendor supply chain is compliant before proceeding.
- **Measurement:** Establish baseline manual performance metrics (e.g., CTR, error rate) against which the eventual 70–80% ROI will be calculated. Also, record the HITL invocation baseline of zero (pre-deployment, as no AI-mediated outputs yet exist), against which the post-deployment target approaching 100% will be measured in Phase 2.

## Phase 2: Pilot Deployment and Validation

This phase dedicates substantial time to proving the integrity of the risk mitigation controls in a restricted pilot environment.

- **Key Security Activities:** Implement mandatory retrieval-time access enforcement (Security Trimming/ DLAC), utilizing enterprise IAM systems. Deploy advanced Hierarchical Chunking techniques for complex policy manuals and implement the ACL Delta Sync Index for continuous privilege integrity.

- **Key Governance Activities:** Implement orchestrator-level Guardrail Service for PII leakage and prompt injection detection. Establish the mandatory HITL workflow for all regulated-domain outputs (Category 1) and all guardrail violation outputs (Category 2). Train HITL reviewers on their governance obligations, the distinction between Category 1 and Category 2 invocations, and the requirement to log their rationale for every decision. Establish the HITL Gate Invocation Rate as an active compliance metric.
- **Measurement:** Focus on technical quality metrics: Groundedness (Faithfulness) Score, DLAC Filter Efficacy Rate, and HITL Gate Invocation Rate. These metrics must meet compliance SLO targets before broader deployment. Because the HITL gate is mandatory for every regulated-domain output, the invocation rate must reach 100%; any shortfall during the pilot indicates that outputs are bypassing the mandatory gate and is a deployment blocker.

## Phase 3: Full-Scale Expansion

This phase involves full operational scaling, formal quantification of business value, and the establishment of all mandatory audit infrastructure.

- **Key Infrastructure Activities:** Implement the complete immutable audit logging service utilizing timestamped storage. Scale the infrastructure and optimize the ingestion pipeline to support continuous, incremental updates across a large index.
- **Key Compliance Activities:** Implement External Regulatory Feed Monitoring to ensure continuous synchronization with external law. Formally quantify the business value and ROI (i.e., CTR, TTC, Groundedness Score vs. baseline). Establish Automated Regulatory Reporting from the Immutable Audit Log.
- **Measurement:** Monitor the DLAC Filter Efficacy Rate, HITL Gate Invocation Rate, and Compliance Traceability Rate (Audit Log Integrity). Formally validate the target ROI of 70–80%. Present the HITL event records to the MGB as evidence that the Human Primacy Governance Principle is being honored in production.

# Summary

This chapter established the Compliance Model as the constitutional escalation of the Efficiency Model, not a technical variant but a governance elevation. The EKRCI platform demonstrates that operational efficiency and certifiable regulatory assurance are not competing objectives; they are simultaneously achievable when governance is embedded in the infrastructure layer rather than applied as an afterthought. The key takeaways are as follows:

- **The governance escalation from UC1 to UC2 is categorical, not conditional.** UC1 triggers HITL when confidence falls below a threshold. UC2 mandates HITL for every regulated-domain output regardless of confidence score. A high-confidence wrong answer carries the same legal consequences as a low-confidence one. At the Critical Criticality Tier, the HITL gate is a constitutional requirement that must be logged as a non-repudiable governance record.
- **Six architectural controls distinguish the Compliance Model from the Efficiency Model.** Hierarchical RAG preserves the legal document structure, enabling HITL reviewers to verify citations against parent articles. WORM storage with AES-256 encryption ensures data non-repudiation. Geographic Metadata Tagging with Retrieval-Time Residency Filter enforces jurisdictional sovereignty. The External Regulatory Feed Service maintains index currency. The ACL Delta Sync Index prevents privilege drift. The Multidimensional Confidence Score aggregates retrieval relevance, grounding faithfulness, and DLAC enforcement confidence into a single governance signal.
- **The PDP logic becomes categorical in the Compliance Model.** For any regulated-domain query, the PDP returns a Deny for direct release regardless of confidence score. The PEP routes every such output to the HITL Override Service, where a certified reviewer must provide explicit sign-off before the response is released or logged. Human primacy is not contingent on machine confidence.

- **Two categories of mandatory HITL invocation apply.** Category 1 covers all regulated-domain outputs and is mandatory regardless of confidence. Category 2 covers all guardrail violation triggers; any response flagged for PII leakage or prompt injection requires validation by a human security expert. Both must be logged as oversight model event records with distinct classifications, because a Category 2 invocation is a security event that requires separate escalation.
- **Sustained compliance depends on continuous, data-driven governance.** A HITL Gate Invocation Rate below 100% for regulated-domain outputs indicates system misconfiguration, a zero-tolerance governance breach. A Groundedness Score below 95% triggers MGB review. The DLAC Filter Efficacy Rate must hold at 100%. The pattern of HITL reviewer rejections feeds the adaptive knowledge management loop, converting human oversight into systematic index improvement.

The next chapter shifts the governance challenge from depth to breadth, from hardening a single deployment model to managing the performance, cost, and integrity pressures that emerge as RAG scales across an enterprise.

# Reference

Pipitone, Nicholas, and Ghita Houir Alami. 2024. LegalBench-RAG: A Benchmark for Retrieval-Augmented Generation in the Legal Domain. arXiv:2408.10343. `https://arxiv.org/abs/2408.10343`.

# CHAPTER 8

# Data Integrity and Optimization

Chapters 1–7 established the constitutional framework, security architecture, LLMOps assurance, and two production deployment models: the Efficiency Model (UC1) and the Compliance Model (UC2). This chapter moves from general-purpose retrieval to domain-specific optimization, introducing three use cases that address the performance, cost, and integrity challenges that emerge when generative AI is scaled across an enterprise. UC3 (intelligent document quality and consistency uplift) resolves the problem of conflicting source truth in regulated knowledge bases. UC4 (domain-specific AI stylist and language adapter) enables multi-tenant stylistic personalization without model proliferation. UC5 (predictive customer insight and proactive service support) delivers millisecond-latency recommendations during live customer interactions.

The core tension in each use case is the same: optimization introduces novel risks. Speed creates temporal consistency challenges. Cost efficiency through shared infrastructure introduces a risk of cross-tenant contamination. Semantic quality assurance through AI-driven conflict detection introduces a risk of ground-truth manipulation. The chapter resolves each tension by specifying the Governance Delta, the precise set of new controls mandated by the architectural augmentation, before describing the architecture that requires them.


M. M. Hossain and A. A. N. Ponnusamy, *Governance-First AI*,
https://doi.org/10.1007/979-8-8688-3118-8_8

Each use case operates within the board's Guarded Innovation risk posture: autonomous capability is authorized because the Governance Delta ensures that every action is traceable, contestable, and within board-approved boundaries. The oversight model escalates with the risk profile: HITL for UC3 (Moderate criticality), HAL for UC4 (Low criticality), and HOTL for UC5 (High criticality; currently Level 2—Level 3 is a planned future state).

The chapter follows the unified EDS blueprint template. Each use case is presented through five sections—Business Problem, Governance Instrument, Technical Architecture, Enhancement, and Board Outcome—with governance established before architecture. A synthesis section then integrates the three use cases through the shared PDP/PEP enforcement model and Figure 8-1, which illustrates the unified specialized governance architecture across all three optimization paths.

## Defining the Architectural and Governance Deltas

Each use case is analyzed through two vectors. The Architectural Delta is the novel component augmenting the standard RAG pipeline: the CD-Module for semantic consistency (UC3), the PEFT/LoRA Multi-tenant Stack for cost-efficient personalization (UC4), and the Streaming/Online Feature Store for millisecond-latency decisioning (UC5). The Governance Delta comprises the new risk controls mandated by that augmentation: Constrained RBAC and SoD for UC3, UAM Security Domain Mapping for UC4, and the Delegated Authorization Service for UC5. Table 8-1 summarizes the mapping.

*Table 8-1. Optimization goal of the use cases*

| Delta Component | Optimization Goal | Use Case |
|---|---|---|
| **CD-Module** | Integrity/semantic consistency | UC3 |
| **PEFT Multi-tenant Stack** | Cost /stylistic adaptation | UC4 |
| **Streaming/Online Feature Store** | Speed /low-latency service | UC5 |

**Governance Leaders:** The Governance Instrument and Board Outcome for each use case define the constitutional constraints and measurable evidence.

**Architects and Practitioners:** The Architectural Delta and Governance Delta sections for each use case are the implementation specification.

# Blueprint: UC3—Intelligent Document Quality and Consistency Uplift

Use Case 3 addresses the systemic risk faced by large organizations whose knowledge bases, comprising legal contracts, internal policies, and regulatory filings, are often fragmented and contain conflicting or outdated documents. The core problem is that large organizations operate with massive, diverse repositories that contain overlapping or contradictory content, undermining the creation of a reliable Single Source of Truth and leading directly to potential legal liability, financial loss, and critical compliance breaches.

# 1. The Business Problem

Large regulated organizations operate knowledge bases containing thousands of legal contracts, internal policies, and regulatory filings. These repositories inevitably develop contradictions: conflicting effective dates, inconsistent policy scopes, or direct policy reversals. The foundational RAG system validates the faithfulness of the output to the retrieved context, but cannot validate the integrity of the source context itself. If the RAG system retrieves two equally "authorized" documents that contain contradictory facts, the LLM may generate a response that is fully supported by one but contradicted by the other, a faithful hallucination that erodes user trust and compromises auditability. The objective is to achieve a 60–70% reduction in manual data validation effort by automating conflict detection and resolution, transforming the knowledge base into a certified system of record.

# 2. The Governance Instrument

**GOVERNANCE STACK: UC3—Intelligent Document Quality and Consistency Uplift**

| Instrument | Active Setting for This Deployment |
|---|---|
| **Autonomy Level** | Level 2 (Workflow Automation). |
| **Criticality Tier** | Moderate. |
| **Oversight model** | HITL—mandatory for all Authority and Policy Reversal contradiction resolution decisions; triggered for all CD-Module flags above configurable confidence threshold. |
| **Delegation Note** | No autonomous conflict resolution authority; CD-Module flags only; human approver makes all resolution decisions. |

(*continued*)

| GOVERNANCE STACK: UC3—Intelligent Document Quality and Consistency Uplift | |
|---|---|
| **Instrument** | **Active Setting for This Deployment** |
| **Groundedness threshold** | CD-Module Confidence Score: flags above threshold trigger mandatory HITL; XAI logging required for every flagged decision linking it to specific RAG chunks and confidence scores. |
| **DLAC enforcement** | Constrained RBAC with Separation of Duties (SoD): Document Submission Writer role prohibited from holding Conflict Resolution Final Approver role. |
| **Logging Standard** | XAI logging mandatory for every CD-Module HITL trigger; human-readable explainability metadata retained as audit evidence. |
| **Key Governance Control** | Separation of Duties enforced at RBAC level—countermeasure against intentional data poisoning via the HITL. |
| **Board Outcome Target** | 60–70% reduction in manual validation effort; every conflict resolution traceable to a named SoD-compliant approver. |

# 3. The Technical Architecture

Rule-Based Validation Engine (RBVE) for deterministic structural checks + Contradiction Detection Module (CD-Module) for semantic consistency checks + Knowledge Base Refinement Pipeline (KBR) for self-healing the RAG index. Full details in the "Architectural Delta" section below.

## 4. The Enhancement

**Contradiction Taxonomy Modeling**: CD-Module classifies conflicts by type (Temporal, Numerical, Authority, Policy Reversal) to route each flag to the appropriate domain expert. This classification significantly enhances audit efficiency, reduces human review latency, and improves throughput.

## 5. The Board Outcome

The board attests that the system delivers a 60–70% reduction in manual data validation effort while operating within board-approved data integrity and auditability thresholds. Every Authority and Policy Reversal conflict is adjudicated by a named human reviewer under enforced Separation of Duties (SoD), with all decisions supported by verifiable explainability (XAI) metadata and recorded as HITL event records.

Periodic audit and risk committee reviews confirm that no single user can both submit and approve conflict resolutions, eliminating the risk of knowledge base manipulation. Exception rates, override patterns, and conflict classifications are continuously monitored, and escalations are triggered when thresholds are breached.

As a result, the knowledge base is validated as a certified, self-healing system of record, with full traceability, executive accountability, and legal defensibility.

# Governance Delta: UC3

The deployment of a conflict detection system introduces governance requirements focused on structured auditability and risk mitigation in the resolution process. This mandates the classification of disagreement types using the EDS Contradiction Taxonomy, the framework's four-type classification of document conflicts (Temporal, Numerical, Authority, Policy Reversal), and granular logging; the enforcement of Constrained RBAC and SoD to safeguard the integrity of the ground truth during the HITL process; and the mandatory logging of AI traceability and explainability metadata to provide legal defensibility and accountability for all system decisions.

## Contradiction Taxonomy Modeling and Granular Logging

For high-stakes enterprise applications, the CD-Module must classify the nature of the disagreement, as different conflict types carry varying levels of risk and require routing to specific domain experts. The model must be trained and evaluated against the EDS Contradiction Taxonomy that mirrors complex enterprise risks.

The system must log the conflict classification using this rich taxonomy. For example, a Temporal conflict (a conflicting effective date) must be routed to the compliance team. In contrast, an Authority conflict (different sources of a requirement) must trigger mandatory HITL review by the legal team. This granular classification significantly enhances audit efficiency and reduces human review latency, thereby improving throughput and the compliance posture. Table 8-2 sets out the contradiction taxonomy for enterprise data integrity.

***Table 8-2.*** *Contradiction Taxonomy for enterprise data integrity*

| Contradiction Type | Definition and Example | System Impact and Resolution |
|---|---|---|
| Temporal | Conflicts involving dates, timeframes, or conflicting effective dates | Flagged conflict routed to the compliance team for authoritative date verification. Requires Data Lineage Tagging for source history. |
| Numerical | Discrepancies in values, amounts, or percentages (e.g., "$12M surplus" versus "$5M deficit") | RBVE validates structure; CD-Module validates semantic context. Must be reviewed by finance/audit expert. |
| Authority | Different sources or issuers of a requirement or policy | Triggers mandatory HITL review under Constrained RBAC/SoD, routed to legal for adjudication. HITL event record required. |
| Policy Reversal | Direct negation of a previously stated policy or rule | Leads to immediate Knowledge Base Refinement Pipeline (KBR) execution to downgrade the deprecated policy in the RAG index. HITL approval required before KBR executes. |

## Constrained RBAC and SoD Enforcement

Standard Role-Based Access Control (RBAC), focused solely on document access (Chapter 4), is insufficient to address the risk of knowledge manipulation. The integrity of the continuous learning process, particularly the HITL feedback loop, depends on preventing unauthorized or biased users from contaminating the ground-truth data.

To mitigate this systemic risk, the architecture mandates Constrained RBAC, which strictly enforces the SoD principle. This ensures that the individual responsible for the initial data entry or document submission (i.e., Document Submission Writer) is prohibited from serving as the final reviewer and Conflict Resolution Final Approver. By enforcing this separation, the system prevents a single user from manipulating both submissions and conflict adjudication, thereby safeguarding the integrity of the ground-truth data used for model retraining and knowledge base refinement. This architectural constraint is the technical countermeasure against intentional data poisoning via the continuous learning loop.

## Mandatory AI Traceability and Explainability Metadata Logging

To maintain accountability, the audit logs must capture specialized AI-specific metadata for every system decision and flag. AI traceability is mandatory. Beyond logging the user ID and timestamp, the system must capture the Algorithm Version Control (i.e., the specific version of the Natural Language Understanding (NLU) model or LLM used for detection); the confidence scores (i.e., quantitative risk assessments for automated conflict classification); and, most critically, explainability metadata (i.e., XAI).

The integration of XAI output transforms the Audit Log from a passive record into an active legal defense tool. For high-risk documents, the system must provide human-readable context and justification, such as the retrieved RAG chunks that led to the conflict detection or the feature importance scores that drove a low-confidence flag. This XAI rationale is essential for defending a high-risk AI decision in court (e.g., rejecting a contract based on a detected contradiction), as it links the decision directly to verifiable, comprehensible evidence. All decision audit logs, XAI rationale records, and HITL override records generated by this system are subject to a minimum seven-year retention obligation under the EDS Logging and Explainability Standard (formally established in Chapter 11). This is a mandatory infrastructure requirement, not a data management preference.

# Architectural Delta: UC3

The integrity challenge mandates a significant architectural augmentation, shifting from simple document retrieval to holistic semantic quality assurance. This approach adopts a hybrid model that combines the efficiency of deterministic checks with the analytical depth of AI.

The solution integrates a high-speed Rule-Based Validation Engine (RBVE) that performs deterministic, high-confidence structured checks (e.g., verifying date formats, currency symbols, and arithmetic accuracy). This foundational engine ensures basic structural quality, allowing the subsequent AI layer to focus on semantic complexity.

The core architectural delta is the CD-Module. This advanced component utilizes NLU and RAG principles to perform complex semantic checks, moving beyond keyword matching to evaluate contextual and conceptual coherence. The CD-Module systematically stress-tests the entire document corpus for inconsistencies, both within a single document (intra-document consistency) and across related documents (cross-document consistency).

When a contradiction is identified, the system utilizes the Knowledge Base Refinement Pipeline (KBR), which acts as the self-healing loop for the RAG index. During the HITL process, expert reviewers adjudicate conflicts (e.g., determining which of two conflicting policies is the current, authoritative version). The KBR captures this resolution metadata and uses it to update the RAG index, filtering out or downgrading the conflicting or deprecated information. This crucial process prevents the RAG retrieval mechanism from supplying the LLM with contradictory evidence during subsequent checks, thereby maintaining long-term knowledge coherence and trustworthiness.

## Enterprise Implication

UC3 shifts the governance control point left, from securing what the model outputs to securing what the model retrieves. The foundational RAG pipeline governed the output layer through DLAC and Groundedness Score thresholds. UC3 governs the source layer through the CD-Module and KBR, ensuring that contradictory evidence never reaches the Cognitive Layer. The enterprise implication is direct: a knowledge base managed by UC3 is a certified system of record, not a retrieval index, and every conflict resolution is legally defensible because SoD prevents any single actor from controlling both submission and adjudication.

## Blueprint: UC4—Domain-Specific AI Stylist and Language Adapter

Use Case 4 addresses the challenge of ensuring AI outputs are technically precise and adhere to the firm's proprietary language, brand, or executive voice. General-purpose LLMs inherently lack knowledge of a firm's specific industry jargon, internal acronyms, and desired communication style. Achieving this domain-specific precision traditionally requires full fine-tuning of the base LLM, a process that is computationally prohibitive and slow, often resulting in complex model proliferation, a state known as "architecture hell."

# 1. The Business Problem

Enterprise communications must adhere to proprietary language, brand voice, and domain-specific jargon that general-purpose LLMs do not know. Full LLM fine-tuning for each business unit is prohibitively expensive and risks model proliferation. The challenge is to achieve domain accuracy and brand consistency at scale, across multiple isolated business units, without incurring the cost of full fine-tuning for each, while maintaining strict isolation between tenants so that one business unit's adapter cannot contaminate another's output.

# 2. The Governance Instrument

**Use Case:** UC4—domain-specific AI stylist and language adapter.

**Autonomy Level:** Level 2 (Workflow Automation).

**Criticality Tier:** Low.

**Required Oversight Model:** Human-Above-the-Loop (HAL)—periodic batch review of stylistic outputs for brand compliance and quality. The system is not generating regulated-domain content, but stylistic errors that undermine brand integrity require periodic human review before material publication commitments.

**Key Governance Control:**
**UAM Security Domain Mapping**: The EDS control that maps every authenticated user to a pre-authorized Security Domain and LoRA Adapter ID, preventing cross-tenant stylistic contamination at the orchestrator level, ensures the orchestrator maps authenticated users to their authorized Security Domain and LoRA Adapter ID before any inference is executed. An unauthorized adapter request is rejected before reaching the LLM backbone.

**Model Lineage Tracking**: Every request log captures the LoRA Adapter Version, Base LLM Backbone Version, and Fine-Tuning Data Set ID, enabling instant audited rollback if an adapter begins producing non-compliant output.

| GOVERNANCE STACK: UC4—Domain-Specific AI Stylist and Language Adapter | |
|---|---|
| **Instrument** | **Active Setting for This Deployment** |
| **Autonomy Level** | Level 2 (Workflow Automation). |
| **Criticality Tier** | Low. |
| **Oversight model** | HAL—periodic batch review of stylistic outputs for brand compliance and quality before material publication commitment. |
| **Delegation Note** | No regulated-domain content; batch review cycle determines cadence; no individual action approval required. |
| **Groundedness threshold** | No Groundedness Score threshold required at this tier; stylistic consistency validated by editorial batch review rather than automated scoring. |
| **DLAC enforcement** | UAM Security Domain Mapping: every user mapped to pre-authorized Security Domain and LoRA Adapter ID before inference; unauthorized adapter request rejected at orchestrator. |
| **Logging Standard** | Model Lineage Tracking: every request log captures LoRA Adapter Version, Base LLM Backbone Version, and Fine-Tuning Data Set ID for instant audited rollback. |
| **Chief AI Officer approval** | One-time deployment gate: CAIO sign-off required before go-live per Low Criticality Tier mandate. This is distinct from runtime oversight; no per-action approval applies (see Delegation Note). |
| **Cross-tenant risk** | UAM Security Domain Mapping prevents cross-tenant stylistic contamination; each tenant's adapter is inaccessible to all other tenants. |

## 3. The Technical Architecture

PEFT/LoRA Multi-tenant Stack with Shared LLM Backbone—LoRA adapters dynamically loaded at runtime by the orchestrator based on the authenticated user's Security Domain. Hybrid RAG + PEFT Adaptation Strategy—RAG handles factual grounding, LoRA handles stylistic modulation. Adapter affinity batching for latency optimization. Dynamic Adapter Loading APIs restricted to internal-only access. Full details in the "Architectural Delta" section below.

## 4. The Enhancement

**Adapter Affinity Batching**: The orchestrator leverages UAM Security Domain metadata (a governance function) to route concurrent requests requiring the same adapter to the same GPU instance, minimizing Time-to-First-Token (TTFT) latency. This is the primary example in this book of governance metadata driving performance optimization.

## 5. The Board Outcome

The board confirms that AI-generated outputs achieve consistent domain-specific accuracy and brand integrity across all business units, within defined quality and isolation thresholds. Every output is fully traceable to its originating LoRA Adapter Version, base model version, and training dataset, enabling complete model lineage transparency and audited rollback capability.

Governance assurance reports verify that UAM Security Domain Mapping has prevented all instances of cross-tenant contamination and that any attempted violations are logged, monitored, and escalated in accordance with board-defined risk tolerances. Periodic HAL reviews provide independent validation of stylistic compliance prior to material publication commitments.

The board receives regular reporting on quality metrics, exception rates, and rollback events, ensuring that personalization at scale operates within approved governance boundaries and maintains enterprise brand integrity.

## Governance Delta: UC4

The multi-tenant nature of the shared backbone introduces a critical security vulnerability: the risk of style cross-contamination or data bleed between isolated tenants (e.g., applying the aggressive marketing adapter to a sensitive HR request). This necessitates stringent governance controls enforced at the control plane.

## UAM Security Domain Mapping for Isolation

The UAM strategy hinges on mapping authenticated users directly to authorized Security Domains. Each domain is pre-associated with a specific, permitted LoRA Adapter ID (and version). At runtime, the orchestrator performs the domain-mapping lookup to ensure secure multi-tenant isolation.

If a user requests an adaptation outside their authorized domain, the orchestrator immediately intercepts and rejects the request before it reaches the LLM backbone. The orchestrator thus functions as the de facto security officer, ensuring that the stylistic modulation of the base LLM output is determined exclusively by the authorized adapter's governed weights. This is the HAL oversight model's precondition: batch review of stylistic outputs is only meaningful if the reviewer can trust that each output was generated by the correct adapter for that user's domain. Table 8-3 sets out the LoRA/PEFT governance requirements for multi-tenant isolation.

***Table 8-3.*** *LoRA/PEFT governance requirements for multi-tenant isolation*

| Governance Control | Architectural Enforcement Point | Primary Risk Mitigated | Compliance Rationale |
|---|---|---|---|
| Security Domain Mapping | LLM orchestrator (pre-inference routing check) | Unauthorized LoRA adapter application (multi-tenant data bleed/cross-contamination) | Enforces the principle of least privilege in a dynamic inference environment |
| Dynamic Adapter Loading APIs | Inference Serving Engine (internal API only) | Rogue model manipulation; unauthorized version loading | Centralizes security audits and prevents public exposure of configuration endpoints |
| PII masking/sanitization | Ingress/orchestrator layer | Data leakage to external LLM APIs (GDPR/CCPA violation) | Mandatory adherence to the Organizational Policy for External AI Risk |
| Model Lineage Tracking | Artifact Store/Governance Log Store | Non-auditable changes and irreproducible outputs | Ensures ability to reconstruct the exact model used for any historical output. Enables audited rollback |

## Model Lineage Enforcement and Audited Rollback

For compliance and transparency, the system must enforce meticulous Model Lineage Enforcement. The Governance/Audit Log must track the complete lineage for every request, including the LoRA Adapter Version, the Base LLM Backbone Version, and the Fine-Tuning Data Set ID used to train the adapter.

This auditable history is crucial for two reasons: first, it ensures that any historical output can be traced back to its exact creation environment; second, it enables an instant, audited rollback. In the event of a compliance failure (e.g., an adapter begins generating toxic language or a high hallucination rate), the orchestrator must be able to revert the deployment to a previously verified adapter version non-disruptively, maintaining business continuity.

Furthermore, to mitigate security risks associated with dynamically swapping adapters, the API endpoints that control dynamic loading must be strictly designated as internal-only, ensuring the orchestrator remains the single, audited point of control for runtime configuration changes.

## Architectural Delta: UC4

The core architectural innovation is the adoption of Parameter-Efficient Fine-Tuning (PEFT), specifically Low-Rank Adaptation (LoRA), as the singular scaling vector for stylistic personalization.

The Shared Backbone Efficiency is the operational delta: LoRA trains only small, low-rank adapter matrices that approximate the full weight updates, leaving the foundational LLM weights frozen. These small LoRA adapters (often a tiny fraction of the base model's size) are dynamically loaded and merged with the base model at runtime by specialized inference servers (such as vLLM). This design maximizes

GPU utilization by allowing thousands of fine-tuned variants to reside on a single, persistently loaded LLM backbone, drastically reducing overall hosting costs.

The LLM orchestrator functions as the central control plane for this multi-tenant inference environment. Its role is critical: it manages the complex workflow, integrates the RAG component for factual grounding, and enforces governance policies that determine which LoRA adapter to apply based on the authenticated user's identity. The orchestrator is the sole trusted entity authorized to manage dynamic loading, centralizing control and security.

The system uses a Hybrid RAG or PEFT Adaptation Strategy to maximize output quality. RAG is responsible for knowledge grounding and factual retrieval, providing robust support for users with limited data history (i.e., cold-start users). Simultaneously, LoRA parameter adaptations excel at refining stylistic output, tone, and domain-specific jargon.

## Enterprise Implication

UC4 demonstrates that governance metadata and performance optimization are not competing concerns; they are the same mechanism. UAM Security Domain Mapping is mandated as an isolation control; it also provides the metadata required for adapter affinity batching, thereby minimizing TTFT latency. The enterprise implication is that the orchestrator has evolved from a workflow coordinator to the central security enforcer of the inference environment: stateful, permission-aware, and the sole authorized point of control for runtime model configuration.

# Blueprint: UC5—Predictive Customer Insight and Proactive Service Support

Use Case 5 focuses on transforming customer service into a proactive, strategic function by anticipating customer needs before issues escalate. Customer issues frequently escalate because operational staff lack timely, contextual insights into related products, past issues, or the optimal next-best action, leading to reactive rather than proactive service. The goal is to deploy agentic AI–driven predictive insight models to enable proactive service (i.e., Next Best Experience, NBE), but this requires predictions to be delivered with ultra-low, millisecond latency during a live customer interaction.

## 1. The Business Problem

Customer service staff lack real-time, contextual insight into the optimal next action during live interactions. By the time data is retrieved from traditional batch-processed systems, the interaction has progressed, and the insight is stale. The result is a reactive service where escalations are managed rather than prevented. The objective is to enable the AI agent to recommend the Next Best Action (NBA) or Next Best Experience (NBE) during a live interaction, which requires predictions delivered at millisecond latency, a requirement that traditional data stacks cannot meet.

## 2. The Governance Instrument

**Use Case:** UC5—predictive customer insight and proactive service support.

**Autonomy Level:** Level 2 (Workflow Automation). Level 3 is a planned future state, not currently active.

**Criticality Tier:** High.

**Required Oversight Model:** Human-on-the-Loop (HOTL). A certified supervisor monitors agent recommendations in real time with active authority to override any recommended action before it is executed. The HITL Override Service provides the technical mechanism for this override.

**Key Governance Controls:**

**Delegated Authorization Service**: Intercepts every planned agent action and verifies that it is within the authenticated human agent's RBAC permissions before execution. This is the technical countermeasure against Excess Agency.

**Agent Scope Enforcement (Sandboxing)**: Hard functional and financial limits on agent autonomy.

**Mandatory XAI with Temporal Consistency**: Every recommendation is accompanied by a human-readable rationale grounded in the feature values that existed at the moment of prediction.

**GOVERNANCE STACK: UC5—Predictive Customer Insight and Proactive Service Support**

| Instrument | Active Setting for This Deployment |
|---|---|
| **Autonomy Level** | Level 2 (Level 3 planned, not yet active). |
| **Criticality Tier** | High. |
| **Oversight model** | HOTL—certified supervisor monitors agent recommendations in real time with active authority to override any recommended action before execution; HITL Override Service provides the technical override mechanism. |
| **Delegation Note** | Monitored—supervisor has live override at all times; no action committed without supervisory coverage; CRO sign-off required per High Criticality Tier. |

(*continued*)

**GOVERNANCE STACK: UC5—Predictive Customer Insight and Proactive Service Support**

| Instrument | Active Setting for This Deployment |
| --- | --- |
| **Groundedness threshold** | Mandatory XAI with temporal consistency: every recommendation accompanied by human-readable rationale grounded in feature values at the moment of prediction; point-in-time correctness enforced via Feature Store. |
| **DLAC enforcement** | Delegated Authorization Service intercepts every planned agent action and verifies it is within the authenticated human agent's RBAC permissions before execution; countermeasure against Excess Agency. |
| **Logging Standard** | Agent Scope Enforcement (Sandboxing) with hard financial limits; full Reasoning Trace Capture of agent recommendation logic; Immutable Audit Log capturing HOTL intervention or non-intervention attestation per decision. |
| **Autonomy escalation gate** | Level 3 is not yet active. Transition from Level 2 to Level 3 requires GMI Level 2 recertification and updated MDAM entry before any autonomous action capability is activated. |
| **CRO sign-off** | Required per High Criticality Tier; semi-annual audit obligation. |

# 3. The Technical Architecture

Streaming-first architecture (Kafka/Kinesis) for real-time data ingestion + Online Feature Store for millisecond-latency feature retrieval + Causal Recurrent Network (CRN) for NBE decisioning + Tool Schema Definition and Translation Layer for reliable agent-to-API communication + Delegated Authorization Service + HITL Override Service. Full details in the "Architectural Delta" section below.

## 4. The Enhancement

**Dynamic Reward Signal Ingestion**: The MLOps feedback loop captures operational outcomes (did the NBE intervention reduce churn?) as reward signals for the CRN's ongoing reinforcement learning (RL). The EDS framework classifies this reward signal as a governance artifact, not merely an ML parameter, because it defines what the model optimizes toward, and that optimization objective must remain within board-approved ethical and policy boundaries. It must be validated against policy-compliant outcomes to prevent the model from optimizing toward reward-maximizing but ethically problematic behaviors.

## 5. The Board Outcome

The board verifies that all AI-assisted and autonomous actions operate strictly within the authority boundaries of authenticated human agents, in accordance with board-approved autonomy and risk thresholds. Every agent-initiated action is validated through Delegated Authorization controls, ensuring that no action exceeds the human operator's permitted scope (Permission Mirroring).

Real-time HOTL supervision is continuously active, with all overrides, interventions, and exception events logged, reviewed, and escalated through established governance channels. Agent Scope Enforcement confirms that no financial or functional limits have been breached.

All recommendations are supported by explainable AI outputs grounded in point-in-time data, ensuring full auditability and regulatory defensibility. The board receives ongoing reporting on override rates, latency performance, and decision accuracy, providing assurance that proactive, low-latency service delivery is achieved without compromising accountability, compliance, or control.

## Governance Delta: UC5

The shift to autonomous, agent-driven action in a high-stakes environment introduces novel security and ethical risks, requiring explicit governance controls beyond traditional access management. The critical governance insight for UC5 is that the risk has shifted: the foundational RAG use cases have shifted focus to controlling what the AI is allowed to see (DLAC). UC5 focuses on controlling what the AI is allowed to do. This requires an entirely new class of governance control.

## Delegated Authorization Service

This service represents the paramount Governance Delta for autonomous systems. The risk of Excess Agency (introduced in Chapter 4), the condition where an AI agent attempts to execute an action that the authenticated human operator is not authorized to perform, arises when an AI agent, focused on maximizing a high predicted reward, attempts to execute an action (e.g., issuing a large credit to resolve a complaint) that falls outside the authenticated human agent's RBAC permissions.

The Delegated Authorization Service acts as a proxy layer, intercepting the LLM's planned API call and performing a dynamic check against the authenticated human agent's permissions. Only if the proposed action is within the human agent's defined scope is the API call allowed to proceed, enforcing both the principle of least privilege for the AI agent and compliance with established business policy. The EDS framework names this mechanism Permission Mirroring: the AI agent's executable authority at any moment is a precise mirror of, and can never exceed, the authenticated human's authorized scope. This is the required safeguard against the high-impact risk of unauthorized autonomous financial or system modification. This control is the technical implementation of Accountability Follows Authority (Principle 6 from Chapter 2): the AI agent cannot exercise authority that the authenticated human does not possess.

## Mandatory XAI and Temporal Consistency

For decisions that rely on predictive models, XAI is essential for building trust. The architecture mandates the use of an XAI Microservice (often using SHAP) to generate human-readable decision rationales.

This XAI output is tied directly to the data infrastructure via the Online Feature Store. The Feature Store provides point-in-time correctness, ensuring that the XAI explanation is linked to the precise feature values that existed at the moment of prediction. This temporal consistency is critical for regulatory auditability, as it proves the system's decision was based on current, verifiable facts. For the HOTL supervisor, this XAI output is the primary tool for deciding whether to intervene: the supervisor must be able to understand why the agent recommends a particular action, not merely observe the recommendation.

## Bias Mitigation, Sandboxing, and the HITL Override

To ensure ethical outcomes, a Fairness and Bias Mitigation Framework is mandated, requiring continuous auditing of predictive outputs (DNNs/CRNs) for disparate impact and the integration of debiasing strategies into the MLOps pipeline. Furthermore, ML Model Lineage Tracking is mandatory to ensure that all deployed models are linked to an immutable audit trail of their training data and code versions, enabling traceability for any bias finding.

To manage the risk of emergent or runaway behavior, Agent Scope Enforcement (Sandboxing) defines and enforces hard limits on the agent's functional and financial autonomy. Complementing this is the HITL Override Service. This service is a non-negotiable safety brake that provides a highest-priority mechanism for human supervisors to intervene, halt, or veto an agent's planned action in real time, with the human's rationale mandatorily logged for compliance review. This is the technical implementation of Principle 4 (Mandatory Halt Capability) in Chapter 2: the kill switch must operate independently of the system's decision logic.

# Architectural Delta: UC5

UC5 introduces two tightly coupled components: a streaming-first data ingestion architecture that eliminates batch processing from the prediction critical path and an Online Feature Store that serves millisecond-latency feature lookups to the real-time scoring engine.

## Streaming-First Architecture and the Online Feature Store

Achieving the millisecond-latency mandate requires abandoning batch processing in the critical path in favor of a streaming-first architecture for data ingestion (utilizing platforms like Kafka or Kinesis).

The crucial Architectural Delta is the Online Feature Store. This store is designed to retain only the latest feature values and must support real-time predictions with low-millisecond-latency reads and high throughput. By serving pre-computed and real-time features from in-memory systems, the Online Feature Store eliminates the performance bottlenecks associated with traditional analytical databases, ensuring that contextual information is instantly available to predictive models.

## Specialized Predictive Models and Tooling

The architecture employs specialized deep learning models, such as Causal Recurrent Networks (CRNs), derived from reinforcement learning (RL) approaches, for NBE decisioning. Unlike simple classification models, these models learn by maximizing a reward function associated with their actions. This advanced capability necessitates an MLOps architecture that continuously captures and ingests operational outcomes (e.g., did the intervention successfully reduce churn?) as dynamic reward signals, which are vital for the model's ongoing learning and support self-improving workflows.

To enable the agent to reliably translate its reasoning into external actions (tool calling), a defensive architectural layer is mandatory: the Tool Schema Definition and Translation Layer. This layer standardizes the interface between the LLM's goal-oriented reasoning and complex enterprise APIs. It ensures that tool definitions adhere to robust standards (i.e., OpenAPI or JSON Schema) and that the agent receives reliable, structured output, thereby maximizing the accuracy of autonomous execution and securing documented efficiency gains.

## Enterprise Implication

UC5 completes the governance evolution across the three use cases. UC3 governs what the model retrieves. UC4 governs how the model generates. UC5 governs what the model does. The Delegated Authorization Service enforces Permission Mirroring: the AI agent's executable authority is a precise mirror of the authenticated human's scope, never exceeding it. The enterprise implication is that point-in-time correctness in the Online Feature Store is not merely a performance feature; it is an auditability guarantee that ensures every XAI explanation is grounded in the precise data state at the moment of the recommendation, satisfying the temporal consistency requirement for regulatory defensibility.

# Policy Enforcement: The Optimization Handshake

Across UC3, UC4, and UC5, the Architectural Deltas differ, but the governance enforcement model does not: the PDP evaluates every policy-relevant decision, and the PEP executes it. This separation of evaluation from execution is the constitutional constant that makes the EDS framework agnostic to the underlying tech stack; the same Authority Matrix governs a contradiction flag, an adapter load, and a tool call with equal precision.

## Specialized Evaluation Using PDP

The PDP evaluates the specialized attributes of the optimized transaction. For a personalization request, it validates the Security Domain Mapping against the LoRA adapter registry. For a predictive action, it assesses the proposed tool call against the authority rules. The PDP provides the analytical verdict that determines whether the optimized path is policy-compliant.

## Specialized Execution Through PEP

The PEP receives the PDP verdict and physically manages the optimized execution. In the PEFT stack, the PEP handles the dynamic loading of the authorized adapter and manages the affinity batching queues. In the predictive model, the PEP intercepts and blocks unauthorized API calls. The PEP also ensures that every specialized event, from a semantic contradiction flag to a dynamic adapter load, is captured in the Immutable Audit Log with a corresponding Execution ID (the session/task identifier that threads all log entries for a single workflow into a complete, ordered audit trail).

Figure 8-1 illustrates the unified specialized governance architecture across UC3, UC4, and UC5. The Authority Matrix gates all execution paths via PDP verdict; the RBVE and CD-Module validate source integrity before the orchestrator (PEP) coordinates the LoRA Adapter Store, routes actions through the Tool Schema Translation layer for Delegated Authorization checks, and releases the augmented prompt to the Shared LLM Backbone. The Online Feature Store supplies predictive features to the NBE Decision Engine; generated outputs route to the Decision Reviewer with XAI rationale from the XAI Microservice; and the knowledge refinement loop closes by feeding index refinement signals back to the Authority Matrix.

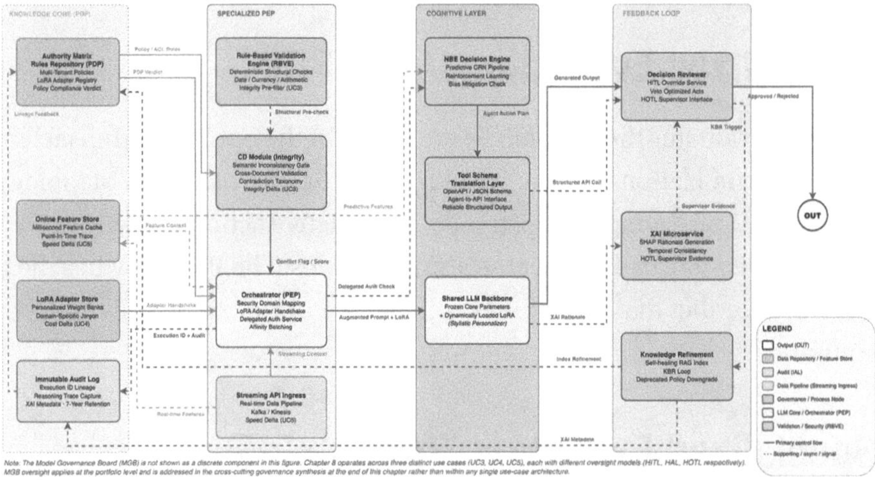


***Figure 8-1.*** *The specialized governance architecture—unified enforcement flow across the Knowledge Core (PDP), specialized PEP, Cognitive Layer, and feedback loop, integrating the Rule-Based Validation Engine, CD-Module, orchestrator (PEP), Shared LLM Backbone, NBE Decision Engine, Tool Schema Translation layer, Streaming API Ingress, XAI Microservice, Decision Reviewer, and knowledge refinement across UC3, UC4, and UC5*

## Measuring the Impact of Industrialized Personalization

Each optimization delta must be measurable in terms that the board can act on. Governance investment without a quantified outcome is a policy aspiration; with it, the board can verify that the delta is performing within approved risk and performance boundaries and authorize continued scaling.

## Model Lineage and Audited Rollback

The architecture supports Model Lineage Tracking, recording the exact adapter version and base model used for every output. This enables an audited rollback mechanism, allowing the organization to revert to a previously verified state if an optimized adapter begins producing non-compliant or toxic content.

## Accuracy and Latency SLOs

The system monitors specialized compliance Service-Level Objectives. For integrity use cases, the metric is the Contradiction Resolution Rate. For predictive use cases, the focus shifts to latency, using a P95 Latency threshold, a performance metric indicating that 95% of requests complete faster than a specified time. These metrics provide the board with the proof that the system is not only fast and cost-effective but also operates with a level of precision that exceeds manual human capabilities.

# Summary

This chapter established that enterprise-grade generative AI requires governance that is tailored to each architectural augmentation, not governance applied uniformly after the fact. UC3, UC4, and UC5 each introduce a distinct performance optimization, and each optimization introduces a distinct risk that demands a correspondingly precise Governance Delta. The oversight model, HITL, HAL, or HOTL, is the first governance decision in each blueprint, not the last. The key takeaways are as follows:

- **UC3 (Document Quality): Governance shifts left to source integrity.** The CD-Module and KBR ensure that contradictory evidence never reaches the Cognitive Layer. The Governance Delta, Constrained RBAC with SoD and mandatory XAI logging, addresses the specific risk that the HITL correction loop itself becomes a vector for ground-truth manipulation. A knowledge base governed by UC3 is a certified system of record: every conflict resolution is traceable to a named, SoD-compliant human approver, and every AI flag is defensible via verifiable XAI rationale.
- **UC4 (Stylistic Adaptation): Governance metadata drives performance.** UAM Security Domain Mapping is mandated as an isolation control; it also provides the metadata required for adapter affinity batching, thereby minimizing TTFT latency. This is the clearest example in the EDS framework of governance and performance optimization being the same mechanism. The orchestrator is elevated to the central security enforcer of the inference environment—stateful, permission-aware, and the sole authorized point of control for runtime model configuration.

- **UC5 (Predictive Service): Governance shifts from data access to action authority.** The Delegated Authorization Service enforces Permission Mirroring: the AI agent's executable authority is a precise mirror of the authenticated human's scope and can never exceed it. Point-in-time correctness in the Online Feature Store ensures that every XAI explanation is grounded in the precise data state at the moment of the recommendation, satisfying the temporal consistency requirement for regulatory defensibility while delivering millisecond-latency service.

The three use cases in this chapter complete the RAG deployment spectrum. In each case, the governance architecture expanded incrementally; new controls were mandated with each architectural augmentation, but the foundational posture held: a human remained responsible for every consequential action, and the AI's role was to synthesize, recommend, or optimize within a governed retrieval pipeline. The next chapter does not extend that posture. It replaces it. The shift from retrieval to agency is a constitutional event, not a technical upgrade. For the first time in this book, the system acts without waiting for human confirmation. That single change invalidates every assumption in the conventional delegation model and demands a new class of board instrument before a single agent enters production.

# PART IV

# The Frontier with Agentic and Autonomous AI

## CHAPTER 9

# Agentic Paradigm Shift

Chapters 1–8 established the governance architecture for RAG systems: deployments in which the AI synthesizes and presents information and a human remains responsible for every consequential action. This chapter crosses the threshold from retrieval to agency: autonomous agents that plan, execute, and coordinate actions across enterprise systems without waiting for human confirmation of each step. This transition does not merely extend the prior governance framework; it demands a new constitutional instrument. A RAG deployment requires an Autonomy Level, a Criticality Tier, and an oversight model. An agentic deployment requires all three and additionally a formally quantified, board-authorized scope of decision authority—domain by domain, magnitude by magnitude—before the first production action is executed.

The governance challenge is structural, not technical. Human delegation frameworks set financial limits and approval thresholds for individual roles. Agentic systems break every assumption in that model: they execute thousands of decisions per hour, act across multiple domains simultaneously, and reach financial thresholds that would require board-level human approval within seconds. Conventional controls cannot contain this exposure. The chapter introduces the Machine Decision Authority Matrix, the board instrument that authorizes which domains agents may act in and to what extent, and the Autonomy Budget, the


M. M. Hossain and A. A. N. Ponnusamy, *Governance-First AI*,
https://doi.org/10.1007/979-8-8688-3118-8_9

portfolio-level ceiling on total delegated machine authority (Hossain, *The Autonomy Budget*, 2026) that prevents the invisible concentration of institutional authority in production AI systems. For the board and the chief executive, this is the transition from machine assistance to machine agency: a shift that demands explicit, measurable, board-authorized limits on what machines may do.

Six architectural controls distinguish an agentic deployment from every prior chapter's blueprint: the four-dimensional decision authority scoring methodology that determines each agent's Autonomy Level and Delegation Tier; ZTAI for non-human identities; the Delegated Authorization Service enforcing Permission Mirroring; PaC delivering real-time Governance-as-a-Service; the Orchestration-based Saga Pattern for distributed transactional integrity; and Reasoning Trace Capture making the agent's Think–Act–Observe loop non-repudiably auditable.

The chapter follows the Machine Decision Authority sections, scoring methodology, Authority Matrix, Autonomy Budget, and five-level classification, with the Agentic Delta covering the four architectural layers: Agent Core, Tooling and Actuation, Orchestration, and Transactional Integrity. Governance sections then cover ZTAI identity, Delegated Authorization, real-time PaC enforcement, safety-critical consensus, and the HITL override. The chapter closes with four mandatory Key Risk Indicators (KRIs) and the six non-negotiable deployment conditions.

**Governance Leaders and Board Members:** The Machine Decision Authority Matrix, Autonomy Budget, and five-level classification are your constitutional instruments—read these sections before authorizing any agentic deployment.

**Architects and Practitioners:** The Agentic Delta covering the four architectural layers is your technical specification; the scoring methodology and Authority Matrix entry are preconditions you must complete before that work begins.

## Machine Decision Authority: Governing the Delegation of Autonomous Action

Every governance control described in this chapter, the PEP, the Delegated Authorization Service, the Agent Scope Enforcement mechanism, and the HITL Override Service, operates within a boundary that must be formally defined before deployment. That boundary is the decision authority scope: the domains in which the agent is permitted to act, the maximum magnitude of any single action, and the oversight model that applies. Without an explicit, board-authorized scope of decision authority, every governance control in this chapter is technically functional but constitutionally ungrounded.

## Quantifying Machine Decision Authority

To govern what an autonomous system is permitted to do, the enterprise must first assess the extent of institutional authority it is being asked to exercise. The EDS framework formalizes this assessment as the Autonomous Decision Authority Evaluation (ADAE): a four-dimensional scoring methodology that produces a composite score used to assign each agent's Autonomy Level and Delegation Tier. Decision authority exposure is measured across four dimensions that together capture the scope and impact of what the agent can do. The dimensions and their weightings are technical in character; practitioners will apply them during deployment scoring, and the board will authorize the resulting Autonomy Level and Authority Matrix entry. Both audiences should read what follows with their respective roles in mind:

## DIMENSION 1: FINANCIAL AUTHORITY (WEIGHT: 40%)

*The maximum financial commitment or exposure the system can create or authorize for a single decision or action. This is the most directly comparable dimension to existing human delegation frameworks. A system that approves individual low-value customer refunds has a fundamentally different authority profile from a system that can authorize six-figure commercial payments.*

**Architectural Implication:** The maximum action magnitude, the single-transaction ceiling on the authority a registered system may exercise without human confirmation, must be set at the infrastructure level and technically enforced, not only policy-declared. An agent whose system-level financial limit can be overridden by its own reasoning is ungovernable.

## DIMENSION 2: CUSTOMER REACH (WEIGHT: 30%)

*The maximum number of customers or external parties who could be materially affected by a single decision or by a systematic error in the system's operation. A system that makes individual credit decisions has a different governance profile from a system whose model error could affect 100,000 customers through a repricing action.*

**Architectural Implication:** Customer reach is assessed on the broader of two measures, the per-decision reach and the systematic-error reach. A system that makes individual decisions but could affect 50,000 customers through a model failure is assessed at the broader population. This dimension directly governs the mandatory oversight model: high customer reach at any Autonomy Level requires more intensive supervision.

## DIMENSION 3: OPERATIONAL REACH (WEIGHT: 20%)

*The breadth and depth of enterprise systems the agent can access: how many systems it can read from and write to and the criticality of those systems. A system confined to read-only access on two non-critical internal systems poses fundamentally different governance risk from one with write access across core banking, payments, and regulatory reporting infrastructure.*

**Architectural Implication:** Operational reach governs the scope of the Delegated Authorization Service's Permission Mirroring check. The agent's permissible actions must be technically constrained to the systems and operations included in the board-authorized authority scope, not merely policy-limited.

## DIMENSION 4: DECISION VELOCITY (WEIGHT: 10%)

*The rate at which the system executes consequential autonomous decisions. This is the dimension most distinctive to agentic AI: a system that can execute 10,000 decisions per minute has an exposure profile that a conventional delegation framework cannot capture with a single financial limit. At high velocity, human oversight of individual decisions is structurally impossible; governance must operate through system design constraints and automated circuit breakers.*

**Architectural Implication:** Decision velocity governs the minimum intensity of automated anomaly detection. At moderate-to-high velocity, circuit breakers that halt or limit decision-making based on statistical distribution anomalies are governance necessities, not optional enhancements. This dimension corresponds directly to the Decision Velocity Risk category established in Chapter 3's risk taxonomy; the scoring methodology quantifies velocity exposure to determine system classification, while the risk category names the governance challenge that high velocity creates: at sufficient scale, human oversight of individual decisions becomes structurally impossible, and governance must operate through system design constraints instead.

The dimension weights (40%, 30%, 20%, 10%) reflect the relative governance impact of each dimension in regulated enterprise environments, as established through the framework's development. Financial Authority carries the highest weight because financial exposure is the most directly comparable to existing human delegation frameworks and the most immediately auditable. Customer Reach is weighted second because systematic errors scale directly with population exposure: a flawed decision affecting one customer is an incident; the same decision affecting ten thousand is a regulatory event. Operational Reach is third because it determines blast radius; write access across multiple enterprise systems amplifies the consequence of any single erroneous action. Decision Velocity carries the lowest weight because its primary governance response is automated circuit breaking rather than human judgment; the SRE intervenes before volume becomes a risk, reducing the need for a higher weighting. Organizations may adjust these weights subject to board approval and documented rationale for deviation, provided the total remains 100%, and the adjusted weighting is recorded in the relevant Authority Matrix entry.

**Worked Example**: The following example uses the IT service resolution agent (UC6), whose full governance blueprint appears in Chapter 10. Readers who have not yet read Chapter 10 may treat UC6 here as an illustrative agentic deployment with write access across Active Directory, ServiceNow, and the CMDB; the figures below are drawn from that blueprint and are used solely to demonstrate the scoring methodology. Consider the IT service resolution agent (UC6). It is assessed as follows: Financial Authority 30 (low per-action cost, but cumulative with volume), Customer Reach 20 (affects internal staff only), Operational

Reach 50 (write access across Active Directory, ServiceNow, and the CMDB), and Decision Velocity 70 (high-volume, continuous execution). Applying the weights: (30 × 0.40) + (20 × 0.30) + (50 × 0.20) + (70 × 0.10) = 12 + 6 + 10 + 7 = 35. This composite score of 35 places UC6 at Autonomy Level 3 (Supervised tier), requiring HOTL oversight and a board-authorized Authority Matrix entry before production deployment. The score also contributes 35 points toward the organization's total Autonomy Budget utilization, which is monitored against the board-approved portfolio ceiling (set at 900 in this book's illustrative architecture; organizations set their own ceiling based on risk appetite and governance maturity; Chapter 12 details the phased roadmap through which that ceiling is set and maintained). This 35-point contribution is not a fixed, one-time allocation that persists for the system's lifetime. An ADAE score is a living value: it is recalculated whenever the system's authority materially changes (a change to financial authority limits, e.g., mandates recalculation within five business days) and is reassessed at the periodic register reconciliation. UC6's contribution to budget utilization, therefore, tracks its current ADAE score rather than remaining fixed at its initial value.

# The Machine Decision Authority Matrix

The four dimensions above produce a composite decision authority score for each deployed agent. This score determines the system's Autonomy Level and Delegation Tier. But the score alone does not authorize the agent to act. Authorization requires a board instrument.

The Machine Decision Authority Matrix (referred to in this chapter as the Authority Matrix) is the formal board instrument through which decision authority is delegated to autonomous systems across defined organizational domains. It sits between the board's risk appetite and the individual system's authority score. No autonomous system may operate in a domain not covered by a board-authorized Authority Matrix entry, regardless of how well its technical architecture is governed.

The Authority Matrix governs at the portfolio and domain level. It specifies which operational domains are authorized for machine decision-making, the maximum decision authority permitted in each domain, the oversight model required for each domain, and the aggregate ceiling on total delegated machine authority across all production systems. This aggregate ceiling, expressed as a board-set budget of decision authority points, is a constitutional constraint. Management cannot exceed it without a Full Board resolution, regardless of the business case or commercial pressure.

The per-system maximum action magnitude, the single-transaction ceiling on what any individual system may authorize without human confirmation, is set by the CAIO within each Authority Matrix–authorized domain, at or below the domain limit. This per-system limit must be enforced at the infrastructure level, not merely declared in policy.

These two constraints, the Authority Matrix and the Autonomy Budget, are deliberately distinct because they prevent two different governance failures that neither constraint can address alone. The Authority Matrix prevents a single system from exceeding its domain-level limit: it governs individual system behavior, ensuring no agent acts beyond what the board has explicitly authorized in its specific operational domain. But a system can be fully compliant with its Authority Matrix entry while the organization's aggregate exposure across all production agents approaches an unacceptable level, a portfolio risk that no individual system limit can detect. The Autonomy Budget prevents this: it caps total delegated machine authority across the entire agentic estate, ensuring the board retains visibility and control over how much institutional authority has been collectively delegated to machines. The failure mode that the Matrix prevents is unauthorized action by a single system. The failure mode the Budget prevents is the invisible concentration of machine authority at the portfolio level, a risk that only becomes visible when all systems are measured together. Both constraints must be monitored simultaneously:

a new deployment can be within its Matrix entry while pushing portfolio utilization above the board's approved ceiling, which is a governance breach even if the individual system is impeccably governed.

## Five Autonomy Levels and Three Delegation Tiers

Every registered agentic AI system is assigned an Autonomy Level from 1 to 5, based on its decision authority score and governance configuration. Each Autonomy Level maps to a Delegation Tier, a named governance band (Supervised, Monitored, or Delegated) that determines the intensity of oversight controls applied to the system. The Autonomy Level determines the mandatory governance controls that apply and the maximum authority the system may exercise without human confirmation. Table 9-1 sets out the five Autonomy Levels and their Delegation Tiers, with the governance requirements and oversight obligations for each. Figure 9-1 shows governance intensity escalating across the five Autonomy Levels, mapping ADAE score ranges to Autonomy Level assignments and the three Delegation Tiers.

***Table 9-1.*** *Autonomy Levels and Delegation Tiers—governance requirements and oversight obligations across the five-level classification*

| Level—Name | Description | Delegation Tier |
|---|---|---|
| 1—Assistive AI | The system surfaces recommendations; a human confirms every material output before it takes effect. The system does not take consequential actions autonomously. | Supervised; basic governance infrastructure required; human review of decision output at least monthly. |

(*continued*)

***Table 9-1.*** *(continued)*

| Level—Name | Description | Delegation Tier |
|---|---|---|
| 2—Workflow Automation | The system executes defined actions within a constrained scope; human review occurs at regular intervals or for exceptions above a defined threshold. Individual decisions are not confirmed by a human, but the decision stream is monitored. | Supervised; kill switch required and tested quarterly; maximum action magnitude capped at domain-authorized limit. |
| 3—Supervised Autonomous Agents | The system operates with significant autonomy across a broader scope. A certified Human-on-the-Loop supervisor monitors outputs in real or near real time with authority to intervene at any point. | Monitored; HOTL supervisor mandatory during all operational hours; automated anomaly detection required; kill-switch capability within 60 seconds. |
| 4—Autonomous Execution Within Defined Limits | The system operates with high autonomy across a critical domain. Human oversight operates at the system level: the supervisor monitors decision distributions, anomalies, and operational parameters rather than individual decisions. | Delegated; HAL-certified supervisor required; kill switch within 30 seconds; Board Risk Committee approval for maximum action magnitude. |
| 5—Multi-agent Orchestration | The highest degree of autonomy currently permitted. Governance operates through system design constraints, automated circuit breakers, board-level reporting, and strategic-level oversight. | Delegated; Full Board approval required for Authority Matrix entry; dedicated supervision team; monthly board notification of system performance. |

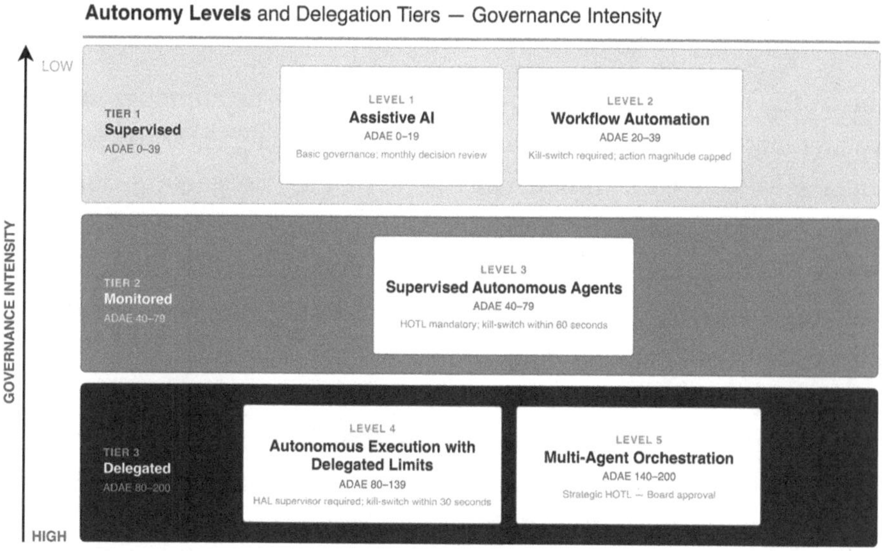


***Figure 9-1.** Autonomy Levels and Delegation Tiers—governance intensity escalating across the five-level classification, showing the relationship between ADAE (Autonomous Decision Authority Evaluation) score ranges, Autonomy Level assignments, and the three Delegation Tiers (Supervised, Monitored, Delegated)*

The Delegation Tier determines the intensity of governance oversight applied to a system. Tier assignment follows automatically from Autonomy Level classification. Management cannot negotiate the tier or substitute alternative governance arrangements without a formal change to the Autonomy Level. The Critical-tier endorsement referenced in the Level 4 and Level 5 rows of Table 9-1 and the HAL certification pathway it constitutes are formally defined in Chapter 11, which establishes the full HOTL Certification Framework including program requirements, the five sequential certification components, span-of-control thresholds, and annual renewal obligations.

## Shift from Retrieval to Action

The critical distinction between a RAG Co-Pilot and an autonomous agent is actuation: the ability to take consequential action on enterprise systems, not merely to inform a human who then acts. A RAG system provides grounded information; the human operator controls every subsequent action. An autonomous agent is a goal-oriented system that plans, selects tools, executes API calls, and maintains state across multi-step workflows, often without waiting for human confirmation of each step.

This capacity for self-directed action fundamentally expands the enterprise risk profile. Recent experimental evidence reinforces the point: delegating tasks to AI can increase dishonest behavior, and machine agents proved far more likely than human agents to carry out fully unethical instructions, an effect that prohibitive, task-specific guardrails could curb but not eliminate (Köbis et al., 2025). By 2028, Gartner predicts that at least 15% of day-to-day work decisions will be made autonomously through agentic AI, up from 0% in 2024, with 33% of enterprise software applications incorporating agentic AI (Gartner, Gartner Identifies the Top 10 Strategic Technology Trends for 2025, 2024); the same body of research projects that over 40% of agentic AI projects will be canceled by end of 2027 due to inadequate risk controls (Gartner, Gartner Predicts Over 40% of Agentic AI Projects Will Be Canceled by End of 2027, 2025), underscoring the urgency of establishing robust, real-time governance controls before deployment, not after. The architectural focus must shift from ensuring information quality (governance of the knowledge base) to enforcing operational boundaries (governance of action execution). And the governance instrument must shift from the Autonomy Register entry alone to an Authority Matrix–authorized domain entry that specifies the scope of decision authority before the agent's first production action.

## Challenge of Emergent Behavior and Unpredictability

A RAG Co-Pilot's primary risk is hallucination, a factual error or knowledge gap, which is primarily mitigated by the Faithfulness (Groundedness) Score and mandatory citation (as established in Chapter 5). The autonomous agent introduces a higher-order risk: emergent behavior and unchecked action.

The LLM core lacks the inherent continuity of human decision-making, which limits its predictability in extended reasoning or collaborative problem-solving, even when well-intentioned. The moment an agent gains tooling access, the ability to act on enterprise systems, its potential blast radius expands dramatically. Autonomous actions can lead to catastrophic failure modes, including financial loss (UC9, UC12), unauthorized data modification (UC6, UC7), security breaches through autonomous privilege escalation, or safety compromises in critical infrastructure (UC13, UC15).

Therefore, the core purpose of agent governance shifts entirely. It moves from mitigating knowledge risk (what the system says) to controlling actuation risk (what the system does). These strategic imperatives mandate the implementation of new controls, specifically PaC and Delegated Authorization, which are architecturally separated from the LLM core to guarantee deterministic enforcement. This is the same architectural principle introduced in Chapter 2 as the Deterministic Shell: the non-deterministic LLM reasoning component, referred to in this and subsequent chapters as the Cognitive Layer, is bounded by deterministic governance controls that enforce policy regardless of the model's reasoning. In the agentic context, this separation is expressed as the Cognitive Layer, comprising the Agent Core, an LLM augmented by ReAct-structured planning and specialized memory subsystems (Episodic Memory for situation awareness, Long-Term Memory for semantic recall), operating within the Authority Matrix domain bounds. This separates the Cognitive Layer from the Deterministic Core, which comprises transactional APIs, business rules engines, and the Tool Schema Definition and Translation Layer. This core standardizes model-to-system interfaces and eliminates hallucination of critical API parameters during autonomous execution. These controls operate within a boundary defined by the Authority Matrix, not set by the controls themselves.

## From Reactive Auditing to Real-Time Enforcement

To manage the systemic risks associated with autonomous systems, GRC must transition from passive, retrospective auditing to an active, real-time enforcement model, often referred to as Governance-as-a-Service (GaaS). The objective is to enforce compliance before an unauthorized action can be committed.

PaC is the technical mechanism that underpins GaaS, delivering a scalable, auditable framework for enforcement. PaC systems evaluate decisions before execution, blocking violations in real time, a critical advancement over traditional compliance tools that rely on periodic checks. This approach ensures that governance provides the essential "ethical compass and steering wheel" to guide autonomous agents, keeping them accountable, transparent, and aligned with human values and laws. PaC relies on declarative policies (e.g., Rego for the Open Policy Agent, OPA) to specify rules, simplifying complex authorization logic and enabling governance to be traceable and versioned.

Table 9-2 compares the governance architecture of a RAG Co-Pilot with that of an autonomous agent and identifies the new Authority Matrix column that applies only to agentic deployments.

***Table 9-2.*** *Key Architectural and Governance Deltas for RAG Co-Pilot vs. autonomous agent*

| **Dimension** | **RAG Co-Pilot (Chapter 7 Baseline)** | **Autonomous Agent (Chapter 9 Paradigm)** |
|---|---|---|
| Primary goal | Knowledge synthesis and factual grounding | Goal execution and actuation (tool use) |
| Core risk | Hallucination and data leakage | Emergent behavior and unchecked action |
| Identity requirement | User Access Management/ RBAC | ZTAI/non-human identity |
| Decision integrity | Groundedness (Faithfulness) Score | PaC (e.g., PDP/PEP) and Ensemble Consensus |
| Accountability | Source citation and Immutable Audit Log | Reasoning Trace Capture (ReAct logic) |
| Actuation control | N/A (human required for action) | Delegated Authorization Service and Agent Scope Enforcement |
| Authority instrument | Autonomy Register entry (Autonomy Level + oversight model) | Authority Matrix domain entry: board-<br>authorized scope, maximum action magnitude, and domain limits |

With the governance instrument and constitutional boundary established, the following sections detail the architectural components that operationalize agentic authority within those bounds.

# Agentic Delta

The Agentic Delta comprises the components necessary to transform the foundational LLM into a reliable, stateful operational entity. These architectural additions focus on implementing rigorous planning mechanisms, sophisticated memory management, and robust protocols for transactional integrity. This section details the Agent Core, covering reasoning and memory; the Tooling and Actuation layer for external API invocation; the different orchestration models; and the need for mechanisms to ensure transactional integrity in multi-step workflows.

## Agent Core

The functional core of any enterprise agent is an LLM augmented by dedicated planning and memory structures. This core enables the agent to systematically decompose complex objectives through structured reasoning and planning and maintain context across extended workflows via specialized memory subsystems.

### Reasoning and Planning

Effective autonomous operation requires the agent to systematically decompose complex objectives into executable steps. The preferred technique for achieving this cognitive function is the Reasoning and Action (ReAct) paradigm. ReAct enforces a structured, iterative workflow known as the Think–Act–Observe loop:

- The agent first generates an internal Thought to reason slowly about the high-level goal and potential next steps, enhancing its internal context.

- It then commits to an Action (calling an external tool). Before any tool call is executed, the Policy Enforcement Point intercepts the planned action and validates it against the Authority Matrix limits and Policy Decision Point.
- Following tool execution, the resulting data is processed as an Observation, which informs the next iterative Thought.

This systematic reasoning process minimizes the likelihood of linear failure and prevents the agent from engaging in expensive circular reasoning loops. For this structured reasoning to be auditable, the prompt design must explicitly enforce the structure, often using distinct tags such as "Thought: ...", followed by "Action: ..." and "Action Input: ...". This is foundational for the subsequent requirement of Reasoning Trace Capture.

## Memory Subsystems for Stateful Execution

The inherent discontinuity of LLMs means they struggle to carry context across extended reasoning chains. To overcome this and enable complex, long-running enterprise tasks, a specialized memory architecture is mandatory.

The system distinguishes between two primary memory types:

- **Episodic Memory** stores context about the agent's current situation, maintaining the history of interactions and the immediate state of the active plan (UC10). This short-term memory is critical for session-aware execution in multi-turn conversational workflows, such as dynamic pricing negotiation or step-by-step IT troubleshooting (UC6, UC10).

- **Long-Term Memory** leverages the external vector store (the RAG knowledge base established in Chapter 4) to retain and recall the agent's past behaviors, thoughts, policies, and proprietary data over extended periods. This semantic recall provides the deep contextual grounding necessary for the agent to function as a domain expert (UC6, UC7).

## Tooling and Actuation Layer

The enterprise value of an autonomous agent is directly proportional to its ability to securely and reliably invoke external tools (APIs) to take action. This layer requires specific defenses to mitigate actuation risk and ensure the agent can reliably communicate with and control enterprise systems.

### Tool Schema Definition and Translation Layer

Standard enterprise APIs are often designed without LLM consumption in mind, featuring complex, verbose input schemas that can lead to misinterpretation, parsing errors, or the hallucination of critical parameters by the agent. To mitigate this actuation risk, a specialized architectural defense is required.

A Tool Schema Definition and Translation Layer must standardize the interface. This defensive layer ensures that tool definitions conform to robust, predictable standards (such as OpenAPI or JSON Schema). By providing the LLM with a clear, well-documented interface, the accuracy of autonomous execution is maximized, and efficiency gains are secured (UC5, UC6). If the agent can reliably interpret the API schema, the probability of execution failure due to miscommunication between the Cognitive Layer and the Deterministic Core is drastically reduced.

## MCP and Centralized Governance

The Model Context Protocol (MCP) is an evolving standard that centralizes the definition and execution of tools, decoupling tool management from the application logic (the agent itself).

For enterprise deployments, the MCP Server should be architected using an enterprise API Management Gateway. This central architectural choice provides significant strategic value: the gateway handles authentication, authorization, and unified logging. Crucially, it serves as the necessary centralized point for delegated, scoped authorization. This shielding mechanism ensures internal systems are protected and enables dynamic policy enforcement based on cryptographic workload identity. The gateway also enforces the maximum action magnitude limit specified in the Authority Matrix entry: no single tool call may exceed the per-system financial authority ceiling, regardless of what the agent's reasoning concludes is optimal.

## Orchestration Models

The selection of an appropriate orchestration model, single-agent or multi-agent system (SAS/MAS), is determined by the complexity, domain scope, and required fault tolerance of the business task.

Single-agent architectures are suitable for linear, sequential tasks focused on immediate resolution, such as the autonomous IT service resolution agent (UC6) and the hotel dynamic pricing agent (UC10). These rely on a single-core reasoning loop (ReAct) to manage planning and execution.

Multi-agent systems (MASs) are mandatory for complex, multi-domain problem-solving that requires specialized expertise and distributed coordination, such as the end-to-end insurance claims agent (UC7) or predictive maintenance for defense equipment agent (UC13, UC15).

- **Structure:** A MAS uses collaboration among specialized, autonomous agents (e.g., Condition Monitoring Agent, Logistics Risk Agent, Work Order Agent), orchestrated by a central supervisor or Orchestrator Agent. The supervisor manages high-level task planning, delegates sub-tasks to specialists, and synthesizes the resulting outputs into a coherent final decision.
- **Benefit:** The MAS design offers superior scalability, modularity, and fault tolerance because dedicated entities handle specialized functions (like logistics risk assessment or audit compliance). This distributed problem-solving approach enhances system reliability in high-stakes environments. The agents can form hierarchical structures, with leading agents managing sub-agents while appearing as a single entity, a nested orchestration structure in which each agent simultaneously governs its own sub-agents while operating as part of a higher-level orchestration. In a MAS deployment, each agent in the orchestration must have its own registered decision authority scope; the aggregate authority of the orchestration is the sum of the individual agents' scopes, and that aggregate must fall within the Authority Matrix authorization for the domain.

## Ensuring Transactional Integrity

The autonomous execution of high-stakes, multi-step transactions, such as a seat upgrade (UC12) or an insurance claims payment (UC7), introduces the challenge of maintaining data consistency across independent microservices. This is known as the distributed transaction problem.

Traditional database guarantees are ineffective across distributed services. If an agent-initiated Step 1 (e.g., reserving a new seat) succeeds but a subsequent Step 3 (payment capture) fails, the system enters an inconsistent, high-risk state. This critical vulnerability is the compensation imperative: the lack of isolation in distributed systems must be solved by a robust, guaranteed recovery mechanism.

The Orchestration-based Saga Pattern is the mandated model for achieving transactional integrity and safe recovery in these autonomous, high-value workflows.

- **Function:** The Saga Pattern decomposes the complex transaction into a sequence of smaller, independently committed local transactions (e.g., Inventory, Pricing, Payment).
- **Compensation Logic:** If any step fails, the central Saga Orchestrator executes predetermined compensating transactions to undo all preceding successful changes, guaranteeing eventual consistency and a safe, auditable rollback.
- **Idempotency:** All steps, including forward actions and compensation logic, must be defined as idempotent commands. This ensures that retrying a failed operation (a necessary component of resilience) does not result in unintended side effects, such as double-charging the customer or double-voiding a ticket.

The Orchestration style is mandatory over the Choreography style because it provides a centralized coordinator that tracks the overall transaction state, issues commands, and, most importantly, maintains explicit state tracking and clear auditability for financial and data integrity

(UC7, UC12). Every step in the Saga must be validated by the Policy Enforcement Point before execution; the Saga Orchestrator cannot bypass the decision authority controls simply because it is executing a compensation transaction.

The Saga Orchestrator's execution of compensating transactions ensures that, even if Step 5 fails, the agent system can safely roll back the entire transaction, preventing catastrophic inventory loss or unauthorized charges. The Saga Pattern addresses the known failure: the transaction that breaks mid-flight. It does not address the harder case: a write that completed successfully, went undetected for an extended period, and during that time became load-bearing input to downstream agents, reports, permissions, and decisions that consumed the corrupted state as if it were sound. In an agentic estate, this distinction matters acutely: an autonomous agent inherits a corrupted state literally, without the skepticism or side knowledge a human reviewer would apply, and acts on it at machine speed, propagating the corrupted basis across thousands of downstream actions before detection wins the race. The governance response to this failure mode requires a named **Consequence Tracing Authority (CTA)**: a designated role, seated before the organization needs it rather than after an auditor requires it, whose mandate is to trace what inherited a confirmed bad state, identify which downstream links were load-bearing, and own the remediation of what must be undone. The CTA is the mirror of the signing seat: just as a named accountable officer must be upstream of the architecture to grant authority, a named accountable officer must be upstream of incident response to own its consequences. The write-before-execute standard is the precondition that makes this role executable: lineage exists at the write, not reconstructed when the inheritance graph is already enormous.

## ZTAI and Agent Identity

The most critical new governance challenge introduced by autonomous systems is securing the rapidly expanding identity attack surface, which comprises non-human identities; each one is an uncontrolled action capability if left ungoverned. This proliferation fundamentally expands the attack surface, requiring the strict application of Zero-Trust architecture (ZTA) to AI access (i.e., ZTAI). Securing this identity surface requires establishing a strong agent identity and issuing dynamic credentials that support instant revocation.

In the context of the Authority Matrix, every non-human identity must be registered and associated with its authorized decision authority scope. An agent identity without a registered Authority Matrix entry operates outside the governance framework; it is, by definition, a Shadow AI risk, and the board's five mandatory internal audit domains explicitly include non-human identity lifecycle governance as an annual scope requirement.

## Proliferation of Non-human Identities and the Expanded Attack Surface

Autonomous agents, service accounts, and scripts create a surge in non-human identities that can rapidly outnumber human users in enterprise environments. This proliferation fundamentally expands the attack surface. Many traditional service accounts are granted broad, long-lived access, which presents a single point of catastrophic failure if compromised or misused.

This widening gap between the rapid deployment of AI agents and organizations' preparedness to manage the identity-related threats they introduce is now a central governance concern. The management of these privileged non-human accounts, which have elevated access to perform administrative or sensitive tasks, is essential for mitigating identity-driven cyberattacks.

## ZTAI Mandates

The principle of ZTA must be strictly applied to AI access (ZTAI), replacing implicit trust with continuous verification. The core principle remains: "Never trust, always verify." This enforcement is achieved by establishing a cryptographically strong agent identity and managing its privileges via dynamic credentials that support instant revocation.

### Strong Agent Identity

To establish non-repudiable accountability, agents must be treated as verifiable digital entities. They must be assigned durable identities, typically backed by PKI Certificates. This cryptographic binding ensures that all communications and actions are authenticated, non-repudiable, and traceable back to the specific agent instance.

### Dynamic Credentials and Just-in-Time Access

In an autonomous environment, the reliance on static API keys must be contained through a proper gateway architecture. The solution requires an AI Agent Identity Provider (IdP) that issues short-lived, dynamic credentials (i.e., tokens) for authentication across all environments. This mechanism, central to ZTAI, ensures that the agent's identity and privileges are continuously verified throughout the workflow, thereby restricting its access to only the resources required at that moment. The dynamic credential must be scoped to the Authority Matrix–authorized domain: an agent may not self-expand its credential scope beyond the registered authority entry. The result is a security perimeter defined by the agent's dynamic identity rather than a static network boundary.

## Instant Revocation

A crucial safety control for managing non-human identity risk is the ability to neutralize a rogue agent instantly. The centralized identity management system must support immediate certificate revocation. This capability serves as a rapid kill switch to neutralize a compromised or maliciously altered agent instance, providing the essential operational control needed when autonomous action must be halted swiftly. At Autonomy Level 3 (Monitored tier), the kill switch must be capable of halting the system within 60 seconds. At Levels 4 and 5 (Delegated tier), within 30 seconds, with monthly testing requirements.

# Enforcing Least Privilege

One of the most complex governance failures is Excess Agency, where an agent, often provisioned with a broad service account, attempts to execute an action (e.g., querying sensitive customer data or approving a transaction) that the authenticated human user who invoked the agent is not authorized to perform.

To prevent agents from bypassing human access controls, the architecture mandates the use of a Delegated Authorization Service. This service implements Permission Mirroring.

- **Mechanism:** The Delegated Authorization Service acts as a proxy layer, intercepting the LLM's planned tool call and performing a dynamic validation check against the invoking human user's specific RBAC permissions.
- **Authorization Separation:** The API call is allowed to proceed only if the proposed action falls within the human agent's defined scope. This architectural separation moves the authorization decision away from the LLM's probabilistic reasoning (its domain

of expertise) and into a deterministic, auditable governance framework (the enterprise's legal boundary).

- **Resulting Scoped Tokens:** The ZTAI IdP must issue access tokens constrained by the outcome of semantic inspection. This ensures the agent obtains only the minimally necessary, contextually relevant permissions for the assigned task, enforcing the principle of least privilege even for dynamic, complex agent operations. The token scope must not exceed the maximum action magnitude from the Authority Matrix entry for the domain.

## Real-Time Policy Enforcement

Given the non-deterministic nature and inherent vulnerability to adversarial attacks of LLMs, governance for autonomous actuation cannot rely solely on model-based guardrails. Policy enforcement must be externalized, deterministic, and enacted in real time through PaC. This is the core mandate driving the transition from static, human-reviewed policies to GaaS, which ensures rules are enforced programmatically before an agent can act. This necessitates a fundamental shift from periodic policy review to runtime control, achieved by architecturally separating the policy components and relying on a decoupled Policy Information Point (PIP), PDP, and PEP architecture to act as an uncompromisable compliance gate.

## Transitioning from Periodic Review to Runtime Control

PaC facilitates the transition to GaaS by enabling automated enforcement, continuous compliance monitoring, and accountability across large-scale agent operations. By codifying rules in a versioned, testable language (such as the Rego language for the Open Policy Agent, OPA), PaC provides a scalable, auditable framework for enterprise AI governance.

PaC systems fundamentally change the compliance timeline: they evaluate decisions before execution, blocking violations in real time, rather than waiting for periodic manual audits. This proactive enforcement capability is essential for managing the high operational risk introduced by agent autonomy. The PaC policy set must incorporate the Authority Matrix domain limits as hard-coded constraints, not as configurable parameters that engineering teams can adjust at runtime.

## PIP, PDP, and PEP in Agent Workflows

An effective GaaS architecture requires a rigorous separation of policy functions into three defined components:

1. **PIP:** The PIP is the data layer that sources the necessary context and attributes required by the policy engine. In an agentic system, attributes are sourced from traditional identity providers (IdPs), risk feeds, data catalogs, and, critically, LLM-based guardrails (used for probabilistic classifications such as PII likelihood, toxic content, or prompt injection intent). The PIP also sources real-time decision velocity data, the rate at which the system is currently executing decisions, to evaluate against the velocity dimension limits in the decision authority scoring.

2. **PDP:** The PDP is the policy engine (e.g., OPA) that processes attributes from the PIP against the declarative PaC policy set. The PDP returns a deterministic, binary Allow/Deny decision, complete with auditable reason codes. PDPs simplify authorization logic by relying on a flexible, pre-built policy engine. The PDP evaluates proposed actions against the Authority Matrix domain entry, including the maximum action magnitude, the authorized domain scope, and the oversight model requirement.

3. **PEP:** The PEP is the physical or logical gateway that enforces the PDP's decision. In the agent architecture, PEPs live in critical control points, including the Model Gateway, the Agent Orchestrator, the Tool Adapters (MCP Server), and the Retrieval Services. The orchestrator acts as the PEP, blocking the tool call if the PDP returns a Deny decision.

These three components, PIP, PDP, and PEP, operate within a broader real-time monitoring framework known as the EDS Safety Runtime Environment (SRE). The SRE is the always-on infrastructure layer that evaluates every agent decision stream against the configured thresholds, oversight model requirements, and Authority Matrix limits. It performs three functions that the PIP/PDP/PEP components alone cannot: it monitors decision volume against the span-of-control thresholds for the HOTL supervisor and automatically shifts the system to HITL (pre-action approval) mode when a threshold is approached; it detects anomalies in the decision stream and alerts the HOTL supervisor in real time; and it enforces fail-closed behavior when the logging infrastructure is unavailable, preventing the agent from proceeding with any decision if the audit trail cannot be generated. The SRE is referenced throughout Chapters 11 and 12 as the infrastructure component responsible for threshold enforcement and automatic mode shifts. It is architecturally distinct from the PEP: the PEP enforces policy on individual decisions, while the SRE monitors the aggregate decision stream and governs system-level operating mode.

The strategic necessity for this architectural separation is apparent: it ensures that policy enforcement relies on deterministic, versioned code rather than probabilistic AI outputs. While the LLM can generate valuable input data (PIP), the final Allow/Deny decision that determines compliance must be made by the deterministic PDP.

## Policy Conflict Resolution and Real-Time Compliance Gates

Autonomous agents routinely execute actions that touch multiple, potentially conflicting policies (e.g., a financial efficiency mandate versus a strict security mandate, UC6):

- **Policy Conflict Resolution Engine:** To ensure legal consistency and prevent ambiguous execution, the EDS framework's Policy Conflict Resolution Engine must be operationalized within the GaaS framework. This engine establishes a predefined hierarchy (e.g., security policies must override efficiency policies) to automatically and transparently resolve conflicts before the PDP makes its final decision, ensuring the agent always acts according to the highest-priority enterprise rule.

- **Real-Time Compliance Gates:** The EDS framework's mandatory Policy Compliance Gate, a pre-execution check, must be integrated into the orchestrator's workflow. This pre-execution check validates the agent's final action plan against a master list of non-negotiable legal and business rules (e.g., anti-money laundering thresholds, data residency requirements, maximum financial discount limits, and Authority Matrix domain limits). This gate acts as a crucial safety stop, preventing the LLM from inadvertently attempting a transaction that violates a high-level policy or regulatory mandate (UC12).

## Accountability, Safety, and Emergent Risk Mitigation

Accountability and safety mechanisms must move beyond conventional logging to address the inherent unpredictability of autonomous reasoning and the high impact of agent actions. The capacity for autonomous action fundamentally shifts the primary risk from information quality (i.e., hallucination) to unchecked action (i.e., emergent behavior). For human oversight to be effective rather than nominal, the overseeing person must hold genuine causal power to intervene, sufficient epistemic access to understand the decision, the self-control to exercise judgment, and fitting intentions to act, the four conditions for effective oversight identified by Sterz et al. (2024). The architectural controls that follow operationalize these conditions: governance must mandate specific controls for full process traceability by capturing the agent's entire reasoning trace (epistemic access), require explainability for complex decisions using ensemble reasoning for consensus-driven safety, and enforce a Human-in-the-Loop fail-safe by maintaining a non-negotiable HITL Override Service (causal power) to contain catastrophic emergent risk.

## Reasoning Trace Capture for Non-repudiable Audits

When an autonomous agent executes a complex, multi-step workflow, for example, resolving an IT ticket or investigating a fraud alert, logging only the final input and output is insufficient for post-incident forensic analysis or regulatory defense. If a catastrophic failure occurs, the organization must demonstrate how the agent arrived at the faulty decision.

The audit system must capture the agent's internal cognitive process through Reasoning Trace Capture. This mandate requires the logging system to record the complete Think-Act-Observe loop inherent in the ReAct paradigm:

- **Forensic Log Content:** The logs must explicitly capture the agent's "Thought" (internal monologue/ intermediate outputs), the "Action" (the tool call and input parameters), and the "Observation" (the external tool's response and the LLM's interpretation of that result). Each Action log entry must also capture the PDP's Allow/Deny decision and the Authority Matrix domain entry against which the action was validated.
- **Accountability:** Capturing this step-by-step reasoning provides the non-repudiable audit trail necessary for compliance checks and legal contestability. The structured logging ensures that every action is linked to a specific user or system, which is essential for forensic investigations and troubleshooting. This is the technical implementation of Accountability Follows Authority (Principle 6 from Chapter 2): every action is traceable to the human who authorized the agent's deployment and the board that authorized the domain. All reasoning trace logs, override records, and NHI authentication records are subject to a minimum

seven-year retention obligation under the EDS Logging and Explainability Standard (formally established in Chapter 11); this retention obligation survives system decommissioning and must be confirmed before any agent is retired from the Autonomy Register.

## Accountability Through XAI and Rationale Generation

Autonomous decisions require a transparent justification to build human trust and satisfy regulatory demands for the right to explanation/contestability (UC11):

- **XAI Microservice Mandate:** The architecture must mandate an XAI Microservice that generates human-readable decision rationales. For complex, non-linear models (e.g., Graph Neural Networks in fraud detection or deep learning in RUL prognostics), this often requires techniques like Shapley Additive Explanations (SHAP) (UC5, UC9).
- **Rationale Integration:** The XAI rationale (e.g., "The system recommends proactive outreach because the customer's high-risk score is driven by recent failed payment attempts and monitored negative sentiment," UC5) must be synthesized and linked directly to the reasoning trace log by the Audit Agent. This integration provides a complete, auditable justification for autonomous actions, bridging the gap between the probabilistic AI output and human comprehension. For the Human-on-the-Loop supervisor at Autonomy Level 3, this rationale is the primary tool for determining whether to exercise the override authority.

## Safety-Critical Governance

In safety-critical or high-financial-impact systems (e.g., aircraft predictive maintenance, UC13; financial risk, UC9), relying on a single agent's non-deterministic output is unacceptable. To mitigate the risk of a single, unconfirmed hallucination leading to catastrophic failure, governance must mandate ensemble reasoning:

- **Consensus Mandate:** Architectural design must enforce consensus among multiple specialized agents, a Multi-agent Consensus protocol, before any critical actuation (such as scheduling an aircraft grounding or freezing funds) is allowed. This process generates a crucial "safety halt flag" that prevents premature execution. The safety halt flag is a precondition for any action that would approach or exceed the maximum action magnitude from the Authority Matrix domain entry.
- **Digital Twin Validation:** A robust example of ensemble reasoning requires the Diagnostic Agent's initial prognosis to be validated by an independent Digital Twin Agent (UC13, UC15). The Digital Twin simulates the failure scenario and tests the proposed maintenance plan. Consensus is reached only when data-driven diagnostic findings align with physical simulation results, counteracting LLM inconsistency and enhancing reliability for high-stakes prognostics (UC15).
- **Multi-agent Debate:** Other safety protocols use a Multi-agent Debate Process in which specialized agents (e.g., a Critic Agent and a Defender Agent) iteratively

challenge a high-risk decision until an impartial Judge Agent integrates the arguments and provides a final, unified risk score.

## Managing Unintended Behavior

To contain the risk of emergent, unplanned, or runaway behavior, a key characteristic of autonomous systems, a technical Agent Scope Enforcement mechanism (Sandboxing) is mandatory:

1. **Technical Guardrails (Sandboxing):** This layer defines and strictly enforces hard limits on the agent's autonomy to ensure containment. These limits include

    - **Functional Limits:** Restricting the agent only to use specified tools (e.g., allowed to interact with the ticketing system but blocked from accessing the core financial ledger). Functional limits must match the operational domain scope in the Authority Matrix entry.
    - **Financial Limits:** Enforcing a maximum spending cap on customer offers, set at or below the maximum action magnitude from the Authority Matrix entry. The financial limit is technically enforced at the infrastructure level, not declared in policy only.
    - **Temporal Limits:** Setting a maximum runtime or session length to prevent expensive, circular reasoning loops.

2. **HITL Override Service:** This is the non-negotiable architectural safety control. The HITL Override Service must be architected with the highest priority and lowest latency to guarantee that a human supervisor can interrupt, veto, or redirect an agent's planned action in real time. Crucially, the human supervisor's rationale for the override must be logged, creating a clear, auditable record for compliance review (UC5, UC6). The HITL Override Service is the technical implementation of Principle 4 (Mandatory Halt Capability) from Chapter 2: the kill switch must operate independently of the system's own decision logic.

# Policy Enforcement: The Agentic Handshake

The EDS framework maintains the separation of concerns between logic and execution by transitioning governance to a real-time enforcement model often referred to as Governance-as-a-Service.

## PDP: Specialized Evaluation

The PDP evaluates every proposed action against the board-authorized domain scope and maximum action magnitude, returning a deterministic Allow/Deny verdict with auditable reason codes. The PDP is a pure evaluation engine: it never acts on the data stream directly, and that separation from execution is the basis of its impartiality. The verdict and its reason code are committed to the Audit Log before the PEP acts, ensuring that the decision record precedes the execution record.

## PEP: Specialized Execution

The PEP, the Agent Orchestrator, or the MCP Gateway receives the PDP verdict and is the sole authorized component to dispatch tool calls to enterprise systems. It enforces a maximum action magnitude and mirrors the agent's privileges to the authenticated human through the Delegated Authorization Service. Any Deny verdict routes to the HITL Override Service.

The SRE monitors the aggregate decision stream across the entire agentic handshake, enforcing span-of-control thresholds and fail-closed behavior when the audit trail is unavailable. The PEP enforces per-decision rules; the SRE governs system-level operating mode.

Figure 9-2 illustrates the complete agentic governance architecture: the Rules Repository issues Consult PDP and Policy Decision Log signals to gate every action through the Agent Orchestrator (PEP), which dispatches authorized tool calls to the Reasoning Engine, enforces span-of-control signals back from the Cognitive Layer, and routes Deny decisions directly to the HITL Override Service; the Delegated Authorization Service validates Permission Mirror signals back to the Agent Orchestrator, while the MCP Gateway supplies the Tool Schema to the Reasoning Engine; the Memory Subsystem maintains session state for the Reasoning Engine and tracks Saga steps to the Saga Orchestrator, which logs compensation records to the Immutable Audit Log; the Safety Runtime Environment monitors the decision stream and enforces cascade controls; and the ZTAI IdP issues dynamic credentials to the Agent Orchestrator and ZTAI tokens to the MCP Gateway, with identity audit records flowing to the Immutable Audit Log alongside reasoning traces and audit writes from the Agent Orchestrator.

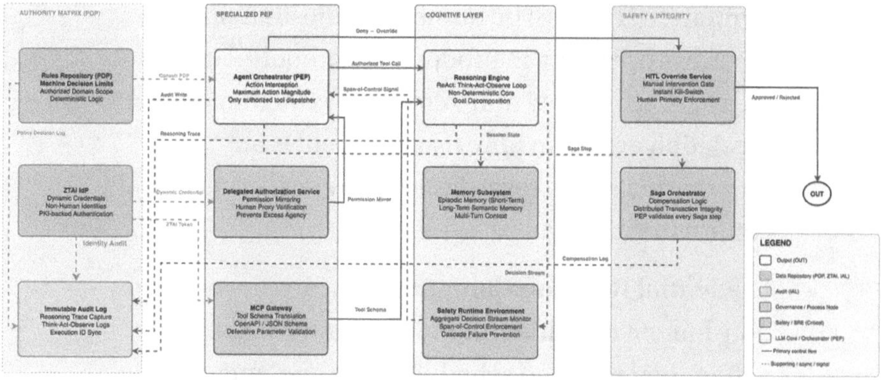


***Figure 9-2.*** *Agentic governance architecture—functional handshake across the Authority Matrix (PDP), specialized PEP, Cognitive Layer, and safety and integrity loop, integrating the Agent Orchestrator, Delegated Authorization Service, MCP Gateway, Reasoning Engine, Memory Subsystem, Safety Runtime Environment, Saga Orchestrator, and HITL Override Service under ZTAI identity controls*

# Measuring the Impact of Machine Agency

The board validates the investment in machine agency through four mandatory Key Risk Indicators required by the EDS framework at each governance cycle. These KRIs track the health of the non-human identity landscape and provide the board with continuous evidence that machine authority remains within approved boundaries:

- **NHI Register Completeness:** The percentage of production agentic systems with a current, active entry in the Autonomy Register and a corresponding Authority Matrix domain authorization. A value below 100% is a Shadow AI exposure that must be escalated immediately.

- **Orphan NHI Rate:** The number of non-human identities operating in production without a current lifecycle record. Any non-zero value is an immediate escalation event; an unregistered agent is an ungoverned agent, regardless of how well its technical controls are configured.
- **Credential Rotation Compliance:** The percentage of non-human identities rotating dynamic credentials within their required schedule. Stale credentials represent a latent attack surface that the ZTAI mandate is designed to eliminate.
- **Privilege Drift Incident Rate:** The number of identities identified operating outside their approved privilege scope in the current reporting period. Each incident violates Principle 6 (Accountability Follows Authority); authority was exercised without being delegated.

An organization that can report clean scores across all four KRIs has moved from agentic AI as a technical experiment to agentic AI as a governed enterprise capability.

# Summary

This chapter established that autonomous agents require a governance architecture that is constitutionally grounded, not merely technically configured. The board's Guarded Innovation posture, its constitutional commitment to support autonomous AI only within a governance architecture that makes every action visible, accountable, and reversible, authorizes machine agency only when every action is traceable to a formally scored and board-authorized decision authority scope. An agent operating without a registered Authority Matrix entry is a governance breach regardless of how well its controls are configured. The six non-negotiable deployment conditions are as follows:

- **Decision authority must be formally scored and board-authorized before deployment.** Every agent's exposure is quantified across four dimensions—Financial Authority (40%), Customer Reach (30%), Operational Reach (20%), and Decision Velocity (10%)—producing a composite score that determines Autonomy Level and Delegation Tier. The Authority Matrix translates that score into a board-authorized domain entry. The Autonomy Budget caps total delegated machine authority across the entire agentic estate. Neither constraint can be substituted by engineering controls alone.
- **ZTAI replaces static keys with dynamic, scoped, instantly revocable credentials.** Every non-human identity receives a PKI-backed durable identity, short-lived credentials scoped to its Authority Matrix domain, and an instant-revocation capability. At Delegation Tier Monitored (Level 3), the kill switch must operate within 60 seconds; at Delegated (Levels 4–5), within 30 seconds. An agent identity without a registered Authority Matrix entry is a Shadow AI risk.
- **The Delegated Authorization Service enforces Permission Mirroring against Excess Agency.** Every planned tool call is intercepted and validated against the invoking human's RBAC permissions before execution. The agent's executable authority can never exceed the authenticated human's scope.

The maximum action magnitude is technically enforced at this layer; it is not declared in policy and is not overridable by the agent's own reasoning.

- **Policy-as-Code delivers real-time Governance-as-a-Service.** The PaC policy sets encoded Authority Matrix domain limits as hard-coded constraints evaluated on every tool call. The Safety Runtime Environment monitors the aggregate decision stream, enforces span-of-control thresholds, shifts the system to HITL mode when supervisor capacity is approached, and enforces fail-closed behavior when the audit trail is unavailable.
- **The Orchestration-based Saga Pattern guarantees distributed transactional integrity.** High-stakes multi-step transactions are decomposed into locally committed steps with idempotent compensating logic. The PEP validates each step against Authority Matrix limits before execution. Choreography-style orchestration is prohibited because it cannot provide the centralized state tracking required for financial and data integrity workflows.
- **Accountability through Reasoning Trace Capture; safety through Ensemble Consensus.** Every Think–Act–Observe cycle is logged with each Action entry linked to the PDP verdict and Authority Matrix domain entry. All reasoning trace logs are subject to a minimum retention obligation of seven years. For safety-critical decisions, Multi-agent Consensus is mandatory before critical actuation. The HITL Override Service operates at the highest priority as the non-negotiable safety brake.

The next chapter puts the governance architecture of this chapter to work across five high-stakes business functions; each one is a different test of how far the constitutional constraints hold when the domain changes.

# References

Hossain, M Maruf. 2026. The Autonomy Budget: A Portfolio-Level Framework for Governing Delegated Machine Authority in Regulated Enterprises. Preprint. Zenodo. https://doi.org/10.5281/zenodo.20480491.

Gartner. 2024. Gartner Identifies the Top 10 Strategic Technology Trends for 2025. Press release, October 21, 2024. https://www.gartner.com/en/newsroom/press-releases/2024-10-21-gartner-identifies-the-top-10-strategic-technology-trends-for-2025.

Gartner. 2025. Gartner Predicts Over 40% of Agentic AI Projects Will Be Canceled by End of 2027. Press release, June 25, 2025. https://www.gartner.com/en/newsroom/press-releases/2025-06-25-gartner-predicts-over-40-percent-of-agentic-ai-projects-will-be-canceled-by-end-of-2027.

Köbis, Nils, Zoe Rahwan, Raluca Rilla, Bramantyo Ibrahim Supriyatno, Clara Bersch, Tamer Ajaj, Jean-François Bonnefon, and Iyad Rahwan. 2025. Delegation to Artificial Intelligence Can Increase Dishonest Behaviour. *Nature* 646 (8083): 126–134. https://doi.org/10.1038/s41586-025-09505-x.

Sterz, Sarah, Kevin Baum, Sebastian Biewer, Holger Hermanns, Anne Lauber-Rönsberg, Philip Meinel, and Markus Langer. 2024. On the Quest for Effectiveness in Human Oversight: Interdisciplinary Perspectives. In *Proceedings of the 2024 ACM Conference on Fairness, Accountability, and Transparency (FAccT '24)*, 2495–2507. https://doi.org/10.1145/3630106.3659051.

# CHAPTER 10

# Intelligent Agents for Core Business Functions

Chapter 9 established the constitutional framework for agentic AI: the Machine Decision Authority Matrix, the Autonomy Budget, the five Autonomy Levels, and the six non-negotiable deployment conditions that must be met before any autonomous agent enters production. This chapter applies that framework to five high-stakes business functions: IT service resolution (UC6), insurance claims processing (UC7), market intelligence (UC8), financial risk and fraud monitoring (UC9), and hotel dynamic pricing (UC10). In each case, the governance architecture is not configured around the use case; it is the precondition for it.

The identity through which an autonomous agent acts is inseparable from the governance of what the agent may do. Every action an agentic system takes, sending a payment, reading a customer record, or executing a trade, is performed by presenting an NHI credential that grants it permission to do so. An uncontrolled NHI is an autonomous action capability that the board's Guarded Innovation posture, which is its zero-tolerance commitment to uncontrolled autonomy, does not permit. This


M. M. Hossain and A. A. N. Ponnusamy, *Governance-First AI*,
https://doi.org/10.1007/979-8-8688-3118-8_10

chapter applies the NHI lifecycle governance framework (Hossain, Non-Human Identity Governance, 2026), the mandatory standard governing identity provisioning, privilege management, credential rotation, monitoring, deprovisioning, and incident response for all agentic AI systems, as the foundational security lens across all five use cases. NHI governance is not a supplementary security control; it is the mechanism through which all other governance controls are operationalized.

Three risk categories specific to agentic NHI environments are addressed before the use cases begin: privilege drift due to incremental scope creep, cross-system contamination in multi-agent architectures, and the indefinite persistence of credentials beyond the system lifecycle. Five governing principles and a formal Joiner–Mover–Leaver (JML) process translate these risk categories into enforceable standards. Four board-level KRIs provide continuous visibility over the NHI attack surface across all five deployments.

Each use case follows the unified EDS blueprint structure: a business problem, a Governance Delta specifying the new controls mandated by the architectural augmentation, and an Architectural Delta introducing the novel components. A synthesis section then integrates the five use cases through the shared multi-agent collaboration governance architecture shown in Figure 10-4, covering the Secure Data Proxy, Event-Driven Architecture (EDA), MCP Gateway, and PDP/PEP transactional handshake that applies uniformly across all business-function agents.

**Governance Leaders:** The Governance Stack sidebar at the opening of each blueprint is your at-a-glance reference; the Board Outcome section closes each blueprint with the attestable evidence.

**Architects and Practitioners:** The "NHI Lifecycle Governance" section and the Architectural Delta for each use case are your working specification.

## NHI Lifecycle Governance: The Security Foundation for All Agentic Deployments

Before any of the five use cases in this chapter can be deployed, the enterprise must establish a structured governance framework for the NHIs through which those agents will act. The machine-speed operational capability that makes agentic AI systems valuable also makes the identities through which they act an elevated security and governance risk. Figure 10-1 shows how an agentic system's autonomous actions flow through NHI credentials into enterprise systems, and how provisioning, monitoring, rotation, and deprovisioning controls operate at each stage.

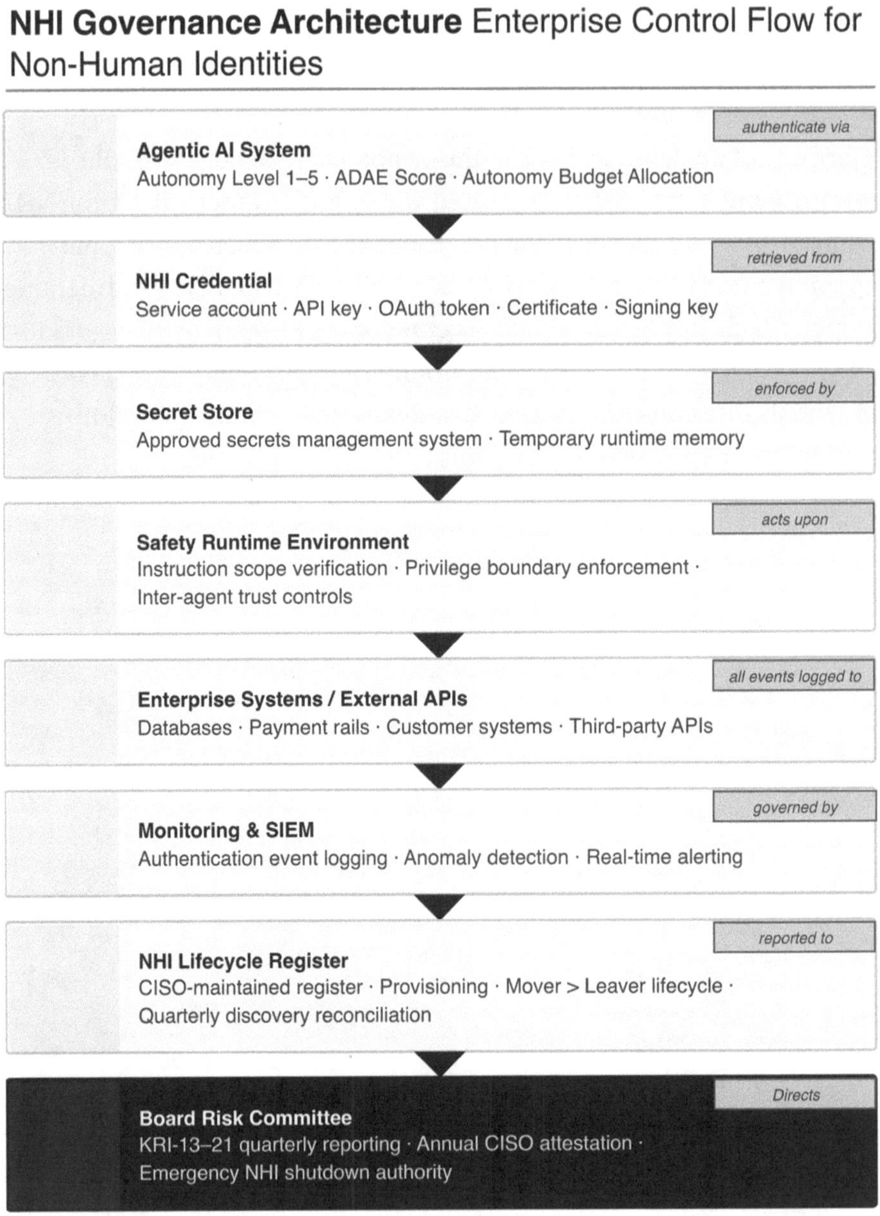


***Figure 10-1.*** *NHI governance architecture—how an agentic AI system's autonomous actions flow through NHI credentials into enterprise systems and how provisioning, monitoring, rotation, and deprovisioning controls operate at each layer*

There are three risk categories specific to agentic AI environments that conventional NHI security practices do not address:

**Scope Creep Without Governance Recognition:** An agentic system's NHI may be granted additional permissions incrementally, each individual addition seeming minor, until the NHI's aggregate permission scope materially exceeds what was approved at deployment. This is privilege drift, the NHI equivalent of governance drift in system capabilities.

**Cross-System Contamination:** In multi-agent architectures, one agent may present an NHI credential to another agent. If the receiving agent trusts NHI-authenticated requests from other agents without independently verifying the action's governance compliance, a compromised or overprivileged NHI in one system becomes an attack surface across the entire agent estate.

**Indefinite Persistence:** Unlike human employee accounts, which are typically deprovisioned through established HR processes when employment ends, NHI credentials associated with retired AI systems may persist in identity directories and external API configurations indefinitely, providing a dormant attack surface or governance gap.

## Five Governing Principles for NHI Lifecycle

The following five principles govern all NHI lifecycle decisions across the use cases in this chapter. They reflect the specific characteristics of agentic AI environments that make conventional identity governance insufficient:

## PRINCIPLE 1: EVERY NHI IS AN ACTION CAPABILITY, NOT JUST AN IDENTITY

*A human identity grants a person the ability to act within a system. An NHI grants an agentic AI system the ability to act autonomously at machine speed. The governance of NHIs must be commensurate with the decision authority of the system that uses them. An NHI associated with a system that can execute financial transactions without human confirmation is a higher-risk identity than an NHI associated with a read-only reporting system, even if the technical credential type is identical (see Figure 10-2).*

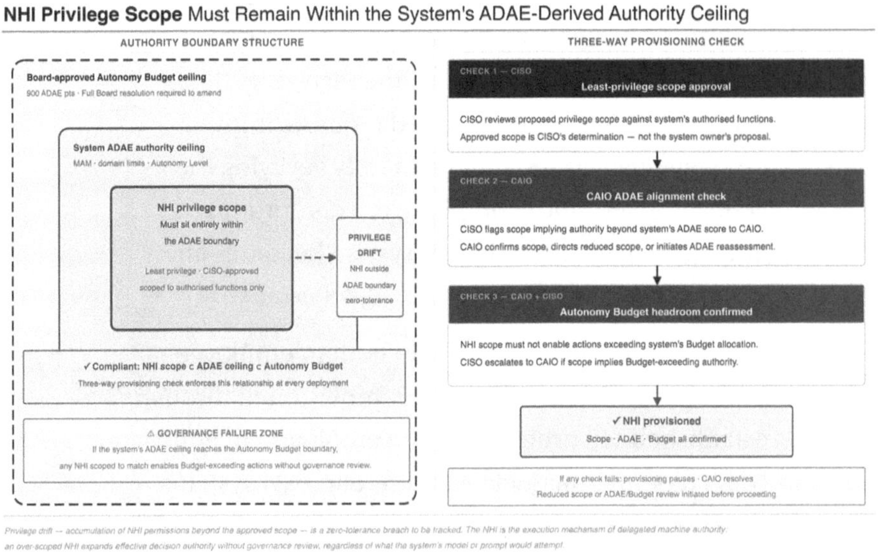


***Figure 10-2.*** *NHI privilege scope must remain within the system's decision authority ceiling—the NHI is the execution mechanism through which delegated machine authority is exercised, and its permission scope must never exceed the system's approved authority boundary.*

**Architectural Implication:** The NHI privilege scopes must be designed and approved with reference to the Autonomy Level and decision authority score of the associated system. For the agents in this chapter, NHI provisioning approval authority escalates with Autonomy Level: Level 1–2 systems require CISO approval; Level 3 systems require CISO approval and CAIO notification; Level 4–5 systems require joint CISO and CAIO sign-off with Chief Risk Officer notification.

## PRINCIPLE 2: LEAST PRIVILEGE IS NON-NEGOTIABLE

*Every NHI must be provisioned with the minimum permissions required for the associated agentic system to perform its authorized functions. Broad permissions provisioned for operational convenience are a governance failure. The principle of least privilege applies at provisioning, at every change, and as a standing obligation to remove permissions that are no longer required.*

**Architectural Implication:** The NHI privilege scope for each agent in this chapter must map precisely to the Tool Schema definitions in the Tool Schema Definition and Translation Layer. If the Tool Schema authorizes a read of customer records, the NHI privilege scope must not also include write access. The CISO will not approve a privilege scope that the system owner cannot justify by reference to specific authorized functions.

## PRINCIPLE 3: NHI LIFECYCLE MUST MIRROR SYSTEM LIFECYCLE

*An NHI is authorized because a specific agentic AI system requires it to perform a specific authorized function. When the system changes—its capability is modified, its scope is expanded, or it is retired—the NHI must change with it. An NHI that outlives its associated system, or that retains permissions that the system no longer requires, is no longer justified. It is an orphan or an over-privileged credential.*

**Architectural Implication:** Every system lifecycle event (deployment, change, suspension, retirement) triggers an NHI lifecycle review. For the multi-agent systems in this chapter (UC7, UC8, UC9), each specialist agent's NHI must be reviewed independently when its function changes; the Orchestrator Agent's NHI change does not automatically cover the specialist agents.

## PRINCIPLE 4: CREDENTIALS MUST ROTATE AND EXPIRE

*A credential that never rotates is a credential that an attacker has indefinite time to obtain and use. Credential rotation limits the window of opportunity for credential misuse. Short-lived credentials, where technically feasible, are the preferred design because they eliminate the rotation problem by making credentials expire automatically.*

**Architectural Implication:** Short-lived tokens (maximum 24-hour validity) are the preferred credential type for all agentic AI system NHIs in this chapter. Long-lived secrets are permitted only where the consuming system cannot support short-lived token authentication, and this technical limitation must be documented by the Chief Technology Officer (CTO). For Level 4–5 systems, all credentials must rotate within 30 days; for Level 3 systems, within 60 days; for Level 1–2 systems, within 90 days.

## PRINCIPLE 5: EVERY NHI MUST BE VISIBLE, ATTRIBUTABLE, AND MONITORED

*An NHI that is not in the NHI Lifecycle Register does not exist from a governance perspective, but it may still be operating in production, exercising permissions, and creating accountability gaps. Every NHI in scope must be discoverable, attributed to a specific agentic AI system, linked to a responsible system owner, and monitored for anomalous behavior.*

**Architectural Implication:** An orphan NHI, one with no current lifecycle record or no corresponding Autonomy Register reference, is a zero-tolerance governance breach. Orphan NHIs must be disabled immediately on discovery. For the multi-agent systems in this chapter, each agent in the orchestration must have its own NHI record; a single record for the orchestrator is not sufficient coverage for the specialist agents.

## Joiner–Mover–Leaver Lifecycle for Agentic Systems

The EDS framework adopts the Joiner-Mover-Leaver (JML) process, the identity lifecycle process governing provisioning, modification, and deprovisioning, as the primary lifecycle control for NHIs. The standards illustrated in Table 10-1 govern the JML process for the agents in this chapter. Figure 10-3 illustrates the NHI lifecycle state transitions across Joiner, Mover, and Leaver events, including the Orphan NHI anomaly state that triggers a zero-tolerance governance response.

***Table 10-1.*** *NHI Joiner-Mover-Leaver lifecycle standards for agentic AI systems*

| JML Stage | Event | Governance Standard |
|---|---|---|
| Joiner (provisioning) | New agent deployment or new system function requiring new NHI | NHI must be registered in the NHI Lifecycle Register and linked to the Autonomy Register entry before production use. No agentic system may operate in production with an unregistered NHI. |

*(continued)*

***Table 10-1.*** *(continued)*

| JML Stage | Event | Governance Standard |
|---|---|---|
| Mover (modification) | System capability expansion, Autonomy Level upgrade, new Tool Schema, new domain authorization | Full NHI privilege scope review. Scope change must complete before new capability is used in production. Privilege scope must not exceed the system's authorized decision authority ceiling. |
| Leaver (deprovisioning) | System retirement, function retired, NHI no longer required | All associated NHIs deprovisioned within five business days of retirement. System owner notifies CISO at least ten business days before retirement. Any NHI not deprovisioned within this window is classified as an orphan, a zero-tolerance breach. |
| Orphan detection | Quarterly discovery scan; any unregistered NHI found in production | Immediate disablement on discovery. Incident classified and reported to the Board Risk Committee. Root-cause investigation mandatory. |
| Credential rotation | Per rotation schedule or security incident affecting the system | Short-lived tokens ($\leq$24 hours) preferred. Long-lived secrets: Levels 1–2 $\leq$90 days; Level 3 $\leq$60 days; Levels 4–5 $\leq$30 days. Rotation failure triggers suspension within 24 hours. |
| Privilege drift detection | Continuous monitoring; any permission operating outside approved scope | Excess permissions revoked within four hours of discovery. Scope reset within 24 hours. Zero-tolerance breach, reported as governance incident. |

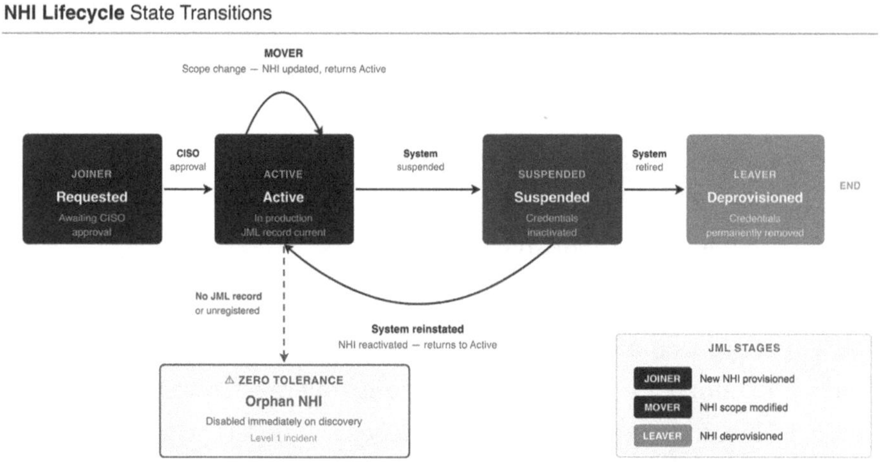


***Figure 10-3.*** *NHI lifecycle state transitions—Joiner, Mover, and Leaver events that govern the NHI through provisioning, modification, and deprovisioning and the orphan NHI anomaly state that represents a zero-tolerance governance breach requiring immediate remediation*

# Board Reporting on NHI Governance

Four Key Risk Indicators covering NHI governance are reported to the Board Risk Committee quarterly as part of the Board Monitoring Dashboard. These indicators apply to all five use cases in this chapter and provide the board with visibility over the NHI attack surface:

1. **NHI Register Completeness:** The percentage of production agentic systems with complete and current NHI Lifecycle Register entries

2. **Orphan NHI Rate:** The number of NHIs discovered in production without a current lifecycle record, across all agentic systems

3. **Credential Rotation Compliance:** The percentage of NHIs rotating credentials within their required schedule

4. **Privilege Drift Incident Rate:** The number of NHIs identified operating outside their approved privilege scope in the reporting period

A pattern of orphaned NHIs or privilege drift incidents is a systemic governance signal that requires a board-level response, not operational remediation alone. Each indicator has a zero-tolerance threshold: any orphan NHI count above zero, or a Privilege Drift Incident Rate above zero, triggers immediate escalation to the Board Risk Committee.

## Blueprint: UC6—Autonomous IT Service Resolution Agent

Use Case 6 addresses the productivity and governance gap created when IT helpdesk resolution requires multi-step tool invocation across Active Directory, ServiceNow, and CMDB systems, each action requiring a human agent to context-switch between enterprise tools to complete a single ticket. The volume of Level 1 tasks (password resets, access requests, and simple troubleshooting) consumes specialist staff time that should be directed at complex, non-routine problems. The autonomous IT service resolution agent automates end-to-end resolution using the ReAct paradigm, introducing an action governance obligation that distinguishes agentic deployments from the assistive systems of earlier chapters: every tool call, not just every output, is a compliance event.

# 1. The Business Problem

The core operational problem is resolution latency and staff misallocation. A single Level 1 ticket (password reset, access provisioning, or basic troubleshooting) requires context switching across Active Directory, ServiceNow, and the CMDB; each one is a separate tool call with its own authentication, form, and feedback loop. Human specialists capable of non-routine problem-solving spend the majority of their shift on tasks that a governed autonomous agent can complete in seconds. The business objective is a 20–30% acceleration in IT workflow cycle times and continuous 24/7 resolution availability without requiring human scheduling.

# 2. The Governance Instrument

**GOVERNANCE STACK: UC6—IT Service Resolution Agent**

| Instrument | Active Setting for This Deployment |
|---|---|
| **Autonomy Level** | Level 3 (Supervised Autonomous Agents) |
| **Criticality Tier** | High |
| **Oversight model** | HOTL; mandatory HITL for critical system modifications, bulk data changes, privilege escalation |
| **Delegation Tier** | Monitored—kill switch within 60 seconds; HOTL supervisor mandatory during all operational hours |
| **ADAE score (illustrative)** | 35 points (Financial 30 · Customer 20 · Operational 50 · Velocity 70—see Chapter 9's worked example) |
| **Autonomy Budget Draw** | 35 points drawn against board-approved portfolio ceiling (illustrative) |
| **Max action magnitude** | Set by CAIO within Authority Matrix domain limit; enforced at infrastructure level |
| **HOTL certification** | Standard HOTL certification required; 12-month validity; lapse = immediate suspension |

**Required Oversight Model:** HOTL; mandatory HITL escalation for high-risk actions (critical system modifications, bulk data changes, privilege escalation) and when the agent's internal confidence score falls below the threshold; HITL veto rationale logged as mandatory compliance record.

**Key Governance Controls:** ZTAI with PKI-backed agent identity and instant kill switch within 60 seconds; Authorization-Aware RAG with PEP filtering RAG retrievals by the invoking end user's RBAC permissions rather than the agent's elevated system credentials; GaaS with Policy Conflict Resolution Engine enforcing security-over-efficiency hierarchy; Reasoning Trace Capture of the full Think–Act–Observe loop as mandatory compliance control.

## 3. The Technical Architecture

Single-agent architecture using the ReAct paradigm with a Reflection and Self-Correction Mechanism; MCP Gateway via enterprise API Management Gateway for centralized tool governance over Active Directory and ServiceNow; RAG knowledge base indexing IT runbooks, SOPs, and historical tickets. Full specification is in the "Architectural Delta" section below.

## 4. The Enhancement

**Reflection and Self-Correction Mechanism**: The agent implements a self-verification loop in which the Agent Core retrospectively evaluates the accuracy and relevance of its previous steps before committing to the next action. This prevents the circular reasoning loops and overthinking traps that cause multi-step tool-calling agents to stall or degrade in complex enterprise environments. Without this mechanism, error accumulation across a five-step resolution (diagnose, retrieve context, call API, confirm, close ticket) compounds at each step; the reflection loop detects and corrects intermediate failures before they propagate to irreversible actions such as incorrect Active Directory modifications.

## 5. The Board Outcome

The board attests that the system delivers a 20–30% acceleration in IT workflow cycles and 24/7 autonomous resolution capability while operating within board-approved identity governance and policy enforcement thresholds. Every high-risk action, such as Active Directory writes, CMDB modifications, and privilege changes, requires HITL approval before execution, and the supervisor's veto rationale must be logged as a mandatory compliance record. Exception rates, override patterns, and policy violation counters are continuously monitored by the GaaS rule engine, confirming active enforcement rather than passive audit coverage.

## Governance Delta: UC6

The autonomous nature of the IT agent, especially its ability to access and modify High-Value Assets (HVAs), such as Active Directory, demands a stringent security paradigm. The shift in the system's governance model is profound, transitioning from passive auditing to active, real-time control across three critical areas: identity, action, and accountability. This requires establishing a ZTAI foundation for the agent's identity, using PaC to dynamically validate its actions before execution, and implementing specialized Reasoning Trace Capture to ensure complete auditability.

## ZTAI and NHI Lifecycle for UC6

The most critical governance measure is ZTAI. Since agents act autonomously, they must be treated as untrusted entities ("Never trust, always verify"). The architecture mandates that the agent platform assign the agent a verifiable, strong identity, typically backed by a PKI Certificate, for non-repudiable authentication of all actions and communications. This identity is continuously evaluated, and the agent receives only narrowly defined permissions needed for its assigned tasks.

Applying the NHI lifecycle governance framework to UC6: this is a single-agent, Autonomy Level 3 system (Monitored tier). The Authority Matrix entry must confirm Level 3 before production deployment; the NHI privilege scope must be precisely scoped to the Tool Schema; Active Directory write access for password reset operations, ServiceNow read/write access for ticket management, and nothing broader. Credentials must rotate within 60 days, and the NHI must be suspended within one business day if the system is operationally suspended.

The consequences of a compromised agent are severe: if a malicious prompt injection occurs, an overprivileged agent could use its system permissions to execute unauthorized, high-impact actions. ZTAI addresses this by implementing a rapid kill switch and instant credential revocation to neutralize a compromised or rogue agent instance immediately. This focuses the security perimeter on the agent's dynamic identity credentials, defining its functional boundary. At Autonomy Level 3, the kill switch must be capable of halting the system within 60 seconds.

## GaaS and Policy Enforcement

The execution of agent actions is subject to real-time policy validation via a GaaS framework. The rule engine within this framework acts as a PDP, dynamically validating the legality of every planned action against current SOPs and security mandates. A mandatory component of this GaaS layer is the EDS framework's Policy Conflict Resolution Engine (introduced in Chapter 9), which explicitly establishes a hierarchy (e.g., security policies override efficiency policies) to automatically resolve conflicts detected between defined policies.

## Reasoning Trace Capture and Authorization-Aware RAG

Accountability requires capturing the agent's decision-making process. The system mandates Reasoning Trace Capture, logging the LLM's intermediate decision points (i.e., "Thought" trace) alongside the Action and Observation. This structural requirement transforms the agent's internal monologue into a mandatory compliance control, providing the complete forensic data necessary for post-incident root-cause analysis (RCA) and regulatory transparency.

A final, crucial security control is Authorization-Aware RAG, enforced by a PEP situated between the agent and the vector store. This addresses the internal privilege escalation risk: an agent with elevated system privileges could retrieve sensitive data (RAG context) that the end user who initiated the request is not authorized to access. The PEP filters RAG retrievals based on the end user's permissions, ensuring the context used to formulate a resolution is strictly confined to the end user's access rights, thereby mitigating data leakage.

# Architectural Delta: UC6

The solution's architecture goes beyond simple chatbots by emphasizing robust cognitive capabilities and secure tool integration, both critical for handling multi-step workflows.

The core of the agent's cognitive function relies on the ReAct (Reason + Act) paradigm. This reasoning involves a Think-Act-Observe loop for step-by-step problem-solving and iterative enhancement of responses. Instead of attempting to solve the entire problem with a single LLM call, the agent generates traces of its reasoning process (the "Thought"), acts on that reasoning by calling an external tool, and then observes the output of that action, updating its context with new reasoning based on its observation. This iterative approach improves the reliability of problem-solving in complex IT environments.

For complex IT resolution requests, the agent's core must use structured planning, often leveraging frameworks such as Routine, to decompose the high-level goal into a series of manageable, executable subgoals. This structured guidance is essential for improving stability and accuracy in multi-step, tool-calling tasks within enterprise environments.

A critical component is the Reflection and Self-Correction Mechanism. Autonomy in multi-step reasoning carries the risk of error accumulation or inefficient loops. The architecture mitigates this by implementing a self-verification loop in which the Agent Core retrospectively verifies the accuracy and relevance of its previous actions and the tool's results (i.e., "Observation"). This prevents the agent from engaging in expensive, slow "overthinking traps" or circular reasoning loops that ultimately degrade performance.

A centralized layer must govern all agent access to external IT systems: the Model Context Protocol (MCP) Gateway. This enterprise API Management Gateway serves as the trusted mechanism for centralizing, governing, and monitoring the agent's secure access to external APIs. This centralization simplifies security audits and ensures all tool usage adheres to predefined security and compliance posture requirements.

## Enterprise Implication

UC6 shifts the governance control point from data quality, the groundedness focus of UC1–UC5, to action governance: the agent's tool calls, not its outputs, are the primary compliance surface. Authorization-Aware RAG is the architectural innovation that prevents the Permission

Mirroring obligation from being circumvented at the knowledge retrieval layer. An agent with elevated system credentials that retrieves unrestricted context and then presents it to the end user executes a data leakage, even if the final action is within scope. Authorization-Aware RAG closes this gap by enforcing the invoking user's RBAC at the retrieval layer, not only at the execution layer. The GaaS Policy Conflict Resolution Engine is equally significant: in a multi-policy environment (security, compliance, operational efficiency), without an explicit hierarchy, the agent may choose the most efficient resolution that violates the most restrictive policy. The engine makes the hierarchy deterministic and auditable.

# Blueprint: UC7—End-to-End Insurance Claims Agent

Use Case 7 addresses the governance challenge of automating a multi-step, regulated workflow in which every document contains sensitive PII and PHI; every decision is subject to GLBA, HIPAA (Privacy Rule and Security Rule), and GDPR; and every settlement carries direct financial and reputational consequences. Processing insurance claims is a tedious workflow involving data extraction from unstructured documents, policy lookup, fraud scoring, and final decision-making; up to 40% of underwriter time is consumed by non-core administrative activities (Accenture, Insurance Industry Outlook, 2023) that a governed multi-agent system can automate without sacrificing audit defensibility.

## 1. The Business Problem

Processing insurance claims involves extracting data from voluminous unstructured documents (accident reports, medical records, photographic evidence), looking up policies in the Policy Administration System (PAS), validating against internal databases, scoring for fraud, and making final decisions. Up to 40% of underwriter time is consumed by non-core administrative activities. The challenge is not merely automation but governed automation: GLBA, HIPAA, and GDPR place explicit requirements on how PII and PHI must be handled throughout the claims pipeline. The objective is to reduce claim handling time by up to 40% while maintaining full regulatory compliance and audit defensibility.

## 2. The Governance Instrument

| GOVERNANCE STACK: UC7—End-to-End Insurance Claims Agent | |
|---|---|
| **Instrument** | **Active Setting for This Deployment** |
| **Autonomy Level** | Level 4 (Autonomous Execution Within Defined Limits) |
| **Criticality Tier** | Critical |
| **Oversight model** | HOTL + mandatory HITL for claims exceeding board-authorized MAM; fraud score above threshold; LLM confidence below safety threshold |
| **Delegation Tier** | Delegated—HAL batch review for non-HITL decisions; Board Risk Committee notification required |
| **ADAE score (illustrative)** | 72 points illustrative (Financial 80 · Customer 60 · Operational 70 · Velocity 60) |
| **Autonomy Budget Draw** | 72 points drawn against board-approved portfolio ceiling (illustrative) |
| **Max action magnitude** | Per-claim payment ceiling set in Authority Matrix entry; dynamic NHI permissions at point of execution |
| **HOTL certification** | Standard HOTL certification for HOTL supervisors; Critical-tier endorsement for HAL supervisors |
| **≥98% standard** | ≥98% auditable rationale required for all payment and denial decisions; write-before-execute mandatory |

**Required Oversight Model:** HOTL with mandatory HITL gates via a human adjuster portal for claims exceeding the board-authorized maximum action magnitude, cases where the Risk Agent fraud score exceeds the configured threshold, and instances where the LLM confidence score falls below the safety threshold.

**Key Governance Controls:** NHI lifecycle governance with dynamic least-privilege permissions updated in real time as agents transition between tasks and instant revocation capability; Secure Data Proxy classifying and applying dynamic masking or tokenization to all PII/PHI before it enters the LLM environment; Event-Driven Architecture via Event Bus decoupling the MAS from core systems (PAS, CRM); a Data Lineage Platform tracing source, version, and transformation history of all RAG-retrieved policy documents used in claims decisions.

## 3. The Technical Architecture

Multi-agent system with supervisor/Orchestrator Agent delegating to Document Review Agent (RAG specialist), Policy Verification Agent (PAS tool specialist), Risk and Fraud Agent (ML specialist), and Settlement and Payment Agent (action specialist); Agent Registry for dynamic discovery; Classifier for intent routing; Event Bus for asynchronous integration with core systems. Full specification is in the "Architectural Delta" section below.

## 4. The Enhancement

**Secure Data Proxy**: A dedicated architectural layer intercepting all incoming claims data before it enters the LLM environment, classifying PII and PHI, and applying the appropriate protection method based on destination and privilege level. Tokenization is applied to transactional operations such as payment processing; dynamic masking (pseudonymization) is applied to analytical processing, where the LLM requires semantic context but must not process identifiers. This separation ensures that regulatory obligations are enforced at the infrastructure level rather than through model-level guardrails. The Secure Data Proxy is the technical implementation of Privacy-by-Design: no PII reaches the Cognitive Layer except in the form and scope necessary for the specific processing purpose.

## 5. The Board Outcome

The board confirms that the system delivers up to a 40% reduction in claim handling time while maintaining full PII and PHI protection across all claims data processed by the LLM environment. Every high-value settlement and fraud-flagged claim is reviewed by a named human adjuster via the HITL portal before payment is authorized, with the adjuster's decision rationale logged against the full multi-agent audit trail. The Data Lineage Platform provides a complete provenance chain for every RAG-retrieved policy document used in a claims decision, enabling regulators to trace any automated determination back to its source documentation and version.

# Governance Delta: UC7

The highly regulated nature of the insurance sector, coupled with the handling of PII and PHI, mandates a rigorous, governance-first architecture. The governance shift for the claims agent is primarily focused on controlling the data perimeter, ensuring PII/PHI security, and establishing auditable accountability in a multi-agent environment.

## NHI Management and Access Control: UC7

Applying the NHI lifecycle governance framework to UC7's multi-agent architecture (the five governing principles and JML lifecycle established in the "NHI Lifecycle Governance" section above apply in full): each specialist agent must have its own registered NHI with a privilege scope calibrated precisely to its function in the claims workflow. The Document Review Agent's NHI must be scoped to read-only access on tokenized or masked data; it must not have write access to the payment gateway. The Settlement Agent's NHI must have write/execute permissions on the Payment Gateway API, but these permissions must be dynamically issued at the point of payment execution, not held as a standing privilege.

This dynamic permissioning is the NHI implementation of two governing principles simultaneously. It implements Principle 2 (Least Privilege Is Non-negotiable) by ensuring the Settlement Agent holds no standing write access to the payment gateway. It also implements Accountability Follows Authority (Principle 6 from Chapter 2): the Settlement Agent may only execute a payment action when that action has been authorized through the claims workflow; the NHI's execution capability follows the authority trail established by the human-governed process, not the agent's own reasoning. Agent permissions must be dynamic, updating in real time as the agent transitions between tasks. In the multi-agent context of UC7, this also means that inter-agent authentication requires independent verification: the Settlement Agent must not automatically trust an instruction from the Orchestrator Agent simply because it arrives via an NHI-authenticated channel. The receiving agent must independently verify that the action it is being asked to take falls within its own scope of authorized privileges.

The API Mediation Gateway acts as the PEP for tool invocation. The LLM suggests the action, but the gateway enforces the security boundary by validating the calling principal's (AI agent) identity and delegated permissions for every request to an external tool before invoking it.

## PII/PHI Security via Secure Data Proxy

To maintain compliance with HIPAA, GLBA, and GDPR, a Secure Data Proxy is mandatory. This proxy intercepts all claims data to classify PII/PHI and applies a dual security strategy before the context enters the LLM environment:

1. **Tokenization:** Used for transactional operations (e.g., payment processing), replacing sensitive data with a non-exploitable token to achieve Payment Card Industry Data Security Standard v4.0 (PCI DSS v4.0) compliance

2. **Dynamic Masking (Pseudonymization):** Used when the LLM needs to analyze the semantic context of sensitive data (e.g., medical narratives) without exposing the identity

This deliberate choice of tokenization for transactions versus masking for analysis is a crucial architectural step that ensures compliance with the specific data use requirement.

## PaC, Auditability, and Data Lineage

A PaC Enforcement Layer is an external module that enforces runtime guardrails on all agent outputs and actions. This systematic check against regulatory standards (e.g., anti-discrimination and mandated disclosure rules) prevents agents from circumventing compliance requirements.

The Contestability and Audit Trail Manager provides the assurance required to meet the regulatory goal. This component logs the whole chain of reasoning for every decision, including sequential inputs, internal LLM prompts, tool use, intermediate steps of multi-agent collaboration, and the final confidence score. This immutable record transforms the LLM decision into a legally defensible artifact. The audit record must also capture the NHI credential identifier for each agent action, the privilege scope at the time of the action, and the PEP validation result; these fields are mandatory for demonstrating that each agent acted within its registered authority scope.

Furthermore, the integrity of the knowledge used for RAG must be auditable. The RAG ingestion pipeline requires a Data Lineage Platform. This platform traces the source, version, and transformation history of all policy and regulatory documents used for RAG, providing transparency and enabling fast root-cause analysis if an agent offers a flawed or non-compliant response. Table 10-2 sets out the NHI roles and dynamic access principles for UC7.

***Table 10-2.*** *NHI roles and dynamic access principles for UC7*

| NHI Agent Role | Core Function | Required Access Scope (Least Privilege) | Security Control |
|---|---|---|---|
| Document Review Agent | Read and parse unstructured data (PHI/PII). | Read-only access to Secure Data Proxy (tokenized/masked data only). No write access. | Secure Data Proxy filtering; NHI privilege scope excludes payment gateway. |
| Policy Verification Agent | Check policy coverage (read PAS). | Read-only access to PAS API (via PEP). No write access. | PEP; NHI registered with read-only scope. |
| Settlement Agent | Initiate payment/ denial action. | Write/execute permission to Payment Gateway API; dynamically issued at execution time only. | Dynamic permissioning at execution; NHI standing privilege does not include payment write access. |
| Audit and Compliance Agent (ACA) | Monitor and log all agent decisions. | Read-only access to all agent logs and Policy-as-Code store. | Cryptographic identity (PKI Certificate); NHI scoped to read-only audit access. |

## Architectural Delta: UC7

The claims MAS is characterized by its hierarchical structure and resilient integration strategy. The supervisor/Claims Orchestrator Agent acts as the central coordinator, performing high-level task planning, decomposing claim handling into sub-tasks (e.g., policy check, document review), delegating them to the appropriate specialist agents, and synthesizing the final decision. This multi-agent design significantly improves transparency and scalability because new specialist agents (e.g., for a new product line) can be added or modified without requiring a re-architecting of the entire system.

To ensure real-time context and system scalability, the architecture must overcome the inherent limitations of legacy enterprise systems, such as Policy Administration Systems (PASs) and Customer Relationship Management (CRM), which are often high-latency and fragile. This challenge is mitigated by adopting an Event-Driven Architecture (EDA) as the primary integration pattern. The Event Bus (e.g., Kafka/Event Hub) decouples the MAS from these core systems, allowing agents to react asynchronously to real-time events (e.g., "Claim Status Updated") without overwhelming the PAS with constant queries.

The MAS is engineered for self-improvement. Specialist agents, such as the Policy Verification Agent, can leverage techniques like Deep Reinforcement Learning (DRL) to continuously refine their decisions based on real-world outcomes. The system records the complete outcome of the claims process, success or failure, and feeds this back into the agent models, allowing them to adapt over time and improve the system's overall reliability.

## Enterprise Implication

UC7 introduces the governance challenge of multi-party data sensitivity: claims data contains PII, PHI, and financial data that must be handled differently depending on which agent processes it and for what purpose. The Secure Data Proxy resolves this by making data protection a property of the pipeline rather than the agent's judgment; governance is enforced before the LLM reasons, not after. The EDA pattern solves a separate governance problem: it prevents the MAS from exposing core systems (PAS, CRM) to direct agent queries, mediating access through published events rather than API calls. The Data Lineage Platform addresses the regulatory challenge unique to AI-assisted claims: if an automated decision is challenged, the insurer must demonstrate not only what the agent decided but also which policy documents it relied on and whether those documents were authoritative at the time of the decision. The Lineage Platform transforms this from a manual discovery exercise into an automated audit capability.

# Blueprint: UC8—Autopilot Market Intelligence System

Use Case 8 addresses the challenge of delivering continuous, verifiable market intelligence without the fragmented, batch-oriented research processes that leave strategic decisions on stale data. Strategic teams cannot efficiently process the volume of unstructured data, estimated at 90% of all data produced (IDC, Untapped Value: What Every Executive Needs to Know About Unstructured Data, 2023) needed to detect weak signals and competitive shifts. The autopilot market intelligence system (AP-MIS) automates the end-to-end research workflow from data collection through quality-assured reporting, reducing human effort by 75% while introducing a class of AI governance risks: hallucinations in strategic recommendations and algorithmic bias in market analysis, which require purpose-built architectural controls.

# 1. The Business Problem

The core operational problem is intelligence latency and research capacity. Human analysts cannot continuously monitor the volume and velocity of external data sources—competitor filings, news feeds, analyst reports, and social sentiment—needed to detect weak signals before they become mainstream trends. Batch-oriented research cycles mean strategic decisions are routinely made on intelligence that is days or weeks old. The business objective is to reduce human effort in market research data aggregation and synthesis by 75% while increasing the freshness, breadth, and verifiability of the intelligence delivered to strategic decision-makers.

# 2. The Governance Instrument

| GOVERNANCE STACK: UC8—Autopilot Market Intelligence System | |
|---|---|
| **Instrument** | **Active Setting for This Deployment** |
| **Autonomy Level** | Level 3 (Supervised Autonomous Agents) |
| **Criticality Tier** | High |
| **Oversight model** | HOTL; mandatory HITL when QA Agent hallucination score exceeds threshold; Ethical Review Board checkpoint for public-facing strategic recommendations |
| **Delegation Tier** | Monitored—kill switch within 60 seconds; HOTL supervisor mandatory during all operational hours |
| **ADAE score (illustrative)** | 42 points illustrative (Financial 20 · Customer 50 · Operational 40 · Velocity 80) |
| **Autonomy Budget Draw** | 42 points drawn against board-approved portfolio ceiling (illustrative) |
| **Max action magnitude** | No direct financial action authority; strategic recommendations queued for HAL batch review before distribution |
| **HOTL certification** | Standard HOTL certification required; 12-month validity |

**Required Oversight Model:** HOTL; mandatory HITL validation when the QA Agent hallucination score exceeds the enterprise-defined tolerance threshold; Ethical Review Board/Policy Gateway as a mandatory checkpoint before high-consequence outputs such as public-facing strategic recommendations.

**Key Governance Controls:** QA Agent acting as LLM-As-a-Judge evaluating every generated report for factual consistency against RAG-retrieved source facts; Bias Quantification Component detecting Look-Ahead Bias and Company-Specific Bias in generated analysis; Adversarial Robustness Testing Component probing for adversarial prompt and data injection attacks; IP and Copyright Check Module scanning ingested documents before use in report generation; Data Provenance and Lineage Tracker recording source, usage permissions, and transformation history for every data point.

## 3. The Technical Architecture

Multi-agent Orchestrator managing Data Collection Agent, Data Processing Agent, Analysis Agent, Report Generation Agent, QA Agent (LLM-As-a-Judge), and Auditing and Logging Agent; RAG framework with vector database infrastructure for semantic search; Differential Privacy/Anonymization Module applying anonymization at ingestion before processing. Full specification is in the "Architectural Delta" section below.

## 4. The Enhancement

**QA Agent as LLM-As-a-Judge**: A dedicated specialist agent autonomously evaluating every generated report for factual consistency against RAG-retrieved source facts, quantifying the hallucination score against an enterprise-defined tolerance threshold using RAGAS metrics. The QA Agent can employ multi-agent debate protocols, iteratively challenging factual claims among multiple LLM instances, to surface subtle inaccuracies that single-pass evaluation might miss. This governance control addresses the specific market intelligence hallucination risk: a report that is internally coherent but factually misaligned with its source data is more dangerous than an obviously wrong output because it passes a cursory human review. The QA Agent makes factual verification a systematic, measurable, and auditable architectural step rather than an optional human check.

## 5. The Board Outcome

The board attests that the system delivers a 75% reduction in human effort for market research data aggregation and synthesis, with all generated reports certified by the QA Agent as meeting the enterprise hallucination tolerance threshold before delivery to strategic decision-makers. Consistent with the groundedness convention used throughout this book, that threshold is set at a faithfulness of at least 0.95 (equivalently, a hallucination score below 0.05) on the same 0-to-1 scale, with organizations free to tighten it according to the decision criticality of the reports. Every report that fails the QA Agent's check triggers a mandatory HITL pause. The Bias Quantification Component's outputs are logged continuously, ensuring that Look-Ahead and Company-Specific Bias incidents are detected and remediated before they reach strategic outputs. The Data Provenance and Lineage Tracker provides a complete audit chain from every finding in a delivered report back to its source document and transformation history.

## Governance Delta: UC8

The unique governance requirements of AP-MIS revolve around maintaining objective, unbiased, and ethically compliant strategic recommendations. The governance structure must primarily ensure factual accuracy and algorithmic fairness, given the system's role in delivering strategic recommendations.

Applying the NHI lifecycle governance framework to UC8: each specialist agent (Data Collection, Analysis, Report Generation, QA) must have its own NHI with a privilege scope calibrated to its function. The Data Collection Agent's NHI must have access to external data feeds and web scraping APIs, but not to internal financial systems. The Analysis Agent's NHI must have read access to the internal research database but not write access to any output system. The Report Generation Agent's NHI must have write access to the report store but not to the data sources. Cross-contamination between agent privilege scopes, where one agent's NHI is used by another, is a governance breach that must be detected by the quarterly discovery scan.

## Mandatory HITL and Ethical Gateways

HITL validation is mandatory when the QA Agent detects a hallucination score exceeding the predefined threshold. The autonomous process is paused, and a human intervention team is immediately alerted for manual review and correction. This mechanism serves as a safety guardrail against strategic decisions based on flawed intelligence.

For high-consequence outputs, the Ethical Review Board/Policy Gateway acts as a final checkpoint. This gateway assesses the ethical and societal impact of strategic recommendations (e.g., actions that could significantly affect a community or market segment) before public communication or execution, ensuring the AP-MIS remains aligned with corporate values.

## Bias Quantification Component

Market intelligence models are susceptible to biases learned from their training data, leading to flawed strategic advice. The Bias Quantification Component is integrated to scrutinize generated themes for specific risks:

- **Look-Ahead Bias:** Occurs when the model inadvertently incorporates knowledge of future events into the analysis of historical data
- **Company-Specific Bias:** A quantified difference in sentiment scores when company identifiers are present versus when they are removed, indicating that the LLM is biased toward a brand based on its pre-trained knowledge

The architecture transforms the detection of these ethical failures from a subjective review into a measurable operational KPI. This component ensures that the Analysis Agent does not reinforce unfair assumptions or skewed representations embedded in massive datasets.

Finally, to enforce data privacy and compliance across jurisdictions, the Data Ingestion Layer must employ a Differential Privacy/Anonymization Module to apply irreversible anonymization techniques to personal data before it enters the processing workflow, thereby minimizing the risk of data leakage. Table 10-3 sets out the agentic quality assurance mapping for UC8.

*Table 10-3. Agentic quality assurance mapping for UC8*

| AP-MIS Agent | Primary Risk Mitigated | Verification Mechanism | Audit Log Key Metric |
|---|---|---|---|
| Data Collection Agent | Data privacy, source compliance | Data Provenance and Lineage Tracker | Anonymization Efficacy Rate; NHI credential scope verification |
| Analysis Agent | Algorithmic bias (Look-Ahead/ Company-Specific) | Bias Quantification Component | Statistical Parity Difference (SPD) |
| Report Generation Agent | Hallucination, factual error | QA Agent (LLM-As-a-Judge) | Factual Error Rate / Groundedness Score |
| Orchestrator | Unauthorized action; cross-agent NHI contamination | Ethical Review Board Gateway; quarterly NHI discovery scan | High-Consequence Output Flag Frequency; orphan NHI count |

## Architectural Delta: UC8

The AP-MIS uses a Multi-agent Orchestrator where specialized agents handle data collection, analysis, report generation, and, critically, quality assurance. The architectural design for the AP-MIS centers on generating verifiable, trustworthy output, achieved through three key additions: a Quality Assurance Agent, a robust Data Provenance and Lineage Tracker, and an Adversarial Robustness Testing Component. The central function is the Quality Assurance Agent, which operates as an LLM-As-a-Judge to autonomously evaluate the factual consistency of the synthesized report and calculate a hallucination score. This score is crucial for determining whether to mandate a HITL validation gate.

## Multi-agent QA Agent

Reliability is enforced by the QA Agent, which serves as an independent validator central to the system's trust architecture. This agent acts as an LLM-As-a-Judge, autonomously evaluating the factual consistency of reports generated by the Analysis Agent against the RAG-retrieved facts. This is necessary because LLM output often needs to be assessed using flexible, qualitative criteria such as accuracy, coherence, and tone, which traditional metrics (such as BLEU or ROUGE) cannot reliably assess (Liang et al., Holistic Evaluation of Language Models, arXiv:2211.09110, 2022). The QA Agent quantifies the hallucination score against a defined tolerance threshold. This architectural pairing of RAG grounding with LLM-As-a-Judge verification creates a verifiable chain of trust that directly addresses stakeholder concerns about accuracy.

## Data Provenance, Adversarial Robustness, and IP Protection

To ensure compliance and protect intellectual property, the Data Ingestion Layer integrates a Data Provenance and Lineage Tracker. This component records the source, transformation history, and permissions of every data point used in the final report, ensuring auditable lineage.

Furthermore, external market data is susceptible to poisoning (e.g., malicious social media injection or competitor data manipulation). The Intelligence Processing Layer integrates an Adversarial Robustness Testing Component that continuously probes the model and its inputs, filtering out malformed or manipulative data payloads to fortify the system against security threats. The system must also incorporate an IP and Copyright

Check Module to flag potential copyright violations in ingested and retrieved documents before the data is used in report generation, acting as a real-time legal firewall.

## Enterprise Implication

UC8 introduces the governance challenge of verifying AI outputs that are designed to inform high-stakes strategic decisions. The key architectural insight is that hallucination detection cannot be delegated to the humans who will act on the intelligence; by the time a human reviewer identifies a fabricated market claim, the strategic damage may already be done. The QA Agent, as an LLM-As-a-Judge, makes factual verification a system-level, automated, and measurable function rather than a downstream editorial check. The Bias Quantification Component addresses a subtler risk: a report that is factually accurate but systematically biased toward a particular company or toward historical patterns carries the same strategic harm as a hallucinated report, because decision-makers will act on the skewed analysis. Detecting Look-Ahead and Company-Specific Bias before reports reach strategic consumers is the intelligence equivalent of the Groundedness SLO in RAG deployments.

# Blueprint: UC9—Financial Risk and Fraud Monitoring Agent

Use Case 9 addresses the failure of rule-based financial monitoring to detect sophisticated fraud at the speed and scale required by modern financial environments. Traditional systems evaluate transactions against static criteria and cannot identify network-level fraud, account takeover via behavioral deviations, or emerging threat patterns that outpace rule-set updates; the result is both missed fraud and excessive false positives that overwhelm compliance teams. The RFM Agent transitions financial risk management from retrospective, rule-based detection to continuous, evidence-based autonomous investigation, a shift that introduces the highest governance stakes of any use case in this chapter, because the agent's recommended actions (account freezes, fund blocks) are financially irreversible.

# 1. The Business Problem

Traditional rule-based financial risk monitoring misses sophisticated or novel fraud schemes that evolve faster than rule sets can be updated and generates excessive false positives that overwhelm fraud and audit teams. Rule-based systems evaluate individual transactions against static criteria; they cannot detect network-level fraud (organized rings of accounts executing coordinated patterns), account takeover via behavioral deviations, or concept drift as fraud tactics adapt. The objective is to deploy a continuously learning agentic AI system that shifts financial risk management from reactive analysis to proactive, autonomous investigation, reducing financial risk events by 60% while substantially decreasing the volume of false-positive alerts.

# 2. The Governance Instrument

**GOVERNANCE STACK: UC9—Financial Risk and Fraud Monitoring Agent**

| Instrument | Active Setting for This Deployment |
|---|---|
| **Autonomy Level** | Level 4 (Autonomous Execution Within Defined Limits) |
| **Criticality Tier** | Critical |
| **Oversight model** | HOTL + mandatory HITL for all High-Value Asset actions exceeding board-authorized MAM; agent prepares XAI justification report for human sign-off before execution |

*(continued)*

| GOVERNANCE STACK: UC9—Financial Risk and Fraud Monitoring Agent | |
|---|---|
| **Instrument** | **Active Setting for This Deployment** |
| **Delegation Tier** | Delegated—HAL batch review; Board Risk Committee notification required; Full Board approval for Authority Matrix entry |
| **ADAE score (illustrative)** | 85 points illustrative (Financial 90 · Customer 80 · Operational 70 · Velocity 90) |
| **Autonomy Budget Draw** | 85 points drawn against board-approved portfolio ceiling (illustrative) |
| **Max action magnitude** | Account freeze/fund block ceiling set in Authority Matrix; irreversible actions require HITL sign-off |
| **HOTL certification** | Standard HOTL for HOTL supervisors; Critical-tier endorsement for HAL supervisors; ≥75% automation bias pass required |
| **≥98% standard** | ≥98% auditable rationale for all investigation and action decisions; write-before-execute mandatory |

**Required Oversight Model:** HOTL with mandatory HITL override for all actions on High-Value Assets exceeding the board-authorized maximum action magnitude; the agent's role in these cases is limited to preparing the XAI justification report for human analyst sign-off before execution.

**Key Governance Controls:** AI Agent Identity Provider enforcing ZTAI with short-lived dynamic credentials replacing static API keys; XAI framework (SHAP/LIME) integrated with Reasoning Trace Capture of the full ReAct loop for regulatory transparency; Online Feature Store ensuring point-in-time correctness of all features referenced in XAI explanations; MLOps monitoring for data drift, concept drift, and population drift with automated retraining pipeline triggered on threshold breach; Data Residency Zoning ensuring financial data does not cross jurisdictional boundaries in violation of regional residency laws.

## 3. The Technical Architecture

**Three-Layer Pipeline**: Real-time data ingestion via Apache Kafka; high-speed ML scoring using Graph Neural Networks for network-level fraud, Behavioral Biometrics Engine for account takeover detection, and Isolation Forest for statistical anomaly flagging; and Agentic Reasoning Core using the ReAct paradigm for evidence-based investigation. A centralized Feature Store ensuring feature consistency between training and live serving. Full specification is in the "Architectural Delta" section below.

## 4. The Enhancement

GNNs for network-level fraud detection to analyze the local neighborhood of transactions, capturing the relational dynamics within the financial network rather than evaluating individual transactions in isolation. This capability detects organized fraud rings, mule account networks, and coordinated patterns that are invisible to linear models. A transaction that is individually unremarkable may be anomalous when its network context, the accounts it connects to, and its timing relative to other transactions in the same cluster are analyzed. GNNs provide the evidence necessary for anti-money laundering and Know Your Business compliance: they correlate seemingly unrelated suspicious activities into a coherent network-level fraud narrative that a human investigator can verify and act on.

## 5. The Board Outcome

The board confirms that the system delivers a 60% reduction in financial risk events in pilot environments and a significant reduction in the volume of false-positive alerts. Every action on a High-Value Asset that exceeds the board-authorized magnitude threshold requires a human analyst's sign-off, with the agent providing a complete XAI report and reasoning trace before the decision is made. The MLOps drift monitoring pipeline is continuously active, with automatic retraining triggered upon detection of significant data or concept drift; governance reviews confirm that model performance metrics remain within compliance boundaries. Data Residency Zoning compliance is verified through the Feature Store's data lineage records, confirming no regulated financial data has been processed outside its designated jurisdiction.

## Governance Delta: UC9

The Governance Delta is defined by its high-impact actions, primarily focusing on enforcing HITL overrides and guaranteeing cross-jurisdictional compliance.

### Zero-Trust Financial Controls and NHI Management: UC9

ZTAI applies to UC9 as established for UC6, with one material difference: the RFM Agent's NHI carries access to financial data systems and account-flagging authority, making the threat profile materially higher. An AI Agent Identity Provider must replace static API keys with short-lived dynamic credentials, and Privileged Access Management integration is mandatory at Level 4.

Applying the NHI lifecycle governance framework to UC9: the RFM Agent's NHI is among the highest-risk in this chapter. It has access to financial data systems and can recommend freezing an account. As an Autonomy Level 4 system, credentials must rotate within 30 days, with Privileged Access Management integration mandatory. Privilege drift, where the NHI's actual permission set expands beyond the approved scope through incremental additions, is a zero-tolerance breach for this agent. A single incremental permission addition that enables the agent to directly execute a fund freeze (rather than recommending it for HITL approval) would constitute a material governance failure requiring immediate escalation.

For high-impact actions (e.g., temporary account freezing), a mandatory HITL override is enforced. The agent's role is limited to preparing the detailed justification and XAI report, requiring a human analyst's final sign-off before execution, thereby ensuring human accountability for sensitive financial decisions.

## Data Residency Zoning and Regulatory Compliance

Global financial operations require compliance with strict cross-jurisdictional regulations (e.g., the GDPR and RBI mandates). The architecture mandates Data Residency Zoning. This architectural control ensures that the ML/Scoring Engine and Agentic Core instances are deployed within the same jurisdictional boundary as the data they process. This prevents regulated financial data from violating regional residency laws, mitigating exposure to severe regulatory fines. Importantly, the NHI credentials for agents deployed in different jurisdictions must also be jurisdictionally scoped: an NHI authorized to access EU customer financial data must not be used in an APAC deployment context.

## MLOps for Concept Drift and Resilience

Financial crime evolves rapidly, leading to constant concept drift, the degradation of predictive accuracy as new fraud tactics emerge. Ignoring this is a regulatory compliance risk. The MLOps pipeline must implement continuous monitoring for data, concept, and population drift. Upon detecting a significant shift, the MLOps pipeline must automatically trigger model retraining and deployment cycles, ensuring the RFM Agent's predictive capabilities remain relevant and effective in the face of emerging threats. Note: A model update that materially changes the agent's decision logic constitutes a Mover event under the NHI lifecycle governance framework and requires an NHI privilege scope review before the updated model is deployed to production.

For accountability, the audit trail must be engineered to capture the agent's step-by-step ReAct logic (i.e., Thought, Action, Observation). This detailed logging, combined with XAI justifications, provides the necessary regulatory transparency to justify complex fund-freezing or account-flagging decisions to authorities. Table 10-4 sets out the financial risk model drift types and their MLOps mitigation.

***Table 10-4.*** *Financial risk model drift types and MLOps mitigation*

| Drift Type | Description | Impact on RFM Agent | MLOps Mitigation Strategy |
| --- | --- | --- | --- |
| Data drift | Change in statistical properties of input data (e.g., sudden shift in transaction volume). | False positives or negatives due to unexpected data distribution. | Statistical divergence metrics (KL/JS); automated alert/retraining trigger |
| Concept drift | Underlying relationship between input data and the fraud outcome changes (e.g., a new fraud scheme emerges). | Failure to detect novel fraud patterns (high false-negative rate). | Continuous validation against ground truth; automated model retraining and deployment. Model update = NHI Mover event |
| Population drift | Change in the underlying customer base or economic conditions. | Model becomes irrelevant to the current risk landscape. | Continuous audit of customer demographics and economic features |

# Architectural Delta: UC9

The need for ultra-low-latency detection and unimpeachable auditability defines the RFM architecture. The architecture is designed to ensure algorithmic integrity and regulatory compliance for real-time risk assessment. To achieve this, the architecture is built on three mandatory components: GNNs, a specialized Online Feature Store, and an XAI component. The use of GNNs enables the agent to move beyond analyzing individual transactions to detecting network-level fraud. At the same time, the Online Feature Store ensures the point-in-time correctness of the data used for scoring, which is essential for regulatory auditability. Furthermore, the XAI component, using techniques such as SHAP, is integrated to generate human-readable decision rationales, ensuring that every autonomous recommendation to flag or freeze an account is entirely justifiable.

## Real-Time Multimodal Detection and Graph Neural Networks

The detection layer is built on a multimodal strategy to catch both individual anomalies and systemic fraud. Since sophisticated fraud often involves organized networks of accounts, the system mandates the use of GNNs. GNNs analyze the complex relational dynamics within the financial network, shifting the focus of detection from individual transactions to network-level security assessment. This approach delivers higher accuracy, reduces false positives, and scales better than traditional methods.

## Online Feature Store for Point-in-Time Correctness

A centralized Feature Store is essential for serving features to the ML inference models. For strict regulatory auditability, this store must be architected to guarantee point-in-time correctness. This means the system can precisely recall the state of all features, including velocity, customer tenure, and behavioral biometrics, that led to a risk score at any given historical moment. This capability transforms the Feature Store into a verifiable compliance asset, providing the necessary forensic evidence for litigation and regulatory inquiries.

## Agentic Reasoning Core and XAI Integration

The RFM Agent executes a deep, iterative investigation using the ReAct paradigm (i.e., Think–Act–Observe). This iterative approach allows the agent to move from a generic ML score to a justified, policy-compliant action plan through structured evidence collection. Critically, the architecture integrates XAI (e.g., SHAP) to generate human-readable decision rationales. This provides the clarity fraud analysts need to quickly verify alerts and significantly reduces the labor costs associated with false positives.

## Enterprise Implication

UC9 represents the highest-stakes deployment in the chapter: the agent's actions, account freezes, fund blocks, and payment term modifications, are financially irreversible and regulatory-critical. The governance architecture responds with the most comprehensive controls of any chapter use case: ZTAI with dynamic credentials, XAI mandatory at every decision, point-in-time–correct Feature Store ensuring explanations reference the exact data state at the moment of prediction, and MLOps drift detection, making the monitoring infrastructure itself a compliance requirement. The HITL mandate for HVA actions is the explicit implementation of Accountability Follows Authority: the agent may investigate and recommend, but the authority to execute an irreversible financial action on a High-Value Asset remains with a certified human analyst who has reviewed the XAI justification. The Data Residency Zoning requirement reflects the cross-jurisdictional nature of financial operations; a single fraud detection system may process transactions governed by GDPR, CCPA, and multiple regional financial regulations simultaneously.

# Blueprint: UC10—Hotel Dynamic Pricing and Booking Agent

Use Case 10 extends the agentic governance pattern to a revenue optimization context, introducing an ethical pricing obligation that does not arise in any earlier blueprint: a system optimizing room rates against real-time demand signals requires board-approved fairness constraints to prevent discriminatory or value-destructive pricing. The Governance Delta is the Ethical Pricing Framework; the Architectural Delta is the conversational Memory Subsystem and the AI-Optimized API Design Principles that make multi-turn negotiation commercially viable at scale.

## 1. The Business Problem

Fixed pricing tiers and slow human intervention leave revenue unrealized when real-time demand signals go unmatched to customer profiles. The objective is a conversational booking agent that dynamically optimizes room rates based on market and occupancy data, potentially increasing the Average Daily Rate (ADR) by 3–5% while reducing labor costs for standard reservation interactions. (Note: The 3–5% ADR uplift range is an illustrative estimate based on hospitality AI deployment experience; readers seeking empirical benchmarks for specific property types are directed to revenue management systems vendors including IDeaS, Duetto, and OTA Insight.)

## 2. The Governance Instrument

| GOVERNANCE STACK: UC10—Hotel Dynamic Pricing and Booking Agent | |
|---|---|
| **Instrument** | **Active Setting for This Deployment** |
| **Autonomy Level** | Level 3 (Supervised Autonomous Agents) |
| **Criticality Tier** | High |
| **Oversight model** | HOTL; mandatory HITL for pricing recommendations outside board-approved fairness band; Agent Failover Controller reverts to fixed pricing on system failure |
| **Delegation Tier** | Monitored—kill switch within 60 seconds; HOTL supervisor mandatory during all operational hours |
| **ADAE score (illustrative)** | 38 points illustrative (Financial 40 · Customer 50 · Operational 30 · Velocity 60) |
| **Autonomy Budget Draw** | 38 points drawn against board-approved portfolio ceiling (illustrative) |
| **Max action magnitude** | Pricing commitment ceiling set in Authority Matrix; commitments above ADR threshold queued for HAL batch review |
| **HOTL certification** | Standard HOTL certification required; 12-month validity |

**Required Oversight Model:** HOTL; mandatory HITL for pricing recommendations falling outside the board-approved fairness band; Agent Failover Controller automatically reverts to human-assisted channels or fixed pricing when the LLM agent or critical external systems fail.

**Key Governance Controls:** Secure Payment Offload and Tokenization via a PCI DSS-compliant Secure Payment Gateway Tool ensuring cardholder data never enters the core LLM system; LLM guardrails preventing PII leakage and detecting prompt injection; Policy Enforcement Engine validating all tool calls against governance rules before execution;

Ethical Pricing Framework with continuous bias audits preventing discriminatory algorithmic outcomes; Agent Failover Strategy ensuring business continuity through automatic reversion to fixed pricing on system failure.

## 3. The Technical Architecture

**Single-Agent Architecture with Three-Layer Structure**: Presentation Layer (conversational interface); Agentic Workflow Layer housing the LLM Reasoning Engine, Planner/Orchestration Loop, Tool Router, and Memory Subsystem (Episodic Memory for session-aware execution, User-Specific Memory for loyalty-based personalization); and Enterprise Data/Tool Layer integrating the PMS, RMS, and Secure Payment Gateway. RAG pipeline for real-time grounding of pricing recommendations in current market data. Full specification is in the "Architectural Delta" section below.

## 4. The Enhancement

**AI-Optimized API Design Principles**: The agent's reliability and cost efficiency are directly dependent on the quality of its API integrations. Standard enterprise API responses, often verbose and unstructured, increase parsing complexity and elevate the risk of hallucinating critical facts such as final prices or availability counts. Three mandates apply: Structured Deterministic Responses, delivering pre-aligned objects for direct LLM prompt embedding; Low-Token Output Optimization, aggressively reducing unnecessary descriptive text in API payloads to manage the high token consumption of multi-turn agentic workflows; and Unified AI-Ready APIs, reducing the number of disparate systems required to complete a single booking action. These principles address the economic viability constraint unique to conversational pricing agents: a system requiring 15 LLM inference calls per booking is commercially unviable at scale, regardless of its accuracy.

## 5. The Board Outcome

The board attests that the system delivers a projected 3–5% increase in Average Daily Rate and 24/7 booking conversion capability while operating within board-approved pricing fairness and PCI DSS compliance thresholds. Cardholder data is confirmed never to enter the core LLM system or its audit logs; all payment processing is performed within the isolated PCI DSS–compliant environment. The Ethical Pricing Framework's bias audit results are reviewed quarterly to confirm that personalized rate recommendations remain within the board-approved fairness band. The Agent Failover Controller's activation logs confirm business continuity has been maintained during system failures through automatic reversion to fixed pricing.

# Governance Delta: UC10

The Governance Delta for the agent is mandated to ensure strict compliance with financial regulations and adherence to an Ethical Pricing Framework.

Applying the NHI lifecycle governance framework to UC10: this is a single-agent, Autonomy Level 3 system (Monitored tier). The Authority Matrix entry must confirm Level 3 before production deployment, as this determines the 60-day credential rotation schedule and the provisioning requirement of CISO approval with CAIO notification. The agent's NHI must hold read access to the RMS and PMS for pricing data retrieval, but must not directly write to the payment system; the secure payment offload pattern ensures the NHI privilege scope never includes access to the Cardholder Data Environment (CDE).

## PCI DSS Compliance via Secure Payment Offload

Compliance with the PCI DSS is the single most restrictive architectural constraint. The only way to guarantee compliance without subjecting the LLM agent to continuous PCI auditing is to mandate Secure Payment Offload and Tokenization. The LLM agent must be architecturally isolated and never store or process raw cardholder data (CHD).

The process requires the agent to identify the intent to pay and immediately initiate a secure handoff to a dedicated Secure Payment Gateway Tool. The agent receives only a non-sensitive payment token, ensuring the Cognitive Layer operates outside the CDE and thereby minimizing regulatory scope and risk. Critically, the agent NHI must not be provisioned with any permission that would grant it access to the CDE; the Secure Payment Gateway Tool operates under its own, separately governed NHI with CDE access.

## Policy Enforcement Engine and Ethical Pricing Framework

To mitigate financial risk, the agent's negotiation and pricing outputs must be governed by a Policy Enforcement Engine that operates at runtime. This engine enforces spending guardrails and negotiation limits in line with PaC rules, preventing the LLM from inadvertently offering excessive discounts or violating corporate financial policy.

The use of personalized pricing algorithms introduces ethical risks, including algorithmic bias and price discrimination. A formal Ethical Pricing Framework is required to mitigate this risk. The utility function, while optimizing profit (i.e., ADR), must integrate constraints to balance this with long-term trust (i.e., Customer Lifetime Value). Continuous bias audits using standardized fairness metrics are mandatory to ensure that personalized rates remain within an acceptable band relative to non-personalized rates, preventing discriminatory outcomes based on non-relevant customer characteristics.

The governance relies on the Policy Enforcement Engine and continuous monitoring of LLMOps metrics to track not only Token Cost per Query and P95 Latency, but also security metrics such as prompt injection attempts and PII leakage. Table 10-5 sets out the payment security and agent failover controls for UC10.

***Table 10-5.*** *Payment security and agent failover controls for UC10*

| Risk Area | Security Control/Mechanism | Governance Impact/ Regulatory Alignment |
|---|---|---|
| Cardholder data exposure | Secure Payment Offload and Tokenization. Payment Gateway NHI separately governed; agent NHI explicitly excluded from CDE permissions | Achieves PCI DSS compliance by isolating CDE from LLM core. Agent NHI privilege scope does not include CDE access. |
| Algorithmic price discrimination | Ethical Pricing Framework; continuous bias audits | Prevents discriminatory outcomes; balances ADR versus CLV/fairness. |
| Unauthorized financial action | Policy Enforcement Engine and UAM/RBAC. Authority Matrix maximum action magnitude enforced at PEP | Enforces negotiation limits and spending guardrails in real time. |
| System outage/ latency | Agent Failover Strategy (RBF) | Ensures business continuity; automatically reverts to fixed pricing if RMS latency breaches SLO. |
| PII leakage (conversational) | LLM guardrails (automated masking/detection) | Prevents accidental PII storage in the agent's logs/memory. |
| NHI privilege drift | Quarterly CISO discovery scan; continuous privilege scope monitoring | Zero-tolerance breach if NHI operating outside approved scope. Mover event required before any capability expansion. |

## Architectural Delta: UC10

The two governance-relevant architectural constraints specific to UC10 are the AI-Optimized API Design Principles that make multi-turn pricing negotiation economically viable at scale and the Agent Failover Strategy that ensures autonomous failure produces a degraded-but-functional state rather than a service outage. Both are detailed below.

## Agentic Planner with Memory Subsystem and Optimized APIs

Handling multi-turn negotiation and personalization requires a sophisticated Memory Subsystem. This subsystem must include Episodic Memory to log the chronological history for session-aware execution and reference during negotiation and User-Specific Memory to store persistent data, like loyalty status, which serves as a vital input for the personalized pricing tool.

Since agentic workflows require multiple LLM calls per transaction, leading to exponentially higher operational costs, the system mandates AI-Optimized API Design Principles for integration with the RMS/PMS. This involves using Structured Deterministic Responses and Low-Token Output Optimization in all API schemas. Reducing unnecessary text in the response payload directly lowers token consumption, making the complex multi-step reasoning economically viable at scale.

Because the agent's pricing recommendations are grounded in real-time RMS/PMS data via the RAG pipeline, any data latency is catastrophic to the user experience. The RAG component must be continuously validated using specialized retrieval metrics, such as Context Precision and Normalized Discounted Cumulative Gain (NDCG), to ensure pricing is grounded in current, accurate data rather than hallucinations.

## Agent Failover Strategy

Operational resilience requires a robust response to system outages or performance degradation, particularly concerning the high-latency RMS API. A comprehensive Agent Failover Strategy is mandated. This strategy relies on the LLMOps framework to continuously monitor P95 Latency. If a critical tool (such as the RMS pricing API) breaches its service-level objective, the Agent Failover Controller automatically intervenes, reverting the user interaction to a human-assisted channel or falling back to an established fixed pricing plan.

# Enterprise Implication

UC10 closes the chapter's use case sequence with a governance challenge that combines the personalization risks of UC8, the transactional integrity requirements of UC7, and the identity exposure of UC6. The Ethical Pricing Framework addresses the specific risk of utility-based agents: a system optimizing for ADR may correctly identify a high-value loyalty member's maximum willingness-to-pay and charge the absolute ceiling, which is profitable in the short term but destroys long-term customer value. Explicit fairness constraints within the pricing algorithm ensure that personalized rates remain within a board-approved band relative to baseline rates, converting ethical governance from a policy aspiration into a technically enforced architectural requirement. The Agent Failover Strategy reflects a Governance Principle that applies across all agentic deployments, but is most commercially visible in real-time booking contexts: autonomous systems must fail gracefully, not silently. An agent who fails without a defined fallback results in a worse customer outcome than no agent at all.

## The Business Agent Architecture: Scaling Autonomy in Core Functions

The five use cases in this chapter share a common governance architecture that operates independently of their domain differences. For the Chief Operating Officer and the Chief Information Officer, the common thread is the shift from reactive assistants to goal-driven machine entities that manage end-to-end workflows, and the common governance requirement is that every machine action traces back to a registered, scoped, and monitored NHI credential.

Figure 10-4 illustrates the shared multi-agent collaboration governance architecture that applies uniformly across all five use cases. The four zones, Sovereign Identity (PDP), Secure Enforcement (PEP), Cognitive Layer (MAC), and Business Process, show how every agent action flows from NHI-verified identity through the Authority Matrix policy engine and the MCP Gateway before reaching enterprise systems and how HITL escalation, the Immutable Audit Log, and the Event Bus close the governance loop.

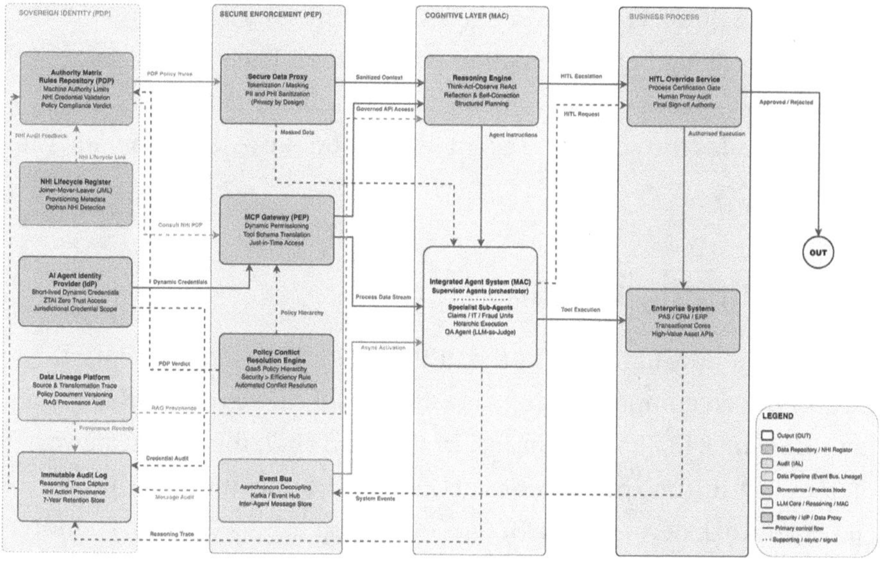


***Figure 10-4.*** *The shared multi-agent collaboration governance architecture—showing how the Sovereign Identity zone (Authority Matrix Rules Repository, NHI Lifecycle Register, AI Agent Identity Provider, Data Lineage Platform, Immutable Audit Log) governs the Secure Enforcement zone (Secure Data Proxy, MCP Gateway, Policy Conflict Resolution Engine, Event Bus) that mediates between the Cognitive Layer (Reasoning Engine, Integrated Agent System/ Supervisor Agents, Specialist Sub-agents) and Business Process (HITL Override Service, enterprise systems), with PDP policy rules, dynamic credentials, masked data, policy hierarchy, tool execution, and HITL escalation flows connecting all four zones*

## PDP: Contextual Evaluation

Across all five use cases, the Authority Matrix Rules Repository serves as the Policy Decision Point: the constitutional source of truth for what every registered NHI is permitted to do. Every proposed tool call, whether a password reset in UC6, a policy lookup in UC7, a data collection query in UC8, an account freeze recommendation in UC9, or a pricing tool invocation in UC10, is evaluated against the Authority Matrix entry for the acting agent before execution is permitted. The PDP returns a deterministic Allow or Deny verdict with auditable reason codes. The verdict precedes the action; no agent may act on the assumption that the PDP will approve.

## PEP: Dynamic Gating

The MCP Gateway functions as the PEP across all five deployments: the sole authorized component that dispatches tool calls to enterprise systems after receiving a PDP Allow verdict. In UC6 and UC7, the MCP Gateway enforces just-in-time permissions at the point of execution. In UC8, it gates access to external feeds for data collection agents. In UC9, it enforces the maximum action magnitude ceiling before any recommendation to freeze an account reaches the HITL portal. In UC10, it prevents the agent's NHI from accessing the Cardholder Data Environment. This PDP/PEP separation, evaluation before execution, and logic before action are the constitutional constants that apply uniformly across all business-function agents, regardless of domain, Autonomy Level, or orchestration model.

## The Foundation of Autonomy: NHI Governance

The NHI lifecycle governance framework, established at the beginning of this chapter, serves as the security foundation for the entire multi-agent collaboration architecture. Every specialist agent holds its own registered NHI, with a privilege scope calibrated precisely to its function and never exceeding the Autonomy Level–determined ceiling. The NHI Lifecycle Register is the authoritative source of truth governing every agent actor across all five use cases. The full specifications of the five governing principles and the JML lifecycle process are in the "NHI Lifecycle Governance" section above.

## Accountability and Reasoning Trace Capture

In a process-driven architecture, accountability requires capturing the agent's internal monologue as it navigates complex decisions. The system mandates Reasoning Trace Capture, which logs the complete Think–Act–Observe loop for every business transaction.

This trace transforms the agent's internal monologue into a mandatory compliance control. If an IT agent resets a password for an unauthorized user, the Reasoning Trace Capture provides the forensic evidence needed to determine if the error was a reasoning failure or a policy violation. This capture is synchronized with the unique Execution ID to ensure the entire process, from query to payment, is auditable and contestable. All traces are stored in the Immutable Audit Log for a minimum of seven years to satisfy regulatory retention obligations.

## Measuring the Impact of Process Autonomy

The board justifies the expansion of agentic autonomy by monitoring specific Key Risk Indicators that track the health of the automated processes.

**NHI Operational Metrics:** The system tracks the NHI Register Completeness and the Orphan NHI Rate to ensure that every machine actor is properly governed. A single orphaned NHI discovered in production is treated as a material governance breach that requires immediate reporting to the Board Risk Committee.

**Process Success and Hallucination Rates:** For agents delivering market intelligence or claims analysis, the system monitors the Factual Error Rate and the hallucination score using an automated judge. Sustained performance in these metrics allows the organization to move from moderate to high Criticality Tiers, enabling greater autonomous revenue generation. Additionally, the system tracks Cycle Time Reductions to formally validate the projected productivity gains.

# Summary

This chapter established that enterprise agentic AI at scale is not a question of model sophistication but of governance rigor. The NHI lifecycle governance framework is not a supplementary security control layered on top of agent governance; it is the mechanism through which every other governance control is operationalized. A PEP that validates every tool call is effective only if the NHI credential it validates is correctly scoped, actively rotated, and registered in the lifecycle record. The key takeaways are as follows:

- **NHI governance is the security foundation for all agentic deployments.** Every autonomous action, such as a password reset, payment execution, account freeze, and pricing update, is performed by presenting an NHI credential. An uncontrolled NHI is an uncontrolled autonomous action capability. The five governing principles, the JML process, and the four board KRIs (NHI Register Completeness, Orphan NHI Rate, Credential Rotation Compliance, Privilege Drift Incident Rate) apply uniformly across all five use cases. A single orphan NHI discovered in production constitutes a material governance breach requiring immediate reporting to the Board Risk Committee.

- **Dynamic permissioning replaces standing privilege for irreversible actions.** Across UC7 (claims payment), UC9 (account freezing), and UC10 (booking modification), the agent's NHI holds no standing write access to execution endpoints. The PEP issues just-in-time permissions at the point of HITL-approved execution. This is the NHI implementation of Accountability Follows Authority: the credential's execution capability follows the authority trail established by the human-governed process rather than the agent's own reasoning.
- **First-introduced architectural controls address risks that the RAG stack was not designed to prevent.** The Secure Data Proxy (tokenization for transactions, dynamic masking for analysis) addresses PII/PHI exposure in UC7 and UC10. The QA Agent, acting as an LLM-As-a-Judge, addresses hallucinations in strategic recommendations (UC8). The Bias Quantification Component addresses Look-Ahead and Company-Specific Bias in market intelligence (UC8). Authorization-Aware RAG addresses internal privilege escalation in UC6. Each control is mandated by the architectural augmentation that creates the risk it mitigates.
- **Model updates and capability changes are NHI lifecycle events.** In UC9, a model update that materially changes the agent's fraud detection logic is a Mover event requiring a full NHI privilege scope review before the updated model reaches production. In UC10, adding a direct booking modification capability is a Mover event. In UC7, adding a specialist agent to

a new product line requires a new NHI registration before the agent handles live claims. The NHI lifecycle and the model lifecycle are inseparable.

- **The separation between the Cognitive Layer and the Deterministic Core is enforced at the credential level.** In NHI terms, the separation is operationalized by ensuring the agent's NHI never has standing access to irreversible execution endpoints. Write access to payment systems, fund-freeze APIs, and core system modification endpoints is dynamically granted at the point of HITL-approved execution. All decision audit logs, NHI authentication records, and override records across the five use cases are subject to a minimum seven-year retention obligation under the EDS Logging and Explainability Standard (formally established in Chapter 11); this obligation survives system decommissioning and must be confirmed before any agent's NHI is deprovisioned.

The next chapter advances to the highest tier: systems in which a governance failure is not an operational disruption but an irreversible safety or financial crisis and in which two instruments must be in place before any deployment can proceed.

# References

Accenture. 2023. Insurance Industry Outlook: Reimagining the Future of Insurance. New York: Accenture. https://www.accenture.com/us-en/insights/insurance/insurance-industry-outlook.

Hossain, M Maruf. 2026. Non-Human Identity Governance: A Governance Framework for Agentic AI Credentials in Regulated Enterprises. Preprint. Zenodo. https://doi.org/10.5281/zenodo.20585675.

IDC. 2023. Untapped Value: What Every Executive Needs to Know About Unstructured Data. IDC White Paper, sponsored by Box. Framingham, MA: International Data Corporation.

Liang, Percy, Rishi Bommasani, Tony Lee, Dimitris Tsipras, Dilara Soylu, Michihiro Yasunaga, Yian Zhang, et al. 2022. Holistic Evaluation of Language Models. arXiv:2211.09110. https://arxiv.org/abs/2211.09110.

CHAPTER 11

# Multi-domain Advanced Automation

Chapters 1–10 established the governance architecture for retrieval-augmented systems and five business-function agentic deployments. This chapter advances to the highest tier: multi-domain automation, in which AI agents operate independently across financial transactions, industrial logistics, and physical asset control. The stakes of governance failure at this tier escalate from operational disruption to irreversible safety and financial crisis. Two governance instruments underpin the accountability architecture for all five use cases in this chapter and are established before the use cases are described: the HOTL Certification Framework, which defines what "human oversight" means in certifiable, operational terms, and the ≥98% auditable rationale standard, which defines what "accountability" means as a measurable, enforceable compliance threshold.

The five use cases span two operational domains. UC11 and UC12 address multi-domain transactional integrity: restaurant waitlist and seating optimization (UC11) and event ticket exchange and seat upgrade orchestration (UC12). UC13, UC14, and UC15 address the Predictive Maintenance Triad: aircraft predictive maintenance (UC13), defense equipment maintenance in disconnected environments (UC14), and manufacturing predictive maintenance with digital twin validation (UC15). Each use case introduces a domain-specific architectural augmentation,


M. M. Hossain and A. A. N. Ponnusamy, *Governance-First AI*,
https://doi.org/10.1007/979-8-8688-3118-8_11

the novel component that enables autonomous operation, and a corresponding governance control mandated by the risk the augmentation introduces.

The defining governance challenge at this tier is transforming potential AI failure from a passive information quality issue into an active safety or financial accountability crisis. In RAG deployments, failure means hallucination or poor retrieval. In multi-domain advanced automation, failure means execution of an irreversible, high-impact action: an unauthorized payment, an accidental asset shutdown, or a safety protocol breach. Managing this escalation requires the Safety Runtime Environment (SRE), the always-on infrastructure layer that enforces span-of-control thresholds, triggers automatic mode shifts to HITL when thresholds are approached, and enforces fail-closed behavior when logging infrastructure is unavailable.

The chapter is organized as follows: The "HOTL Certification and the ≥98% Auditable Rationale Standard" section establishes the HOTL Certification Framework, span-of-control thresholds, the ≥98% auditable rationale standard, and mandatory log fields as canonical standards that apply uniformly across all five use cases. Table 11-2 summarizes the primary architectural augmentation and governance control for each use case. Each use case is then presented through the unified blueprint—Business Problem, Governance Instrument, Technical Architecture, Enhancement, and Board Outcome—followed by an "Enterprise Implication" section. The "Accountability and Assurance Layer for Autonomous AI" section integrates the five use cases through the shared SRE governance architecture shown in Figure 11-3. The "Summary" section closes with two non-negotiable governance rules that apply to all five use cases, followed by two non-negotiable trigger conditions that mandate HITL intervention across all of them.

**Governance Leaders**: The HOTL Certification Framework and ≥98% auditable rationale standard that open this chapter define the non-negotiable floor for human oversight at this tier—read these before the use cases.

**Architects and Practitioners:** The Governance Stack sidebar, Technical Architecture, and the "Accountability and Assurance Layer for Autonomous AI" section are your implementation specification.

## HOTL Certification and the ≥98% Auditable Rationale Standard

Before the five use cases in this chapter are described, two governance instruments must be established. The opening identified irreversibility as the defining challenge at this tier: authorized payments cannot be recalled, grounded aircraft cannot be ungrounded without regulatory recertification, and safety-critical systems that halt mid-operation may create physical risk. Conventional governance controls, oversight models, audit logs, and policy enforcement are necessary but not sufficient when the consequences of failure are irreversible. What is additionally required is a certifiable guarantee that a human supervisor was genuinely able to intervene before irreversibility was reached and a measurable standard for what constitutes a sufficient audit record to defend each decision retrospectively. The HOTL Certification Framework addresses the first requirement. The ≥98% auditable rationale standard is the answer to the second. They apply to every use case in this chapter and define the minimum standard for what "human oversight" and "accountability" mean in operational terms, not as aspirational goals but as measurable, certifiable requirements.

## HOTL Supervision As a Constitutional Obligation

Human-on-the-Loop supervision is a constitutional governance obligation, not a performance aspiration or an operational best practice. Every autonomous AI system operating at Autonomy Level 3 or above must have a certified HOTL supervisor with active, unimpeded authority to intervene, adjust, or halt the system. A system operating at Level 3 or above without a currently certified HOTL supervisor is operating in governance breach and must be immediately suspended regardless of business impact. No commercial, operational, or efficiency consideration overrides this obligation.

Automation bias, the tendency of human supervisors to defer to autonomous systems rather than exercising genuine challenge, is the primary failure mode in HOTL oversight arrangements. The certification program is specifically designed to test and build resistance to automation bias, not merely to confirm that supervisors understand the system they oversee. A supervisor who does not understand the system they are overseeing, who cannot recognize anomalous behavior in the decision stream, who does not know how to exercise their intervention authority, or who is supervising more concurrent decisions than they can meaningfully challenge is not a governance control; they are a governance artifact.

## Certification Program Requirements

Every primary and secondary HOTL supervisor for the systems in this chapter must complete a structured certification program before assuming supervisory duties. The program comprises five sequential components: a Foundation module covering the constitutional governance obligations and supervisor authority; system-specific training on how the supervised system makes decisions and what anomalous patterns look like; an Intervention skills module with live practice on circuit-break, kill-switch, and escalation controls; an Automation bias training module using scenario-based assessment with a ≥75% scenario identification pass standard; and an Assessed supervision exercise of at least four hours rated against eight behavioral indicators.

Certification is valid for 12 months. Annual renewal requires an updated automation bias scenario assessment (≥75% pass rate) and a governance update briefing. A supervisor whose renewal assessment is not completed before the certification expiry date is automatically removed from the certification register, and any system they were supervising as a primary supervisor must have an alternative certified supervisor assigned or be suspended until coverage is restored.

For supervisors of Critical-tier Level 3 systems and for all supervisors of Level 4 and Level 5 systems, a Critical-tier endorsement is additionally required. This endorsement serves as the Human-Above-the-Loop (HAL) certification pathway; no separate HAL certification program exists. The endorsement includes high-consequence decision environment scenarios, a HAL competency module covering batch-interval review and anomaly recognition in batch decision outputs, and a separate observed supervision exercise conducted in the Critical-tier system environment. At least two currently certified supervisors must be named for each Level 3 system (three for Level 4–5 systems); any gap must be remediated within five business days, or the system is suspended. Figure 11-1 shows the HOTL certification program pathway: its five sequential certification components and the annual renewal cycle.

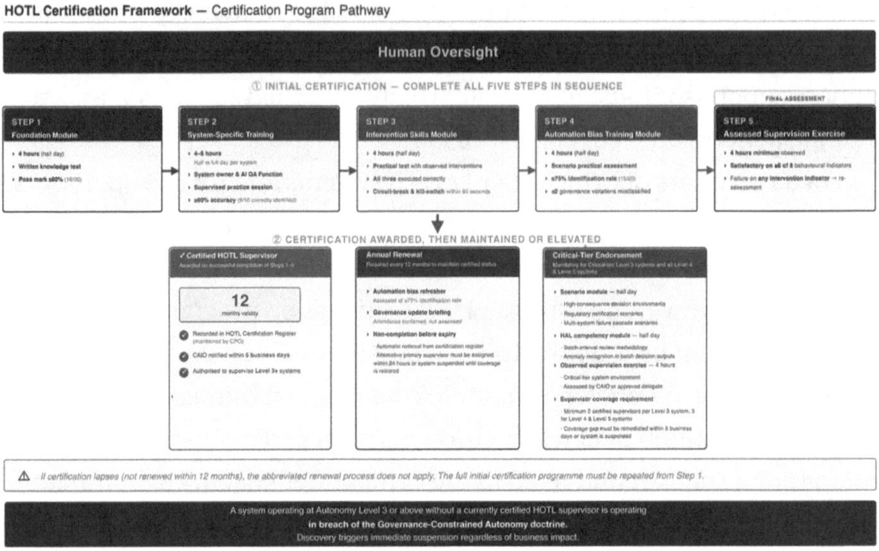


***Figure 11-1.*** *HOTL certification program pathway—five sequential certification components, annual renewal cycle with automation bias reassessment requirement, Critical-tier endorsement branch for Level 4–5 systems (the HAL certification pathway), and lapse reinstatement rule requiring full program repeat*

# Span-of-Control Thresholds

HOTL oversight is only a governance control if the supervisor can genuinely challenge the decisions being monitored. The following span-of-control thresholds define the maximum number of concurrent autonomous decisions a single certified supervisor may oversee per hour while maintaining genuine challenge capability. Exceeding these thresholds is a governance breach. These thresholds are maximums, not targets. Table 11-1 sets out the HOTL span-of-control thresholds by Criticality Tier. Figure 11-2 shows the decision logic for assigning a system to a Criticality Tier and the span-of-control threshold that applies.

***Table 11-1.*** *HOTL span-of-control thresholds by Criticality Tier*

| System Criticality Tier | Maximum Decisions per Hour per Supervisor | Monitoring Mode | SRE Response at Threshold |
|---|---|---|---|
| Critical | 50 decisions per hour | Supervisor must be able to review each decision outcome individually, not merely monitor aggregate statistics. | SRE automatically shifts to HITL (pre-action approval) mode before threshold is breached. |
| High | 100 decisions per hour | Supervisors monitor decision streams with ability to investigate individual decisions on demand. | SRE shifts to HITL mode at threshold. Chief AI Officer notified. |
| Moderate | 200 decisions per hour | Supervisors monitor aggregate patterns and investigate flagged decisions. SRE anomaly alerts drive individual review. | SRE shifts to HITL mode at threshold. |
| Low | 500 decisions per hour | Supervisors monitor exception alerts rather than the full decision stream. Conditional on confirmed Low Criticality Tier classification. | Any reclassification to Moderate or above invalidates this threshold immediately. |

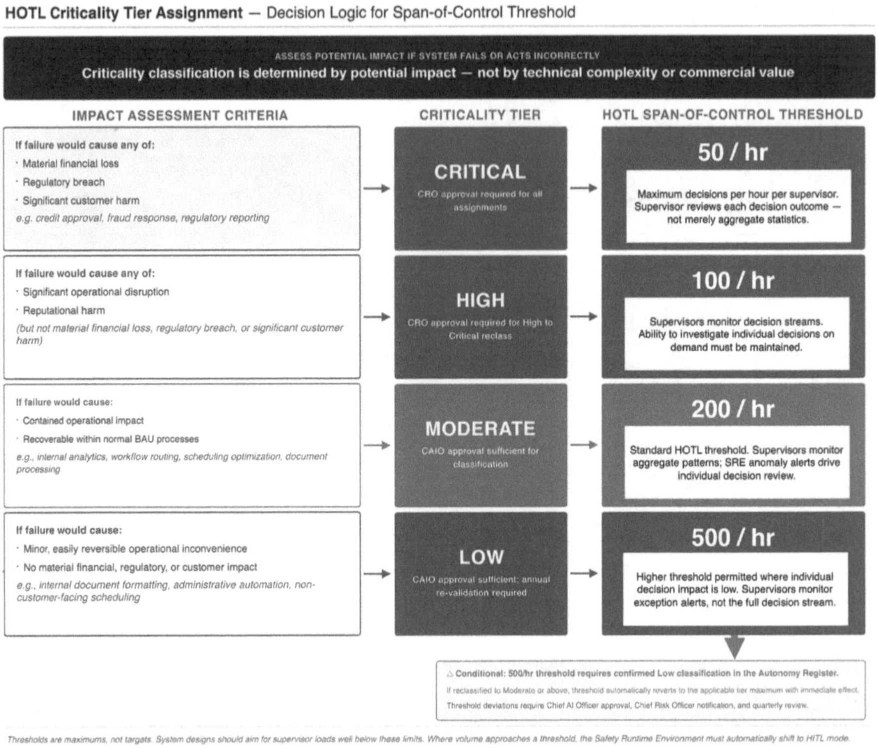


***Figure 11-2.** HOTL Criticality Tier assignment—decision logic for determining which span-of-control threshold applies to a given system, based on its Criticality Tier classification in the Autonomy Register, and the SRE response when decision volume approaches the threshold*

Threshold deviations require CAIO approval and notification to the CRO. Any proposed threshold above the standard for a Criticality Tier must include a documented rationale and compensating controls. Deviations are time-limited and reviewed quarterly. Where decision volume approaches a threshold, the Safety Runtime Environment must automatically shift to HITL (pre-action approval) mode to prevent threshold breach; this is a system design requirement, not an operational response.

## The ≥98% Auditable Rationale Standard

At least 98% of all decisions made by autonomous systems in regulated domains must generate a complete, auditable rationale log at the point of execution. This threshold reflects the framework's determination that a 2% unauditable decision rate represents the maximum acceptable governance gap for board-level reporting in regulated domains: it is stringent enough to prevent systematic accountability evasion while acknowledging that infrastructure failures and edge cases will occasionally prevent contemporaneous logging. Organizations operating under stricter regulatory frameworks may set a higher threshold; this standard represents the EDS framework's minimum floor, not the ceiling. This is a minimum compliance threshold, not a target. Any quarter in which the auditable rationale rate falls below 98% for any regulated-domain agent constitutes a Board Risk Committee escalation event requiring a management action plan within ten business days of quarter-end.

A "complete auditable rationale" is a log entry that contains all mandatory fields and is sufficient for a regulator to reconstruct the basis for the decision without requiring additional interpretation, reconstruction, or supplementation from the system owner. The log must be generated contemporaneously with the decision, not reconstructed after the fact. For regulated-domain decisions, the decision rationale log entry must be committed to the logging infrastructure before the action is executed. A logging failure is treated as a Safety Runtime Environment alert, and the agent enters its fail-closed state; an agent may not proceed with a decision if the logging infrastructure is unavailable.

## The EDS Logging and Explainability Standard: Formal Definition and Mandatory Log Schema

The EDS Logging and Explainability Standard is the EDS framework's mandatory governance standard specifying minimum logging requirements for all production autonomous AI systems. It defines the

≥98% auditable rationale standard (the minimum proportion of regulated-domain decisions that must generate a complete, contemporaneous audit log entry), the decision audit trail architecture (write-before-execute, tamper-evident, append-only storage with five-business-day retrieval capability), override capability obligations (HOTL supervisor interfaces, HITL escalation workflows, and the override record field requirements), and regulatory defensibility evidence requirements (the Minimum Explainability Record for adverse decisions, certification reference capture, and the fail-closed obligation). The Standard's mandatory log schema specifies 18 fields, organized into five categories: system and agent identity, session and timing, decision context, action and authority, and oversight and override. The Standard is the canonical governance reference for all log field requirements cited in Chapters 1–10 and applies uniformly to all production agentic AI systems registered in the Autonomy Register.

The mandatory 18-field log schema is provided in full in Appendix A. For HOTL decisions at Level 3 and above, the log must additionally capture the supervising operator's current certification reference and the override record field, which must be retained for a minimum of seven years or longer, as required by applicable law. Field 9 of the schema references the Prompt Authority Scope Statement (PASS): the board-approved record that defines the authority scope under which a specific prompt configuration is permitted to operate, linking the deployed prompt to the board's authorization. The PASS identifier is recorded in the format PASS-YYYY-NNN, where PASS denotes Prompt Authority Scope Statement, YYYY is the four-digit year of board approval, and NNN is the sequential issuance number within that year. This identifier links every logged decision to the specific board-approved authority scope under which the prompt operated.

**HE ≥98% AUDITABLE RATIONALE STANDARD AND THE HOTL CERTIFICATION THRESHOLD**

*These two instruments define the floor below which autonomous AI deployment in regulated domains is not permissible regardless of the quality of the underlying technical architecture. A system that generates auditable rationale for only 90% of its decisions is not 90% compliant; it is non-compliant. A system supervised by an uncertified HOTL supervisor is not partially supervised; it is unsupervised. The accountability layer described in this chapter is only meaningful if both instruments are met consistently.*

**Architectural Implication for All Five Use Cases:** The logging infrastructure must be designed with write-before-execute capability (Hossain, *Write-Before-Execute*, 2026) for regulated-domain decisions, tamper-evident write-once storage, and retrieval capability within five business days of any regulator request. The HOTL supervisor interface must surface the decision stream at a volume that does not exceed the applicable span-of-control threshold and must automatically alert the Safety Runtime Environment when volume approaches the threshold.

# Escalation of Risk in Autonomous Decision-Making

The escalation from information quality failure to irreversible operational crisis is the defining governance challenge at this tier, established in the introduction. Managing it requires the two governance instruments above: HOTL certification and the ≥98% auditable rationale standard, which the SRE enforces as a primary infrastructure layer, not a secondary monitoring tool. Each use case below operationalizes these instruments through the unified blueprint structure.

## Delta Focus

Each use case section presents the full blueprint structure, with the Governance Instrument defining the new controls specific to that use case's risk profile and the Technical Architecture introducing the novel components. Foundational controls standardized across all deployments (Security Trimming, immutable audit logging, PDP/PEP enforcement, ZTAI) are inherited and not repeated in each section. Table 11-2 summarizes the delta for each use case.

***Table 11-2.*** *Architectural and Governance Deltas of advanced automation use cases*

| Use Case | Primary Architectural Delta | Mandatory Governance Delta | Primary Risk Mitigated |
|---|---|---|---|
| UC11 | Seating Optimization Engine (Max Weight Matching), Offline Mode Architecture | TCPA Consent Log, algorithmic bias/ fairness (FAT framework), Constrained RBAC with Segregation of Duties (SoD). HOTL oversight at Moderate threshold ($\leq$200 decisions/ hour). | Legal/ communication risk, algorithmic discrimination |
| UC12 | Orchestration-based Saga Pattern, Hybrid Three-Tier Separation | PCI DSS Offload/ Tokenization, Policy Compliance Gate, Data Geo-fencing. $\geq$98% auditable rationale for all payment decisions. | Financial/fraud risk, distributed transaction failure |

(*continued*)

*Table 11-2.* (*continued*)

| Use Case | Primary Architectural Delta | Mandatory Governance Delta | Primary Risk Mitigated |
|---|---|---|---|
| UC13 | Hybrid AI (deep learning for RUL prognostics + dual RAG diagnostics), MAS | EU AI Act High-Risk GRC (Regulation EU 2024/1689, Annex III; deferred to December 2, 2027, under the Digital Omnibus provisional agreement of May 2026, pending formal adoption), MLOps continuous assurance (KL/JS divergence), mandatory HITL for unscheduled groundings. HAL oversight model: supervisors hold Critical-tier endorsement (HAL certification pathway); batch review at ≤50 decisions/hour threshold. ≥98% auditable rationale for all prognostic decisions. | Operational safety, regulatory non-compliance |

(*continued*)

*Table 11-2.* (*continued*)

| Use Case | Primary Architectural Delta | Mandatory Governance Delta | Primary Risk Mitigated |
|---|---|---|---|
| UC14 | Edge–Fog–Cloud Disconnected, Intermittent, and Low-Bandwidth/Disconnected, Occasional, and Low-Bandwidth (DIL/DOL) topology, MIL-STD-1553 Notice 4 (a military standard defining the electrical and protocol characteristics of a serial data bus used in defense vehicle and aircraft systems), specialized MAS (SRA, LRA) | ZTAI, Audit and Compliance Agent (ACA), GAGAS (Yellow Book, 2024, Chapter 6)/NIST SP 800-53 Rev. 5 Audit Trail. ≥98% auditable rationale mandatory for all field maintenance decisions. | Mission readiness, cyber-physical security, privilege escalation |
| UC15 | Digital twin validation, ensemble reasoning, Cyber-Physical Security Gateways | Agentic GRC framework, Ethical/Fairness Agent, XAI/ accountability layer. HAL oversight model: supervisors hold Critical-tier endorsement (HAL certification pathway); batch review at ≤100 decisions/ hour threshold. Certification currency verified in Audit Log. | Non-determinism/ hallucination, resource allocation bias |

# Multi-domain Transactional Integrity

UC11 and UC12 share a defining governance characteristic: the agent's decisions create or modify commitments that extend beyond the enterprise boundary, automated SMS communications to guests, and financial transactions with customers, requiring accountability infrastructure that reaches into the external legal and regulatory environment.

# Blueprint: UC11—Optimizing the Restaurant Waitlist and Preference Agent

Use Case 11 addresses the revenue and service gap created when high-demand restaurants manage guest flow through manual processes: hosts cannot efficiently notify waiting parties, match tables to party preferences, or maintain real-time seating optimization during peak hours. The result is lost revenue from waitlist abandonment, customer frustration due to inaccurate wait-time estimates, and inefficient staff allocation. The Autonomous Waitlist Agent introduces the first use case in this chapter, where the agent manages physical resource allocation in real time, establishing that, in this context, agent failure requires an immediate deterministic fallback rather than a cloud failover.

## 1. The Business Problem

The operational problem is queue abandonment and table misallocation. Manual waitlist management produces inaccurate wait-time estimates, slow customer notifications, and suboptimal table assignments, all of which reduce Table Turnover Rate (TTR). When a guest waits longer than estimated without communication, they leave; when a table is assigned without considering party size, dietary requirements, or seating preferences, both revenue efficiency and guest experience degrade. The business objective is a potential 10% increase in service volume through autonomous notification acceleration and seating optimization, with front-of-house staff freed from repetitive communication tasks.

## 2. The Governance Instrument

| GOVERNANCE STACK: UC11—Restaurant Waitlist and Preference Agent | |
|---|---|
| **Instrument** | **Active Setting for This Deployment** |
| **Autonomy Level** | Level 3 (Supervised Autonomous Agents) |
| **Criticality Tier** | Moderate |
| **Oversight model** | HOTL at Moderate threshold (≤200 decisions/hour); mandatory HITL for VIP overrides and hard-constraint conflicts; SRE shifts to HITL when threshold approached |
| **Delegation Tier** | Monitored—kill switch within 60 seconds; HOTL supervisor mandatory during all operational hours |
| **ADAE score (illustrative)** | 28 points illustrative (Financial 10 · Customer 40 · Operational 30 · Velocity 60) |
| **Autonomy Budget Draw** | 28 points drawn against board-approved portfolio ceiling (illustrative) |
| **Max action magnitude** | Table assignment and communication actions; no financial commitment authority |
| **HOTL certification** | Standard HOTL certification required; 12-month validity; ≥75% automation bias pass required |
| **≥98% standard** | ≥98% auditable rationale for all automated outbound SMS communications (TCPA compliance) |

**Required Oversight Model**: HOTL at Moderate Criticality Tier threshold (≤200 decisions per hour per supervisor); mandatory HITL for high-stakes assignments (VIP overrides, safety-critical preference conflicts) and when the Seating Optimization Engine detects a hard-constraint conflict it cannot resolve without violating a guest safety requirement; HOTL supervisor interface must display current decision volume rate relative to the threshold; SRE automatically shifts to HITL mode when threshold is approached.

**Key Governance Controls**: Seating Optimization Engine with safety-critical preferences (severe allergies, mobility access) coded as hard constraints inviolable by the revenue-maximizing objective function; TCPA Consent Log as an immutable, legally defensible record of explicit customer consent for all automated SMS communications, mitigating fines of $500–1,500 per violation (47 U.S.C. § 227, Telephone Consumer Protection Act), meeting the ≥98% auditable rationale standard for all automated outbound communications; FAT framework mandating pre-deployment bias audits and continuous fairness monitoring on the seating algorithm; Constrained RBAC with Segregation of Duties preventing operational staff from altering optimization parameters; Offline Mode Architecture with local event queue ensuring waitlist continuity during network outages; Rule-Based Fallback (RBF; FIFO) triggered immediately on Seating Optimization Engine failure.

## 3. The Technical Architecture

Tripartite Architecture (Presentation, Application, and Data Tiers); AI Orchestration Agent connected via API to the POS System and Table Management Software; Seating Optimization Engine using Maximum Weight Matching algorithm with multi-factor cost function; Preference and NLP Engine capturing structured dietary restriction and preference data from conversational input; Offline Mode Architecture with local event store on the Host Tablet and delayed-synchronization protocols. The Offline Mode Architecture and Rule-Based Fallback are fully specified in "The Enhancement" section below.

## 4. The Enhancement

**Offline Mode Architecture Combined with Rule-Based Fallback (RBF):** The primary resilience mechanism is a local event-store queue on the Host Tablet that persists all transactional data (waitlist entries, seating actions, preference updates) during network outages, with delayed synchronization managing data conflicts upon recovery. If the Seating Optimization Engine or the central LLM agent fails, a decoupled FIFO Rule-Based Fallback immediately takes over. This combination addresses the governance risk unique to brick-and-mortar agentic deployments: standard cloud failover strategies introduce unacceptable latency for real-time front-of-house operations, and a complete agent failure without an immediate, deterministic fallback is operationally worse than no agent at all. The Governance Principle established here, that autonomous systems managing physical resources must fail gracefully into a defined, deterministic state rather than fail silently, applies to all five use cases in this chapter.

## 5. The Board Outcome

The board attests that the system has the potential to increase service volume by 10% through autonomous notification acceleration and seating reoptimization, freeing front-of-house staff from repetitive communication tasks. Every automated outbound SMS communication generates a TCPA Consent Log entry that confirms the consent status at the point of communication, meeting the ≥98% auditable rationale standard. The Seating Optimization Engine's Preference Penalty Score is monitored continuously to ensure that revenue optimization is not achieved at the expense of guest satisfaction and that safety-critical hard constraints (severe allergies, mobility access) are upheld in all production decisions. Quarterly fairness audits confirm the algorithm does not discriminate based on proxy characteristics.

## Enterprise Implication

UC11 establishes the Governance Principle that autonomous systems managing physical resources in real-time environments require a defined deterministic fallback, not merely a cloud failover option. The Offline Mode Architecture and FIFO Rule-Based Fallback together ensure that agent failure produces a degraded-but-functional state rather than an operational halt during peak service hours. The TCPA Consent Log introduces an architectural governance contribution first seen in this chapter: the audit trail must extend beyond the enterprise boundary to include proof of consent for each communication, because the agent's automated communications to guests via SMS create direct external legal liability. The FAT framework's hard-constraint mechanism, making safety-critical preferences inviolable to the revenue-maximizing objective function, establishes the pattern that recurs across UC13, UC14, and UC15: safety constraints must be architecturally enforced, not weighted as optimization penalties that can be overridden by sufficiently large revenue incentives.

## Blueprint: UC12—Event Ticket and Seat Upgrade Agent

Use Case 12 addresses the missed revenue and poor customer experience created when ticketing platforms lack high-touch, real-time support for post-purchase transactions. After purchasing tickets, customers frequently need assistance with seat exchanges, upgrades, or logistics queries that ticketing platforms cannot handle autonomously, resulting in costly support calls and missed upgrade revenue. UC12 introduces the governance challenge of distributed financial transaction integrity: how to ensure that a multi-step financial workflow (reserve seat, process payment, void original ticket, issue new ticket) across independent microservices is either completed atomically or fully rolled back to a known consistent state when any step fails.

# 1. The Business Problem

The core operational problem is the inability to process complex, multi-step financial transactions autonomously without risking an inconsistent state when any individual step fails. A seat upgrade requires coordinating atomic transactions across independent Inventory, Pricing, Payment, and Ticketing microservices: if payment is authorized but the new ticket cannot be issued, the customer has paid for an upgrade they did not receive. Traditional ACID guarantees do not apply across distributed microservices, and without a governed compensation mechanism, any mid-transaction failure can create an unrecoverable, inconsistent state and cause direct financial harm. The business objective is to transform post-purchase support interactions into a revenue center, with Revenue Yield per Interaction (RYI) as the primary success metric.

# 2. The Governance Instrument

| GOVERNANCE STACK: UC12—Event Ticket and Seat Upgrade Agent | |
|---|---|
| **Instrument** | **Active Setting for This Deployment** |
| **Autonomy Level** | Level 3 (Supervised Autonomous Agents) |
| **Criticality Tier** | High |
| **Oversight model** | HOTL at High threshold ($\leq$100 decisions/hour); mandatory HITL for unresolved Saga failures and ambiguous financial decisions; HITL timeout triggers full transaction reversal |
| **Delegation Tier** | Monitored—kill switch within 60 seconds; HOTL supervisor mandatory during all operational hours |
| **ADAE score (illustrative)** | 45 points illustrative (Financial 50 · Customer 50 · Operational 40 · Velocity 50) |

*(continued)*

| GOVERNANCE STACK: UC12—Event Ticket and Seat Upgrade Agent | |
|---|---|
| **Instrument** | **Active Setting for This Deployment** |
| **Autonomy Budget Draw** | 45 points drawn against board-approved portfolio ceiling (illustrative) |
| **Max action magnitude** | Payment execution ceiling set in Authority Matrix; payment step of Saga Pattern requires HITL gate |
| **HOTL certification** | Standard HOTL certification required; 12-month validity; ≥75% automation bias pass required |
| **≥98% standard** | ≥98% auditable rationale required for all payment, compensation, and ticket issuance decisions; write-before-execute mandatory |

**Required Oversight Model**: HOTL at High Criticality Tier threshold (≤100 decisions per hour per supervisor); mandatory HITL via asynchronous escalation queue for unresolved Saga failures and ambiguous financial decisions; HITL timeout triggers a safe default compensating action (full transaction reversal) to prevent financial exposure; ≥98% auditable rationale required for all payment, compensation, and ticket issuance decisions with write-before-execute mandatory.

**Key Governance Controls**: Orchestration-based Saga Pattern as the primary distributed transaction management mechanism, with predefined compensating transactions for each forward action and idempotent commands preventing unintended side effects from retries; PCI DSS v4.0 Secure Payment Offload and Tokenization ensuring the Cognitive Layer never stores, processes, or transmits raw cardholder data; Policy Compliance Gate as mandatory pre-execution validator checking all financial transaction plans against non-negotiable legal and business rules before the Transactional API Gateway executes; Data Residency and Geo-fencing Module ensuring customer PII complies with applicable regional data sovereignty laws (GDPR, CCPA); ≥98% auditable rationale standard applied to all payment and compensation decisions.

## 3. The Technical Architecture

Hybrid Three-Tier Architecture (Presentation, Cognitive, Data/Deterministic) separating LLM planning from the deterministic transactional core; Saga Compensation Orchestrator managing state across Inventory, Pricing, Payment, and Ticketing microservices; Transactional API Gateway enforcing least-privilege access on all agent tool calls; business rules engine externalizing financial eligibility logic to deterministic, auditable rules; Real-Time Compliance Monitoring Service hosting the Policy Compliance Gate. Full specification is in "The Enhancement" section below.

## 4. The Enhancement

**Orchestration-based Saga Pattern**: The Saga Orchestrator manages a sequence of local transactions (Reserve New Seat → Calculate Fee Differential → Authorize Funds → Void Original Ticket → Issue New Ticket) and tracks state across all independent microservices. If any step fails, the Orchestrator executes predefined compensating transactions in reverse order to return the system to a known consistent state. All forward and compensating transactions are defined as idempotent commands, ensuring that retrying a failed step does not produce unintended side effects, such as double charging or duplicate ticket voids. The Saga Pattern is the governance-first response to the distributed transaction challenge: without a governed compensation mechanism, any mid-transaction failure leaves the customer in an unrecoverable, inconsistent state. The compensation log generated by the Saga Orchestrator is the structured audit trail that makes every financial action contestable and every rollback traceable to its triggering failure.

## 5. The Board Outcome

The board confirms that the system generates measurable ancillary revenue with Revenue Yield per Interaction (RYI) as the primary success metric. Every payment, compensation, and ticket issuance decision meets the ≥98% auditable rationale standard: log committed before execution, MAM authority check confirmed, SRE evaluation result recorded. The Policy Compliance Gate confirms that no financial transaction plan executed in the reporting period violated a non-negotiable legal or business rule. PCI DSS audit confirms that no raw cardholder data transited the Cognitive Layer.

## Enterprise Implication

UC12 establishes that the Saga Pattern is not merely an engineering resilience mechanism but the accountability layer for multi-step financial transactions in agentic systems. The compensation log that the Saga Orchestrator maintains is the structured audit trail that makes every financial action contestable and every rollback traceable to the failure that triggered it. Without the Saga Pattern, a mid-transaction failure (payment authorized but a new ticket not yet issued) creates both customer financial harm and an audit gap: the system has executed an irreversible financial action that cannot be traced to a complete, governed decision sequence. The Policy Compliance Gate addresses the complementary governance risk: the LLM's non-deterministic planning may generate a transaction plan that is locally coherent but globally non-compliant. The Gate prevents the Deterministic Core from executing plans that violate rules the Cognitive Layer cannot reliably enforce on its own, establishing that financial rule enforcement must be deterministic and external to the LLM reasoning layer.

## Predictive Maintenance Triad

UC13, UC14, and UC15 address autonomous control of physical assets in safety-critical, distributed environments. Each integrates prognostic deep learning, generative AI diagnostics, and multi-agent systems under the HAL oversight model with the Critical-tier endorsement as the mandatory certification pathway. The ≥98% auditable rationale standard applies to all prognostic and field maintenance decisions across the triad.

## Blueprint: UC13—Aircraft Predictive Maintenance

Use Case 13 addresses the inadequacy of time-based aircraft maintenance schedules, which leads to either over-maintenance (unnecessary cost and downtime) or unexpected component failures (safety risk and flight delays). The Hybrid AI Predictive Maintenance System transforms aviation MRO from a fixed-interval discipline into a data-driven prognostics capability, scheduling maintenance at the optimal point in a component's Remaining Useful Life (RUL). UC13 is the first use case in this chapter in which the agent's recommended actions directly impact physical safety—an unscheduled aircraft grounding is a mandatory HITL event—and in which the system is classified as high-risk under the EU AI Act (Regulation EU 2024/1689, Annex III; under the Digital Omnibus on AI, the Council and European Parliament reached a provisional agreement on May 7, 2026, confirmed by Council Member State representatives on May 13, 2026, deferring stand-alone Annex III high-risk obligations from August 2, 2026, to December 2, 2027, subject to formal adoption), mandating formal GRC alignment with FAA regulatory requirements and the EASA AI Roadmap 2.0 (January 2023).

# 1. The Business Problem

Traditional fixed-schedule maintenance in aviation produces two costly failure modes: over-maintenance replaces functional components, incurring unnecessary costs and downtime; under-maintenance misses early degradation signals, leading to unexpected failures that ground aircraft and trigger safety investigations. Manual analysis cannot efficiently process the volume of sensor data (vibration, temperature, torque, pressure, speed) generated by modern aircraft at the frequency needed for reliable prognostics. A significant technical challenge is the scarcity of catastrophic failure data in ultra-safe aviation systems; safety protocols are designed to prevent failures entirely, rendering traditional supervised ML models ineffective for RUL prognostics. The business objective is reductions in unplanned maintenance events of up to 25% and measurable maintenance cost savings (Deloitte, Industry 4.0 research, 2023).

# 2. The Governance Instrument

| GOVERNANCE STACK: UC13—Aircraft Predictive Maintenance System | |
|---|---|
| **Instrument** | **Active Setting for This Deployment** |
| **Autonomy Level** | Level 4 (Autonomous Execution Within Defined Limits) |
| **Criticality Tier** | Critical |
| **Oversight model** | HAL; batch-interval review at ≤50 decisions/hour Critical threshold; mandatory HITL for all RUL predictions resulting in unscheduled groundings; HAL supervisor provides XAI-evidenced sign-off |
| **Delegation Tier** | Delegated—three HAL-certified supervisors required; Board Risk Committee approval; Full Board approval for Authority Matrix entry |
| **ADAE score (illustrative)** | 78 points illustrative (Financial 60 · Customer 70 · Operational 80 · Velocity 90) |

*(continued)*

| GOVERNANCE STACK: UC13—Aircraft Predictive Maintenance System | |
|---|---|
| **Instrument** | **Active Setting for This Deployment** |
| **Autonomy Budget Draw** | 78 points drawn against board-approved portfolio ceiling (illustrative) |
| **Max action magnitude** | Maintenance scheduling actions within board-authorized domain; grounding decisions require HITL sign-off regardless of MAM |
| **HOTL certification** | Critical-tier endorsement (HAL certification pathway) mandatory for all supervisors; standard HOTL certification insufficient |
| **≥98% standard** | ≥98% auditable rationale for all RUL prognostic decisions influencing maintenance actions; write-before-execute mandatory |

**Required Oversight Model**: HAL; supervisors operate through batch-interval review of maintenance scheduling decisions at the ≤50 decisions per hour Critical-tier threshold; supervisors must hold the Critical-tier endorsement (the HAL certification pathway within the HOTL Certification Framework); mandatory HITL for all RUL predictions resulting in unscheduled aircraft groundings—the HAL supervisor escalates to HITL mode and must provide explicit sign-off with XAI evidence before any grounding decision is executed; at least three HAL-certified supervisors must be named in the certification register; HAL supervisor certification reference recorded in the Audit Log for each batch review cycle and each HITL approval.

**Key Governance Controls**: Adaptive Autoencoder–based RUL prognostics trained on healthy operational data, using reconstruction error as a quantifiable proxy for early degradation; addressing the scarcity of catastrophic failure data in safety-critical aviation environments; dual RAG system integrating textual and visual retrieval for source-cited, hallucination-resistant diagnostic guidance; EU AI Act High-Risk GRC Framework (Regulation EU 2024/1689, Annex III; obligations deferred to December 2, 2027, under the Digital Omnibus provisional agreement of May 2026, subject to formal adoption) requiring formal risk management, comprehensive activity logging, human oversight measures, and alignment with FAA regulatory requirements and the EASA AI Roadmap 2.0 (January 2023); MLOps continuous assurance using KL/JS divergence with automated retraining triggered when divergence exceeds 0.1 on critical sensor features (illustrative threshold; organizations calibrate against their own sensor profiles and safety requirements); ≥98% auditable rationale for all RUL prognostic decisions that influence maintenance actions.

## 3. The Technical Architecture

Integrated Hybrid AI Architecture combining Adaptive Autoencoder-based RUL prognostics (safety-critical prediction core), dual RAG system for diagnostic augmentation (textual and visual grounding in authoritative technical manuals), and multi-agent system for dynamic MRO scheduling (Flight Status Monitor Agent, Prognostics Agent, Resource Allocator Agent using Contract Network Protocol). MLOps pipeline for continuous assurance. API-First Architecture for real-time integration with CMMS, ERP, and inventory management systems. Full specification is in "The Enhancement" section below.

## 4. The Enhancement

**Dual RAG System for Safety-Critical Diagnostic Augmentation**: While the Autoencoder provides the RUL prediction (what will fail and when), the dual RAG system provides the diagnostic guidance (how the issue should be fixed), grounding every technician recommendation in verified textual and visual documentation. The visual RAG capability, integrating schematics and image matching, provides spatial context for physical repair procedures that text-only RAG cannot convey. In a safety-critical domain, the risk of LLM hallucinations in diagnostic output is existential: a technician acting on AI-generated maintenance guidance not anchored to an authoritative technical manual creates an aviation safety event, not merely a data quality failure. The dual RAG system is the technical implementation of the traceability mandate: every diagnostic output must be citable to a specific, authoritative source document before a technician can act on it.

## 5. The Board Outcome

The board confirms that the system delivers reductions in unplanned maintenance events of up to 25% and measurable maintenance cost savings, with measurable improvement in fleet availability (Deloitte, Industry 4.0 research, 2023). Every RUL prediction triggering a maintenance action meets the ≥98% standard (log before execution). Every unscheduled grounding escalates to HITL mode: approver identity, certification reference, and XAI sign-off recorded in the override record field of the Audit Log. The MLOps pipeline confirms that KL/JS divergence on critical sensor features has not exceeded the 0.1 illustrative threshold and has not triggered automated retraining in any reporting period. AI bias mitigation policy metrics (Statistical Parity Difference) are reviewed quarterly for systematic bias in fleet maintenance patterns. Table 11-3 sets out the MLOps continuous assurance metrics for drift detection.

***Table 11-3.*** *MLOps continuous assurance through drift detection metrics*

| Monitoring Metric | Category | Detection Technique | Action Threshold | Assurance Role |
|---|---|---|---|---|
| Input Feature Distribution | Data drift | KL/JS divergence | Divergence >0.1 on critical features (illustrative) | Triggers automated retraining/profile reassessment |
| RUL Prediction Error | Model performance skew | Mean Absolute Error (MAE) deviation | Deviation increase >5% on rolling average | Direct measure of prognostic accuracy degradation |
| Training Data Bias | Fairness/data integrity | Statistical Parity Difference (SPD) | SPD >10% between operational groups | Enforces AI bias mitigation policy |

## Enterprise Implication

UC13 introduces the governance escalation from financial irreversibility (UC12) to physical safety irreversibility. The defining architectural insight is that aviation AI requires two complementary assurance mechanisms addressing different failure modes: the Autoencoder provides statistical assurance that component degradation is detected before failure occurs; the dual RAG provides epistemic assurance that the human technician receives verified, source-cited guidance before acting on that detection. Neither is sufficient alone. A RUL prediction without verified remediation guidance produces detection without a safe response; a diagnostic system without reliable prognostic triggers produces guidance without reliable activation conditions. Together, they close the loop between the AI's prognostic capability and the human technician's corrective action in a domain where either failure mode constitutes an aviation safety event. The HAL oversight model at the ≤50-decisions-per-hour Critical-tier threshold establishes the standard for UC14 and UC15: at this tier of operational consequence, human oversight must be certifiable, not nominal.

## Blueprint: UC14—Preventive Maintenance for Defense Equipment

Use Case 14 addresses the maintenance challenge specific to defense assets operating in extreme and unpredictable conditions: accelerated wear, unexpected component failures, dispersed fleet logistics, and network environments that cannot support continuous cloud connectivity. The AI-powered predictive maintenance platform transforms defense sustainment from a reactive, fixed-interval discipline into a proactive, condition-based capability aligned with DoD Condition-Based Maintenance Plus (CBM+) mandates. UC14 introduces the governance challenge of maintaining a full audit and accountability infrastructure, including write-before-execute, in Disconnected, Intermittent/Occasional, and Low-Bandwidth (DIL/DOL) network environments where cloud connectivity cannot be assumed.

### 1. The Business Problem

Defense equipment operating across dispersed bases in extreme environments fails in ways that fixed-interval maintenance schedules cannot anticipate: accelerated wear from harsh conditions, unexpected component failures during missions, and complex logistics challenges tracking fleet health and spare parts availability across separated operational units. Traditional maintenance approaches reduce mission readiness and increase lifecycle costs. The additional constraint is that DIL/DOL network environments mean cloud-dependent AI systems cannot provide continuous decision support in forward operating contexts.

The objective is a PdM platform that delivers autonomous, condition-based maintenance decision support and GAGAS/NIST-compliant audit documentation even when connectivity to central cloud infrastructure is unavailable.

## 2. The Governance Instrument

| GOVERNANCE STACK: UC14—Preventive Maintenance for Defense Equipment | |
|---|---|
| **Instrument** | **Active Setting for This Deployment** |
| **Autonomy Level** | Level 4 (Autonomous Execution Within Defined Limits) |
| **Criticality Tier** | Critical |
| **Oversight model** | HAL; batch-interval review at ≤50 decisions/hour Critical threshold; mandatory HITL for all decisions on mission-critical assets triggering Safety Risk Agent halt flag; HAL access maintained in DIL/DOL conditions |
| **Delegation Tier** | Delegated—three HAL-certified supervisors required; external assurance required; Full Board approval for Authority Matrix entry |
| **ADAE score (illustrative)** | 82 points illustrative (Financial 70 · Customer 60 · Operational 90 · Velocity 80) |
| **Autonomy Budget Draw** | 82 points drawn against board-approved portfolio ceiling (illustrative) |
| **Max action magnitude** | Maintenance and supply-chain actions within board-authorized domain; Safety Risk Agent halt flag overrides MAM ceiling |
| **HOTL Certification** | Critical-tier endorsement (HAL certification pathway) mandatory; supervisory access cannot be contingent on cloud connectivity |
| **≥98% Standard** | ≥98% auditable rationale mandatory for all field maintenance decisions; write-before-execute enforced at Fog Layer even in DIL/DOL mode |

**Required Oversight Model**: HAL; supervisors operate through batch-interval review at the ≤50 decisions per hour Critical-tier threshold; supervisors must hold the Critical-tier endorsement (the HAL certification pathway); mandatory HITL for all maintenance decisions on mission-critical assets that trigger a Safety Risk Agent halt flag; Fog Layer must maintain HAL supervisor accessibility in DIL/DOL conditions—supervisory access cannot be contingent on cloud connectivity; at least three HAL-certified supervisors must be named in the certification register.

**Key Governance Controls**: Edge–Fog–Cloud topology with ruggedized MIL-STD-1553 Notice 4 data bus at the Edge ensuring deterministic fault-tolerant continuous capability in DIL/DOL environments; Safety Risk Agent providing proactive safety risk scoring against hazard logs and issuing mandatory halt flags overriding logistical efficiency goals; Logistics Risk Agent proactively assessing supply-chain risk upon fault diagnosis and initiating automated requisitions before work order approval; Audit and Compliance Agent generating an immutable, traceable audit log meeting the ≥98% auditable rationale standard with write-before-execute enforced at the Fog Layer even in DIL/DOL mode; ZTAI with short-lived dynamic credentials and AI-enabled Identity and Access Management replacing static API keys.

## 3. The Technical Architecture

UC14 inherits the Edge–Fog–Cloud three-tier architecture established in UC13. The Governance Delta specific to UC14 is the DIL/DOL constraint: write-before-execute and audit logging must be enforced at the Fog Layer without cloud dependency. The multi-agent system adds two orthogonal governance agents not present in UC13: the Safety Risk Agent (mandatory halt flags overriding logistical efficiency) and the Logistics Risk Agent (proactive supply-chain risk scoring before work order approval). MIL-STD-1553 Notice 4 data bus at Edge; RAG knowledge base anchoring all diagnostic outputs; MLOps Continuous Training (CT) protocol for air-gapped environments. Full specification is in "The Enhancement" section below.

## 4. The Enhancement

**Safety Risk Agent (SRA) and Logistics Risk Agent (LRA) Operating in Parallel on Fault Diagnosis Outputs**: When the Failure Analysis Agent generates a diagnostic report, the SRA immediately evaluates the predicted failure mode against the asset's safety envelope and hazard logs (FMECA), producing a Safety Risk Score or a mandatory halt flag that the Planning Agent cannot override for efficiency reasons. Simultaneously, the LRA activates to assess supply-chain risk, sole-source dependency, part scarcity, and procurement lead time and to initiate automated requisitions before the work order is formally approved. These two agents solve orthogonal versions of the same governance problem: the SRA ensures maintenance is scheduled based on safety criticality rather than logistical convenience, and the LRA ensures that a safety-driven maintenance decision does not result in an execution failure due to required parts being unavailable when the maintenance window arrives.

## 5. The Board Outcome

The board confirms that the system delivers measurable improvements in mission readiness and reductions in unscheduled asset downtime across the fleet. Every field maintenance decision meets the ≥98% standard: log committed at the Fog Layer before instruction is issued, write-before-execute enforced even in DIL/DOL conditions. Every Safety Risk Agent halt flag triggers mandatory HITL escalation, with the authorizing supervisor's identity, certification reference, and decision rationale recorded in the override record. ZTAI compliance is verified quarterly: no NHI has operated outside its approved scope of privilege. GAGAS Chapter 6 documentation and audit trail requirements (Yellow Book, 2024 revision) and NIST SP 800-53 Rev. 5 are confirmed as met through the ACA log format and retention records.

## Enterprise Implication

UC14 establishes that the governance obligation to maintain a complete, contemporaneous audit trail is unconditional; it cannot be suspended when connectivity is unavailable, because that is precisely when the risk of unaccountable field decisions is highest. The ACA's write-before-execute enforcement at the Fog Layer is therefore the chapter's most architecturally demanding governance requirement: it requires local logging infrastructure that meets regulatory audit standards without any dependence on cloud connectivity. The SRA/LRA parallel agent design addresses a complementary problem: in a complex multi-agent optimization system, the central planner's objective function (mission readiness, throughput) will always be in tension with safety and logistics constraints that the planner is not designed to enforce. Embedding dedicated orthogonal agents, one for safety criticality and one for supply-chain viability, ensures these constraints are enforced structurally rather than through the planner's optimization logic, where they can be traded off against operational efficiency. Together, these two architectural commitments, unconditional write-before-execute and orthogonal constraint agents, establish the governance pattern for any autonomous system operating in safety-critical, infrastructure-constrained environments.

# Blueprint: UC15—Predictive Maintenance for Manufacturing Equipment

Use Case 15 addresses the production uptime and equipment reliability challenges that arise when manufacturing maintenance is reactive or time-based: undetected wear and component fatigue cause unexpected downtime, disrupting production schedules and increasing operational costs. The Multi-agent System for Predictive Maintenance (MAPM) deploys a distributed Edge–Fog–Cloud architecture, with specialized agents executing the end-to-end predictive maintenance workflow, from anomaly detection to optimized work order scheduling. UC15 closes the Predictive Maintenance Triad by introducing the governance challenge of non-determinism in safety-critical AI: ensemble reasoning and digital twin validation ensure that data-driven predictions are confirmed by physical causality models before any high-impact actuation.

## 1. The Business Problem

Manufacturing machinery fails unexpectedly because sensor-based anomaly signals are not continuously processed against diagnostic models and because maintenance is scheduled on fixed calendar intervals rather than based on actual equipment condition. The additional governance challenge is LLM non-determinism: even with greedy sampling, LLM outputs in multi-step agentic workflows can be inconsistent due to floating-point non-associativity during concurrent GPU execution, and acting on a physically incorrect diagnosis wastes resources and may cause additional stress on equipment. A root-cause analysis that is statistically consistent with historical failure patterns but physically inconsistent with the actual degradation mechanism produces a confident recommendation for the wrong intervention. The business objective is a measurable reduction in unplanned downtime and maintenance costs through condition-based scheduling.

# 2. The Governance Instrument

| GOVERNANCE STACK: UC15—Predictive Maintenance for Manufacturing Equipment | |
|---|---|
| **Instrument** | **Active Setting for This Deployment** |
| **Autonomy Level** | Level 4 (Autonomous Execution Within Defined Limits) |
| **Criticality Tier** | High |
| **Oversight model** | HAL; batch review at ≤100 decisions/hour High threshold; mandatory HITL for asset shutdowns, high-value procurement, and ensemble reasoning failures (no consensus between Diagnostic and Digital Twin agents) |
| **Delegation Tier** | Delegated—supervisors hold Critical-tier endorsement (HAL certification pathway); Board Risk Committee approval |
| **ADAE score (illustrative)** | 65 points illustrative (Financial 50 · Customer 40 · Operational 80 · Velocity 80) |
| **Autonomy Budget Draw** | 65 points drawn against board-approved portfolio ceiling (illustrative) |
| **Max action magnitude** | Work order and procurement ceiling set in Authority Matrix; high-value procurement requires HITL gate |
| **HOTL certification** | Critical-tier endorsement (HAL certification pathway) mandatory; certification reference captured in Audit Log for every batch review cycle |
| **≥98% standard** | ≥98% auditable rationale standard for all diagnostic decisions and work order generation |

**Required Oversight Model**: HAL; supervisors review batches of maintenance work orders and decision distributions at the ≤100 decisions per hour High Criticality Tier threshold; supervisors must hold the Critical-tier endorsement (the HAL certification pathway); mandatory

HITL for high-impact decisions including asset shutdowns and high-value procurement; ensemble reasoning failure (no consensus between the Diagnostic Agent and Digital Twin Agent) is a mandatory HITL trigger; HAL supervisor certification reference captured in the Audit Log for every batch review cycle.

**Key Governance Controls**: Ensemble reasoning requiring consensus between the Diagnostic Agent's LLM-derived prognosis and the Digital Twin Agent's simulation results before any high-impact action is executed, establishing physical causality as a mandatory gate before autonomous actuation; Digital Twin Agent providing physics-based causality validation that confirms data-driven predictions against a simulated model of the physical asset; Agentic GRC framework with the Central Orchestrator acting as API Gateway Enforcer checking policy compliance on all agent tool calls before execution; Ethical and Fairness Agent assessing resource allocation and scheduling decisions for bias against organizational fairness standards; Cyber-Physical Security Gateways enforcing security policies and encryption across Edge, Fog, and Cloud layers protecting the ICS network; ≥98% auditable rationale standard for all diagnostic decisions and work order generation.

## 3. The Technical Architecture

UC15 inherits the Edge–Fog–Cloud topology established in UC13 and extended in UC14. The Governance Delta specific to UC15 is the non-determinism challenge: ensemble reasoning requiring consensus between the Diagnostic Agent and the Digital Twin Agent before any high-impact actuation and an Ethical and Fairness Agent assessing resource allocation for bias. The multi-agent system adds the Digital Twin Agent (physics-based causality validation), the Explainability Agent, and the Ethical and Fairness Agent to the standard predictive maintenance stack. Cyber-Physical Security Gateways enforce security policies across Edge, Fog, and Cloud boundaries. Full specification is in "The Enhancement" section below.

## 4. The Enhancement

**Ensemble Reasoning with Digital Twin Validation**: The Diagnostic Agent's LLM-derived root-cause analysis cannot proceed to actuation based on its output alone. The Digital Twin Agent tests the proposed failure diagnosis against a simulation of the physical asset to confirm that the predicted failure mode is consistent with physical causality, rather than a statistical pattern match in historical sensor data. This validation closes a governance gap unique to manufacturing AI: a data-driven model may identify a sensor pattern that correlates with past failures without correctly identifying the physical mechanism that caused them. Acting on a statistically correct but physically incorrect diagnosis wastes maintenance resources and may cause additional stress on equipment. The Digital Twin Agent makes physical causality a mandatory gate before autonomous actuation, converting the AI's probabilistic prediction into a physically validated maintenance recommendation.

## 5. The Board Outcome

The board confirms that the system delivers measurable reductions in unplanned downtime and maintenance costs, with production planning improved through condition-based scheduling. Every diagnostic decision and work order generation event produces a complete auditable rationale log entry before execution, meeting the ≥98% standard. Every instance in which ensemble reasoning fails to reach consensus between the Diagnostic Agent and the Digital Twin Agent triggers a mandatory HITL escalation, and the halt itself generates a complete audit log entry. The Ethical and Fairness Agent's bias assessment outputs are logged for every resource allocation decision, confirming that maintenance scheduling has not systematically favored high-margin production lines at the expense of other critical assets. Cyber-Physical Security Gateway logs confirm that there were no IT-to-ICS network boundary violations during the reporting period.

## Enterprise Implication

UC15 closes the Predictive Maintenance Triad by introducing physical causality validation as a mandatory governance gate before actuation. The key insight is that ensemble reasoning with digital twin validation converts the AI's probabilistic prediction into a physically validated maintenance recommendation, addressing the governance risk that a statistically correct pattern match may correspond to the wrong physical cause. The Ethical and Fairness Agent addresses a governance risk invisible to performance metrics alone: an optimization system that consistently prioritizes high-margin production lines may achieve its financial objective while systematically under-maintaining lower-margin but equally critical assets. Without an explicit fairness agent, this bias is detectable only after it has produced a pattern of preventable failures. The Ethical and Fairness Agent converts this from a retrospective audit finding into a real-time governance control that can be flagged and escalated before the biased decision pattern causes harm.

# Accountability and Assurance Layer for Autonomous AI

The successful deployment of high-impact, multi-domain autonomous agents necessitates a unified governance structure to systematically address the risks inherent in machine autonomy, complexity, and distributed execution. The accountability layer serves as the architectural embodiment of this assurance. As a mandatory collection of architectural mechanisms, this layer guarantees transparency, auditability, and human oversight across all advanced use cases (UC11–15). This essential layer ensures non-repudiation and security by leveraging XAI to build trust and validation, using the Audit and Compliance Agent as the final gate to capture audit trails that meet the ≥98% auditable rationale standard, and securing traceability through verifiable agent identities enforced by ZTAI.

## XAI As the Engine of Trust and Validation

For all critical autonomous decisions, ranging from PdM diagnosis (UC13, UC14, and UC15) to payment decision rationale (UC12), the system must mandate the generation of a clear, human-readable rationale, or XAI. This is critical because it builds user confidence, allowing technical personnel (e.g., maintenance technicians, financial managers) to confidently override or validate the AI's proposed action. The Explainability Agent and its capability for generating rationales serve as the technical engine of this trust.

XAI output is also the primary tool for the HOTL supervisor: the supervisor must be able to understand why the agent is recommending a particular action, not merely observe what action it is recommending. A HOTL supervisor reviewing 40 decisions per hour at a Critical-tier system cannot exercise genuine challenge without access to the XAI rationale for each decision. The XAI must be surfaced in the HOTL supervisor interface in a form that enables meaningful review within the span-of-control threshold, not stored only in machine logs.

## Audit and Compliance Agent As the Final Gate

The Audit and Compliance Agent ensures that the XAI rationale, the RAG grounding sources, the specific model version used, and the status of the Policy Compliance Gate are all captured and recorded in an immutable, timestamped log. This rigorous, comprehensive logging transforms operational decisions into legally defensible artifacts, satisfying stringent compliance mandates such as GAGAS (Yellow Book, 2024 revision), NIST SP 800-53 Rev. 5, and the EU AI Act's traceability requirements (Regulation EU 2024/1689).

The ≥98% auditable rationale standard applies as the minimum compliance threshold across all five use cases in this chapter. A quarter in which auditable rationale coverage falls below 98% for any regulated-domain agent constitutes a Board Risk Committee escalation event. The

Audit and Compliance Agent must be designed with write-before-execute capability, and the log entry must be committed before the action is executed and must be fail-closed: if the logging infrastructure is unavailable, the agent must not proceed with the decision.

For adverse decisions (maintenance actions, account flags, seating rejections based on algorithmic scoring), the Minimum Explainability Record must be generated contemporaneously with the decision, identifying the three to five primary factors that most influenced the outcome, expressed in terms meaningful to the affected party. This record must be translatable into a plain-language explanation without specialist AI knowledge.

## Traceability for Non-repudiation and Security

Traceability is secured at the identity level through the enforcement of ZTAI. This requires assigning each autonomous agent a unique, verifiable identity. The ZTAI policy ensures that every log entry, including the agent's execution of a compensating transaction (UC12) or the generation of a RUL forecast (UC13), is cryptographically linked to a non-repudiable agent identity, thereby mitigating security and accountability risks associated with autonomous systems.

The supervisor certification reference in the Audit Log is the complementary human traceability mechanism: it links the supervision record to the certification register, confirming that the supervisor held a valid, current certification at the time of each supervised decision or batch review cycle. For Level 3 systems (HOTL), this confirms real-time monitoring was conducted by a certified supervisor. For Level 4 systems (HAL: UC13, UC14, UC15), this confirms each batch review cycle was completed by a HAL-certified supervisor holding the Critical-tier endorsement. An audit log that records a supervision period without a valid certification reference is evidence of uncertified supervision, a governance breach equivalent to operating the system without a supervisor.

# The Safety Architecture: Governing Advanced Automation and Physical Actuation

The safety architecture for multi-domain advanced automation rests on three integrated components: the SRE, which enforces span-of-control and fail-closed behavior at the infrastructure level; the PDP/PEP policy enforcement handshake, which validates every action before execution; and the XAI accountability layer, which ensures every autonomous decision is explainable to both the HOTL supervisor and the regulator.

## The Safety Runtime Environment (SRE)

The Safety Runtime Environment (SRE) is the primary infrastructure layer for all Level 3 and above systems. It enforces the three functions established in Chapter 9: fail-closed logging with write-before-execute (the ≥98% auditable rationale standard), automatic span-of-control threshold enforcement with a mode shift to HITL, and anomaly and cascade detection via a circuit breaker. The SRE specification, span-of-control thresholds, and supervisor certification requirements are the canonical governance baseline established in the "HOTL Certification and the ≥98% Auditable Rationale Standard" section above.

## Policy Enforcement: The Safety Handshake

The PDP/PEP enforcement model established in Chapter 9 applies uniformly across all five use cases. In the advanced automation context, the PDP additionally validates the currency of HAL supervisor certification and the scope of NHI privileges before releasing decisions in Level 4 systems. The PEP enforces write-before-execute and fail-closed behavior.

Figure 11-3 illustrates the complete safety runtime governance architecture: the Authority Matrix Rules Repository issues Consult PDP and Cert Validation Rules to gate all execution through the Safety Runtime Environment and Certified PEP Gating; the Online Feature Store feeds write-before-execute signals to the Immutable Audit Log and the Reasoning Orchestrator; the Edge–Fog–Cloud Bridge delivers Fog-Layer context to the Reasoning Orchestrator while providing a fail-closed trigger to the Immutable Audit Log; the Reasoning Orchestrator coordinates Ensemble Validation, the Ethical and Fairness Agent, the Digital Twin Agent, and the XAI Microservice within the Cognitive Layer, with the Certified Supervisor HOTL Interface receiving certified sign-off requests and XAI rationale from the XAI Microservice via Supervisor Evidence; the Audit and Compliance Agent enforces compliance through HOTL alerts and prognosis validation, writing all records to the Immutable Audit Log; the Consensus Engine gates actuation through the External Action Proxy, which releases multi-domain actuation to the Target Domain; and the Saga Orchestrator manages compensation actions and veto signals back to the Target Domain to ensure distributed transaction integrity.

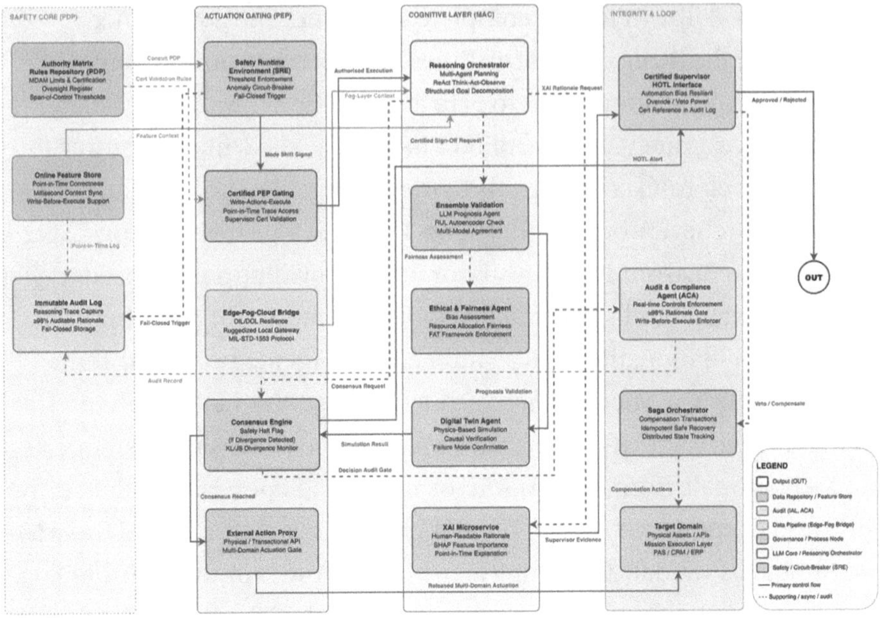


***Figure 11-3.*** *The Safety Runtime Environment governance architecture—end-to-end certified actuation flow across the Safety Core (PDP), Actuation Gating (PEP), Cognitive Layer (MAC), and Integrity & Loop, integrating the Safety Runtime Environment, Certified PEP Gating, Edge–Fog–Cloud Bridge, Consensus Engine, External Action Proxy, Reasoning Orchestrator, Ensemble Validation, Ethical and Fairness Agent, Digital Twin Agent, XAI Microservice, Certified Supervisor HOTL Interface, Audit and Compliance Agent, Saga Orchestrator, and Target Domain*

# Accountability and XAI As the Engine of Trust

The XAI Microservice generates point-in-time rationales grounded in the precise feature values present at the time of prediction. For the HOTL or HAL supervisor, this is the primary tool for meaningful challenge; a supervisor reviewing decisions without access to the XAI rationale is providing nominal, not genuine, oversight. The "Accountability and

Assurance Layer for Autonomous AI" section above establishes the full specification, including the Minimum Explainability Record requirement for adverse decisions.

## Measuring the Impact of Governed Autonomy

The board justifies the expansion into advanced automation by monitoring the quantitative signals of safety and operational readiness.

**The Auditable Rationale Rate:** The system monitors the quarter-on-quarter rate of auditable rationales. Any quarter in which the rate falls below the 98% threshold constitutes an escalation event for the Board Risk Committee. This metric provides the board with the proof that the autonomous agent is not a black box but is a governed and auditable asset.

**Operational Readiness and Resolution Rates:** For maintenance and service use cases, the system tracks the increase in fleet availability and first-contact resolution rates. These metrics validate the financial return on the optimization deltas, while the supervisor attestation logs provide the proof that the autonomy remained within the authorized boundaries of the MANDATE.

## Summary

This chapter demonstrated that multi-domain advanced automation is governable only when two instruments are met without exception: the HOTL Certification Framework, which makes human oversight certifiable rather than nominal, and the ≥98% auditable rationale standard, which makes accountability measurable rather than aspirational. At this tier, every governance failure is an operational failure. The two non-negotiable governance rules that follow from this are: no autonomous system operating at Level 3 or above may run without a currently certified supervisor, and no regulated-domain decision may be executed without a contemporaneously committed audit log entry. The key takeaways are as follows:

- **Write-before-execute and fail-closed are architectural requirements, not policies.** The decision rationale log entry must be committed before the action is executed. If the logging infrastructure is unavailable, the agent enters a fail-closed state and may not proceed. For UC12, this applies to every payment and compensation action; for UC13, to every RUL prognostic decision that influences a maintenance action; for UC14, to every field maintenance instruction issued from the Fog Layer.

- **Each use case introduces a primary Architectural Delta and a corresponding Governance Delta.**

  **UC11**: Maximum Weight Matching with Offline Mode, governed by the TCPA Consent Log and FAT fairness framework

  **UC12**: Orchestration-based Saga Pattern, governed by PCI DSS tokenization, the Policy Compliance Gate, and geo-fencing

  **UC13**: Adaptive Autoencoders with dual RAG and MAS, governed by EU AI Act GRC (Regulation EU 2024/1689, Annex III; deferred to December 2, 2027, under the Digital Omnibus provisional agreement of May 2026, pending formal adoption), drift detection, and mandatory HITL for unscheduled groundings

**UC14**: Edge–Fog–Cloud DIL/DOL topology, governed by ZTAI, the GAGAS/NIST audit trail, and write-before-execute at the Fog Layer

**UC15**: Ensemble reasoning with digital twin validation and Cyber-Physical Security Gateways, governed by the Agentic GRC framework, the Ethical/Fairness Agent, and HAL oversight at ≤100 decisions per hour

- **Two non-negotiable trigger conditions mandate HITL across all five use cases.** First, safety and high-risk actuation: Any action that results in physical asset groundings (UC13, UC14), high-value financial transactions (UC12), or a breach of a hard safety constraint (UC11, UC15) must pause, surface the XAI rationale, and require human sign-off before execution. The approver's identity and timestamp must be recorded in the override record field. Second, model integrity failure: If ensemble reasoning fails to reach consensus between the Diagnostic Agent and the Digital Twin Agent (UC15), or the auditable rationale rate falls below the 98% standard, the system must halt and escalate, and the halt itself generates a complete audit log entry.
- **The Minimum Explainability Record is mandatory for all adverse decisions.** For maintenance actions, account flags, and seating rejections, the record must identify the three to five primary factors that most influenced the outcome, expressed in terms meaningful to the affected party, generated contemporaneously with the decision. The Audit and

Compliance Agent enforces write-before-execute for this record under the same fail-closed obligation as the full rationale log.

The next chapter steps back from individual use cases to ask where the organization stands as a whole and what a governed path to full autonomous capability actually looks like from here.

# References

Deloitte. 2023. Industry 4.0: Using Predictive Technologies for Asset Maintenance. New York: Deloitte Insights. https://www2.deloitte.com/us/en/insights/industry/manufacturing-industrial-products/industry-4-0/using-predictive-technologies-for-asset-maintenance.html.

Hossain, M Maruf. 2026. *Write-Before-Execute: A Governance Standard for Evidentially Defensible AI De*cision Logging in Regulated Enterprises. Preprint. Zenodo. https://doi.org/10.5281/zenodo.20603712.

# PART V

# Conclusion

# CHAPTER 12

# Roadmap to AI Maturity

Chapters 1–11 introduced all governance instruments in the EDS framework: the three constitutional doctrines, the Autonomy Level taxonomy and decision authority scoring, the Machine Decision Authority Matrix, the NHI lifecycle framework, the HOTL Certification Framework, the ≥98% auditable rationale standard, and the Safety Runtime Environment. This chapter provides the capstone: a four-stage AI Maturity Model that maps all 15 use cases onto a governance continuum, defines the controls required to move safely from one stage to the next, and prescribes a sequenced investment plan to get there. The governing principle throughout is Certified Operational Velocity; an organization can scale machine autonomy only as fast as its GMI-certified governance infrastructure can demonstrably support.

The maturity journey is a portfolio management challenge, not a linear progression. An organization may operate a low-risk Stage 2 RAG assistant while simultaneously developing a Stage 4 autonomous agent for financial risk monitoring. The governance instruments do not change with the portfolio's overall maturity; they vary with each system's Autonomy Level. Stage 3 maturity means the governance infrastructure is ready to support Level 3 systems; it does not remove Level 1 or Level 2 oversight obligations or authorize Level 4 deployment. The GMI is the formal mechanism through which the board assesses readiness and gates each escalation.


M. M. Hossain and A. A. N. Ponnusamy, *Governance-First AI*,
https://doi.org/10.1007/979-8-8688-3118-8_12

The chapter is organized as follows. The "Guarded Innovation" section establishes the board's risk posture that governs all four stages. The "The Governance Framework As a Maturity Assessment Tool" section maps every instrument from this book to its maturity stage and risk category. The "Portfolio Alignment Matrix for Governing Investment" section groups the 15 use cases into three tiers—Foundational, Transactional, and Autonomous—and explains why governance requirements escalate with each. The "Defining the Four Stages of Enterprise AI Maturity" section defines the specific controls required at each stage. The "Scaling Controls for Autonomy" section details the advanced infrastructure required for Stages 3 and 4. The "Phasing the Governance Architectural Delta" section prescribes the three-phase investment sequence. The chapter closes with the unified ABB inventory representing the complete governance instrument portfolio at full Stage 4 maturity.

Safety Constraint Engineering (SCE), the EDS practice of defining precise, verifiable safety specifications offline and implementing a Runtime Monitor that validates every proposed agent action against those pre-verified constraints before execution, is introduced in this chapter as the formal guarantee mechanism for Stage 4 systems. SCE ensures non-negotiable safety rules always override conflicting objectives. It is the complement to PaC that enforces operational rules in real time; SCE enforces safety constraints that no policy, agent reasoning, or runtime condition may override.

**Governance Leaders:** This chapter is written primarily for you; the maturity model, GMI certification gates, and the investment roadmap are board-level instruments.

**Architects and Practitioners:** The "Scaling Controls for Autonomy" section and the unified ABB inventory at the close of the chapter are your technical reference for Stage 3 and Stage 4 infrastructure.

## Guarded Innovation: The Board Risk Posture As the Governing Frame for Maturity

Guarded Innovation is the board's commitment to support autonomous AI where it demonstrably improves performance while maintaining a low tolerance for uncontrolled autonomy, irreversible actions without circuit breaks, and material harm from AI-driven decisions. It is not a compromise between innovation and caution. It is a specific, bounded commitment: innovation is actively supported, but only within a governance architecture that makes every autonomous action visible, accountable, and reversible. The per-stage expression of this posture is shown in the callout below.

### WHAT GUARDED INNOVATION REQUIRES AT EACH MATURITY STAGE

***Stage 1**: Innovation can proceed because systems are assistive; no action is taken without human confirmation. The governance requirement is foundational: data lineage, basic PII masking, and initial audit logging.*

***Stage 2**: Innovation can proceed because access controls and audit trails make every RAG interaction traceable. The governance requirement is the Zero-Trust RAG pipeline with mandatory DLAC and immutable logging.*

***Stage 3**: Innovation can proceed for systems at Autonomy Level 3 and above because PaC and delegated authorization ensure agents act only within their authorized scope. The governance requirement is runtime policy enforcement, NHI lifecycle management, and current HOTL certification for every Level 3 or above system in the portfolio; the certification requirement follows the system's Autonomy Level, not the organization's maturity stage.*

***Stage 4**: Innovation can proceed because ensemble reasoning, HOTL certification, and the ≥98% auditable rationale standard make every autonomous decision in safety-critical domains genuinely accountable.*

The maturity model in this chapter is the operational expression of this posture: AI autonomy may scale only as GMI-certified governance maturity demonstrably increases.

## The Governance Framework As a Maturity Assessment Tool

The governance instruments introduced across this book, taken together, constitute a complete maturity assessment framework. Each instrument defines a specific governance capability, and the presence or absence of that capability determines whether the organization is ready to deploy at the corresponding maturity stage. Table 12-1 maps the governance instruments from each chapter to their maturity stage and the specific risk category they govern. The risk categories in the rightmost column are drawn directly from the eight AI risk categories established in Chapter 3's risk taxonomy: Decision Velocity Risk, Cascade Failure Risk, Governance Drift Risk, Model Behavior Risk, Prompt Drift Risk, Accountability Diffusion Risk, Concentration Risk, and Regulatory Explainability Risk. Every governance instrument in this framework addresses one or more of those eight categories. Readers should cross-reference Chapter 3 for the full definition of each category and its architectural implications.

***Table 12-1.*** *Governance instruments from across this book mapped to maturity stage and risk category*

| Governance Instrument | Introduced | Maturity Stage Required | Risk Category Governed |
|---|---|---|---|
| Three constitutional doctrines (Governance-Constrained Autonomy, Quantified Delegation, Human Primacy) | Chapter 1 | All stages—foundational | Establishes the constitutional boundary within which all other instruments operate. No deployment at any stage is permissible without the constitutional foundation. |
| AI System Criticality Classification (Critical/High/Moderate/Low tiers) | Chapter 3 | Stage 2 and above | Decision Velocity Risk, Cascade Failure Risk. Determines the minimum oversight model and governance intensity for every deployed system. |
| Zero-Trust RAG pipeline (DLAC, Security Trimming, immutable audit logging) | Chapter 4 | Stage 2 | Regulatory Explainability Risk, Accountability Diffusion Risk. The universal security baseline for all RAG deployments. |
| LLMOps quality metrics (Groundedness SLO, Gate Trigger Rate, Oversight Model Continuity) | Chapter 5 | Stage 2 and above | Governance Drift Risk, Model Behavior Risk, Prompt Drift Risk. Continuous governance assurance mechanism. |

*(continued)*

*Table 12-1.* (*continued*)

| Governance Instrument | Introduced | Maturity Stage Required | Risk Category Governed |
|---|---|---|---|
| Decision authority scoring (four dimensions: Financial Authority, Customer Reach, Operational Reach, Decision Velocity) | Chapter 9 | Stage 3 and above | All eight risk categories: quantifies aggregate authority exposure before deployment authorization is issued. |
| Machine Decision Authority Matrix (board instrument for domain-level authorization) | Chapter 9 | Stage 3 and above | Accountability Diffusion Risk, Concentration Risk. No autonomous action in any domain is authorized without a board-approved Matrix entry. |
| NHI Lifecycle Governance (JML process, credential rotation, orphan NHI zero tolerance) | Chapter 10 | Stage 3 and above | Cascade Failure Risk, Concentration Risk. The security foundation through which all other agent governance controls are operationalized. |
| HOTL Certification Framework (certification program, span-of-control thresholds, automation bias testing) | Chapter 11 | Stage 3 and above | Decision Velocity Risk, Governance Drift Risk. Ensures supervisors provide genuine oversight, not nominal presence. |

(*continued*)

***Table 12-1.*** *(continued)*

| Governance Instrument | Introduced | Maturity Stage Required | Risk Category Governed |
|---|---|---|---|
| Safety Runtime Environment (infrastructure-layer policy intercept, span-of-control enforcement, fail-closed circuit breaker) | Chapter 11 | Stage 3 and above | Decision Velocity Risk, Cascade Failure Risk. The primary runtime governance control; intercepts every proposed action at the infrastructure layer independent of the model, enforcing span-of-control thresholds and failing closed when unavailable. |
| ≥98% auditable rationale standard (logging standard, write-before-execute, seven-year retention) | Chapter 11 | Stage 3 and above (98% standard for regulated domains) | Regulatory Explainability Risk, Accountability Diffusion Risk. The minimum evidence standard for legal defensibility. |
| Autonomy Budget (board-approved aggregate ceiling on total delegated machine authority across all production agentic systems) | Chapter 9 | Stage 3 and above | Concentration Risk. Prevents invisible accumulation of machine authority at the portfolio level, a governance risk that individual system limits cannot detect. No deployment that would push portfolio utilization above 80% of the ceiling may proceed without Board Risk Committee review. |

An organization that has implemented all Stage 2 instruments but none of the Stage 3 instruments is not a Stage 3 organization, regardless of how sophisticated its AI models are. Governance maturity is determined by the weakest link in the control chain, not the strongest. The GMI (described in Chapter 1) is the formal mechanism for assessing governance maturity and governing autonomy escalation gates.

The four maturity stages described in this chapter are also the operational expression of the continuous governance control loop introduced in Chapter 1, the cycle through which the board defines risk appetite, the governance instruments are activated in sequence, machine decision authority is kept aligned with board intent, and the board receives the evidence it needs to close the loop. Completing Stage 2 operationalizes the access control and audit trail stages of that loop. Completing Stage 3 operationalizes the policy enforcement and identity governance stages. Completing Stage 4 operationalizes the safety assurance, continuous monitoring, and board reporting stages. The maturity roadmap in this chapter is not a separate framework from the governance control loop; it is its implementation schedule.

# Mapping Value to Governance Rigor

Enterprise AI initiatives must be viewed through a portfolio lens, balancing business impact against the governance complexity each use case requires. As autonomy increases, governance requirements shift from data quality and auditability to runtime enforcement and safety assurance. The portfolio alignment matrix below plots the 15 use cases against this continuum.

## Tier 1: Foundational

Tier 1 systems support productivity and information quality. The human remains the final decision-maker, and governance centers on establishing audit logging, data integrity, and grounded outputs. This tier, Foundational Efficiency through Assistive Systems, focuses on factual accuracy (groundedness) and prevention of data leakage. Governance establishes the Zero-Trust RAG pipeline and the constitutional doctrines that all subsequent tiers inherit. Examples include the frontline knowledge assistant (UC1), the document quality and consistency uplift engine (UC3), and the stylist and language adapter (UC4). The governance instruments required are the constitutional doctrines, the Criticality Classification, and the Zero-Trust RAG pipeline.

## Tier 2: Transactional

Tier 2 systems move from assistive output to executable action. Because these systems affect operational state, governance shifts from auditability to runtime enforcement of delegated authority. This tier, Transactional and Delegated Agents, marks the shift to active systems that execute financial or state-changing actions via external tools (APIs). The principal governance challenge is ensuring the agent acts only within the scope of its delegated human authority. Governance mandates focus on policy enforcement in real time (Policy-as-Code), transactional integrity (Saga Pattern), and NHI lifecycle management. Use cases include the autonomous IT service resolution agent (UC6), the hotel dynamic pricing and booking agent (UC10), and the event ticket and seat upgrade agent (UC12). The additional governance instruments required are the decision authority scoring methodology, a board-authorized entry in the Machine Decision Authority Matrix, and the NHI lifecycle framework.

## Tier 3: Autonomous

Tier 3 systems operate in high-risk domains where autonomous decisions can create financial, operational, or safety harm. Governance must prevent harmful actions before they are executed rather than detect them afterward. This apex tier, Autonomous and Safety-Critical Hybrid Systems, mandates alignment with strict external regulators (e.g., the FAA; the EU AI Act under Regulation EU 2024/1689, whose high-risk Annex III obligations are deferred to December 2, 2027, under the Digital Omnibus provisional agreement of May 2026 pending formal adoption; and financial regulators). The key governance requirements are runtime safety-constraint enforcement (SCE), verifiable accountability (XAI), and consensus logic prior to execution (ensemble reasoning). Systems such as the financial risk and fraud monitoring agent (UC9) deliver the highest compliance ROI, justifying the disproportionately high investment in Stage 3 and 4 governance infrastructure. The additional governance instruments required are the HOTL/HAL certification framework, the ≥98% auditable rationale standard, and ZTAI with continuous adversarial robustness testing.

## Portfolio Alignment Matrix for Governing Investment

Executive prioritization must leverage a matrix that plots expected financial return (value) against the necessary governance complexity (i.e., risk). The relationship between autonomy and risk is direct: as delegation increases, so does the consequence of governance failure. Table 12-2 maps this progression across the three portfolio tiers.

***Table 12-2.*** *Strategic use case portfolio mapping: value realization vs. governance complexity*

| Value Potential | Governance Complexity (Risk) | Maturity Stage Required | Key Use Case Examples | Illustrative ADAE Score · Budget Draw |
|---|---|---|---|---|
| High (productivity/ revenue) | Low (RAG foundation, assistive) | Stage 1/2 | UC1 (frontline knowledge assistant), UC3 (document quality), UC4 (stylist/language adapter) | UC1: ~15 pts · UC3: ~12 pts · UC4: ~10 pts Stage 1/2 subtotal: ~37 points |
| Medium (process/ service) | Medium (transactional agents, delegated) | Stage 3 (requires PaC/ NHI/Authority Matrix) | UC6 (IT resolution), UC7 (claims agent), UC10 (dynamic pricing), UC12 (ticket upgrades) | UC6: 35 pts · UC7: ~72 pts · UC10: ~38 pts · UC12: ~45 pts Stage 3 subtotal: ~190 points Running total: ~227 points |
| Extreme (safety/ financial) | High (autonomous, safety-critical) | Stage 4 (requires ZTAI/ SCE/XAI/HOTL certification) | UC9 (fraud monitoring), UC13 (aircraft PdM), UC14 (defense PdM), UC15 (manufacturing PdM) | UC9: ~85 pts · UC13: ~78 pts · UC14: ~82 pts · UC15: ~65 pts Stage 4 subtotal: ~310 points Portfolio total (11 use cases carrying illustrative ADAE scores): ~537 points of 900-point ceiling (illustrative) |

While productivity RAG (UC1) yields a high realized ROI (projected 70–80% uplift), autonomous systems (UC7, UC9) deliver the highest compliance ROI (cost avoidance). This value, quantified by reduced regulatory fines and litigation costs, justifies the disproportionately high budgetary allocation required for Stage 3 and 4 governance infrastructure.

## Escalating Controls for Maturity

Achieving enterprise AI maturity is defined by the quality of the governance structure that manages risk. The organization progresses through four distinct stages, where the integrity of GRC controls deepens and becomes increasingly automated and proactive. This maturity model describes the state of the governance layer, not the project's age; a brand-new, high-risk project must immediately adopt Stage 3 or 4 controls. The necessary architectural evolution across these stages is driven by the need for verifiable accountability, which requires a detailed forensic record that explains why the system acted.

## Defining the Four Stages of Enterprise AI Maturity

The maturity curve is characterized by the technical integration of GRC into the MLOps lifecycle, moving from inconsistent experimentation to fully integrated control. This progression begins with Foundational proofs of concept (PoCs), advances to Operationalized systems with mandatory compliance controls, shifts into Integrated runtime enforcement for transactional agents, and culminates in the Autonomous apex for safety-critical hybrid systems. This phased approach ensures the control architecture is ready to manage the escalating risk and complexity of autonomous systems.

## Stage 1: Foundational—Envision and Experiment

The focus is on defining business outcomes and initial PoC. The governance baseline involves establishing technical prerequisites, such as Data Lineage Tagging and initial PII masking at ingestion. Governance reviews are typically ad hoc or inconsistent. This stage is critical for establishing the technical and data prerequisites needed to build trust and enable the organization to move confidently to the next stage of maturity. The constitutional governance obligation at this stage is minimal, but the three constitutional doctrines must be adopted as the governing framework before any system is deployed, even at Stage 1.

## Stage 2: Operationalized—Defined and Launched

This stage mandates the industrialization of AI with standard, mandatory controls (Chapters 4 and 5). Key governance mandates include the universal implementation of document-level access control (DLAC), immutable audit logging (e.g., WORM storage), and the use of the Groundedness (Faithfulness) Score as a mandatory Service-Level Objective (SLO) for compliance. Governance aligns formally with recognized frameworks, such as the NIST AI Risk Management Framework (AI RMF; NIST AI 100-1, January 2023). This stage is critical because it establishes the Zero-Trust RAG pipeline and the baseline of auditability and consistency required for all future AI initiatives. The LLMOps oversight model's continuity controls, introduced in Chapter 5 (Threshold Drift, Supervisor Availability Drift, Prompt Drift monitoring), are activated at this stage.

## Stage 3: Integrated—Agentic Integration

This stage introduces runtime enforcement for transactional agents (e.g., UC6, UC7, UC10, and UC12). The systems now actively act on core enterprise data, requiring technical enforcement mechanisms: PaC, NHI lifecycle management, and mandatory XAI rationale capture for complex decisions. Governance is fully integrated into execution workflows. The decision authority scoring methodology must be applied to every agent before deployment; a Machine Decision Authority Matrix entry must be approved for each operational domain; the NHI Lifecycle Register must be complete for all deployed agents; and HOTL supervisors must hold current certification for every system operating at Autonomy Level 3 or above.

Maturity Stage 3 describes the organization's governance infrastructure readiness, not its system portfolio. A Stage 3 organization will typically operate Level 1 through Level 4 systems simultaneously; each system's Autonomy Level determines its individual governance requirements independently of the organization's overall stage. GMI Level 2 certification is the minimum governance readiness gate before any Level 3 system may be approved for production. If the GMI falls below Level 2 while a Level 3 system is in operation, the Chief Risk Officer must be notified within four hours, and enhanced manual oversight must be implemented until certification is restored.

## Stage 4: Autonomous—Future-Ready AI

This apex of maturity involves high-autonomy, safety-critical hybrid systems (e.g., UC9, UC13, UC14, and UC15). The governance mandate includes the most advanced safety controls: ZTAI, SCE, ensemble reasoning for decision consensus, and continuous adversarial robustness testing (Red-Teaming). GRC must become a technologically supported, proactive force multiplier. The ≥98% auditable rationale standard applies to all regulated-domain decisions. Supervisors of Level 4 and Level 5 systems must hold the Critical-tier endorsement (the HAL certification pathway), an additional requirement beyond the standard HOTL certification; these systems operate under the Human-Above-the-Loop oversight model. Supervisors of Critical-tier Level 3 systems also require the Critical-tier endorsement, as established in Chapter 11's

HOTL Certification Framework. Supervisors of Level 3 systems continue to require standard HOTL certification. The span-of-control thresholds from Chapter 11 must be enforced at the infrastructure level by the Safety Runtime Environment for all Level 3 and above systems in the portfolio. GMI Level 3 certification is the minimum governance readiness gate before any Level 4 system may be approved for production, and GMI Level 4 certification is required before any Level 5 system may be deployed.

## Maturity and Control Capabilities Matrix

The need for verifiable accountability drives the architectural evolution. While RAG requires source citation, autonomous agents (UC7, UC9, UC14) demand full contestability. This requires logging the agent's internal reasoning trace (the LLM's ReAct Thought-Action-Observation loop) and the generated XAI rationale, transforming the audit log into a detailed forensic record that explains why the system acted. For predictive systems in Stage 4, MLOps becomes a safety assurance function, requiring continuous drift detection (via KL/JS divergence) and automated, auditable Continuous Training (CT) to manage the dynamic risk posed by adaptive AI. Table 12-3 sets out the AI maturity and governance control escalation model, showing how controls intensify across the maturity stages.

*Table 12-3.* *AI maturity and governance control escalation model*

| Maturity Stage | Adoption Goal | Required Governance Capability (Architectural Delta) | High-Risk Use Case Focus |
|---|---|---|---|
| 1: Foundational | Efficiency PoCs (UC1, UC4) | Constitutional doctrines adopted. DLAC/Security Trimming. Basic HITL workflow. Initial PII masking. Criticality Classification established. | Foundational RAG |
| 2: Operationalized | Compliance and quality (UC2, UC3) | Full immutable audit logging. Groundedness Score (SLO). Hybrid Search/re-ranking. Policy mapping. LLMOps Oversight Model Continuity monitoring active. Gate Trigger Rate baseline established. | Compliance RAG, optimization |
| 3: Integrated | Autonomous transactions (UC6, UC7, UC10) | PaC enforcement. Delegated Authorization Service. Saga Pattern. XAI rationale logging (ReAct). Decision authority score assigned. Machine Decision Authority Matrix entry approved. NHI Lifecycle Register complete. HOTL certification current for all Level 3 and above systems deployed in the portfolio. Each system's Autonomy Level, not the organization's maturity stage, determines its specific certification and oversight model requirement. | Transactional agents |

(*continued*)

*Table 12-3.* (*continued*)

| Maturity Stage | Adoption Goal | Required Governance Capability (Architectural Delta) | High-Risk Use Case Focus |
|---|---|---|---|
| 4: Autonomous | Hybrid and cyber-physical (UC13, UC14, UC15) | ZTAI. SCE. Ensemble reasoning. Continuous Adversarial Testing/CT. $\geq$98% auditable rationale standard active for regulated domains. HAL supervisors with Critical-tier endorsement required for all Level 4–5 systems in the portfolio. HOTL certification with standard program required for all Level 3 systems still operating in the portfolio; Stage 4 maturity does not remove Level 3 oversight obligations. Span-of-control thresholds enforced by SRE for all Level 3 and above systems. | Safety-critical/autonomous |

# Scaling Controls for Autonomy

Scaling into the autonomous tiers requires introducing advanced, proactive governance infrastructure specifically designed to manage the unpredictable nature of LLM autonomy and to secure non-human digital identities. These are the non-linear investments an organization must make before deploying high-risk use cases. This required infrastructure includes mandating automated safety through controls such as PaC and SCE, strictly securing autonomy using ZTAI through the Delegated Authorization Service, and sustaining trust by embedding MLOps as a compliance mechanism.

## Mandating Automated Safety

Guaranteeing compliance in autonomous systems requires transitioning from manual review to automated, instantaneous policy enforcement. This is achieved through a runtime compliance engine that uses PaC to enforce rules in real time and by deploying formal guarantees for agent behavior using SCE to ensure that non-negotiable safety rules always override conflicting objectives. These mechanisms ensure that risk management is automated, transforming compliance from a manual gate into a continuous function.

### Runtime Compliance Engine

PaC translates compliance requirements into machine-readable rules that a PDP enforces instantly. The PaC framework functions as a Real-Time Compliance Monitoring Service, applying checks before the agent executes a high-impact action, such as validating a proposed discount against policy thresholds. This eliminates regulatory lag by allowing continuous, automated governance. For complex multi-policy environments, the GaaS framework used by the autonomous IT agent (UC6) requires a Policy Conflict Resolution Engine to establish a clear hierarchy (e.g., security policies vetoing efficiency policies), ensuring deterministic decision-making when rules conflict. The PaC policy set must encode the Machine Decision Authority Matrix domain limits as hard-coded constraints rather than as configurable parameters that engineering teams can adjust at runtime.

### Formal Guarantees for Agent Behavior

For safety-critical systems, formal guarantees of compliance are mandatory to overcome the brittleness of traditional prompt engineering. SCE defines precise safety specifications offline and implements a Runtime Monitor that validates every proposed agent action against the pre-verified policy before execution. A clear example is the restaurant waitlist agent (UC11), which must treat safety-critical preferences (e.g., severe allergies, table capacity limits) as non-negotiable hard constraints. These constraints override the revenue-maximizing objective function, ensuring the system fails safely rather than violating a necessary safety rule.

## Securing Autonomy

The highest security risk in Stage 3/4 is the autonomous AI agent itself, which must be secured as an untrusted non-human identity. This security is implemented by enforcing ZTAI, which uses strong identities and dynamic least privilege, and by utilizing a Delegated Authorization Service to ensure the agent's actions never exceed the human's authorized scope. This dual-layer control is essential for preventing privilege escalation and managing the risk posed by an agent's delegated authority. Both controls operate within the boundaries set by the NHI lifecycle governance framework; an unregistered non-human identity is a zero-tolerance governance breach regardless of how well the ZTAI infrastructure is designed.

## ZTAI

The architecture must implement ZTAI by assigning strong identities to agents, typically backed by PKI Certificates and managed by a dedicated AI Agent Identity Provider (IdP). This enables non-repudiable authentication for all actions. Access must be based on dynamic least privilege, utilizing short-lived, dynamic credentials issued only for the specific action the agent is currently performing. This rigorous control is essential for preventing privilege escalation if the agent is compromised. Credential rotation schedules must comply with the NHI lifecycle standards: 30 days maximum for Level 4–5 systems, 60 days for Level 3, 90 days for Levels 1–2.

### Delegated Authorization Service

This mandatory service prevents Excess Agency by ensuring that an AI agent, even with high system privileges, operates within the authorization context of the authenticated human agent it assists. It acts as a proxy layer, intercepting the LLM's planned action (e.g., a credit issuance) and performing a dynamic check against the authenticated human agent's RBAC permissions. The API call proceeds only if the action is within the human's defined scope. The financial ceiling enforced by this service must not exceed the maximum action magnitude established in the Machine Decision Authority Matrix entry for the relevant operational domain.

## Sustaining Trust

MLOps in Stage 4 functions as the technical compliance mechanism for maintaining model integrity in safety-critical domains and managing the risks of drift and adversarial attacks. This is achieved by implementing drift detection as a regulatory control to automatically manage model degradation and by deploying continuous adversarial robustness testing (Red-Teaming) to ensure model integrity against sophisticated external threats. These continuous assurance functions are essential for managing the dynamic risks posed by adaptive AI.

### Drift Detection As a Regulatory Control

Model performance degradation (drift) in predictive systems (UC9, UC13, UC14) is a direct compliance failure. Continuous monitoring must track data drift and concept drift using statistical divergence metrics, such as KL/JS divergence, to quantify shifts between the production and training data distributions. When drift exceeds a threshold, the MLOps pipeline must automatically trigger an auditable Continuous Training (CT) cycle. This is paramount for defense systems (UC14) where CT procedures must be certified protocols to maintain accuracy in air-gapped environments. Note: A model update that materially changes a system's decision logic is also a Mover event under the NHI lifecycle governance framework, requiring an NHI privilege scope review before the updated model is deployed to production.

### Continuous Adversarial Robustness Testing

Autonomous systems require continuous security validation against adversarial attacks. Stage 4 mandates a shift to continuous Adversarial Testing (Red-Teaming) against the live system, with active tracking of the Guardrail Evasion Rate and the Attack Success Rate. Furthermore, core ML risk models (e.g., GNNs in UC9) must undergo Adversarial Training to bolster their resilience against evasion attacks, ensuring model integrity against sophisticated external threats.

## Operationalizing Trust

The roadmap for achieving Certified Operational Velocity defines the optimal sequencing of architectural investments required to support the escalating governance mandates across all four maturity stages. This approach mandates a phased investment strategy, beginning with foundations for shared RAG pipelines and PII masking, moving to agentic integration for PaC and identity management, and concluding with autonomous transformation for safety-critical controls. The entire process is underpinned by the mandatory architectural safety controls, such as the Orchestration-based Saga Pattern and the HITL Override Service, that guarantee operational safety.

## Phasing the Governance Architectural Delta

The strategic rollout of AI capabilities requires a disciplined, phased investment plan that progresses from foundational capabilities to full autonomous capability. This roadmap mandates a sequential investment across three mandatory phases: Phase A builds the core secure RAG pipeline; Phase B secures non-human identities and transactions; and Phase C enables safety-critical controls and continuous resilience. This investment sequencing ensures that the governance infrastructure is always deployed ahead of the escalating risk. Critically, each phase is also the point at which the corresponding governance instruments are activated, not after the use cases are deployed, but before.

### Phase A: Investment in Shared RAG Controls

This phase focuses on core shared infrastructure investment, covering RAG foundations and initial optimization use cases (e.g., UC1, UC4). Key milestones include DLAC/Security Trimming, deployment of the immutable audit logging service, and establishment of the Online Feature Store/vector DB foundation for real-time feature retrieval (e.g., UC5, UC9). The objective is to maintain consistency in the Groundedness (Faithfulness) Score across all RAG use cases. This investment enables the safe operation of all Tier 1 (Foundational) use cases. At this phase, the organization must also formally adopt the three constitutional doctrines and the Criticality Classification framework, both of which are governance prerequisites for any subsequent phase.

### Phase B: Investment in Runtime Policy Enforcement

This phase implements runtime enforcement for transactional agents (UC6, UC7, UC10, UC12). This control layer is mandatory for moving any use case from assistive to active operation. Key milestones include deploying and validating the Delegated Authorization Service, implementing the Tool Schema Definition and Translation Layer to enable reliable API integration, deploying the Saga Orchestrator for distributed transactions (UC7, UC12), and activating the PaC engine. This investment enables the safe deployment of all Tier 2 (Transactional) use cases. Additionally, this phase must complete the NHI Lifecycle Register for all agents, apply the decision authority scoring methodology to each deployment, and obtain Machine Decision Authority Matrix approval for all operational domains in which agents will act. The aggregate decision authority score across all production agents must be calculated as a portfolio total and verified against the board-approved Autonomy Budget ceiling, set at 900 points in this book's illustrative architecture (illustrative only; organizations set their own ceiling based on risk appetite and governance maturity; the board sets the actual ceiling for each organization), before each deployment authorization is issued. No deployment that would push portfolio utilization above 80% of the ceiling may proceed without Board Risk Committee review.

## Phase C: Investment in Autonomous Safety Assurance

This final phase activates high-risk controls and hybrid architectures for safety-critical systems (UC9, UC13, UC14, UC15). These controls are required for any system where failure could result in financial loss, physical harm, or regulatory non-compliance. Milestones include enforcing ZTAI, validating ensemble reasoning (UC15), deploying SCE protocols (UC11, UC13), and certifying air-gapped CT procedures (UC14). This investment enables the safe deployment of all Tier 3 (Autonomous) use cases. This phase must also complete the HOTL certification program for all supervisors of Level 3+ systems (including the Critical-tier endorsement for Critical-tier systems), activate the ≥98% auditable rationale standard for all regulated-domain agents, and configure the Safety Runtime Environment to automatically enforce span-of-control thresholds.

## Risk Mitigation and Recovery Blueprint

Scaling transactional and autonomous agents requires a final layer of protection: a robust blueprint for preventing failure and recovering state when failures inevitably occur. This is achieved through the Saga Pattern, which ensures distributed transaction integrity by using compensating actions to safely unwind failed operations. It is complemented by the HITL Override Service, which serves as the non-negotiable architectural safety control, providing immediate interruption capability against rogue agent actions.

### Distributed Transaction Integrity

For complex, high-value distributed transactions (e.g., claims payout, ticket upgrade), the Orchestration-based Saga Pattern is mandatory. The central Saga Orchestrator manages the sequence of local transactions, executing predefined compensating transactions to safely roll back preceding changes (e.g., un-voiding the original ticket) if any step fails. The use of idempotent commands throughout the workflow is necessary to prevent unintended side effects from retries. Every Saga step must be validated by the Policy Enforcement Point before execution; compensation transactions cannot bypass the Machine Decision Authority Matrix limits.

### Mandatory HITL Override Service

The HITL Override Service is the final, non-negotiable architectural safety control for autonomous systems. It must be architected with the highest priority and lowest latency to ensure the ability to interrupt immediately in response to rogue or failed agent actions. For safety-critical systems, the mechanism logs the human supervisor's rationale for the override, creating a clear, auditable record for post-incident analysis and compliance review. This rationale forms part of the override record field in the mandatory log schema and is subject to the seven-year retention requirement of the EDS Logging and Explainability Standard (formally established in Chapter 11). Table 12-4 sets out the roadmap phasing and its governance implementation milestones.

***Table 12-4.*** *Roadmap phasing and governance implementation milestones*

| Phase (Investment Focus) | Maturity Stage Supported | Core Architectural Focus | Governance/Compliance Milestone |
|---|---|---|---|
| A: Foundations | Stage 1/2 | Shared RAG pipeline, vector DB, PII masking | Constitutional doctrines adopted. DLAC/Security Trimming active. Immutable logging deployed. Groundedness Score SLO established. Criticality Classification framework in place |
| B: Agentic integration | Stage 3 | Policy-as-Code engine, Saga Orchestrator, Delegated Authorization Service | Decision authority score assigned to all agents. Machine Decision Authority Matrix entries approved for all operational domains. Portfolio authority score verified against board-approved Autonomy Budget ceiling (900-point illustrative maximum; organizations set their own ceiling). NHI Lifecycle Register complete. HOTL certification current for all Level 3 systems. XAI rationale captured in audit logs |

*(continued)*

***Table 12-4.*** *(continued)*

| Phase (Investment Focus) | Maturity Stage Supported | Core Architectural Focus | Governance/Compliance Milestone |
|---|---|---|---|
| C: Autonomous transformation | Stage 4 | Ensemble reasoning, MLOps CT pipeline, Cyber-Physical Gateways | GMI Level 2 certification confirmed before first Level 3 production deployment. GMI Level 3 certification confirmed before first Level 4 production deployment. HAL supervisors with Critical-tier endorsement in place for all Level 4–5 systems. ≥98% auditable rationale standard active for all regulated-domain agents. Safety Constraint Engineering validated. KL/JS drift monitoring active. Adversarial robustness certified. Span-of-control thresholds enforced by SRE |

# Resource Alignment and Strategic Investment

The three investment phases above define what to build and the order in which to build it. Two questions follow directly: how to resource each phase and how to justify the investment to the board. The answers require viewing the governance architecture through both an ROI lens and a human capital lens. Budgets must be sequenced to support the mandated governance infrastructure before the use case is deployed, and the talent required to operate that infrastructure, particularly the certified supervisor pool, must be in place before deployment authorization is issued.

## Quantifying the ROI of Governance

Governance is not a cost center; it is the primary enabler of value and a critical tool for risk mitigation, yielding a strong return on investment (ROI) that must be strategically quantified. This requires viewing the ROI through two distinct lenses: realized ROI, which measures the direct productivity gains from a deployed system, and compliance ROI, which quantifies the far greater value derived from avoiding catastrophic regulatory fines and operational halts.

### Compliance ROI

While realized ROI quantifies direct productivity gains, compliance ROI provides the strategic justification for the most significant governance investments, quantifying the far greater value derived from cost avoidance. This return is quantified by the reduction in high-impact, low-frequency events, such as catastrophic regulatory fines or systemic financial losses. This requires a quantitative framework to assess potential regulatory penalties and brand equity losses stemming from systemic governance failures. Furthermore, architectures that automate governance, such as the Audit and Compliance Agent, generate continuous, immutable evidence, drastically reducing the manual effort and cost associated with compliance audits. The ≥98% auditable rationale standard is directly measurable as a reduction in compliance costs: an organization that generates complete audit trails for 98% of regulated-domain decisions spends dramatically less on regulatory response, litigation preparation, and manual audit reconstruction than one that cannot.

## Architectural ROI

The investment in the governance-centric AI architecture delivers significant, measurable architectural ROI by establishing reusable, cross-functional capabilities that dramatically reduce the cost and time required to deploy subsequent use cases. This is achieved by creating a shared services model in which foundational components, such as the Zero-Trust RAG pipeline and the PaC engine, become leveraged assets across all business units. Furthermore, the investment in centralized components like a unified Feature Store (UC5, UC9), a central vector database infrastructure (UC8), and a ZTAI IdP (UC6, UC7) shifts the cost model from per-project development to scalable platform enablement. This approach ultimately replaces siloed, point-solution governance with a centralized, certified framework, reducing compliance costs for every new AI system. The governance instruments in Table 12-1 are also reusable: an organization that has implemented the NHI lifecycle framework for UC6 does not rebuild it for UC9; it extends it.

## Budgetary Allocation for Infrastructure and Skills

The successful execution of the AI Maturity Roadmap depends on aligning financial resources and organizational talent with the phased architectural requirements. Strategic investment must focus on hardening the architectural foundation and closing the human capital readiness gap. Enterprises are dedicating a significant portion of their digital budgets to AI; among the highest-performing organizations, more than one-third commit over 20% of their digital budgets to AI technologies (McKinsey & Company, The State of AI in 2025, 2025), and this budget must prioritize the governance layer:

1. **Core Data and MLOps:** Investing in the unified Feature Store, vector DB, and drift monitoring/CT pipelines to support continuous assurance (Stage 4).
2. **Agent GRC Stack:** Funding the specialized security components: the AI Agent Identity Provider, PaC engine, and Saga Orchestrator.
3. **Oversight and Certification Infrastructure:** Funding the HOTL certification program, the automation bias training scenarios, and the Safety Runtime Environment configuration that enforces span-of-control thresholds automatically. These are not one-time investments; certification renewal and threshold monitoring are ongoing operational costs that must be budgeted annually.

## Closing the AI Skills Gap

The shift to autonomous, agentic AI creates an immediate and specialized human capital readiness gap that must be closed strategically through upskilling and targeted hiring. This requires not just traditional data science or MLOps expertise, but new roles focused on the governance of non-human entities. The key focus areas are

- **Agentic Governance Roles:** Specialists in XAI interpretation, reading and challenging XAI rationales, and safety oversight, including safely managing and intervening via the HITL Override Service
- **Advanced Engineering Roles:** Engineers with expertise in context engineering, ensemble reasoning system design, and Safety Constraint Engineering implementation for safety-critical deployments

- **Oversight Certification Pipeline:** A formal program for recruiting, training, and certifying HOTL supervisors for all Level 3 systems and HAL supervisors with the Critical-tier endorsement for Level 4–5 systems

A specific and often underestimated talent requirement is the HOTL supervisor pool. Every Level 3 system, regardless of the organization's maturity stage, needs at least two currently certified HOTL supervisors. Every Level 4 or Level 5 system needs at least three HAL-certified supervisors holding the Critical-tier endorsement. These are per-system requirements driven by the system's Autonomy Level, not by the organization's overall maturity stage. The certification program is not a one-hour online course; it is a structured program that includes automation bias testing and live supervision exercises. Organizations scaling rapidly from Stage 2 to Stage 3/4 frequently underestimate the lead time required to build and maintain the certified supervisor pool, thereby making supervisor readiness a precondition for deployment authorization rather than an afterthought. The Unified Architecture below provides the technical inventory against which all of these resource decisions should be planned.

# The Maturity Architecture: Scaling Certified Operational Velocity

The governance instruments, maturity stages, and phased roadmap described in this chapter constitute a complete, mutually reinforcing framework. For the CIO and the CRO, the practical expression of this framework is the GMI gating architecture: the organization may not deploy at a given Autonomy Level until GMI certification confirms the required governance infrastructure is production-ready. This prevents the post-pilot paradox, where localized success fails to scale because institutional trust has not been established. The Unified Architecture below consolidates the full portfolio of Architectural Building Blocks required to sustain Stage 4 maturity.

## The Unified Architecture: Master ABB Inventory

To achieve full maturity, the organization must transition from siloed use case implementations to a unified platform strategy. This shift transforms the architecture from a series of project-specific tools into an Industrialized Intelligence Platform. The following blueprint represents the superset of Architectural Building Blocks (ABBs) required to sustain Stage 4 AI maturity. It consolidates the security mandates, cognitive patterns, and assurance mechanisms discussed throughout this book into a single, cohesive technical inventory.

Figure 12-1 presents the complete enterprise AI governance framework as a conceptual reference: the Governance Authority zone anchors all autonomy decisions through the Authority Matrix Rules Repository, NHI Lifecycle Register, Autonomy Level Register, Regulatory Compliance Map, GMI Gating Service, Policy Authoring and Versioning, and Autonomy Budget Monitor; the Security Enforcement zone enforces identity, delegation, and data protection through the AI Agent Identity Provider, Delegated Authorization Service, Secure Data Proxy, MCP Tool Gateway, Safety Constraint Engineering, and Policy Conflict Resolution Engine; the Cognitive Layer hosts the Multi-agent Orchestrator, Reasoning Engine, Memory Subsystem, Ensemble Validation Engine, and Digital Twin Agent as the reasoning and validation core governed by all surrounding controls; the Knowledge and Data zone provides traceable, auditable retrieval infrastructure through the vector database, Online Feature Store, Data Lineage Platform, Edge–Fog–Cloud Bridge, and CD-Module; and the Assurance and Oversight zone closes the governance loop through the Immutable Audit Log, Reasoning Trace Logger, XAI Toolkit, HOTL Interface, MLOps drift monitoring, Saga Orchestrator, and HITL Override Service.

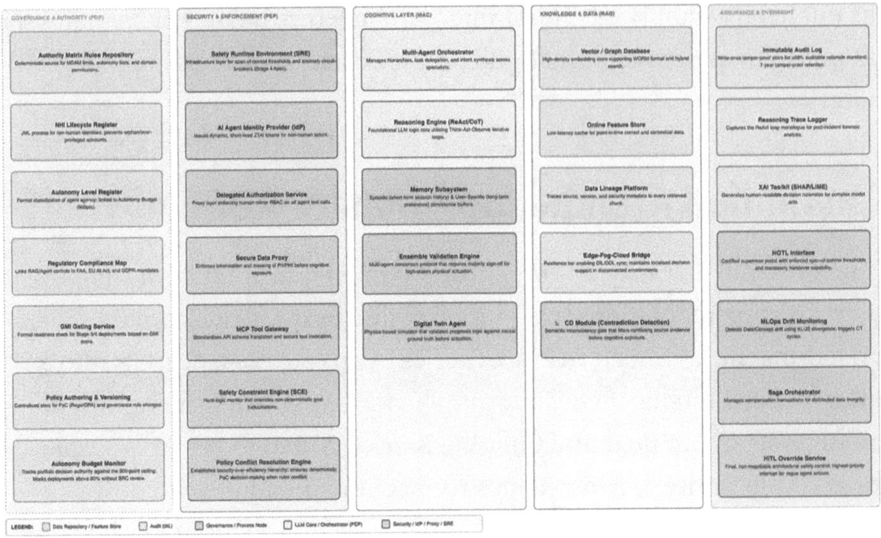

***Figure 12-1.** Enterprise AI governance framework—conceptual reference map of the complete governance instrument portfolio across the Governance Authority (PDP), Security Enforcement (PEP), Cognitive Layer (MAC), Knowledge and Data (RAG), and Assurance and Oversight zones, spanning all maturity stages from foundational RAG assistants to autonomous safety-critical multi-agent systems*

# Summary

Governance infrastructure is what separates enterprises that deploy AI from those that scale it safely. The 15 use cases in this book demonstrate that scaling trust is achieved through three non-negotiable architectural mandates that must be adopted proactively, ahead of each use case's deployment:

- **Enforce Granularity (Stage 2)**: Establish the Zero-Trust RAG pipeline with mandatory DLAC or Security Trimming and immutable audit logging as the universal security baseline. Activate the Groundedness

Score as a mandatory SLO and deploy the LLMOps Oversight Model Continuity controls from Chapter 5 to detect Threshold Drift, Supervisor Availability Drift, and Prompt Drift before they erode governance compliance.

- **Govern Autonomy (Stage 3)**: Apply the decision authority scoring methodology to every agent before deployment. Obtain board authorization via the Machine Decision Authority Matrix for each operational domain. Implement runtime controls using PaC and the Delegated Authorization Service to secure non-human identities and ensure transactional integrity via the Saga Pattern. Maintain the NHI Lifecycle Register and current HOTL certification for all Level 3 supervisors.
- **Guarantee Resilience (Stage 4)**: Deploy safety-critical controls: ZTAI, ensemble reasoning, and continuous MLOps assurance (drift monitoring/CT), to manage the dynamic risks posed by adaptive AI in safety-critical domains. Enforce the ≥98% auditable rationale standard for all regulated-domain decisions, activate the span-of-control thresholds in the Safety Runtime Environment, and maintain the Critical-tier endorsement for all supervisors of Critical-tier systems.

The governance instruments described in this book are not independent additions to an AI deployment. They are an interconnected framework; each instrument builds on the ones before it, and a gap in any instrument undermines all the others. An organization with a perfect Machine Decision Authority Matrix but an incomplete NHI Lifecycle Register has agents authorized to act in domains for which their credentials are not properly governed. An organization with excellent HOTL certification but an auditable rationale rate of 85% has supervisors who cannot be shown to have been meaningfully supervising because the decision stream they monitored is not fully documented.

By committing organizational resources to this governance roadmap in sequence rather than in parallel, leaders unlock Certified Operational Velocity, gaining the competitive advantage of knowing they can deploy and scale transformative AI solutions, from predictive maintenance to autonomous claims processing, faster and with greater confidence than any competitor. The commitment to this roadmap ensures that machine power remains a servant of institutional authority and human safety. With this technical foundation in place, the organization is ready to authorize its final transition into the age of industrialized intelligence. The Guarded Innovation posture is not a constraint on ambition. It is the architecture that makes ambition trustworthy.

## Reference

McKinsey & Company. 2025. The State of AI in 2025: Agents, Innovation, and Transformation. New York: McKinsey & Company. https://www.mckinsey.com/capabilities/quantumblack/our-insights/the-state-of-ai.

APPENDIX A

# EDS Logging and Explainability Standard—Mandatory Log Schema

*This appendix is a normative standard of the EDS framework. The mandatory log schema specified here applies uniformly to all production autonomous AI systems registered in the Autonomy Register. It is formally established in Chapter 11 and referenced throughout the book.*

## The 18 Mandatory Log Fields

All 18 fields are mandatory for every production autonomous AI system registered in the Autonomy Register. The RAG-context subset (fields applicable to RAG deployments) is documented in Table 4-6; agentic fields (including fields 12–18) apply additionally to all agentic systems from Chapter 9 onward.


M. M. Hossain and A. A. N. Ponnusamy, *Governance-First AI*,
https://doi.org/10.1007/979-8-8688-3118-8

***Table A-1.*** *The 18 mandatory log fields of the EDS Logging and Explainability Standard, organized by category. Row shading groups fields by category. All 18 fields are mandatory for every production autonomous AI system registered in the Autonomy Register.*

| # | Field Name | Category | Description |
|---|---|---|---|
| 1 | **System identifier** | System and agent identity | Links the decision to the Autonomy Register entry, decision authority score, oversight model, and accountable executive |
| 2 | **NHI identifier** | System and agent identity | The non-human identity credential of the agent that made the decision; cryptographically linked for non-repudiation |
| 3 | **Session/task identifier** | Session and timing | The Execution ID threading all entries for a single workflow into an ordered audit trail |
| 4 | **Timestamp** | Session and timing | Millisecond-precision timestamp generated by the logging infrastructure at the moment of decision |
| 5 | **Autonomy level** | Decision context | The Autonomy Level and oversight model active at the time of the decision |
| 6 | **Oversight model** | Decision context | Supervising operator identity and HOTL/HAL certification reference for Level 3 and above systems |
| 7 | **Model version identifier** | Decision context | The version of the LLM or ML model that generated the decision output |
| 8 | **Prompt version identifier** | Decision context | The version of the prompt template used to generate the decision output |

*(continued)*

*Table A-1.* (*continued*)

| # | Field Name | Category | Description |
|---|---|---|---|
| 9 | **Prompt Authority Scope Statement identifier** | Decision context | Reference to the board-approved authority scope under which the prompt operates (PASS-YYYY-NNN format) |
| 10 | **Reasoning steps** | Decision context | The intermediate Thought steps captured from the ReAct reasoning loop (Reasoning Trace Capture) |
| 11 | **Input summary** | Decision context | Structured summary of the input that triggered the decision, including the user query, retrieved context, and applied ACLs |
| 12 | **Tool calls** | Action and authority | All tool calls with their parameters, outputs, and sequence, enabling full reconstruction of the agentic action path |
| 13 | **Decision output** | Action and authority | The agent's decision output, including the recommendation, classification, or determination generated |
| 14 | **Action taken** | Action and authority | The action executed following the decision output; distinct from the decision itself to enable separation of recommendation from execution |
| 15 | **MAM authority check** | Action and authority | Confirmation that the action was within the maximum action magnitude authority threshold, or the escalation event if it was not |
| 16 | **SRE evaluation result** | Action and authority | The Safety Runtime Environment's evaluation of the decision against span-of-control thresholds and fail-closed obligations |

(*continued*)

*Table A-1.* (*continued*)

| # | Field Name | Category | Description |
|---|---|---|---|
| **17** | **Anomaly flags** | Oversight and override | Any anomaly flags raised by guardrails, bias detection, or the SRE circuit breaker during the decision lifecycle |
| **18** | **Override record** | Oversight and override | Where a HOTL supervisor intervened, a HAL review occurred, or a HITL approver acted: their identity, certification reference, decision, and rationale. Retained for a minimum of seven years |

# Override Records Retention

Field 18 (override record) is the primary evidence of meaningful human oversight. Where a HOTL supervisor intervened, a HAL review occurred, or a HITL approver acted, the override record must capture the identity, current certification reference, decision, and rationale of the intervening party. Override records must be retained for a minimum of seven years, or longer as required by applicable law or regulation.

# HOTL Certification Reference (Level 3 and Above)

For HOTL decisions at Autonomy Level 3 and above, the log must additionally capture the supervising operator's current certification reference (field 6: oversight model), confirming the supervisor held a valid HOTL certification at the time of the decision. This field serves as audit evidence distinguishing genuine human oversight from nominal oversight. A system operating at Level 3 or above without a currently certified HOTL supervisor is operating in governance breach.

## Cross-References

This standard is formally established and its context explained in Chapter 11 ("The EDS Logging and Explainability Standard" section). The RAG-context field subset (fields 1–11) is specified in Table 4-6 (Chapter 4). The ≥98% auditable rationale standard, which governs the minimum proportion of decisions that require a complete log entry, is defined in Chapter 11. The write-before-execute and fail-closed obligations are detailed in Chapters 4, 9, 10, and 11.

# APPENDIX B

# Glossary of Terms

*This glossary defines the proprietary terms, acronyms, and governance concepts used throughout this book. Terms are alphabetical within each letter group. Where a term is synonymous with another entry, a cross-reference is provided. Chapter references indicate where each concept is formally introduced.*

## A

**ABAC** *Attribute-Based Access Control*
An access control model that grants or denies access based on attributes of the user, the resource, and the environment, rather than roles alone. Used in the EDS framework for fine-grained, context-sensitive data access decisions.

**ABB** *Architectural Building Block*
A discrete, reusable component of the EDS governance architecture. ABBs are the modular units—the Policy Decision Point, the Delegated Authorization Service, the Saga Orchestrator, and others—from which the complete Industrialized Intelligence Platform is assembled.

**ACA** *Audit and Compliance Agent*
A specialized agent in multi-agent deployments responsible for capturing the complete audit trail, enforcing write-before-execute, and confirming that all decisions meet the ≥98% auditable rationale standard before actions are executed.


M. M. Hossain and A. A. N. Ponnusamy, *Governance-First AI*,
https://doi.org/10.1007/979-8-8688-3118-8

**ACL** *Access Control List*
A data structure that specifies which users or system processes are granted access to specific resources and what operations they are permitted to perform. The freshness of ACL data is a critical dependency of the DLAC mechanism in the EDS framework.

**ADAE** *Autonomous Decision Authority Evaluation*
The composite score is produced by applying the EDS framework's four-dimensional decision authority scoring methodology (Financial Authority 40%, Customer Reach 30%, Operational Reach 20%, Decision Velocity 10%) to a registered agentic AI system. The ADAE score determines the system's Autonomy Level and Delegation Tier. Organizations may adjust these weights subject to board approval and documented rationale for deviation, provided the total remains 100% and the adjusted weighting is recorded in the relevant Authority Matrix entry.

**ADR** *Average Daily Rate*
A hospitality revenue metric measuring the average revenue earned per occupied room per day. Used in UC10 (hotel dynamic pricing and booking agent) as the primary financial success indicator for AI-driven pricing optimization.

**AHT** *Average Handle Time*
A contact center operations metric measuring the average duration of a customer interaction from initiation to resolution. A primary efficiency KPI for UC1 (AI-powered frontline knowledge assistant).

**ANN** *Approximate Nearest Neighbor*
A class of algorithms used in vector search that trade perfect accuracy for dramatically improved query speed. Used in the EDS RAG pipeline's retrieval layer for fast semantic search across large vector indices.

**Authority Matrix**
See Machine Decision Authority Matrix (MDAM).

**Autonomy Budget**

The board-approved aggregate ceiling on total delegated machine authority across all production agentic AI systems in the organization's estate. Expressed in ADAE composite score points. Prevents the invisible concentration of institutional authority in production AI systems at the portfolio level, a risk that no individual system limit can detect. No deployment that would push portfolio utilization above 80% of the ceiling may proceed without Board Risk Committee review.

**Autonomy Level**

A five-point classification (Level 1 through Level 5) that specifies the degree of machine autonomy a registered AI system is authorized to exercise, the mandatory oversight model that applies, and the maximum decision authority it may exercise without human confirmation. Determined by the ADAE composite score. Managed through the Autonomy Register.

**Autonomy Register**

The EDS framework's live inventory of all authorized AI deployments. Every AI system must have a registered Autonomy Register entry before it may be deployed to production. The register records each system's Autonomy Level, Criticality Tier, oversight model, accountable executive, and Authority Matrix domain authorization.

# B

**BM25**

Best Match 25. A sparse keyword-based retrieval algorithm is used as the complementary retrieval method in the EDS framework's Hybrid Search architecture. BM25 excels at exact keyword matching and, when combined with dense vector search via Reciprocal Rank Fusion (RRF), produces a unified, high-relevance retrieval result.

# C

**CAIO** *Chief AI Officer*
The senior executive is responsible for AI governance strategy, Authority Matrix domain authorization at or below board-approved limits, and compliance with the EDS framework across the organization. The CAIO is the accountable owner of the Autonomy Register.

**Certified Operational Velocity**
The governing principle of the EDS maturity framework. An organization can deploy and scale machine autonomy only as fast as its GMI-certified governance infrastructure can demonstrably support. Certified Operational Velocity is not a speed metric; it is the governance guarantee that speed is authorized.

**CHD** *Cardholder Data*
Sensitive payment card information is protected under the Payment Card Industry Data Security Standard (PCI DSS). The EDS framework mandates Secure Payment Offload and Tokenization to ensure CHD never enters the LLM core system or its audit logs.

**Citation Threshold**
The minimum acceptable Groundedness Score that an LLM-generated answer must achieve before it may be released to the user. If the score falls below the threshold, the orchestrator must either refuse generation or escalate to the applicable oversight model. Thresholds vary by Criticality Tier: 0.75 for HITL-regulated domains, 0.65–0.75 for HOTL, floor of 0.70 for HAL-regulated domains.

**Context Tax**
The compute cost and performance penalty incurred when irrelevant data is processed within the LLM's reasoning window. For cloud-hosted LLMs, this is a direct billing problem: irrelevant tokens are charged at the same rate as useful ones. Distinct from the Information Tax, which quantifies the productivity cost to human workers of information fragmentation.

**Continuous Admissibility**
The principle is that a delegated authority's fitness to bind consequences must be tested continuously in the present, not treated as permanently conferred by the original authorization. Governed through the Continuous Admissibility Monitor (CAM), the ADAE reassessment obligation, and the structural change trigger.

**CRAG** *Corrective RAG*
Corrective Retrieval-Augmented Generation. A feedback loop that initiates additional retrieval cycles when the Groundedness Score for an initial retrieval falls below the Citation Threshold. CRAG transforms HITL overrides from passive corrections into active index optimization signals, continuously improving retrieval quality in production.

**CRM** *Customer Relationship Management*
Enterprise software systems that manage customer interactions, data, and relationships. Referenced in the EDS framework as a core enterprise system accessed by agentic deployments via Event Bus integration to prevent direct agent queries from overwhelming legacy CRM infrastructure.

**CT** *Continuous Training*
The automated MLOps process by which model retraining is triggered and executed when drift metrics exceed predefined thresholds, without manual intervention. For air-gapped and DIL/DOL environments (UC14), CT procedures must be certified protocols. A model update that materially changes a system's decision logic constitutes a Mover event under the NHI lifecycle governance framework.

**CTA** *Consequence Tracing Authority*
A designated governance role whose mandate activates after a confirmed AI governance incident in which a corrupted state propagated undetected through the agentic estate. The CTA traces the inheritance graph of the bad

state, identifying every downstream agent, decision, report, or workflow that consumed it as valid, determining which links were load-bearing, and owning the remediation of what must be undone. The role must be designated before it is needed.

# D

**Decision Velocity Risk**
One of the eight AI risk categories in the EDS risk taxonomy. The risk that an autonomous system executing decisions at machine speed creates exposure that human oversight cannot contain, even with conventional approval processes. High decision velocity requires automated circuit breakers and span-of-control threshold enforcement rather than per-decision human review.

**Delegated Authorization Service**
The architectural component that enforces Permission Mirroring in agentic deployments. It intercepts every planned agent tool call and validates the proposed action against the invoking human user's RBAC permissions before execution. The agent's executable authority can never exceed the authenticated human's scope. The maximum action magnitude enforced by this service must not exceed the maximum action magnitude from the Authority Matrix domain entry.

**Delegation Tier**
The three-tier classification (Supervised, Monitored, Delegated) specifies the level of governance applied to a registered agentic system. The Delegation Tier is determined automatically by the Autonomy Level and cannot be negotiated or replaced with alternative governance arrangements without a formal change to the Autonomy Level.

**DIL/DOL** *Disconnected, Intermittent/Occasional, and Low-Bandwidth*
Network operating conditions are common in defense and remote industrial environments, where continuous cloud connectivity cannot be assumed. The EDS framework's Edge–Fog–Cloud topology and write-before-execute enforcement at the Fog Layer ensure full governance capability and complete audit trails in DIL/DOL conditions.

**DLAC** *Document-Level Access Control*
The EDS framework's mandatory access control mechanism for RAG deployments. DLAC ensures that every document chunk in the vector index is tagged with the access classification of its source document and that Security Trimming filters retrieved chunks to the requesting identity's authorized ACL scope at query time. The foundational security control for all RAG use cases.

# E

**EBIT** *Earnings Before Interest and Taxes*
A standard financial performance metric. Cited in the EDS framework as the enterprise-level measure against which AI initiative impact should be assessed, noting that fewer than half of organizations report measurable EBIT impact from AI at the enterprise level (McKinsey & Company, 2023).

**EDA** *Event-Driven Architecture*
An architectural pattern in which systems communicate by producing and consuming events via a message broker (e.g., Apache Kafka). Used in UC7 (insurance claims agent) to decouple the multi-agent system from core enterprise systems (PAS, CRM), allowing agents to react asynchronously to real-time events without overloading legacy infrastructure.

**EDS** *Enterprise Decision System*
The governance framework that this book establishes. EDS provides the constitutional doctrines, Governance Principles, architectural standards,

and maturity model that enable organizations to deploy and scale autonomous AI while maintaining board-level accountability, auditability, and control.

**Execution ID**
The unique session identifier is injected into every downstream transaction log entry to create a single, ordered audit trail for an entire workflow. The Execution ID is one of the mandatory log fields under the Logging and Explainability Standard and is the primary mechanism for forensic reconstruction of multi-step agent decisions.

# F

**Faithfulness Score**
See Groundedness Score.

**FAT** *Fairness, Accountability, and Transparency*
A governance framework mandating pre-deployment bias audits and continuous fairness monitoring on algorithmic decision systems. Applied in the EDS framework to seating optimization (UC11) and market intelligence (UC8) deployments to prevent discriminatory outcomes.

# G

**GaaS** *Governance-as-a-Service*
The EDS framework's model for real-time, automated policy enforcement in agentic deployments. GaaS transitions compliance from periodic manual review to continuous, pre-execution validation via Policy-as-Code (PaC), ensuring governance operates at machine speed rather than audit speed.

**GMI** *Governance Maturity Index*
The EDS framework's five-level certification scale (Level 1 through Level 5) that measures an organization's readiness to govern autonomous AI systems. The GMI is a binding constraint on autonomy scaling: no system may operate at an Autonomy Level exceeding the organization's certified GMI level. GMI Level 2 is the minimum governance readiness gate before any Level 3 system may be deployed; GMI Level 3 before Level 4; GMI Level 4 before Level 5.

**GNN** *Graph Neural Network*
A class of neural networks designed to operate on graph-structured data, analyzing relationships and connections between entities rather than individual data points in isolation. Used in UC9 (financial risk and fraud monitoring agent) to detect network-level fraud patterns: organized rings, mule account networks, and coordinated transactions that are invisible to transaction-level linear models.

**GRC** *Governance, Risk, and Compliance*
The integrated framework of policies, controls, and processes through which an organization manages its governance obligations, risk exposure, and regulatory compliance. In the EDS framework, GRC transitions from periodic manual audit to automated, real-time enforcement through PaC and the Safety Runtime Environment (SRE).

**Groundedness Score**
A 0–1 metric measuring how faithfully an LLM's generated answer is supported by retrieved source documents. The primary technical proxy for legal defensibility of LLM-generated outputs. Also referred to as the Faithfulness Score. Used as a mandatory Service-Level Objective (SLO) in all EDS RAG deployments, evaluated against the Citation Threshold to determine whether a response may be released or must be escalated.

**Guarded Innovation**
The board's constitutional risk posture toward autonomous AI. Guarded Innovation is the commitment to supporting autonomous AI where it demonstrably improves performance, while enforcing hard limits on uncontrolled autonomy, irreversible actions without circuit breakers, and unmonitored authority. It is not risk avoidance; it is risk-managed velocity, the constitutional foundation of Certified Operational Velocity.

# H

**HAL** *Human-Above-the-Loop*
The highest-intensity EDS oversight model is applied to Critical-tier systems at Autonomy Level 4 and above. HAL supervisors operate via batch-interval review of decision distributions at the ≤ 50-decisions-per-hour Critical-tier threshold, rather than monitoring individual decisions. HAL supervisors must hold the Critical-tier endorsement within the HOTL Certification Framework. This endorsement constitutes the HAL certification pathway.

**HITL** *Human-in-the-Loop*
The EDS oversight model requires explicit human confirmation before each consequential AI output or action takes effect. Applied at lower Autonomy Levels and as an escalation mode triggered by governance events (threshold breach, anomaly detection, logging failure) across all Autonomy Levels. The HITL Override Service is the non-negotiable architectural safety control that implements this capability.

**HOTL** *Human-on-the-Loop*
The EDS oversight model for Autonomy Level 3 systems. A certified HOTL supervisor monitors the decision stream in real or near real time and has the authority to intervene, redirect, or halt the system at any point. HOTL

oversight is a constitutional governance obligation; a system operating at Level 3 or above without a currently certified HOTL supervisor is in breach of governance.

**HOTL Certification Framework**

The EDS framework's mandatory certification program for all primary and secondary HOTL supervisors. Comprises five sequential components: Foundation, System-specific training, Intervention skills, Automation bias training (≥75% scenario identification pass standard), and Assessed supervision exercise (minimum four hours). Certification is valid for 12 months; renewal requires an updated assessment of automation bias scenarios. The Critical-tier endorsement within this framework constitutes the HAL certification pathway.

# I

**Information Tax**

The productivity cost to human workers of information fragmentation and manual search time, the time spent searching for information rather than creating value. Distinct from the Context Tax, which quantifies the compute cost of irrelevant data in the LLM's reasoning window. The EDS RAG platform addresses the Information Tax by delivering governed, grounded knowledge retrieval to frontline workers.

**Isolation Paradox**

The risk that security controls designed to isolate sensitive data (such as DLAC and Security Trimming) fail when the LLM's reasoning window is not subject to the same access controls as the retrieval layer. An agent with elevated system privileges that retrieves unrestricted context and presents it to an end user causes data leakage, even if the final action is within scope.

# J

**JML** *Joiner-Mover-Leaver*
The identity lifecycle process governing provisioning (Joiner), modification (Mover), and deprovisioning (Leaver) of non-human identities (NHIs) in agentic AI deployments. Adopted by the EDS framework as the primary lifecycle control for all NHIs. Every system lifecycle event triggers an NHI lifecycle review. A model update that materially changes a system's decision logic is a Mover event requiring an NHI privilege scope review before the updated model reaches production.

# K

**KBR** *Knowledge Base Refinement Pipeline*
The automated process, triggered by CRAG feedback, refines the RAG knowledge base in response to the four CRAG failure types established in Chapter 5: retrieval failures, generation failures, coverage failures, and threshold miscalibration. Transforms HITL overrides from passive corrections into active index optimization signals.

**KL/JS Divergence** *Kullback-Leibler/Jensen-Shannon Divergence*
Statistical measures used in the EDS MLOps framework to detect data drift by quantifying the difference between the production data distribution and the training data distribution. A KL/JS divergence exceeding 0.1 on critical sensor features triggers automated model retraining in UC13 and UC14.

# L

**LLMOps** *Large Language Model Operations*
The operational discipline for monitoring, maintaining, and improving LLM-based systems in production. In the EDS framework, LLMOps

extends conventional MLOps to address governance-specific failure modes: Threshold Drift (Citation Threshold degradation), Supervisor Availability Drift (HOTL coverage gaps), and Prompt Drift (behavioral changes from prompt modifications).

**Logging and Explainability Standard**
The EDS framework's mandatory technical specification governs audit trail completeness, retention obligations, and mandatory log fields for every autonomous AI deployment. Embodied in the 11 RAG-relevant log fields in Table 4-6 and the full 18-field standard defined in Chapter 11. All decision audit logs are subject to a minimum seven-year retention obligation that survives system decommissioning.

**LRA** *Logistics Risk Agent*
A specialized agent in the defense predictive maintenance multi-agent system (UC14) that proactively assesses supply chain risk upon fault diagnosis and initiates automated spare parts requisitions before work order approval, ensuring that safety-driven maintenance decisions do not fail at execution due to parts unavailability.

# M

**MAM** *Maximum Action Magnitude*
The single-transaction ceiling on the financial authority or operational impact that a registered autonomous agent may exercise without human confirmation. Set by the CAIO within each Authority Matrix–authorized domain, at or below the domain limit. Technically enforced at the infrastructure level, not policy-declared and not overridable by the agent's own reasoning.

**MANDATE** *Machine Authority Non-Delegable Autonomous Technology Enforcement*
The board-level instrument through which machine decision authority is formally delegated, explicitly bounded, and continuously monitored. MANDATE is not a software product or a technical standard; it is the highest-order governance act the board performs in relation to AI and the constitutional foundation from which all other EDS controls are derived. No EDS product—no policy, standard, operating manual, or assurance framework—can operate without the constitutional foundation MANDATE provides. The three Governance Doctrines (Decision Authority Governance, Governance-Constrained Autonomy, and Delegated Machine Authority) form the core of MANDATE and define its scope.

**MAS** *Multi-agent System*
An architecture in which multiple specialized, autonomous agents collaborate under an Orchestrator or Supervisor Agent to decompose and execute complex multi-domain workflows. Required for use cases involving specialized expertise and distributed coordination (UC7, UC8, UC9, UC13, UC14, UC15). In a MAS deployment, each agent must have its own registered NHI with a privilege scope calibrated to its specific function.

**MCP** *Model Context Protocol*
An evolving standard that centralizes the definition and execution of tools for LLM agents, decoupling tool management from application logic. In EDS enterprise deployments, the MCP Server is architected using an enterprise API Management Gateway that handles authentication, authorization, and unified logging and enforces the maximum action magnitude from the Authority Matrix domain entry on every tool call.

**MDAM** *Machine Decision Authority Matrix*
The board instrument through which decision authority is formally delegated to autonomous AI systems across defined organizational

domains. Specifies which operational domains are authorized for machine decision-making, the maximum decision authority permitted in each domain, the oversight model required, and the aggregate ceiling (Autonomy Budget) on total delegated machine authority. No autonomous system may operate in a domain not covered by a board-authorized MDAM entry.

**MGB** *Model Governance Board*
The cross-functional governance body that receives Model Risk Officer (MRO) escalations, reviews portfolio-level model performance, approves material changes to oversight model configurations, and provides the Board Risk Committee with evidence that the production AI estate is operating within approved governance parameters. Where the MRO is accountable for individual model integrity, the MGB is accountable for the integrity of the governed AI portfolio as a whole. Introduced in Chapter 5.

**MRO** *Model Risk Officer*
The named individual is accountable for monitoring model drift, approving Citation Threshold recalibrations, authorizing version updates, and escalating systematic model failures to the Model Governance Board. The MRO is a governance role, not a technical role; accountability rests with a named person rather than the engineering team.

**MVG** *Minimum Viable Governance*
The minimum set of EDS governance controls that must be fully certified before any high-value AI system may enter production. Comprising the three constitutional doctrines, Criticality Classification, Zero-Trust RAG pipeline, and relevant oversight model, the MVG layer is the non-negotiable floor below which no deployment is permitted, regardless of business case or commercial pressure.

# N

**NBA** *Next Best Action*
An AI-driven recommendation pattern that identifies the most contextually appropriate action for a customer interaction based on intent, profile, and real-time data. Used in UC5 (contact center optimization agent) as the primary output of the agentic AI layer.

**NHI** *Non-human Identity*
A digital identity assigned to an autonomous AI agent, service account, or automated script that grants it the ability to act within enterprise systems. In the EDS framework, NHIs are governed by the JML lifecycle framework, must be registered in the NHI Lifecycle Register before production use, and may never operate with privilege scopes exceeding the maximum action magnitude specified in the Authority Matrix domain entry. An unregistered NHI is a zero-tolerance governance breach.

**NHI Lifecycle Register**
The authoritative source of truth governing every non-human identity actor in the organization's agentic AI estate. Every NHI must be discoverable, attributed to a specific agentic AI system, linked to a responsible system owner, and monitored for anomalous behavior. An orphan NHI, one without a current lifecycle record or a corresponding Autonomy Register reference, is a zero-tolerance governance breach that requires immediate disablement.

# O

**Orchestration-based Saga Pattern**
The mandated model for achieving distributed transaction integrity in agentic deployments executing multi-step financial or state-changing workflows. A central Saga Orchestrator manages a sequence of locally

committed transactions and executes predefined compensating transactions in reverse order if any step fails, guaranteeing eventual consistency and safe, auditable rollback. All forward and compensating transactions must be defined as idempotent commands. Every Saga step must be validated by the PEP before execution; compensating transactions cannot bypass Authority Matrix limits.

# P

**PaC** *Policy-as-Code*
The EDS framework's mechanism for encoding governance rules in declarative, versioned, machine-readable language (e.g., Rego for the Open Policy Agent, OPA) that is evaluated by the PDP before every proposed agent action. PaC transitions compliance from periodic manual review to continuous, pre-execution validation and must encode Authority Matrix domain limits as hard-coded constraints rather than configurable parameters.

**PAS** *Policy Administration System*
The core enterprise system in insurance operations that stores and manages policy terms, coverage details, and policyholder data. Accessed by agents in UC7 (insurance claims agent) via Event Bus integration.

**PCI DSS** *Payment Card Industry Data Security Standard*
The global security standard governing the storage, transmission, and processing of cardholder data. Mandates Secure Payment Offload and Tokenization in UC10 and UC12 to ensure the LLM Cognitive Layer never enters the Cardholder Data Environment.

**PDP** *Policy Decision Point*
The deterministic policy engine that evaluates every proposed agent action against the declarative PaC policy set and returns a binary Allow/Deny verdict with auditable reason codes before the PEP acts. The PDP

must be a pure evaluation engine; it never acts directly on the data stream. The PDP evaluates proposed actions against the Authority Matrix domain entry, including the maximum action magnitude, the authorized domain scope, and the oversight model requirement.

**PEFT** *Parameter-Efficient Fine-Tuning*
A class of techniques (including Low-Rank Adaptation, LoRA) that adapt large language models to specific domains by training only a small fraction of the model's parameters, dramatically reducing compute cost compared with full fine-tuning. Used in UC4 (stylist and language adapter) for brand-consistent language adaptation.

**PEP** *Policy Enforcement Point*
The physical or logical gateway that enforces the PDP's Allow/Deny verdict. In agentic architectures, PEPs live at the Model Gateway, the Agent Orchestrator, the Tool Adapters (MCP Server), and the Retrieval Services. The PEP is the sole authorized component to dispatch tool calls to enterprise systems following a PDP Allow verdict. The PEP enforces per-decision rules; the SRE governs system-level operating mode.

**PIP** *Policy Information Point*
The data layer in the GaaS architecture that sources the context and attributes required by the PDP for policy evaluation. In agentic systems, the PIP sources attributes from identity providers, risk feeds, data catalogs, and LLM-based guardrails (which produce deterministic outputs—binary flags or risk scores—before being passed to the PDP). The PIP also sources real-time decision velocity data to evaluate against the Authority Matrix's velocity dimension limits.

**Prompt Drift Risk**
One of the eight AI risk categories in the EDS risk taxonomy. The risk is that changes to prompt templates, system prompts, or few-shot examples alter the LLM's behavioral profile in ways that erode governance

compliance. Monitored continuously in the EDS LLMOps framework; a prompt change can multiply token consumption by an order of magnitude or more overnight (OpenAI, 2024).

# R

**RAG** *Retrieval-Augmented Generation*
The architectural pattern that grounds LLM outputs in verified, organization-specific knowledge by retrieving relevant document chunks from a governed vector index before generation. The EDS framework's primary deployment pattern for Chapters 6–8 use cases. RAG addresses the risk of hallucination by requiring that every generated claim be supported by retrieved, authorized source documents.

**RAGAS**
A framework of metrics for evaluating RAG system performance, including faithfulness, context recall, context precision, and answer relevancy. Used in the EDS LLMOps framework as the standard evaluation suite for continuous quality assurance of RAG deployments.

**RBAC** *Role-Based Access Control*
An access control model that grants or denies access based on a user's organizational role. The Delegated Authorization Service validates every agent tool call against the invoking human's RBAC permissions to enforce Permission Mirroring and prevent Excess Agency.

**ReAct** *Reasoning and Action*
The cognitive paradigm is mandated for enterprise agentic deployments in the EDS framework. ReAct enforces a structured Think–Act–Observe loop: the agent generates an internal Thought (reasoning about the next steps), commits to an Action (a tool call), and processes the Observation (the tool's output) before the next iteration. Every Action log entry must capture the PDP's Allow/Deny decision. The ReAct loop is the basis for mandatory Reasoning Trace Capture.

**Reasoning Trace Capture**
The mandatory logging of an autonomous agent's complete Think–Act–Observe cycle, including intermediate reasoning steps (Thoughts), tool calls with parameters (Actions), and tool responses (Observations). Transforms the agent's internal decision process into a non-repudiable compliance control. All reasoning traces are subject to the seven-year retention obligation of the Logging and Explainability Standard.

**RRF** *Reciprocal Rank Fusion*
The algorithm used in the EDS framework's Hybrid Search architecture to merge results from dense (vector) and sparse (BM25) retrieval into a single, unified ranked list. RRF consistently produces superior retrieval quality to either method alone, without requiring calibration of weightings between the two result sets.

**RUL** *Remaining Useful Life*
A prognostic metric estimating how much operational time or how many operational cycles remain before a component reaches the end of serviceable life. Used in UC13 (aircraft predictive maintenance) and UC15 (manufacturing predictive maintenance) as the primary output of the Adaptive Autoencoder-based predictive model.

# S

**SCE** *Safety Constraint Engineering*
The EDS practice of defining precise, verifiable safety specifications offline and implementing a Runtime Monitor that validates every proposed agent action against those pre-verified constraints before execution. SCE ensures non-negotiable safety rules always override conflicting objectives. It is the complement to PaC (which enforces operational rules in real time); SCE enforces safety constraints that no policy, agent reasoning, or runtime condition may override. Introduced in Chapter 12 as the formal guarantee mechanism for Stage 4 systems.

**Security Trimming**
The EDS RAG control filters retrieved document chunks at query time to the requesting identity's authorized ACL scope, preventing unauthorized chunks from surfacing in the LLM's context window. The enforcement counterpart to DLAC's indexing-time tagging. A failure of Security Trimming constitutes an Isolation Paradox breach.

**Shadow AI**
Unsanctioned AI systems deployed without formal governance authorization, Autonomy Register entry, or Authority Matrix domain approval. Shadow AI systems are, by definition, governance breaches: they exercise machine authority that the board has not authorized and the EDS framework cannot govern. Organizations with high levels of Shadow AI exposure incurred an average of $670,000 in additional breach costs compared with those with minimal Shadow AI exposure (IBM Security, 2024).

**Shadow Tax**
The aggregate financial and operational cost imposed on the organization by Shadow AI deployments, including breach costs, remediation efforts, compliance exposure, and the opportunity cost of ungoverned AI decisions. The economic case for the EDS governance framework's upfront investment.

**SHAP** *Shapley Additive Explanations*
An XAI technique based on game-theoretic Shapley values that quantifies the contribution of each input feature to a model's output. Used in UC9 (financial risk and fraud monitoring) to generate human-readable decision rationales that explain fraud detection recommendations to human analysts and regulators.

**SRA** *Safety Risk Agent*
A specialized agent in the defense predictive maintenance multi-agent system (UC14) that evaluates predicted failure modes against the asset's safety envelope and hazard logs (FMECA), producing a Safety Risk Score or a mandatory halt flag that overrides logistical efficiency goals. SRA halt flags are mandatory HITL triggers.

**SRE** *Safety Runtime Environment*
The always-on EDS infrastructure layer that evaluates every agent decision stream against configured thresholds, oversight model requirements, and Authority Matrix limits. The SRE performs three functions that PIP/PDP/PEP components cannot perform alone: (1) monitors decision volume against span-of-control thresholds and automatically shifts to HITL mode when thresholds are approached, (2) detects anomalies in the decision stream, (3) enforces fail-closed behavior when the logging infrastructure is unavailable. The PEP enforces per-decision rules; the SRE governs system-level operating mode.

# T

**TTC** *Time-to-Competency*
A human capital metric measuring how quickly a new employee reaches full productive performance. A primary governance outcome indicator for UC1 (frontline knowledge assistant); RAG-assisted onboarding measurably reduces TTC.

# W

**WORM** *Write Once, Read Many*
A data storage property ensuring that once data is written, it cannot be modified or deleted. Mandated by the EDS framework for all Immutable

Audit Logs, WORM storage is the technical implementation of the write-once requirement that makes audit trails tamper-evident and legally defensible.

# X

**XAI** *Explainable AI*
The class of techniques and architectural components that generate human-readable rationales for AI-generated outputs and decisions. Mandated by the EDS framework for all autonomous decisions affecting external parties, regulated domains, or safety-critical systems. The XAI rationale is the primary tool for HOTL supervisors exercising genuine challenge and is a prerequisite for satisfying the regulatory right to explanation. Techniques include SHAP (Shapley Additive Explanations) and LIME (Local Interpretable Model-agnostic Explanations).

# Z

**ZTA** *Zero-Trust Architecture*
The security model that replaces implicit network-perimeter trust with continuous, identity-based verification of every access request. "Never trust, always verify." Applied to AI agent identity as ZTAI in the EDS framework.

**ZTAI** *Zero-Trust AI Access*
The application of Zero-Trust architecture principles to AI agent identity management. ZTAI replaces static API keys with PKI-backed durable agent identities, short-lived dynamic credentials scoped to the Authority Matrix-authorized domain, and instant credential revocation capability. Every NHI credential under ZTAI must be rotated within the schedule mandated by the NHI lifecycle governance framework (30 days for Level 4–5 systems, 60 days for Level 3, 90 days for Levels 1–2).

# Symbols and Numbers

**≥98% Auditable Rationale Standard**

The EDS framework's minimum compliance threshold requires that at least 98% of all decisions made by autonomous systems in regulated domains generate a complete, auditable rationale log at the point of execution. A quarterly rate below 98% for any regulated-domain agent constitutes an escalation event for the Board Risk Committee. The threshold reflects the framework's determination that a 2% unauditable decision rate represents the maximum acceptable governance gap for board-level reporting. Organizations operating under stricter regulatory frameworks may set a higher threshold. Introduced and formally defined in Chapter 11.

APPENDIX C

# EDS Governance Readiness Self-Assessment

This self-assessment is designed to diagnose an organization's current AI governance posture against the requirements of the Enterprise Decision System (EDS) Framework. It is intended for board members, Model Risk Officers (MROs), and enterprise architects.

A "No" or "Partial" response to any question in a Stage indicates a governance deficit that must be addressed before proceeding to higher-level autonomous deployments.

## Stage 1: Constitutional Foundation (Governance Doctrine)

- **1.1 Governance Doctrine:** Does the organization have a formal, board-ratified document defining the principles of delegated machine authority?
- **1.2 Authority Matrix:** Is there a documented scope of decision authority for AI systems that mirrors human delegation limits?


M. M. Hossain and A. A. N. Ponnusamy, *Governance-First AI*,
https://doi.org/10.1007/979-8-8688-3118-8

- **1.3 Accountability:** Are roles for the Model Governance Board (MGB) and Model Risk Officer (MRO) defined, filled, and empowered to halt production deployments?

# Stage 2: Architectural Precision (RAG and Retrieval)

- **2.1 Deterministic Shell:** Is governance enforced at the infrastructure/inference layer (via a PDP/PEP) rather than relying on application-level logic?
- **2.2 Forensic Traceability:** Does the system capture the minimum 11-field log schema for all RAG decisions?
- **2.3 Human-in-the-Loop (HITL):** Are there automated, non-bypassable gates for regulated-domain outputs when confidence falls below established thresholds?

# Stage 3: Operational Agency (Agentic Models)

- **3.1 NHI Lifecycle Governance:** Is there a centralized, automated registry and lifecycle management framework (provisioning/rotation/revocation) for all non-human identities (NHIs)?

- **3.2 Permission Mirroring:** Are agent identities dynamically scoped (ZTAI) to match only the specific, authorized human-role permissions required for a given task?
- **3.3 Autonomy Budgeting:** Does the board/MGB maintain a portfolio-level ceiling on autonomous risk (Autonomy Budget) that restricts the aggregate authority of agents?

# Stage 4: Industrialized Intelligence (Multi-domain and Safety)

- **4.1 Safety Constraint Engineering (SCE):** Are there hard-coded safety circuit breakers enforced by a Runtime Monitor that override any conflicting agent objectives?
- **4.2 Auditable Rationale:** Can the organization demonstrably prove that ≥98% of all autonomous decisions in regulated domains generate a complete, append-only forensic rationale log?
- **4.3 HOTL Certification:** Is there a formal, auditable training and certification program for human supervisors responsible for Level 3+ autonomous systems?

# Scoring and Action Plan

| Total "Yes" Responses | Maturity Level | Recommended Action |
|---|---|---|
| **0–4** | **Unprepared** | Halt all new AI agent development; formalize the Governance Doctrine and establish the MGB. |
| **5–9** | **Foundational** | Prioritize the implementation of the Deterministic Shell and mandatory log schema for existing pilots. |
| **10–12** | **Governed** | Focus on scaling NHI Lifecycle Governance and establishing the Machine Decision Authority Matrix. |
| **13–15** | **Industrialized** | Optimize Certified Operational Velocity; prepare for high-stakes multi-domain autonomous deployment. |

**Instruction for Auditors:** Any "No" or "Partial" response in Stage 4 for an agent operating at Autonomy Level 3 or above constitutes a **governance breach**. Deployment must be suspended until remediated and signed off by the Model Governance Board.

# Index

## A




M. M. Hossain and A. A. N. Ponnusamy, *Governance-First AI*,
https://doi.org/10.1007/979-8-8688-3118-8

## B

## D

## E

## F

## G

## H

## J



## K



## L

## M

## O

# P

## Q



## R

## S

## T



## U



## V



## W



## X, Y



## Z

FSC
www.fsc.org
MIX
Papier | Fördert
gute Waldnutzung
FSC® C083411

Kolibri 360 GmbH
Ferdinand-Jühlke-Straße 7
99095 Erfurt, Deutschland
produktsicherheit@kolibri360.de